CROSSINGS

SELECTED TRAVEL WRITINGS

Spruce Coast Press
Oregon, U.S.A.

First Edition: March 2012, Peathead Publishing, USA
This Edition: June 2018, Spruce Coast Press, U.S.A.

ISBN 978-0-9975085-2-9

Book design by Maureen Cutajar
Cover art by Trevor Gordon
Cover design by Jennifer Sirchuck

Manufactured in the United States of America

michaelkew.com

To my family

CONTENTS

PART I

Gaels

1

WHISKY WINS

2010

"DON'T YOU KNOW that Islay offers more than *whisky*, Michael?"

She was a red-eyed coffee drinker, a kombucha brewer, an organic juice squeezer, a rare Scottish hippie—possibly an ex-drug addict—working the reception desk of my Port Charlotte hostel. She was pale, Meryl Streepish, about 35, wearing a purply tie-dyed T-shirt, brown leather sandals, a long blonde ponytail, no bra, no makeup, jangly earrings, tight black jeans, and large oval eyeglasses that telescoped the center of her face. I was a whisky pilgrim, ferry-fresh from mainland Scotland via Kennacraig, onto the Hebridean isle of Islay to taste its single-malts and tour some distilleries—Laphroaig, especially—after my surfy outing in Orkney and a jaunt across the misty panoramas of Shetland.

"Bloody strange that people will travel all the way here *just* to drink whisky," she said. "It's like going to England *just* to drink tea." I told Heather that, for me, Islay's whisky was cerebral, not mere drink, and Laphroaig's aroma and palatal complexity—iodine, peat, salt, ocean, seaweed, smoke—flung my psyche afar.

I also theorized that whisky was not little Islay's sole lure, but, anyway, I did need a bed. She pointed to my room: a narrow cell with a metal bunk and sink and wall heater, comfortable enough, but overpriced at 30 quid per night. No matter—out the hostel's front door and 45 seconds on foot led me to the small bar of the lochside Port Charlotte Hotel, its smiling, rosy-cheeked drinkers downing pints of Angus Og Ale and sipping drams of the 227 available single-malts from Islay's eight distilleries: Lagavulin, Ardbeg, Caol Ila, Bruichladdich, Bowmore, Bunnahabhain, Kilchoman, and Laphroaig, whose name meant "beautiful hollow by the broad bay."

Outside, the air was crisp, the wind briny, the rain imminent—winter loomed. The hotel's bar, crowned Whisky Pub of the Year in 2009's Good Pub Guide, was certainly a snug nook to imbibe for the evening. That morning I had lucked into a rocky right-hand reefbreak on the left flank of a scenic bay, a special place where sheep and Highland cattle grazed green grass and flocks of geese honked high overhead. The wan sun shone and there were no humans anywhere. The waves were glassy and blue, head-high and playful, the water clear and about 45°F. Ireland, a black smear, lay low in the distance.

After the session I had a pleasant guided tour of Laphroaig's seaside distillery; on the malting floor I chatted with a friendly employee named David, who'd been with Laphroaig for three years; his prior eight were spent with Bowmore. "There're no hard feelings," he said. "Aye, we're all friends in this industry."

I wondered if he knew of any Islay surfers.

"Nay, not much surfin' here. But me mate is into windsurfin', aye. He does it at Machir Bay. He says there are often some big breakers. Have you been to Machir?"

After the tour I drove straight there and saw my first local surfer after four weeks of exploring Scottish islands. He was arguing—something about making coffee—with a girl inside his yellow kombi before he waxed a red egg-shaped thruster and attempted to paddle out, but was annihilated by the large, junky windswell. Then a squall appeared, so I left and drove north for a bit of coastal hiking and birding (Islay supported more than 200 species).

En route, bumping along the empty one-lane dirt tracks and enjoying somber hymns on Radio nan Gàidheal, BBC Scotland's Gaelic language station, I passed groves of brown-leafed maple and skinny birch, thorny bramble hedges, mirrorlike lochs, babbling brooks, bogs, heathlands, moorlands, gold grasslands, sweeping farm vistas, mildewed street signs, deer, geese, horses, cows, sheep, grouse, ducks, elusive cats, and old stone walls. By the time I reached the thin beach trail the sun was low, the light pastel, and the rustic traits of autumn harkened to a quiet time in my travel memory. Certainly, Islay was of the purest, prettiest places on Earth.

I walked holding a green 35cl bottle of Laphroaig's flagship 10-year-old whisky, taking intermittent swigs while absorbing the environs. A cool, light breeze blew offshore, and flocks of birds squawked overhead; I strode through swampy fields and across untracked dunes, and all afternoon I saw just one other person.

"Lovely day!—a fine day," the old bearded man said to me. His brogue was loose and breathy. Binoculars hung from his neck—we'd been observing the same pair of golden eagles. He pointed at my bottle. "I see you've been sampling our local."

"Laphroaig's my favorite. I drink it all the time back home. Basically, it brought me to Islay."

"Aye, many people come for the whisky foremost. It's our 'water of life,' so the saying goes. You Americans, you have your bourbons and that. I really fancy a drop of Maker's Mark. Have you had it?"

"Countless times."

"Aye, and I've had that Laphroaig countless times," he said, chuckling. "I reckon it's better than water!"

With dusk the sky flared ocher; thin clouds threaded the rural twilight. In lieu of light pollution, vast constellations appeared, followed quickly by a vigorous cold front. It was time to repair to the sandy shore of Loch Indaal and Port Charlotte, its classic whitewashed village slated for the site of Islay's ninth whisky distillery, a retrospective push by Bruichladdich, Islay's "sophisticated" single-malter. Like Port Charlotte Hotel, Bruichladdich was within walking distance from my hostel, but the distillery had no bar, which didn't matter because Port Charlotte's was aglow warmly with drink and peat fire and live bagpipe with fiddle, a boozy clime of Scottish cliché. And I was excited to drink in a pub where no one knew my name.

"Well, if it isn't Michael Kew!" Heather sat on the barstool nearest the doorway; she cocked her head and looked at me slyly. "I thought I might find you here," she said. Her hair was up, her glasses gone, and she looked sassy, somewhat lubricated, yet she was sober. In a utopia of booze, the woman didn't drink. This was unfathomable.

"What brings you here this stormy night?" I asked.

"The live music. And I could walk here. You?"

"To drink whisky, and I walked here, too. This bar recently won a whisky award, you know."

"I had no idea," she said, rolling her eyes. She patted the stool next to her. "But if you want to get to know me better, why don't you sit and have some tea with me?"

"No thanks. I'm going to sink a few drams by the fire, near the musicians."

"You don't want to talk to me?"

"Not really."

"Has anyone ever called you an arsehole?" she asked.

I nodded to the barkeep, who'd heard the exchange. "I'll have a dram of Octomore 140, please."

"Whisky wins, mate," he said, laughing. "Whisky *always* wins."

2

DWR CYMRU

2001

LLANFAIRPWLLGWYNGYLLGOGERYCHWYRNDROBWLLLLANTYSILIOGOGO GOCH.

My eyes snuck a double-take at the relief map tacked to the kitchen wall. This 58-letter word is the name of a village in North Wales—the longest place name in Great Britain. I later learned that the first 20 letters formed the name until the 1880s, when a cobbler invented the new name, meaning "Church of St. Mary in a hollow of white hazel, near to a rapid whirlpool, and St. Tysilio's Church of the red cave."

Croeso i Gymru: Welcome to Wales. But don't try to learn the language.

"THIS IS THE BEAUTY for which you've traveled all this way, Mr. Kew."

The mustachioed Paul Gill cracked a coy grin, gesturing through the narrow sliding glass door in his kitchen. The sky was dark and leaky. The 2000 season had twice as much rain as last year, the wettest since records commenced in 1766, and I happened to be in Wales to absorb most of it. Fifty knots of wind, 20 shades of gray.

Aged 47 years and healthy, Paul resides with his wife Sara in a slim, multi-storied affair, one of those turn-of-the century jobs with loose door handles and creaky wooden staircases. Weather-proofed and heated, Paul's is a good hideout from the natural elements of Mumbles, a quaint seaside burg moonlighting as the surfing polestar of Wales.

Arriving yesterday via the relaxing National Express bus line from Bristol, England, I'd disembarked late afternoon into the Welsh maritime hub of Swansea, a teeming dimple of industry and higher education flanked by Swansea Bay and the idyllic Vale of Neath, also the birthplace to Dylan Thomas, Wales's most prolific writer and poet.

From Swansea, I'd boarded the South Wales-Gower Peninsula bus route, geared for Mumbles Corner, wherever that was. An elderly lady motioned to me at the correct stop, so I stepped off the bus and walked the streets with my two bulging backpacks, searching for Paul's address.

Linked to Swansea in 1807 by the globe's first consistent passenger rail transport with horse-drawn cars, Mumbles evolved into a voguish resort for Victorian society before morphing into a contemporary surf/college town brimming with talent and good intent.

I had arranged the meeting with Paul the prior eve back at Alex Williams's home down in Bantham, a timeless South Hams outpost of England's County Devon. An ace sports photographer, Alex had put me up the previous week in his 400-year-old farm house cloaked by muddy one-laners, impenetrable hedges and smooth, green hillsides. For the sake of exercise and saltwater therapy in the midst of near-constant rain, we killed time by surfing mushy, cold, windpocked Bantham beachbreak, later huddling near his fireplace, thumbing through a worldly array of surf magazines and downing scads of tea.

Paul and I aimed to rendezvous in Mumbles with Welsh surfing icon Carwyn Williams, who now resides in southwestern France (alas, Carwyn never arrived due to personal problems in Seignosse). From there, it was proposed to become a two-week bonanza of Welsh secret-spot glory iced with an intimate relationship with alcoholic beverages, smoky Mumbles nightlife and mud-caked shoes. Indeed it became.

"It's looked down upon here if you don't *go drinking."—John Purton, Welsh surfboard shaper*

HOT TEA AND frigid Mumbles tap water were my lubricants by day, warming drams of ten-year-old Laphroaig whisky and copious pints of Guinness Extra Cold by night. Meander down to the White Rose on the bayfront corner and eye the same nightly patrons of all epochs yet with seamless backgrounds—that of Welsh, rather extrinsic in relation to my pasteurized, saturated, white-toothed California crib. Young women and men sucking on cigarettes, smiling, laughing.

Bar closes at 11. Stumble along the wet concrete sidewalk up to Bentley's, open until 2 a.m., housing a lively DJ spinning the same frantic beats nightly. Catch the blue eyes of that bubbly blonde lass you chatted with Sunday, the one who slithered up closely and, through hot, boozy breath, wondered aloud why in the hell you'd come from sunny California to sodden Wales, and why you chose to enter this stinky nightclub on a Thursday night, drunk off your ass from Scotch whisky and Irish stout.

Scott,

I'm in South Wales right now, reasoning with Jessica, local lass, age 25, blonde hair down to her waist, carries an affinity for the demon liquid. Not quite rocket fuel like rum, but formidable quantities of Guinness and cabernet sauvignon.

The pubs here are soaked in stale cigarette smoke and human sweat; the accents are exotic and there are no other Americans here. We've surfed some decent spots with loads of other surfers out. Nobody said South Wales was uncrowded. The women are of the nicest I've ever met. Jessica is fantastic. I told her she should come visit California in the springtime.

Been swilling enormous amounts of ale, out-drinking nearly everybody. You'd like the bitters and session beers. Guinness tastes like nothing else.

People smoke everywhere around here. It is a religion. They eat almost anything, it seems. The breakfasts are slimy and salty: fatty bacon, pork sausages, cockles, runny eggs, limp toast, fried tomatoes, hot tea, laverbread (mashed seaweed), glistening hash browns. Curry is big over here, for some reason. Loads of grease.

Meat is everywhere. Pork is popular. I had ostrich the other night. Scrumptious, like venison. MK

WALES...*CYMRU* IN Welsh, "land of compatriots," pronounced *CUM-ree*. The national symbol has been the red dragon since King Arthur's regime 2,000 years back. A rainy, wind-swept landscape of rugby, football (known as soccer in America), cricket, agriculture, and the world's finest coal. Roughly the same size as Massachusetts. The origins of the Welsh stretch back further than most civilizations on the planet, much further than the Iron Age Celts, who established themselves in Wales and Europe circa 500-700 B.C., or the Beaker Folk, who sailed here from the Iberian coast in Central Europe some 5,000 years ago.

Evidence vouches that some man-made Welsh structures pre-date the ancient pyramids of Egypt by as much as 1,500 years, notably cromlechi (burial chambers), Roman forts, Celtic artifacts, Norman castles, and stone churches. Wales has more castles per square mile than any other country in the world. The word Wales was first used in the eighth century, spawned from the Anglo-Saxon word wealas, meaning foreigners.

Europe's oldest language, Welsh has been spoken daily for centuries, used today by more than a half million of the nation's three million residents. Hovering on the brink of extinction a generation ago, the language was revived in the mainstream with the aid of Welsh governmental planning. These days, schoolchildren are required to learn English and Welsh, and official public documents are composed in both languages. Road signs are now all bilingual, displaying Welsh and English renditions of place and street names.

Scott,

It rained endlessly last night. The wind was fierce; Force 10 (55-63 mph) on the Beaufort Scale, I'd reckon, but no one here seems to mind. Welsh coastal dwellers are well-acquainted with conditions like these. Think U.S. Pacific Northwest in February with much smaller surf

The people are kind and the air sharp. Hours are spent aside the fireplace with a good book or decent magazine. Conversations of photography, British politics, weather, icons, tea. Lots of tea-drinking as of late. Hot and black; warms the soul. Summer is gone and so are the tourists; a rural landscape pacifies whatever mind-set which was roughened during the travel from France to Norway to London to here. Nothing but the Swansea sprawl and long, green fields, tractors, animals, rain and wind.

The ocean is oatmeal-gray and torn by the gale. A hot shower sounds good, followed with a hot tea and a hot wood fire.

A place where the younger buildings are 400 years old is humbling to our relatively juvenile American nation. I can only imagine the things these walls have seen. Time is unending and unchanging for nature and the seasons. It is different for humans. MK

THE WEST-SOUTHWEST wind is cold, merciless. Paul and I have been surfing in insanely windpocked Langland beachbreak, sharing the quasi lineup with shortboarding kids freed from school and the odd older longboarder. Windsurfing is the quest on days like these.

Memorable surf in Wales typically spawns from a distinct batch of meteorological whimsy, requiring a deep low pressure system to situate in the mid-North Atlantic; the further south the low, the better. Pairing this with a ridge of high pressure over the country to block the low from moving onshore, the result can be clean, small-to-medium-sized swell á la Southern California. Rarely does Wales endure large surf.

The best season overall is late summer and early autumn, when the ocean temperature can warm into the 60s and air temperatures can reach the low 80s. The Welsh also reap some of their finest waves during the hurricane season, when the U.S. East Coast hurricane swells steam across the Atlantic.

ANOTHER RAIN DAY, this one with a tinge of swell. A gargantuan low pressure bulb was wreaking havoc in the middle of the Atlantic, and Ireland was getting hammered. With thoughts geared toward surf potential on the Gower Peninsula (the Peninsula was designated Britain's first "Area of Outstanding Natural Beauty," coined more than four decades ago, remaining unspoiled today), Paul, his mate Mark and I ventured out to Oxwich Bay, a sweeping fetch of windblown beachbreak spiked by a long, rocky headland. Requiring a big swell and able to handle large doses of wind, we could see that, upon arrival, Oxwich Point had awakened from months of flatness.

A 13th century church and a Norman castle overlook the point at Oxwich—quite the backdrop for a novelty session at one of Wales's rarest arenas. Strolling out along the point was a lesson in ancient geography, what with the twisted slate, funky mosses and decayed bits of maritime waste at our feet. Booties proved invaluable.

Oxwich was a shotgun of a wave, dishing up a few bowl sections and several sketchy boils frighteningly close to the rock shelf. Paul lurked onshore with his telephoto lens and camera as Mark and I leapt from the ledge, stroking into the quirky lineup now teeming with 15 other surfers, mostly students from Swansea University. Apparently, the institution advertises itself as "the surfer's university" considering its proximity to rideable waves, usurping England's Plymouth University claim as Britain's premier surfer school.

"Just drop in on all of the bloody fuckin' wankers," Mark told me. I could tell he'd long ago capped his fill of novices surfing advanced spots, getting in the way of others and invariably displaying poor surfing etiquette and ability.

Hard rain and wind ensued mid-way through the session as the tide pushed, shutting the waves off like a faucet. Oxwich only works with a slim tide window at low tide, good for perhaps an hour or two before vanishing on either side of the shift. Tides in the Bristol Channel have a range of 30 feet, hence the fickle disposition of all Welsh surf spots.

"You've got to get it while you can," winked Paul post-session.

Scott,

Skies are dark and leaking hard here in West Wales. The dialect is peculiar. Very difficult for this Californian to pronounce or decipher. Swilling a few pints of bitter ale with Alf Alderson, editor of Britain's Surf magazine. We're out in northern Pembrokeshire, an enchantingly ancient landscape. Wind is intense.

The Welsh are of the nicest folk I've ever come across. The women are exceptionally friendly. One stranger invited me in for a pint. Another offered me a bed. A culture unsaturated with McDonald's and Wal-Mart survives. Celtic tradition speaks boldly at these beaches surrounded by 800-year-old chapels and cathedrals. Endless sheep and cattle. Rain and narrow streets. MK

DAY TWO OF the swell found me in the passenger seat of Alf's new plum-colored Volkswagen station wagon, gunning westward from Mumbles into pastoral Pembrokeshire, where Alf has planted his roots in the ancient hamlet called Solva, neighboring St. David's, Britain's smallest city replete with a landmark cathedral. Overloaded were the sandbars at Freshwater West, Newgale and Whitesands Bay, so we opted for the northbound track, bound for a rare left at New Quay.

"I'd say that there's still a feel of the old days about (Pembrokeshire), outside of the busiest summer weekends," Alf said as we sped along the A487. "It still isn't too crowded. We have some of the clearest water and cleanest beaches in the U.K., and the surroundings are usually pretty cool. It's a place where you can still catch a head-high peak on a sunny day with just a few mates in the water."

Existing on the crook of the United Kingdom geographically spared Pembrokeshire from modern development, leading to its designation as Britain's sole coastal national park in 1952.

Lingering evidence suggests mankind has inhabited Pembrokeshire for more than 10,000 years. The Vikings and Romans paid regular visits to the region, naming towns and offshore islands like Fishguard and Tenby before the Normans arrived, who erected several impressive castles (Pembroke Castle is the birthplace of Henry Tudor, who became Henry VII, King of England, in the 15th century) and effectively halving the country with the Landsker Line, a string of castles and strongholds. Dividing Anglo-Norman Pembrokeshire in the south to Welsh Pembrokeshire in the south, the Landsker remains a cultural waypost to this day, with the Welsh-speaking denizens hovering primarily to the north of the line.

Dodging wide rain puddles and fording towns with anomalous names like Eglwyswrw, I asked Alf if Pembrokeshire's surf occasionally equaled the land's exquisite beauty.

"If we could tow Ireland out of the way, we'd have the best surf in Europe," he replied. "It is fickle compared to other parts of Europe, but then on the whole, we don't have the crowds or the hassles at more popular spots such as Cornwall and southwestern France.

"The Irish Sea isn't as consistent as the Bristol Channel, but, as all the locals know, when it's working—usually in winter as it needs big swells—Pembrokeshire has some excellent pointbreaks. We try not to give any specific details, though, to keep the crowds down."

Scott,

Surfed a clandestine left-hand pointbreak up the coast today. Slate-gray sea and sky. Several takers, many of them bodyboarders. Surf was a consistent head-high with the odd larger line, flattening through the middle before zipping over the inside sandbar. Wind was straight offshore and the rain steady.

Drinking loads of black tea and wearing a smile for the classic Pembrokeshire old-timers. You should hear them speak. It's like a real-life film. Nobody gives a damn if you're rad or cool or shy or drunk. It's life. The Welsh endure through the storms and England's superiority complex.

Off to the neighborhood pub tonight under the rain and southwesterly gale. Alf's abode offers a fantastic view of the Irish Sea and all its windblown glory...the Irish Sea is the most radioactive sea on the planet, though not this far south.

The Welsh are deep—Pembrokeshire is not quite Southern California. Harshness breeds hardiness. Time to think. This is good.
MK

THE WELSH ARE sparse, their land wee, and they have grappled through the centuries to sustain their identity. In North America, we are still debating what ours will become.

"It is not easy to be Welsh," Jan Morris wrote in *The Matter of Wales.*

"There are many now, as there always have been, whose lives are guided by...the passions of a powerless people, in a small country, trying to honour their deepest instincts."

Wales is one of Western Europe's poorest nations, constantly existing in the shadow of the wealthier landscape of neighboring England, which, by-and-large, views the Welsh to be of second-class citizenry. Bordering England for more than 150 miles, the Welsh remain fiercely loyal to their heritage, especially when it comes to rugby, a veritable religion in Wales.

"I have two favorite rugby teams," Carwyn Williams once told me back in France. "Wales and any team playing against England."

One afternoon, following a glutton of crisp tube-rides over the shallow rock bottom of Porthcawl Point, a small coterie of Welsh surfers and I convened inside of a cozy, stone-walled pub in Porthcawl proper. With firewood crackling and pints steadily consumed, conversation flowed around our small wooden table aside Celtic paraphernalia, rugby posters and grinning, grizzled men fresh off work, ripe for happy hour. Everyone seemed to know one another.

To my left sat Johnny James, a 31-year-old gardener with a boyish face and a friendly, calm demeanor.

"Peoples' perception from London or wherever haven't a clue about Wales," he said between sips of Guinness. "Fuck, you know, it's bullshit. They think we're just completely ass-backwards. We're on the periphery as well as it were in economic terms in the U.K.—pretty poor—but we're grateful for what we have."

Across the table sat Herbie, age 43, a jovial Porthcawl surf shop owner with a striking resemblance to famous Italian tenor Luciano Pavarotti.

"(The surf) might be a bit shitty on days, but we're pretty proud of who and where we are," he said. "I don't think there's a better country in the world, and I've been to quite a few."

Two days later, I found myself basking in weak sunlight down at Langland Bay, swilling a beer beside Pete Jones, the European surfing champion in 1977 and British champ in 1978 who now runs a surf shop in Llangennith. Fresh from a dip in the sloppy beachbreak peaks, the 51-year-old Jones was amiable and articulate, a widely respected elder statesman for Welsh surfing.

"I'm proud to be Celtic," he said. "Yeah, of course I am. We have got a lot of in-grown determination, you know? As a nation, I think we are quite determined. Celtic identity is good."

Finishing the beer, I asked Jones to assess Welsh surfing considering his extensive global travels through the years.

"Surfing in Wales is definitely really hard-core because of the weather; it's so cold that you've got to be super keen," he said. "And the waves we get are not brilliant. You've got to be keen to go in on days like today—there's waves, but if you were in California or Hawaii, they'd be looking at this 3-4' chop and they wouldn't go in. They'd think, Ah, shit, this is crap, you know? But Welsh surfers really go for it in all conditions. I suppose you've got to, really.

"We do have surf conditions that are below average on a world level, and considering the surf we surf, I think we're doing pretty well," he continued. "You cannot get beyond a certain level of surfing in conditions like we get because the waves just don't allow you to. You don't get barrels very often; you get faces, but you can't really learn how to ride the tube and stuff like that."

I point out that, in his 30-something years of surfing in Wales, he must have witnessed substantial growth within the sport, considering the Langland waves we were watching had roughly 40 surfers (mostly young shortboarders) all vying for rideable scraps.

"It's definitely gotten bigger, yeah," Jones said, surveying the scene. "It's probably grown in parallel with surfing growing around the world, but we'll never get super crowded because it's too cold. There's more to surfing than just surfing in warm water with perfect waves. I enjoy surfing for what it is—to be out in the elements, feeling the wind in your face. Cold-water surfing is fantastic. There's something more to it."

Back in the pub, Johnny James voiced what perhaps every surfer on the planet would say about their backyard, hinting at his dedication to Wales despite its elemental adversities.

"A lot of the boys try to go away in the winter if they can, because it does get cold here. But that's when we get most of our surf: in the winter. It's cold, yeah. It would be a bit nicer if it was a bit sunnier, a bit warmer…The grass is always greener on the other side, isn't it?" He grinned. "We always come home, though. Home is always home."

3

THE SHETLAND SPIRIT

2009

NO STORM COULD smash the cold burgh of 7,000 souls. Edging the North Sea, Lerwick was low and old, windswept and valiant, stone-structured and combat-proofed. Its people walked in heavy clothing, its narrow roads slick with rain, and come evening the streetlights cast orange glows onto the glistening gray brick of Harbour Street outside my guesthouse window, below the black battlements and looming clock tower of Fort Charlotte, tolling hourly, ominously, in Scotland's most Norwegian of towns.

Yet Lerwick, capital of the Shetland Islands, was 130 miles northeast of the Scottish mainland and 225 from Norway. "Mind, it would be a bit fookin' weird if we was still Norwegian," Sigurd, the guesthouse's cook, had told me two hours prior. He was Shetlandic, tall and red-headed, freckly and foul-breathed, a descendent of the Norse vikings who colonized Hjaltland in the 9th century. The archipelago became Scottish after a marriage was arranged between Margaret, the 13-year-old daughter of Norway's King Christian I, and Scotland's 18-year-old King James III. For dowry, Christian I pledged Shetland to the young James, planning to reclaim his archipelago by giving 8,000 gold coins to Scotland. Christian I was broke, however, so in 1469 Shetland was annexed to Scotland.

"Any talk of seceding?" I asked Sigurd.

"From Scotland? Oh, god no. Aye, it's far from here, but we've no need for autonomy." He flipped a steaming pink steak of salmon; the iron pan's grease popped loudly; smoke fluffed the ceiling. The tiny kitchen reeked of fish. "Look at *your* country, mate. Would Hawai'i secede? Fook no!" He dabbed his sweaty forehead with a blue rag. "Everybody knows we'd never survive on our own. Scotland provides our roads, post, petrol, absolutely everything except sheep, cows, horses, and fish."

"And oil," I said, noting the North Sea's rich reservoirs and recent oil exploration in the Atlantic between Shetland and the Faroe Islands, an autonomous Danish province.

"Aye, and what if the Faroes weren't part of fookin' Denmark?" he asked. "They'd be shite!"

After I mentioned the Norse translation on every road sign announcing a town, Sigurd spoke of Shetlandic elders being able to converse with the Faroese. "That's the *old* Shetland," he said. "Speaking of old, Shetland used to be down near the equator."

"Shetland would be a bit different if it was on the equator," I said.

"Aw, and it'd be nice, aye?"

Though overdone, his salmon was a fine meal, and later, upstairs in my small room, I gazed through the window and listened to rain patter the roof. My wetsuit hung dripping in the shower. With an unchilled pint of Sjolmet Stout I lounged on a comfortable chair, absorbing quietude of the autumnal Lerwick eve, nuances of old Norway abound—nearby streets were called King Erik, St. Olaf, King Haakon; the cook's name was Norwegian (and he was a participant in Up Helly Aa, Lerwick's viking fire festival); my beer was made by a brewery named after Valhalla, the mythological Norse "hall of the slain." With an aura perhaps more Nordic than Scottish, Shetland seemed complex and compelling, even cryptic.

But it is bad for surfing. Unlike Norway, an arctic wave garden with a burgeoning surf populace, Shetland cannot accommodate. Teasingly loaded with North Atlantic energy, the archipelago is rife with swell but bereft of surf spots. Its best surf-geography lies along the 23 east-coast miles between Gulberwick and Sumburgh Head, yet for the two or three Shetlandic surfers (whom I never saw), east swells are almost nonexistent and, if they do appear, are typically created by—and thus arrive with—onshore gales. Typically, roads don't go where you want them to; hiking distances are vast and often require fording deep bogs. Elsewhere stand vertical cliffs and vertical drops into deep sea with virtually no continental shelf, offering swells no chance to break until they collide with sheer rock. The few beachbreaks are generally formless, surfable reefs are scant, and you can forget about finding a Shetlandic Thurso East.

"Just turn down that track, boy, and you should find some surfin' waves." Early that morning, dangling a lighted cigarette between his middle and index fingers, the stout uniformed man had leaned inside the passenger window of my small blue rental car, pointing at the thin lane to my right. I was parked behind two cars, awaiting a plane to take off—the man guarded the gate and traffic light spanning the A970 South Road because, for a few dozens meters, it crossed Sumburgh Airport's runway. Two days prior, my Loganair Saab 340 had landed dangerously here inside a southeast gale and horizontal rain; what appeared to be a messy right-hander slid into my porthole view seconds before touchdown.

Heeding the guardsman, I turned onto the track and within seconds faced that same right-hander—wobbly, smallish, in a rocky cove, very funky but surfable. Black ponies grazed on the adjacent green hillock, flecked with old wooden barns and bales of hay; fog slid to and fro in the bight, hiding and revealing jagged black skerries offshore, haloed by white squawking gulls. The wind was lightly onshore, the tide high, and there was no one around. Drizzle and brief sunlight created a photogenic double rainbow that arced over the surf spot, one of Shetland's few. Enya's "Water Shows the Hidden Heart" floated from the car stereo, apt for the scene, a cold cove flanked by rural island idyll and the butt of an asphalt runway.

Quickly the hooded 5-mil was found and the surfboard waxed, but reality spoke in the voice of a rough session: many rocks, a ding or two, bumpy chest-high waves, disorientating fog, and whitecapping wind.

The hillside ponies whinnied and one aircraft—a Dash 8—landed in the hour I surfed. My body grew numb, a consensus and somewhat erstwhile deference to viking life because the vikings had no wetsuits, yet they blasted in and claimed Shetland's shores, spiritually Nordic, innate muscle of the region's humanity.

Under inky mid-morning skies I drove many northbound miles atop wide, manicured roads, then remote one-laners, targeting a right-hand slab wave I'd seen in *Surfing* magazine. Though a hoax, the wave looked interesting. The route to it sliced through settlements like Aith, Voe, and Bixter, where I mailed a Shetland pony postcard to my parents—longtime owners of such ponies—in California. Onward through Brae, past Sullom and Tanwick, out toward the primordial cliffs of Eshaness, I passed browny-black peat fields and deep glens, coppery creeks, desolate lochs, rabbits, horses, birds, and sheep scampering across the road—or laying on it. Wide space, few cars. Mist blurred the windscreen and I listened to BBC Scotland talk radio: lectures about Alcohol Awareness Week, 18th-century diary readings, news of a parliament scandal.

I found the slab barreling over the shallow reef in the bay fronting an old croft where, strangely, there was a green Volvo wagon with a surfboard inside. The car had Norway license plates. For a surfer, driving to this bay was a peripheral drift west from the nearby hamlet of Hamnavoe, wide open to swell, an alcove with particular promise.

I walked out onto the grassy headland above the wave and met Anders, a tall, bearded Norwegian who had taken the ferry ("Was a very rough ride.") up from Aberdeen. He'd brought his car from his Stavanger home and had been exploring Shetland for the last 10 days, living in his Volvo, thrice attempting to ride the slab, which he too had seen in *Surfing*. The wave wasn't hard to find—Shetland was small—but it didn't matter because the wave was a farce.

"I surf this other right reef," Anders said in a thick accent, showing me photos on his digital camera. I had checked the spot but it was flat, needing rare conditions to fire. I envied his score. "Is the best wave in Shetland, I think," he said, "but I want to surf places that nobody has ever surfed." He pointed to Muckle Ossa, an offshore sea stack. "Maybe there are waves out there?"

"Doubtful," I said. "Have you found any other good waves?"

"Not really."

"Where have you looked?"

"All over. Here, Sandness, Yell, Unst. But I want to also see Fair Isle and Foula, maybe Out Skerries and Papa Stour. Those islands might have something."

"I've heard otherwise."

Anders laughed and lit a cigarette. "I think that for surf, Shetland can be called *Shitland*. Ha!"

"This used to be part of your country," I said.

"*Ja*." He blew smoke toward the clouds, then smiled. "But we Norse surfers, we do not think we miss it. No, no—Scotland can keep this beautiful place."

4

WATER BECOMES YOU

2002

"PEACE AND QUIET...there's no peace like here. We've got a peace you can feel when you come aboard. A lot of people are looking for peace, by the way, and they don't even know it. But the people who are looking for peace who know they are looking for peace, well...they find it here."

He paused, drawing a long pull from a canned pint of lager as the autumnal moon lifted from the cliffs behind us.

"I'd been out on the sea fishing all my life and had no life at all. Just been working away in madness in the tempests at sea. And every time I closed my eyes, I could see the reefs I worked year after year. That's when I realized what was going on with surfing."

Peering into the flames, I wedged my elbows comfortably between driftwood scree, shoes stirring the course, gray beach sand, once consolidated as metamorphic rock transformed by the heat and pressures of distant geological traumas. Opposite the firepit, through the torquing yellows and oranges, sat new friend Roderic: Burly, stubble-faced and densely clothed, alternating between beer and cigarette, he looked more like a typical commercial fisherman than surfer. Yet this was no typical surfscape.

"I have a life now. When I was fishing, I had a lot of money and bits and pieces of whatever, but now, I've got far more than that."

With a firm handshake, we'd met on this wild beach a month prior, the gleam in his hazel eyes hinting he knew things as we exchanged pleasantries that stellar mid-November morning. Plans were made to dine at his cabin come nightfall; I brought two fresh haddock fillets, a spiny lobster and a fifth of Ardbeg single-malt whisky. Late into the night, society, boating, climate and local history were canvassed as the bottle was drained.

Roderic and I had a sage yet brief relationship, feeding off of each other's interests and expertise. His aim was to continue an ardent father, mine to exist a nomadic freelance journalist. He spoke of fishing and rural self-sufficiency, as I was a man of endless questions and inadvertent myopia reaped from a lifetime as a one-track-minded surfer. I elucidated the intricacies of photography and syntax, both of which fascinated him, yet Roderic and his cherished isle would deeply enrich through ways I cannot define. Of these, life.

> *"A strange and beautiful sight to see the fleet put silently out against a rising moon, the sea-line rough as a wood with sails, and ever and again and one after another, a boat flitting swiftly by the silver dusk."*
>
> *—Robert Louis Stevenson, 1875*

FISHING HAS ALWAYS been economically critical to Roderic's island—more than forty percent of its fishing fleet is based in his hometown. Here, on the fringe of the continental shelf, lie some of the planet's richest fishing arenas. Cold North Atlantic waters are warmed by the Gulf Stream along this serrated coast, hosting a formidable diversity of habitat for fish and shellfish. The shallows are abundant with shellfish, while the westerly depths yield a vast range and quality of seafood.

I assumed the harvest of these volatile waters is not easily won.

"We fished all year," Roderic quipped during a lull at a hollow reefbreak near home. "You've got to pay your mortgage all twelve months of the year, you know. There's no seasons at the bank—it's just pay pay pay pay."

Sea was smooth as possible, sparkling green. Pure oil.

"I'd have to calculate some things when I was put into a situation; I'd have to make a level-headed decision, and I'd have to have it right or else we were all dead. Dead. If I didn't pull the right call, it was over. I've been airlifted, shipwrecked, tossed overboard, badly injured, what have you—all humbling experiences. They'll bring you down to the speck of sand you are, mate."

Painfully inconsistent, slightly overhead rights sucked and bowled hard before collapsing into the channel. Late elevator drop into a barrel, nothing more. Nothing desired.

I ask Roderic what separates his reality from the modern world.

"Nothing. We don't stand out. We don't want to stand out. We stand in the back."

Reef was a shallow mushroom of jagged gneiss, ancient bedrock forty feet across, looped by deep water. We surfed in solitude surrounded by miles of empty Atlantic and soggy moorlands full of sheep.

Two hours into the session, a gray seal poked through the surface, cartwheeling into the air, streaking inside cresting waves. Large white gull circumnavigated the commotion before plummeting toward cuisine. I caught its eye prior to.

"There are finer fish in the sea than have ever been caught." Old proverb.

I nodded. Prolonged lulls cast us in this meditative contemplation of lucid surrealism: the emerald right-hand tubes, the thick kelp, the blinding afternoon sun and its scintillations off water. Following lulls, I was afraid to catch a wave as to hold the spell. Roderic sensed it, rising and falling over the swells, rhythm intact with the pace of his reality…rising through life, falling from both despair and grace, feeling the water, absorbing the brine as he did life itself. Inhaling, measuring, processing, digesting.

"Everything has come to us from the sea," he said. "It is the water of life."

"That's a funny piece of water," said Captain Hamilton.
—Joseph Conrad, The Shadow Line

NEVER BEFORE HAD I witnessed snowfall. Morning treat this day, powder white atop fence posts and dune grass and seaside cemeteries and the indifferent rumps of sheep. Arctic gales blow down this afternoon and the ferry was canceled, Roderic's younger brother Derek booked to board. Thoughts shifted to waves and sheltered nooks.

One way leads north, one way leads west, one way leads south. We threw in the gear and embarked westward, nursing Roderic's sputtering, tobacco-fumed kombi from the driveway to the thoroughfare traversing the island's spine to the turn-off to the grade down to the beach. We conversed passionately, at length. One topic stuck with me.

He called them his 'journeys to the stars,' granted nightly through whisky, fatigue, and a piercingly silent, black house. Cerebral fairytales….to go beyond his reality, but not quite. Dreams. Mere mind-blink.

The merlin soars with the arctic wind, surveying Earth. No retreats nor hollows adorn the machair land. Rabbit, pygmy shrew and field mouse are raptor's motive, conceivably ill-fated aside the stormy vastness of the North Atlantic, a dusky carpet of whitecaps sweeping far beyond the merlin's eye. Countless nooks gouge into the shoreline, greeted with an opaque ribbon of sand sequed into velvety green hillock.

Perhaps the merlin is too starved, too expectant of fodder. Perhaps it is admiring the northern beauty, or perhaps it is merely all a skipper's dream trapped at sea in the midst of a Force 9 gale.

As it was.

"Water is the biggest part of our lives up here. It becomes you."

He lowered his eyes. I raised mine. For raptors they scanned the sky, a uniform wash-gray, not a blotch in sight, draped low over distant white hills. The sea was tarnished silver, the swell flaccid, sleepy. Ceaseless wind scoured the island's opposite side, here strangely absent. Thick drizzle fogged the windshield.

Sitting at the beach in his rusted van, parked in muddy slush, the setting haunted me—an elemental beauty, of sorts. We'd just motored across the island's snow-laced expanse, listening to Enya albums over and over; first "Shepherd Moons," then "The Celts," "Watermark" and "The Memory of Trees." Roderic upped the van's stereo volume during one particular piece. It was "Miss Clare Remembers," a stirring piano instrumental. Roderic's mother was Clare, rest in peace. Through Enya, she lulled us as we faced this muted beachbreak.

What does Enya say? I ask.

"Her synths and song envelop the truth."

He exhaled, then lilted.

"What do *you* say, Kew? Speak no more. What do *we* say? Listen and react, react and listen, feel and sense, smell and hear. Listen to her echoes. It's like flowing water from a cold, fresh rain."

Up here, in the course of a single day one can see, in that immensity of sky, the dance of rain, sun, cloud, sea mist and thunder. The Gaelic language is rich in proverbs about weather. One caught my eye: *Latha na Seachd Sian—goath is uisge, cuir is cathadh, tarnanaich is dealanaich is clachan meallainn.* 'The Day of Seven Storms—wind and rain, snowfall and blizzard, thunder, lightning and hailstorms.'

No surfing today. Roderic owned all of Enya's albums. He chose "A Day Without Rain" for the drive home.

"A lot of people upset themselves with the weather here," he gestured, "but at the end of the day, you can't let it beat you. It blows me away all the time, when the sun's out or when there's a storm. When you see this place in a storm, it's as impressive as when it's blue sky. You go up to the north and you've got 100-foot waves hitting the cliffs.

"You are on a mission in life to have happiness, to have three-course meals every day. If you get your uptightness in the way, then you will have no three-course meals. Accept what is in front of you and make the best of it—that's the essence of leading a happy life."

What does this coast know about sorrow? So serene and melancholy at one glance, healthy and pungent the next. Air swollen with nutrition, a substantial difference from my own person. Another timeless, unspoiled turf, so detached and impartial to emotion. Yearning that I could say the same, but, born human, this cognition was rendered moot long ago. A life wasted.

For once in my decrepit, estranged existence, I hereby fall witness to an exquisite place, somewhere I should have relocated myself prior to marriage. Then, and only then, I fancy to think I may have saved myself from this moment of vacancy, of shame, of defeat.

A DUSTED INK passage from Miss Clare, dead six years. Roderic kept the endearing journal in a stout lockbox below his cabin, cellared amongst family photo albums, the final dress she wore, and an unfinished bottle of merlot, the last she'd uncorked. Red wine was her lifeblood, something she'd literally bequeathed both sons.

In most cases an inherited condition, members of a family will often be found to carry Long QT Syndrome, as Miss Clare did, transferring it to Roderic at birth. She eventually expired to lung cancer.

It was a time bomb in his chest. Increasingly common, yet most doctors seem unaware of the syndrome's existence and it often strikes without warning, killing humans in life's full bloom.

Long QT Syndrome—Roderic's demise—is an abnormality of the heart's electrical system. The heart's mechanical function is normal, but the electrical problem stems from defects in heart muscle cell structures, predisposing those affected to a rapid heart rhythm which is too fast for the heart to beat effectively. Thus, blood flow to the brain falls precipitously, inducing sudden unconsciousness and cardiac death.

The syndrome draws its name from the distinctive signature or shape of the wave—an unusually long interval between the 'Q' and 'T' wave points—shown on an electrocardiagram. The interval depicts how long it takes for the heart to return to normal after contracting and thrusting blood through body.

Typically, there is no presage to unconsciousness; often the sole indications are fainting or unexplained collapses. Roderic had merely retired to bed following a surf, a healthy meal and two drams of whisky.

Last words to me before stepping into his bedroom:

"Sustenance comes from the sea, you know. It's part of our heritage. G'night, Kew."

I reflected. It was all water, and is. Beatha eileanach, he once said—island life. There are many different lives we could be leading besides the one we do.

I WOKE INTO a slight daze. The waves....a visceral rumble. The air....cold, heavy. The sky....black, full of stars. Dense gray when I last saw it several hours ago. Laying alone on this seductively empty beach, a long way from anywhere, fire snapping loudly after a bracing surf session, dank chill easing...I'd watched the wood sparks fly and fall. Sleep ensued.

Now....awake. Roderic's face was gone but the water of life remained, just a few yards from my feet, rolling up onto the beach as white foam. I closed my eyes again. The vivid dream of four weeks never returned.

5

SCOTTISH DEPTH, VIKING SOUL

2009

THE COLD WESTERN gale, a vile wind, had corrugated the peat-red loch and doused the pub's windows with rain. Flocks of greylag geese honked and soared high, wildfowl celebrating the equinox, daylight fading to gauze gray, the hours of darkness growing with the death of each windswept dusk. Above the black cattle in the green grass field, symbolizing the archipelago's heritage, the Nordic-cross flag was horizontally stiff from the gale spawned by an Icelandic depression that tonight was exiting Orkney, eastbound to Norway, fanning the cow fields and shredding the North Sea, murmurs of winter etching deep into autumn's quintessence.

Aside the fireplace with a dram of whisky, I mulled the scene. Surfing Orkney was not customary—its spots were few and fickle, its weather inclement. It is a nearly unsurfable place. In a week's time our sole day of chance lay in a sheltered bay, a rough reef that really wasn't a surf spot but, briefly, before the tide drained, had lips, walls, rows of whitewater. Yet closeouts, strong onshores, and severe squalls were generally prohibitive of everything but duckdives and endurance paddling. The session was loud and cold; a few overhead corners were whacked and the island's first air-reverse was pulled. Outside the bay, the swells were 50 feet high. Passersby pointed and stared at us from their heated car seats, the sight of surfers both rare and ridiculous.

"Beyond Britannia, where the endless ocean opens, lies Orkney."
—Orosius, 5th century

ORKNEY IS NOT a household word. If you're European—Swedish or French, say—perhaps you've held a map and studied the small archipelago above Thurso East, one of Scotland's best waves, and you may have thought the treeless islands opposite the Pentland Firth, on Thurso's horizon, might have something good to ride. If you're Irish, British, or mainland Scottish, one might assume you've actually surfed among Orkney's 70 isles. But that's unlikely—why make the effort?

Axiom redirects you. Mainland Scotland is cheaper and endowed with high-quality waves easily accessible by car. Thurso's County Caithness enjoys one of Europe's best surf spans, miles of it stretching west to County Sutherland, beachbreak by pointbreak by picturesque cove. Yet the triumvirate of North Sea, Norwegian Sea, and North Atlantic Ocean provides Orkney with consistent swell, because those winds do blow.

Before you land at tiny Kirkwall Airport, where an oak barrel and whisky bottles adorn the baggage belt, you may see myriad setups far below, grassy pointbreaks and shelfy reefs and crescents of sand yawning into an open sea. But the airline doesn't take surfboards, and the swell direction is skewed or the wind is wrong, or the tide is out, or there is no way to get down the cliff to reach that triangle of white. Orkney's elements work against you. When you set foot on Orcadian soil, however, you inhale the briny air and feel the fresh breeze on your face, and the scruffy old sheep farmer in black boots and blue coveralls shuts his red tractor off, smiles, and tells you that trespassing is accepted here. He'd never seen a surfboard in person. Across his mucky field is a possible right point, and over there is a flawed left blasting over flagstone reef. But what about the stone walls and barbed wire and electric fences? No problem, the farmer says—you can go. His brogue is dense, almost undecipherable, lexically influenced by a Gaelic substratum that penetrated neolithic Scotland, a Viking era, an Iron Age, a scene that visually wasn't much different from the Orkney Islands of today.

It was with boardbags and hooded 5-mils, then, heralding the Hatston Ferry Terminal arrival of central California's Josh Mulcoy, north Oah'u's Daniel Jones, and transient American Warren Smith this first night of October. For seven hours from Aberdeen the 410-foot-long *MV Hrossey* had steamed through a violent North Sea, at last rumbling into Kirkwall's harbor five minutes to midnight. "That was weird," Mulcoy said, collecting his bags. "Definitely the closest I've ever come to being seasick." Smith too was nauseous. Jones just laughed as we loaded the rental car. The cold wind flung sleet around us, and it was the first time his duffel had housed so much wetsuit. "I'd love to come and freeze my ass off with you guys," he'd told me a week prior. The humble Hawaiian was keen for something new.

> *"Tonight: Rain clearing to showers as strong SE'ly winds veer strong to gale SW'ly. Towards morning the showers becoming heavy and squally as winds veer NW to N'ly and increase gale or severe-gale."*

NORTH ATLANTIC STORMS are never fake.

One morning dawned unusually calm and clear—the day would be the sun-dappled Orkney of its tourism brochures—so we strapped boards to the car roof and took a sunrise drive. "I'm *incredibly* happy to be here," Smith said in Floridian drawl as we motored through the golden hues of dewy farmland, past livestock grazing along narrow tracks under an azure sky. The panoramas moved him. "Back to my roots, man. This place is simply unreal." Smith was of a lengthy Scottish lineage; it was his first and long-overdue trip to Europe. Mulcoy, a coldwater specialist, had never seen this nook of the world. And Jones had not surfed in an ocean colder than 60°F; Orkney's was far below that.

Considering the day's weather, two pointbreaks in the bay nearest our B&B would have been excellent had the swell been larger and more direct. But for us the points were flat. Their surrounding views were sublime, the sea a deep glassy blue, the sweep of flaxen fields to the east and north, the gentle inclines and greeny-beige checkerboard farms, the rabbits and well-fed feral cats, the cackling ravens, the round hay bales, the rusty barbed-wire fences, the raptors preying from telephone poles, the silhouettes of cows and sheep with the tractors and ancient flagstone barns. In this rural paradise, just one thing was missing.

Perhaps there were waves elsewhere—on this island or another—or perhaps not, because in Orkney you never knew what to expect, even if a local directed you to it. En route to another iffy surf spot, we stopped for gas (US$9 per gallon). The elderly cashier saw our surfboards; she told us her house overlooked a bay we'd seen on the map. "Last week we had some nice waves there," she said. "Have you lads found some nice waves yet?"

"No," Mulcoy said, opening a Snickers bar. "But hopefully we will in a few minutes."

"Aye, needn't worry," the lady said. "The sea is usually quite rough this time of year. But look at this weather!"

"It's nice, isn't it?" Mulcoy said.

"Aye. Twenty years ago it used to snow a lot more in autumn, but now it snows rarely. We're not sure what to make of it, whether it's global warming or something else. But the past few Octobers have been mild as I can remember."

"That must be good for the fishermen, yeah?" Smith asked. "A smoother ocean?"

"Oh, aye. But you wouldn't catch me sailing around out there." She smiled, revealing brown teeth as she palmed our change to Jones. "Best of luck to you, lads. Hopefully the fishermen won't be able to go out during your time here."

We found nothing that day—most days, in fact. Surfing in Orkney meant being on it at all hours, even if the forecast looked bad, even if you knew you would fail. Early bedtimes barred need for an alarm clock. Tomorrow we would sip strong coffee in frosty 6 a.m. darkness, waiting for the 8 a.m. high tide at a strange, sectiony left; the next day we would be caffeinated and hot-chocolated by 5:30 a.m., speeding through fog to catch an inter-island ferry. With so much coast and so many variables, there was nowhere to fixate, no lingering, our movement fluid and ceaseless like the Orcadian wind.

> *"In the days of Harold Fairhair, King of Norway, certain pirates…stripped these races of their ancient settlements, destroyed them wholly, and subdued the islands to themselves."*
>
> *—anonymous monk,* Historia Norwegiæ, *16th century*

> *"The Vikings rode channel bottoms."*
>
> *—Sam George,* Surfer *magazine, 20th century*

ARMED, BEARDED, AND loudly impetuous, perhaps the Vikings really were assholes. In 875 AD, after 8,000 tranquil years of Orkney humanity, the pagan Norsemen blazed into Orcadian harbors aboard massive wooden longships, eager to expand their turf westward. They smiled at islands' assets (fertile farmland, relatively temperate climate, central location, wanton Pict women) and instantly claimed them. But historical records are sparse and nobody really knows what the Vikings did to the Picts, and whether they coexisted is anyone's guess, but one truth is the raiders overwhelmed them. The Picts were peaceful pious souls, sophisticated yet simple, shy of unsolicited pillage; yet their quiet home soon lay under the spiked fist of Norway, a mere day's sail east.

Viking rule bloomed until the year 1469, when a royal bicultural marriage was booked. Margaret, the 13-year-old daughter of Norway's King Christian I, was to wed Scotland's 18-year-old King James III in Edinburgh. For dowry, Christian pledged Orkney to the young James, planning to reclaim his Norse islands by giving 50,000 gold coins to Scotland. Christian was broke, however, so Orkney was annexed to Scotland in 1472, instantly bolstering the nation's wave chest. Not that anyone cared.

One sunny morning 537 years later we surfed an idyllic beachbreak that was a landing for the Vikings—they surfed their longships right onto the sand. It was likely a raucous and perhaps bloody scene in medieval times. But today it was seabirds and pinnipeds, not a human in sight, because the beach was obscure and ill-accessed. "Just go down that farm track aways," a fat red-cheeked man told us, pointing at an impassable-looking lane fording a muddy field. "Don't try the track next to it, though—too many bumps and rabbit holes. Aye, lads, you'll get 'er stuck for certain!" We chose the latter and didn't get stuck but popped a tire and hit a fence, adding a few expensive scrapes to the rented sedan.

The sandbar sets were overhead, shifty, somewhat hollow. Curious fur seals cruised the lineup, and the water was perfectly clear. The air felt mild and the breeze blew offshore briskly, strengthening as our session waned. After a quick snack on the beach, Smith and Jones sampled a punchy left that broke on a shallow ledge next to the beachbreak; the two goofyfooters were thrilled about Orkney's trove of frontside options. The spot snapped Smith's leash on his first wave, and Jones almost ollied his 5'3" bonzer over one of the 30-something seals milling around, their heads bobbing in the trough.

The left held promise but was quickly slain by the tide. Anyway, there were more reefs around; up the beach and fronting vertical bluffs was one, a genuine right-hand slab exploding with stunning regularity, a sight which impressed Mulcoy, who, working the peaks at the beachbreak's far end, had the best view into the bowl. "Hey, that wave is *ridiculous*," he said, pointing at another spitter. "We have to go look at it up close."

Two days later, for Mulcoy that meant a frightening "shortcut" paddle through a narrow cave at the base of cliffs violently sloshed with whitewater and strong current. There was no beach, so once the waves broke outside, the whitewater, losing no speed, steamrolled straight into sheer rock, blasting through the cave. Had Mulcoy mistimed his entry, he could have been seriously injured or perhaps killed, and we were in the remotest recesses of the archipelago. "That was by far the scariest thing I've ever done." Initially I thought he was referring to the wave. Smith and Jones took the long route out, paddling over from the next headland.

Superlatives ensued. Jones: "Maybe that's the gnarliest wave around?" Smith: "That was so fucking rad, man. Just the heaviest surfing experience ever." Before the trip Smith told me he would be "absolutely useless at a big right slab." Also interesting was the fact there wasn't a real swell running that day but the sets were triple-overhead, vomiting repeatedly over the shallow flagstone. Unfortunately there was no way to backdoor the peak, so no true glory holes were bagged. Mulcoy had a few slots. A tow rope was the answer, but no jet skis were available. In this era of ubiquitous slab-wave/tow-in exploits, Scotland remains virgin.

> *"It would be no true or, at least, no very discerning lover of whisky who could enter this almost sacred zone without awe."*
> *—Aeneas MacDonald, 20th century*

"HOW CAN YOU drink this shit?" Mulcoy wrinkled his nose and handed his full tasting glass to me, which I gladly took. We were touring the grounds of Kirkwall's Highland Park, world's northernmost Scotch whisky distillery, maker of fine single malts that parallel those of Islay, the southern Hebridean island worshiped by single-malt purists. But Highland Park maintains an elegance with its standard 12-year-old whisky and particularly its special cask-strength edition called "Hjärta," sold only at the distillery and in Scandinavia. Smartly, after our hour-long tour, Daniel Jones personally exported a bottle for his uncle on Oah'u.

In Orkney, worlds from Hawaii, Scandinavian spirit still penetrates (*hjärta*, for example, is Norse for "heart"), and nearly all place names are Norwegian, not Scottish, because in Orkney the Gaelic language never stuck. But what if Orkney hadn't become Scottish? If the islands were still Norwegian, I wondered, how would the soul differ?

"Ha! Boy, we're all from the same stock." This was John, our jovial barkeep in town who served lunch and drinks with a cleft right hand. "Viking, Scotsman, Norwegian....around here, mate, everybody came from somebody else. It's all the same blood. See, there's not a lot to do here besides fishin', drinkin', and shaggin', and things wouldn't be much different around here if we was Norwegians—different language, aye, but the fishin', farmin', and drinkin' would still be here."

"And shagging," Smith said.

"Aye, that too!"

I told John that I felt a bit groggy from my previous eve's solitary whisky binge. "You know what the best cure for a hangover is?" he asked in his singsong Orcadian dialect. "A tin of Coke. You open it the night before, so by mornin' it's flat. You drink it. Or Zantac. You pop a Zantac before you drink, and out you go. The next mornin'? Aye, no hangover, no grogginess, and that's after 15 or 16 pints of lager and some right drams."

"You can drink 15 or 16 pints in one night, plus whisky?" I asked.

He nodded, smiled, winked. "And that's on a *slow* night, boy."

Not that there was reason for hangovers—Mulcoy, Smith, and Jones typically shied from drink, and Orkney was not Oslo. Nightlife was nil and we had coast to comb.

After lunch Smith suggested we inspect a few miles of jagged shore on the island's leeward side—the wind would be offshore there—so we left the village and drove along bumpy wet lanes into isolation, eventually cresting a knoll from where we could see a covert cove, the mouth of a green vale with a lonesome overhead left reeling along a nearshore shelf, an ambiguous slab with bumps and boils. The water was gray but gin-clear, the waves dredging thick brown seaweed as they cracked along the ledge. The spot looked fun and challenging. Beyond it were several latent reefs, too, and the cove's opposite side had a right-hand setup that would need more swell—a big swell, swell winter could serve.

The sky was gunmetal gray smeared with black—an hour of daylight left. I stopped the car in a puddle on the side of a muddy track at the bottom of the vale, fronting two decaying barns, disused farm tools, and a low flagstone wall that enclosed dozens of grazing sheep. The air smelled of wet hay and livestock dung.

"Damn, another left?" Mulcoy said half-jokingly, watching another lurch toward the channel. "Man, I *never* go backside." (This was actually true.) Goofyfooters Smith and Jones laughed as they pulled their wet 5-mils on. "Sure is a lot of work getting ready to surf these cold places," the grinning Hawaiian said, noting the effort for getting into the mounds of rubber that kept him warm and loose. "But it's worth it—so worth it." And until darkness, it was Orcadian zen.

> *"A tongue here and there was touched to enchantment by starlight and peat flame."*
> *—George Mackay Brown*

ANOTHER UNSURFABLE DAY. Accordion and fiddle were apt din for a cozy mid-afternoon teatime in the small pub of our B&B aside a coal fire with pints of cask-drawn ale 'round the dark wooden table. Then the CD started skipping and so was switched off, allowing for soothing rain patter on the room's double-paned windows, the wind whistling around the pub's old stone perimeter, the soft lilting voices in the room augmenting ours. Main courses were fatty and caloric—Jones's broiled, seaweed-fed lamb, Mulcoy's battered haddock, Smith's beef pie with black pudding—and there were the soft fillets of wild brown trout, hooked hours ago in the adjacent loch; then the selection of Grimbister Farm cheese on a tray, the chewy warm oatcakes, the flaky butter biscuits, the gooey fudge from Stromness, the unfiltered pints of Quoyloo ale, the drams of peaty whisky from the outskirts of Kirkwall.

Dusk was a slit of ochre pressed between distant low hills and dark rain clouds. Early night was wet, a gale from the south, its constant low rumble like the hymn of waves. The rain intensified from a patter to a pelting of hail, a woodfire crackle, the tiny balls sticking to the ground like snow. White in the night. Surely the glass of the small room's window had seen fairer eves.

Outside...pitch-black. Eventually the storm's vigor killed the town's wattage, so we used candlelight, a fitting glow for Orkney, islands steeped in sentimentality despite the 21st-century trappings on the far end of that Atlantic horizon. In the tiny B&B we pored over the maps, drew arrows, made plans. The boys would turn in early, not long after 9, satiated with artisan fare, comfortable in the old warmth that only a Scottish isle could grant.

Later—the wee hours. Drowsing supine with Enya's "And Winter Came" in my ears, there was a meditation on the archipelago's 59°N latitude and our position in surf travel. North Atlantic austerity had only allowed for recent navigation of the region's surf wealth. Scotland has many locals now—new wetsuit technology has fostered a gestation of surfers in places like this. Abroad, too, temperate surfers have begun to search far beyond the tropical fray, the traditional heart of surf trips—the equatorial score, the Third World junket, the generic lust for barrels in boardshorts. But our Orkney nonce was dissimilar, a cerebral levitation into the northern wilds, chased by weather and lured by maps. It was emotional and risky, a long and expensive journey.

The next morning's newspaper said the sea-and-sky forecast was good, but not for another 72 hours. Winter was near. There would be more time to burn, more setups to consider. If anything it was a chance to dry the wetsuits and study some historic decor—Viking ruins, standing stones, medieval churches, brochs, castles, cairns, tombs. It was all there, an archeologist's dream. Sometimes, like Enya sang, dreams are more precious. We had ours, too.

PART II

Polynesia

6

PASIFIKA VAILIMA

2002

HER SMILE. THOSE eyes. Round, black, soothed by thick salt air and mossy, spicy, rotted-earth tang of tropical rain forest.

"Tofa soifua."

Goodbye. A chance encounter with a South Pacific beauty. Ensconced in ivory, off solo to evening church, flower adorning her left ear, she broke from the beach with a final back glance, casting another sultry, soft smile as I waded into the turquoise lagoon for a swim.

Tofa soifua, yes. Forgotten?....no.

Dusk now. Coconut palm fronds sweep over the pearly beach as I pick barefoot over coral and lava, drawing deeper into the 87-degree saltwater, clear as air. First immersion and I'm away from the North Pacific and all of its frigid reverences, springtide gales, redwoods, white sharks and hypothermia. One-third of Earth is Pacific, larger than all lands combined, and here was its lower half—a warm wet, unlike the March gray I'd abandoned in California days prior.

As was the rough midnight drop through the clouds into Faleolo Airport, Apia. Last off the jet, through the emptied Air New Zealand rows and farewelling stewardesses, I pressed straight into Upolu's sublime stickiness—another warm wet, this one nosed with sweat, bloom and soil. A grand entrance to the unspoiled heart and swell of Polynesia.

> *"Long time ago, there's a man name Lu. He's the first one to have a chicken in Samoa, so he's very strict to anyone who touch his chicken. He have a chicken zoo. One day, the young men who served godfather Taloalang…they come in nighttime and try to attack Lu's chicken zoo. So Lu's very angry because he have a rule: not allow anyone to touch his chickens. The young men come to get his chickens for them. But Lu was very angry to find them trying to kill chickens. So a girl of the godfather named Taloalang lay down on the way where Lu tried to find the men to kill them. There's a Samoan proverb, very popular: The lady lying in the way. So stop Lu from killing the men. That's the end of Lu's angry.*
>
> *"So that's the meaning of the name Samoa. Sa means 'forbidden.' Moa means 'chicken.' Samoa means "forbidden chicken."*
>
> *—Saia Tui*

EACH DAY BRINGS another boat trip. Aside from a pair of epic sessions at Boulders, it is Nu'usafee Island or Siumu or Coconuts or Spot X for this California posse, guests of classy Sa'Moana Resort in Salamumu, south shore Upolu. Ideal striking distance to several hazardous reef waves, one of them fronting the guest quarters, or fales. A carload reconnaissance mission circling Upolu reveals north shore potential in the language of heavy-duty coral barrels with no one to surf them.

The boat is freedom. Ticket to ride. Alternative to long, sketchy paddles from shore. The 7'6" pintail is either gore or glory. Our boat stays at port; we settle back into the van and resume driving.

Imagine traveling the world and owning the ability to surf anything encountered. This person could conceivably live on Upolu for one year and surf its dozens of unsurfed breaks and never share a lineup. A helmet and reef booties are required for the waves we viewed, absolutely reeling over distant reefs under scorching midday sun. Upolu—some of the world's heaviest lineups unridden—scar reefs, dreamscape waves from shore, terror in close range. User-friendly for the trigger finger. Or Tom Carroll.

Then there's Leper Colony Left at Upolu's southeast fringe, flanked by an island and a headland. Gorgeous symmetry. Sharky. Lethal. Risk your life if you dare. Or get back into the van and drive away.

> *"But we are so fond of life that we have no leisure to entertain the terror of death. It is a honeymoon with us all through, and none of the longest. Small blame to us if we give our whole hearts to this glowing bride of ours, to the appetites, to honour, to the hungry curiosity of the mind, to the pleasure of the eyes in nature, and the pride of our own nimble bodies."*
>
> *—Robert Louis Stevenson*

SAMOA. ARCHIPELAGO OF black lava crowns strung along an east-west axis roughly 14 degrees south of the Equator. Eons ago, these islands sprouted from the seabed, hissing and gurgling hot as crustal plates jockeyed below. An old yarn claims this is where the world began when the creator, Tagaloalagi, first bellowed forth earth, sea and sky from rock. Then he made the first human being.

Language links and artifacts suggest the first distinctly Polynesian culture may have evolved here some 3,000 years yore. Spanning the ensuing centuries, Polynesian men piloting double-hulled sailboats packed with pigs, dogs and fruit scattered their culture across much of the Pacific, colonizing lands as distant as Hawaii, New Zealand and Rapa Nui.

Through the modern colonial era, the western islands succumbed to Germany, then New Zealand (introducing the now-immensely popular Samoan rugby), both nations disregarding local kings and customs in classic colonialistic form. Come 1962, following a granted proposal to the United Nations, the islands of Savai'i and Upolu became the independent nation of Western Samoa, known simply as Samoa since 1995.

All was not smooth, however. Dependence on foreign aid and vicious labor disputes meant the dream was tainted, and life steeply deteriorated after the nation was thrashed by successive cyclones, and its main export crop, taro, was decimated by a fungal curse. Samoa ebbed into an economic impasse from which it has never fully recovered, though tourism is easing the blow.

CORAL REEF: RAIN forests of the sea, breadbaskets sustaining a massive ecosystem, among Earth's oldest and most biologically diverse, emerging some 200 million years ago. One hundred thousand species of coral have been cataloged out of a possible two million. A crucial nexus in the maritime food chain, these microcosms of color and life are a highly sensitive barometer of the tropical environment's well-being.

The serrated kaleidoscope shallows off Nu'usafee Island felt healthy to me. Lower back reef bounce in two feet of water so clear, depth discernment is challenging. A harsh wound appears. Our regularfooted skipper Brent, Australian expat, eyes the roping head-high lefts and shrugs. "Mate, I couldn't ride backside barrels worth a shit when I first moved here," he says. "Figured I'd have to learn painfully, eventually."

Yes. Weaving deeply through bending blue vortexes, crouched with one hand on the nose, one grabbing rail, he emerges more often than not. It is an excellent demonstration.

That afternoon, a perfect double rainbow arcs atop Nu'usafee, Upolu's tried-and-true offshore savior during the southeast trades. No cameras; consistently beautiful yet unmakeable backside tubes and a dangerously shallow inside section. Blistering shortboard speed lines, warm trade wind whistling through the hair and ears. Bloodshot, salt-stung faces glare into the westward-setting sun, highlighting the rainbow like a postcard or fantasized oil painting. It is almost too cliché, this Robinson Crusoe factor. So we surf over sharp coral and the boat waits at anchor, framing the island scene, a fine ocular repast. Polynesian zen.

"Yesterday, which was Sunday—the Quantieme is most likely erroneous; you can now correct it—we had a visitor—Baker of Tonga. Heard you ever of him? He is a great man here: he is

accused of theft, rape, judicial murder, private poisoning, abortion, misappropriation of public moneys—oddly enough, not forgery, nor arson: you would be amused if you knew how thick the accusations fly in this South Sea world. I make no doubt my own character is something illustrious; or if not yet, there is a good time coming." (Letter from R.L.S. to Henry James. Apia, Samoa, Dec. 29, 1890.)

A SHIMMERING, SWEATY blue Sunday morn. Sa'Moana Resort guests marshal inside the resort's van en route to church service at the end of the three-minute coral commute to Salamumu's dapper new house of worship, an example of good Samoan architecture fitted with elegant wood ceilings and pews, fanned by the ubiquitous overhead spiral blur. And packed to the walls with those of Salamumu, all in white, many stone-faced, gripping The Word, ripe for prayer. Same deal, different week.

I enter then sit. Conceal the Canon with the removed wide-brimmed hat. Three-hundred pounds of elder Samoan occupies the aisle seat to my left. Nobody to the right.

The pastor begins his sermon. I unveil the camera. Three-hundred pounds of elder Samoan notices, eyes my intent, raises a brow, then leans over and whispers.

"You tek a piktcha?"

A peculiar moment. I nod vaguely with a forced grin. Blasphemy?

Suddenly his face morphs into a huge, white smile and he stands, motioning for me to take his place with a better view. We switch seats and I shake his vast hand.

"Thank you, sir."

"God bless," he grinned with sincerity.

Missionaries waltzed onto Upolu more than a century ago, and as the church evolved into a preeminent role of village life, Samoa became the Bible Belt of the South Seas, embracing the transposed Christian religion with gusto. Sunday service is a pinnacle event each week.

This belies the region's reputation for being quite flexible of inhibitions and attire, an image brewed from lusty sailor tales later bolstered by Margaret Mead's "Coming of Age in Samoa," a popular read of adolescent sexuality. Many a foreigner is nonplussed to discover it is deemed offensive for females to bear shorts or scant tops in a village. Definitely no bikinis. And one mustn't swim or surf or indulge in any other form of recreation near villages on Sundays, set aside for family visits, feasting and worship.

The hour comes and Salamumu's congregation lethargically files out. I catch Sa'Moana barkeep Saia for a question about the Christian influence.

"The missionaries arrived here in our land and we then knew the real god," he says. "Samoans had a god they prayed for, a traditional god. But the god is unknown. Who's that god? At the time the missionaries arrived here, they explain well, and we know that it's the real god they pray for."

Staunch traditionalism saturates Samoa, adhering to a knotty set of social hierarchies, courtesies and customs dictating social, religious and political livelihoods. There is no crime; homes have no walls. Etiquette rules abound, with a sharp grasp of propriety and respect.

Here is the South Pacific's epicenter of tribal tattooing, an intrinsic step of initiation into Samoan culture. The markings are made come puberty; at age 12 or 13, Samoan males visit the tufuga, or tattooist, and get inked from waist to knee. Tattoos represent the strength of a man's heart and his spirituality. If you can bear the pain of a month's worth of tattooing, you can bear anything.

Culture is hinged on a *fa'amatai*—a governmental system boasting a chief, or matai, who reigns an entire aiga, or extended family. Necessities are rationed on a needs basis, while honor and social standing are shared by all in the aiga. Their matai represents the family on the village council, doles out justice and ensures customs are abided. He is also a living encyclopedia of all that is Samoan, responsible for narrating ancient folklore, family genealogies and tales of the old gods.

Each village has a certified orator, his words braiding long, elaborate sinews of family ancestry and spiritual prowess, speaking also of everyday affairs on behalf of the village's high chief. Donning traditional tattoos and a floral sarong-ish lavalava, Saia is our orator tonight at Sa'Moana's weekly 'ava ceremony, or fiafia, in the dining fale. Saia is a descendent of highly ranked men in Salamumu. Full name's Saia Tauiliili Tui, the latter two translating into "high chief" and "king," respectively.

While the women of Salamumu prepare a feast inside, Saia wrings root liquid into a wood bowl. Hoisting the bowl in gratitude then draining it with one gulp, I'm served the result in a sweeping flourish accompanied by a warrior's whoop. Deep words flow from Saia proceeded by taro leaf platters of fish, breadfruit, taro root, lobster and baked coconut cream.

Legend claims the premier 'ava ceremony occurred twixt the world's first man and Tagaloalagi, his creator, who concocted a drink from roots of the kava, a strain of pepper plant. Offering this bitter, milky brown beverage has exemplified Polynesian welcome and communion ever since.

"THERE IS A two different people here in Samoa. Lots of Samoan, they know how fishing. They're the people who not afraid about the ocean. But the people who not know how to fish, they afraid about the ocean. But Samoan island is still same as the Hawaiian people—they like ocean."

Magenta floods the early sky as I converse with Vai, Sa'Moana employee and one of Samoa's native surfing handful. We are aboard the resort's 34-foot aluminum twin-hulled vessel engulfed by the absolute essence of morning: sunrise at sea.

South shore's Aganoa Point. Built of jagged black lava, it is robed in rain forest, further softened by summit mists and verdant skylines spilling to the ocean. Accruing daylight reveals empty triple-overhead lefts detonating against deep-set lava reef. Stand-up barrels for anyone with experience and a pintail. With a leap of courage over the gunwale, we are surfing.

Nine hours later, I swill a lager and muse about the virtual nonexistence of native Samoan surfers. Saia describes it this way:

"Many surfers from overseas ask me about any Samoan surfing before. They try to find the history—is there anyone here in Samoa who took place in surfing? Well, there's a legend story about the one Samoan surfing. It is a true story. We use it here now for our speeches.

"So, in American Samoa, there's a village named Afono. One day, the people wake up in the morning and look out to the ocean. There's a man who's surfing the waves, from the reef, going back beyond the reef, go back…like that. And the people stand on the beach and wave their hands. They try to chase him. 'Who's that man? Get off! Get off!' Like that. So the man run away from that island of American Samoa from the village of Afono and stay here in a village on Upolu. The village is very straight from American Samoa to here.

"At that time there was a very big fight in the villages here on Upolu. That man came and lived here in this village where that fight happens. All the villages, they prepared for a fight. So this man included in this group. They don't know who he is, where he from. When the fight ended, he's a different man. This a man who won the fight. But this a man from Afono, from the village of American Samoa, so they chase him out.

"Afono villagers, they know the stories about the fights here. They know that's the man they chased out from their village, so there's a Samoan proverb which means Afono missed their blessing. They're lucky from this man. That man surfing, the one who surfing is a very hero man. And I know that this history of surfing is a very long time ago took place. Because there's a man in American Samoa who surf. He's a hero man, know everythings. Good in a tide, in a ocean. When he go out there, he know how to surf. When he go on land, he know how to fight. He's a hero.

"That is the story and history I know from long time ago. Lots of Samoans, they know it. We have a special proverb like if you missed something, or you just throw something away, the people say, 'Ah, you missed your blessing' or 'You missed your lucky.' They missed chance to learn surfing."

POLYNESIAN TRANQUILLITY COMES with a sinking sun into palm silhouettes. Four more breaststrokes and I can't touch lagoon bottom. Stop and tread water, blink the eyes clear and see the girl vanish into riotous vegetation, from the beach back onto the coral road. It was a pleasant stroll for us. A detour.

Many attend church at this hour. Others commune in social centers, rugby fields, dinner mats in spartan homes. Down at the resort, now a faint glow to the east, Saia serves cocktails. "I surf the waves with my eyes," he'd stated earlier, pointing to his face then to the ocean. One day, he claims, it will be with a surfboard. Still treading, I think of this and peer seaward. Dim horizon fuzz grows pale with broken swell hitting the barrier reef. No surfing out there.

The girl is gone and so is the sun. Twilight resplendence suffocates all else. Here, just offshore Salamumu, I drift on my back, ears filled with muffled wave energy. Close the eyes then open them to the evening star. I try to envision these people at war once with Tonga, or with the rough sea and reefs in fishing canoes, with the Christian white man invasion, with natural disasters, with the tattoo needle. All overcome. For now, it is Samoan idyll.

Fa'afetai tele.

7

WELCOME TO MEATLAND

2011

9:46 a.m.
Fua'amotu International Airport

FIRST THING: CANNIBALISM.

"Naked houris—cannibal banquets—groves of cocoa-nut—coral reefs—tattooed chiefs...carved canoes dancing on the flashing blue waters—savage woodlands guarded by horrible idols—*heathenish rites and human sacrifices.*"

Page four of *Typee*. Ink brilliance amid airport drone. But I can't quote Herman Melville on a photograph for this article—the Marquesas Islands are 4,000 kilometers northeast. We're not going there. I'd like to. During the past two boozy days of flight from LAX, I was inspired by Melville's pen.

By 1842, when he wrote *Typee*, Tonga had been pierced by Captain Cook and forever soiled by Western traders and missionaries. The Marquesas were big and culturally wild, unlike the slow, homogeneous vibe in Tonga's biggest airport where we sit on big blue benches near the luggage carousel, awaiting our big surfboard bags to get burped from the big plane that flew us from a big Fijian isle. But Tonga's airport isn't actually big. Besides the local humans and humpback whales, nothing here seems to be. Except the many Mormon churches we saw on the descent.

Patrick Millin removes his big black headphones and looks up. His head is bald. He's 24 and sports a mustache. His green eyes are jet-lagged.

"Do you think our boardbags are gonna be too big to get into our next plane?" he asks me quietly.

"Why wouldn't they make it?"

"Check it."

He points to the small Chatham Pacific aircraft on the tarmac, a Convair 580 twin-prop seating 50. It's our domestic mule to a possibly unsurfed haven. Back home, with Google Earth, we'd mapped out some left reef passes. A goofyfoot, Millin likes left reef passes. So do goofyfooters Ryan Burch and Daniel Jones. Motionless, they sit on Millin's right. A tall Tongan man carrying a suitcase trips over Burch's foot.

"No sweat," I tell Millin. "They'll fit. Chatham Pacific never carries surfboards, so we won't get hosed. They don't know how to screw surfers."

He shrugs and resumes iPodding to techno beats. I reach into my dirty red backpack and trade *Typee* for *The Happy Isles of Oceania*. In chapters 14 and 15, author Paul Theroux describes his experience in Tonga, to where he traveled in 1990, first to the main island of Tongatapu. There he visited the Royal Palace and yakked with 375-pound King Taufa'ahau Tupou IV. (Tonga is the Pacific's dinosaur of constitutional monarchism. The king was a sedentary fat-ass with unlimited power.) Then he flew up to the jellyfish-shaped Vava'u Group, where he rowed his collapsible kayak and tent-camped solo, mostly in the rain.

"It was said that these islands were among the most beautiful in the Pacific," Theroux writes, "and many of them were desert islands, utterly inhabited but pristine—dream islands, each one like a little world."

His chapter details dog-eating, annoying mosquitoes, downpours ("It was though I were paddling beneath a waterfall. . . ."), wildlife, local residents, and chatty Caucasian yachties in the Port of Refuge, a fine anchorage. Hence, we will be going nowhere near it. But I like something else Theroux wrote about Vava'u at the bottom of page 318:

"Each was just what you imagined a tropical island to be—palms, woods, surf on the bright beach, limpid green lagoons."

I stop and tap my finger on the sentence.

"Millin. Look."

He leans over and reads aloud: "'Surf on the bright beach.'" He grins calmly and repeats. "Surf on the bright beach! Yew! Maybe a reef? A slab? Let's do this!" He high-fives me. It's a loud slap. Burch and Jones flash sleepy thumbs-ups.

"Barrels," Burch says.

"Wait," Jones says. "Is that where we're going?"

I don't know.

7:32 a.m.
South Pacific Ocean, 40 fathoms

OUR BOAT DRIVER is drunk. Sateki's glazed, red eyes focus on nothing. He didn't sleep last night and was in a messy quarrel with his wife until dawn. Something about not drinking on Sundays. Today is Monday.

Still Sateki drinks. His forearms are gray with faded tattoos. In the chest pocket of his dirty black shirt is a small glass bottle of whiskey ("Jack Daniel's! Don' tell nobody."). With a fat brown hand gripping the wheel, he pounds us through the blue wind chop over two-meter swells and a deep, dark sea outside a small island's barrier reef. The drop-off is sheer. The boat ride is loud and blustery and spine-jolting and we are soaked in salt spray.

Low and green, this island looks deserted. But, viewing the abundance of baitballs and splashes, an angler here would have it made. Tonga is known for rich fisheries. And we're really not far from the Tonga Trench, which, at its deepest, drops to 35,702 feet—nearly seven miles.

"One time here I see tiger shark longer than dis boat!" Sateki yells, slurring a bit but nodding slowly as he sways. He wipes sweat from his face. "Come right up to da side and sit, waiting for us to bring fish up on da line. *Hooo-wee!*"

"How big's this boat?" I yell back.

"Six, eight meter? I dunno!" He laughs and picks his nose.

Armed with print-outs of Google Earth grabs, I pinpoint our location. Amid the bounce, I almost lose a few precious sheets of paper to the wind. But it's a good wind. It's offshore. We need it. These swells are not clean.

Ryan Burch steadies and stands. His eyes gape when he sees a gap in the reef.

"Ahoy!" he yells. "Is this the spot?"

It's one I'd marked with a red pen arrow, the coffee cup stain two inches away. Tongan coffee is particularly good, akin to French roast.

"Sateki, will you please steer us into that channel?" I show the map to him. We've reached the end of the reef at the end of the island. In the distance are several more, like stepping stones, and nothing but soaring birds, spindrift, and bouncy blue water. Lifting and lowering our little boat, the swells are from the southwest, the wind from the east, and as Sateki motors us around the reef and into the pass, it becomes joyously clear that Google Earth is indeed our best friend.

"Yes!" Millin shouts, clenching a fist. "We love Google Earth!"

This morning, it's led us to a hollow, slightly overhead left that rises from deep water and trips at the top of the reef, where the wind hits it sideways. The wave then bends 90 degrees 'round the reef and faces the wind, trimming some size but tidying the place up. It looks like a fun spot for a goofyfooter who isn't afraid falling onto urchins and sharp, shallow, living coral. And it's much better than the wave we'd surfed during the last two days. We were being lazy.

"Are we out there?" Jones asks, waxing his little single-fin.

Pensive now, slouched on the transom, Sateki takes a swig from his whiskey bottle. His sight is askew. He pushes the bottle at me, and since I love whiskey, I have a drink. This pleases him.

"Dis where I saw the big tiger shark," Sateki says calmly, as if disclosing a great secret. "Dis channel. Right here."

"Right here?" I ask.

"Yes! Right here!" Suddenly he seems defensive and glowers at me, like I doubt him. "You don't believe me? What! What you gonna do?"

Tongans are known for orneriness. I recall a Theroux quote from *The Happy Isles of Oceania*: "Many of the Tongans I met were unreliable, and some outright liars. This could be tiresome in a hot climate. My solution was to take my boat to a part of Tonga where there were no Tongans."

We couldn't do that. We needed a boat and a human to drive it. We could drive a boat ourselves, but we didn't know the area and no one would loan or rent one to us.

Certainly Sateki is the only Tongan near us, and, since he's a large, drunk man and owns the boat we're sitting in, I smile and say, "Of course I believe you, my friend. There are many tiger sharks around here."

"How you know this?" he asks. "You have never been here before!"

"Because you just told me."

"You don't believe me!"

"Hey, man, we believe you," says Millin the mediator. "It's cool. Can you toss the anchor in over there? Like, inside, facing the wave? We'd like to surf here."

"Why I anchor if you guys are like fools? Dis guy call me liar."

"Sateki, I never called you a liar," I say. "All I said was I was surprised by how big tiger sharks can get here. That's impressive. And the fact that you were right there next to a huge one? That's really cool."

"No!" He points a stubby finger at me. "You don' believe. I see big tiger shark here, and you don' believe. You call me a liar." He sways and takes a quick pull of whiskey. He's very drunk now. "Why you do this? What!"

"I didn't call you anything, man. Relax."

"Yeah," Millin says, "Mike didn't call you anything. It's cool. Of course there are lots of huge tiger sharks around here. Why wouldn't there be?"

A three-wave set stacks over the reef.

"Are we out there, or what?" Jones says, about to leap overboard.

"I am," Burch says as he hops off the gunwale with a short, self-shaped asymmetrical board underarm. He brought four of them to Tonga. The splash from his jump douses Sateki's fat face.

3:04 p.m.
Remote cove on another isle

BUSHWHACKING THROUGH TALL weeds and sticky spider webs makes us dirty and sweaty. Two spiders hide in Burch's hair. Jones inhales a wisp of silk. Our clothing has unwittingly transported many small arachnids from their fragile airborne homes to the beach, though this isn't really a beach. It's a notch of ragged volcanic rock, sharp as broken glass, dug into the low bluff that we're standing on.

"Check that one!" Burch says, pointing at the hollow, bluey-green left 300 yards offshore. The wave spits. "What?"

Jones too is enthused. We are going to score. As far as we know, this wave is unnamed and unsurfed. Both surfers leave their shirts and sandals with me and crab down the bluff. I'm going to video them. The sun is dropping—we've got time for tubes.

Peeling around an elbow of coral, the waves are slightly overhead, fast and clean, with humpback whales cruising beyond, spouting water as they surface to exhale. Tonga is a breeding ground for these massive cetaceans which migrate from Antarctica each June, reversing in November, 12,000 kilometers round-trip. A major tourist draw, Tongan whale-watching is superb, especially in Vava'u.

To cap the scene, Millin and lensman Billy Watts migrate to the lineup in the aluminum skiff. Sateki, its driver, is not drunk—but today is Friday and tomorrow will likely be painful for him. It's a sensitive portrait of a deep Polynesian ilk poisoned by the ills of the West. Pre-contact, his creed was avidly cannibalistic, sexually gleeful, unstained by Spam or Marlboro or Diet Coke. Tongans have always had kava, but kava is not and will never match Jack Daniel's Tennessee Whiskey.

Tongans have and will always have sun and surf on their side.

5:18 p.m.
Small grassy yard behind a palm-thatch hut

THEROUX, PAGE 294: "I could just imagine a sick Tongan's sense of doom when he or she looked out the hut window and saw the family pig being fattened."

Rigor mortis doesn't make you pretty, but it's tough to look good when a big metal pole has been shoved into your ass, through your body, and out your mouth. You're being roasted clockwise over a pit of coals. You've been eviscerated. Your eyeballs have evaporated. Your legs and skinny tail are stiff. Your long tongue is sticking out. You actually appear to be laughing. You've got a gaping red hole in your belly, where your organs once were, now being wolfed by a big brown dog in a corner of the yard. Your neck features another red hole with boiling blood bubbling from it, trickling around your shiny, pink corpse.

"And then what kind of meat do you get off of it?" Burch asks the man turning the pig. "Ham?"

"Yeah, ham," the man says.

"Is it nice ham?"

"It's like pulled pork," Watts says. "But I can honestly say I've never had a pig like this."

A fat woman in a bright orange dress sits on dirt near the pig. She's using aluminum foil to wrap onions and pieces of taro and breadfruit to be set in the umu ("earth oven") to be cooked by hot rocks. Tonight we will feast Tongan style to celebrate the first birthday of the daughter of the guy who's cooking the pig. His wife is the one doing the umu stuff. Neither has a problem with roasting the family pet.

"Many more where this came from," the man says.

"Not sure if I got a pig on a spit when I turned one year old," Daniel Jones says. But it's possible since he's Hawaiian and they do this sort of thing there and throughout Polynesia. I guessed that umu was a far healthier and wholesome alternative to the usual modern Polynesian diet of Pacific Brand corned beef and other imported junk.

But dog is modern fare, too. All meat is fair game (no pun intended), and Tongans have been eating Fido for millenia. Back in the day, dog was a delicacy, far tastier than pork, and both species were raised domestically. To sweeten their flesh, dogs were fed only vegetables and, in 1774, when Captain James Cook landed in Tonga, he likened the meat to English lamb. But ol' Jimmy was weird since his colleagues thought that barbecuing household pets was terrible.

I glance across the yard to the dog chewing pig intestines.

"Are you guys going to eat that mutt?" I ask the pig-roasting man.

"Yeah. But not tonight."

With his teeth, he removes the cap from a green bottle of beer. Back home I was told that, since Tonga is home to thousands of Mormons, drinking was bad. But this man was Mormon and visibly buzzed whilst swilling from his bottle of Mata Maka, the weak so-called "Tongan" lager that's only available in Tonga but is actually brewed in and imported from New Zealand, 2,000 kilometers away.

"This beer sucks," Watts says to me. He's just finished his second; I'm on my fifth of the afternoon. Watts and I are the drinkers of this trip. Burch and Jones rarely booze. Millin has been voluntarily dry for six months.

Mata Maka is also the name of a low hill on Nomuka Island in Tonga's Ha'apai Group, clamped between Vava'u and Tongatapu, an archipelago my guidebook described as being a "sleepy, seductive place." Nobody really surfs Ha'apai, but I know of at least one excellent left. Nomuka and its surrounding reefs might have good waves, too. So might nearby Mango, Kelefesia, and Tonumeia, green stars on a galaxy of blue. There are dozens more—Ha'apai has many secrets. A boat is required. Viewed from space, the group looks like two big atolls with no western sides, which would be clean and offshore most of the year. Yet another cruelty for surfers since east swells are painfully rare. Our boat is small, so we won't visit Ha'apai this week.

Starting with Ha'apai, Captain Cook spent three months in Tonga. He commanded the *HMS Resolution* while his colleague manned the *HMS Discovery*. When the two ships landed on the isle of Lifuka, a lively food festival was underway. Cook and his men were so gaily greeted that he dubbed Tonga "the Friendly Islands," a motto still used by the Tonga Visitors Bureau.

Cook didn't know the warm welcome was actually bullshit and that Lifuka's opportunistic chiefs planned to kill and eat him and all his men, then loot the two ships. But the nobles couldn't agree on a plan, so they shined the whole thing.

I'm drunk by nightfall. Finally, with equally drunk Tongans, we eat the pig. The white meat is leatherlike, unchewable. Under my chair, I feed most of mine to the big gut-eating dog. He's happy. He's not on the menu—yet.

8

CORAL REFUGE, OCEAN DEEP

2003

SUSTENANCE FLOPS ONTO the stern, hook embedded. A wooden club is found, and the large fish is beaten to death. *Poisson cru*, Hinano, and buttered rice soon flow. Come twilight, drifting off a deserted swath of sand and palm deep within the lagoon, a harmony-with-life notion seems apropos.

Our chaperon speaks.

"Definitely the best fishing in the world, no two ways about it. For sure. I've never had a trip when we haven't caught a marlin. It's completely alive here. There are fish everywhere. You cannot go fishing and not catch fish."

Coral crowns on the rims of ancient sunken volcanoes; 78 constellations of land on a universe of sea. Gluttony of blues, a hundred shades of green....

"On the last trip, we got this really good lefthander that I hadn't got on before. Just epic, just unreal...unbelievable. The whole wave is a barrel from take-off to the end. It's really long—the whole wave is a tube, and it doesn't section. You just take off—and it's an easy take-off—and straight away, it hits this shelf and you just ride at the same speed of the wave. You don't have to pump or anything—you just stay there. You actually have to try and slow down. If you can slow down, you can stay in the barrel the whole wave. Every wave's the same—absolutely mechanical. It's the best wave we've got, for sure. Basically a 10- or 12- second barrel."

The essence of French Polynesia exotica begins and ends with L'Archipel Dangereux, a fragrantly humid coconut palm escape fondly examined aboard the *M/V Cascade*, 64 feet of seaworthy repose. Acquired by our Australian guide Chris O'Callaghan specifically for L'Archipel reconnaissance, this fine vessel administers pristine, vacant perfection amongst a maze of atolls at the end of the Earth.

> *"On every side of us swam sharks innumerable, and so voracious that they bit our oars and rudder, and I actually stuck my saber into the back of one while he had the rudder in his teeth."*
>
> *—Diary of James Trevenen, Captain Cook's midshipman, negotiating a L'Archipel reef pass in 1777.*

LIFE AT SEA epitomizes calm balance with nature while thin, deep reef passes rage with current. Case in point as the *Cascade* shifts on tidal whim, grating anchor along serrated seafloor, threatening either seaborne aimlessness or shipwreck on the pass's elbow. Instinctively, deckhand Francois clears the gunwale and free dives 60 feet to reposition the hook. A fearless ex-pearl diver with minutes of lung capacity, Francois is well-accustomed to such tasks, later surfacing with his broad, white grin, keen to repeat the exercise if need be.

Fletcher is particularly impressed. Line-fishing, he lands a small parrot fish and a few trevally before stroking out to negotiate the throaty, ledgy right-hander blasting into the pink rock shelf. Chris reckons we are the first to surf this wave, referring to an ancient local fisherman who assures us he has not seen a surfer before we appeared.

"Pink Rock, mate—that's what we'll call it," Chris beams, christening the spot in deference to a mutant slab near his Australian home. An expat to Tahiti Nui and wed to a Tahitian woman, Chris possesses an extensive intelligence cache about surfing L'Archipel Dangereux, likely more than anybody.

"There are a lot of waves that nobody's surfed," he assures. "We've got heaps more exploration to do. Out of the 78 atolls, we only know about 20. For sure, there is real epic stuff out here; it just takes a little train of thought to piece it all together, but we're slowly getting there. By this time next year, we'll know two or three times what we know now."

> *"This hypocritical consideration of liberty, equality, fraternity under a French flag becomes a remarkable irony when applied to this disgusting spectacle of humanity who are no more than the flesh from which all kinds of contributions are extracted by the arbitrary gendarme."*
>
> *—Paul Gauguin*

WOULD THEY DO IT IN PARIS?

The second T-shirt in this village I've seen today carrying this question, lingering evidence of animosity toward France's three decades of nuclear testing in L'Archipel. France ignored a 1973 World Court request to stop the practice, sparking protest worldwide, including New Zealand's delegation of a naval ship to the main atoll, and Peru's severance of their French diplomatic relations.

Relentless global opposition to nuclear testing saw the French drilling bomb shafts beneath the lagoon in 1975. Rather than blasting motus in plain view, replete with ominous, "harmless" fallout, the endeavor cloaked the tests submarine.

In 1995, French president Jacques Chirac announced a fresh line of tests, igniting severe global protest. New Zealand and Chile yanked their ambassadors from Paris and heavy rioting ensued in Papeete, yet the French cast a blind eye to the opposition, lounging comfortably in Europe, light-years distant. France stopped the testing in 1996.

French authorities claim the tests pose no ecological threat, though in 1998, plutonium leakage was discovered in one lagoon, and France's director of its Atomic Energy Commission admitted to the existence of cracks in the coral cones of two atolls. Still, French officials insist there is no cause for concern.

"If nuclear testing so safe," a villager says to me, "why didn't they do in their water?"

Motoring out of the pass late that afternoon, bound for the next atoll, another sort of explosion is viewed port side. Flawless 10' lefts detonating onto damp coral, fiery and backlit, seething mechanically, beckoning sadistically.

"Now there's some *real* gold, boys," Chris grins. "Anyone up for a go?"

Resting a small metal case on the saloon table, he unveils a more salable Archipel treasure: black pearls. Valentine's Day loomed, after all. More famous than this region's surf, black pearls are larger, fatter, and rarer than the white Japanese variety, spawned naturally in nearby lagoons, unlike Japan's hatchery-spawned oysters.

"Certainly can make your girl happy with these, mate."

Sold worldwide, the pearls can fetch up to tens of thousands of dollars, showcased as everything from opulent jewelry to à la carte. Fletcher and I, the boat's token bachelors, scoff at the theory and elect to pursue our nightly beer quota astern.

Francois, a decidedly non-single local Paumotu, regales us with stories of his ladyfriends throughout the atolls and on Tahiti Nui, likely accumulated from his notoriety as a champion ukulele player. Festooned with ink ("You come my island? My brother give you free tattoo.") and wrestler-thick, Francois verbally depicts life's rhythm within his arcadian culture, encompassing pearl culture, fishing, coconut harvest, Sunday worship, boat schedules, and, for him, surfing.

His culture varies slightly to Tahiti's, yet the authentic Paumotu cultural origin is unclear. In the 14th to 16th centuries, history suggests that civil conflict led the peace-oriented Paumotu people to the then-uninhabited atolls from the Marquesas and Leeward Islands. History also claims the atolls were populated around 1000 A.D., when the major Polynesian diaspora shuffled onward to Rapa Nui, the Marquesas, and the Gambiers.

Undoubtedly, wholesome L'Archipel culture has persevered through the French occupation due to distance from Tahiti, the acknowledged hotbed of a yearning for independence. Many feel these atolls could not make it on their own without the French backbone, but others, like the villager I met, want out. Still, L'Archipel Dangereux pleasantly feels far more Polynesian than French.

> *"The question of independence from France—could it happen? might it happen? should it happen?—seeped into nearly every conversation. Among Polynesians, animosity toward what was perceived as French hegemony was, if not universal, at least pervasive. The French, meanwhile, struggle to maintain a façade of serenity: Let Hong Kong slip away from Great Britain, let the world ride a wave of decolonization; Tahiti would remain not merely French but France."*
>
> *—Peter Benchley*

POLITICS ASIDE, FRANCOIS seamlessly learns the basics on thrashed boards at black-diamond spots. Leather-footed, naturally gifted and impervious to razor coral or death barrels, Francois is a legit waterman, likely to evolve into a premier L'Archipel surfer. Speaking excitedly about his family's atoll in the south, he paints a pretty picture.

"At my home, you wake up…and there is the wave," he smiles, enunciating slowly for effect, spreading his arms and opening his hands for vision. Reputedly, an ultra world-class left pinwheels at his doorstep during south swell season—yet another digit among a bevy of uncounted atoll perfection.

Always a sketchy seascape for navigators, formal L'Archipel Dangereux surf exploration, however unconventional, commenced for Chris O'Callaghan in the mid-1990s. Also a legendary waterman, Chris assimilated several shimmering, alluring lineups ultimately devoid of locals, carparks, pollution, or prior cataloging—he'd be the first.

"I would take my Zodiac onto freighters from Papeete. The freighter would drop me off on a few of the atolls—I did quite a few trips—and I'd camp out and see what was going on. With maps, I'd already sussed out where could be good. The freighters had these big cranes, and when we'd come to a good spot, they'd pick me up in the Zodiac and dump me into the water, and I'd go into the pass and set up camp on the beach. I knew when the freighter was coming back, so I'd make sure that I was ready when it came. They'd crane me back up onto the deck, and I'd move on.

"One time after they dropped me off, everything was going well until, for no apparent reason, my motor decided to konk out right in the middle of this pass, while the current raged like Victoria Falls rapids. Meanwhile, this right-hander was piping at around six to eight feet just over from me.

"You see, the current was only in the middle of the pass, and where the waves were—next to the reef—there was no current. I just couldn't get to (the wave), instead drifting back out to sea, only to fix the motor. Within five minutes, I motored back in toward the spot only for the motor to konk out again, and I ended up in the same position. I just couldn't believe that this was happening—three times in a row.

"After hours of frustration, I decided to motor back out to sea as I saw that the freighter was making its way to another chain of islands. Problem was, they were not expecting me, and it was getting very close to dark. One of the deckhands spotted me frantically powering alongside the huge ship. He notified the captain, who stopped and craned me out of there. Just then, the motor konked out again.

"After sleeping through the night, I repaired the motor, problem being there was a small hole in the fuel line. When I was going through the rapids, water would come inside the boat, saturating the fuel line, which would choke up the motor; 250 pulls of the rope would exit the water from the cylinders, and she would seem as good as gold, only until I hit the rapids again.

"I came back to the pass at a later date, and it was a very playful four feet, which I surfed for two days. But I will always remember this spot for being the biggest, cleanest right-hand barrel I have ever witnessed, and I've surfed and traveled for 25 years."

L'ARCHIPEL'S ENTIRE LAND mass constitutes just 435 square miles, but the thin links of low-lying motu comprising the atolls encircle 3,720 square miles of placid lagoon. Free from distractions and wildly idyllic, the fragile L'Archipel Dangereux exemplifies utter isolationism.

Knowing this, we go bonefishing.

This atoll is on the way to nowhere—except the crossroads of romance and adventure. Après-surf and brunch, Yvon and I board the skiff and buzz into close range; Francois kills the motor. Adrift within the lagoon's turquoise comfort, far from the roily pass and its fish traps, a broad, sandy flat is declared quintessential bonefish domain. Nearby, a few decayed fishing shacks face dense coconut palms—Polynesia's most important tree—hinting a wistful regard to overfishing and a once-seemingly endless bounty.

"Well, there's no fish here compared to...I mean, you can go all day trolling out there and you don't catch a fish sometimes," Yvon says, absorbing the scene. "If you were at a place like Christmas Island or some of the less-inhabited places—or some places that haven't been fished out—you can't go a quarter-mile without hooking up with something. There's still some pelagic fish here and stuff, but it's pretty well fished-out, especially the closer you get to Tahiti."

Exiting the skiff, we infiltrate with fly rods, cameras, and dim expectancy. Yvon wades and searches, casting over the sand and coral knobs.

"Bonefishing is like a combination of hunting and fishing," he says. "You're just searching all day. Your perception gets real acute looking for these fish. When you finally get one, they're so strong—they're just amazing."

Casting several times on different days in different lagoons, not a single bonefish is landed during the voyage. Yvon shrugs. "Hell, I don't know. Maybe it's like Hawaii...maybe bonefishing here is a seasonal thing, too."

The surf is not. Year-round, L'Archipel is blitzed with swell from all directions. Winter, spring, summer, autumn—doesn't matter. To date, several diamonds have been mined and more await discovery. On our first day at sea, Chris spells it out:

"Since I've had my boat, we've been able to go to many places the freighters don't go to, because they only go where there's civilization. There's no other way to explore other than the way we're doing it, because there's no other way to get here. No planes, no boats, no nothing—you've *got* to have your own boat."

A MORNING LATE in the voyage. Terns aloft, first light burns the horizon—the edge of infinitude. Roused by warm sun on my face, awakening unfolds to a dream outside my porthole. Oily-glass lagoon resonates, ablaze with dawn. Sole sounds are muffled wave action and the gentle lapping of water against hull. Rising, I exit the bunk and head for the bow.

The young air is heavy, windless, hot. Sweat ensues. This, an odyssey through time, represents volumes from my pre-travel life, knowing that this exists somewhere, but lacking memories and passport stamps. Storybook longing over seductive tropical imagery and lucid tales of the South Pacific precede anyone's baptism in Polynesian seas.

Yvon, a veteran traveler, appears from below.

"Ah, this is paradise for me," he nods. "When I was a kid, I read every book I could find on the South Pacific, and this is what I wanted to do. I wanted to disappear out here someday (laughs). My wife doesn't like the tropics, though. Otherwise, I'd be here all the time. Go with my fly rod and my surfboard; find some island that had good surf on it, good bonefishing...."

The entire image is erased as the fantasy gives way: Slicing toward the pass in the dinghy, an azure right-hander sprouts from the depths and heaves onto the reef, visible through the wave itself. Francois idles us into the lineup.

Cracking an iced Hinano with twilight, Chris reflects.

"I think it's every surfer's dream...I see the same kind of waves that we all used draw during math class in school. The teacher's talking up at the front, and you're drawing little palm trees hanging over with these lines peeling around the point. I actually get to see waves like that in real life, on a regular basis, with nobody out.

"And the *colors* here, mate—every single shade of blue in the spectrum. From the sky all the way down to the depths of the sea, the blues are just amazing...."

We motor into Tahiti's Marina Taina 30 hours later, Fa'aa International Airport beckoning beneath dreary overcast and the sticky grime of tropical civilization. The others soon depart for Los Angeles; tonight, my journey remains.

"For a moment I might have been back in the oldest Polynesia, where virgin islands could still surprise the voyager. The haunting Polynesia of Western dreams, of the writer Melville and the painter Gauguin; the Polynesia of Rousseau's "noble savage," heaven-sent for philosopher, poet, and adventurer."
—Maurice Shadbolt, 1967

WHEREVER HE WENT, he would be a stranger. A desolate fisherman, hidden by the island's profound insularity and lost in an infinity of sea, he was a person one reads about, no one anybody actually knew.

"They always say we came from them, but we keep reminding them, that, no, they came from us. This has been proven. They are our younger brothers and sisters—there no two way about that."

He clarified his relation with New Zealand's Maoris, ancient blood brothers of most modern Cook Islanders. Was the 'Great Migration,' circa 1350 AD, when the Maori canoes voyaged 2,200 miles from Rarotonga's Avana Harbor to New Zealand, then known as Aotearoa, the land of the long white cloud. Today, the seven-canoe fleet is commemorated at Avana Harbor with a circle of seven stones: Mataatua, Te Arawa, Tainui, Aotea, Kurahaupo, Tokomaru, and Takitumu. Each tracing their genealogies to ancestors who arrived from the crossing, New Zealand's Maori tribes are named after these seven 'Great Canoes,' immortalized in paint on Air New Zealand's seven Boeing 747s.

"*They* came from *us*."

Piri has never left Rarotonga, inheriting a sublime immunity to the hazards of the world. He traveled the the globe vicariously via the white Western cultures arriving from cruise ships and airplanes, passing through these beachfront rooms. I am American—a somewhat rare breed down here as most patrons are Kiwi, Australian, Canadian, or European—and my world to Piri seemed unmanageable, unimaginable. He'd watched The O'Reilly Factor, danced to Madonna, swilled Pepsi and smelled CK1, yet a palpable, succulent slice of America lay far from reach. Its soil was impure and arcane; I imagined he'd tote a film canister home full of it if he ever visited California, mirroring my desk collection of South Pacific sand.

With beers on my hotel balcony, we watched pallid, pink-skinned tourists wallow in the lagoon, sunbathe below the palms, stroll for token shells. It was colder where they lived, after all—icy in Reykjavik, snowy in Winnipeg, drafty in Dunedin. And beyond them, past the lagoon and barrier reef, a double-overhead left explodes, slightly marred by the tradewind but treacherously impressive. Fast and sectiony, the wave peaked way up at the reef's tip and bent around the shelf for 200 yards before thwacking onto a horrendous ledge. Looked thrilling, but not my style.

Piri gleamed. "You will meet him, I promise," he said warmly. "You will surf together."

The wave *was* Luc's style—Piri's son and one of Rarotonga's few stand-up surfers. Because new surfboards are unavailable in the Cooks and because the waves' ferocity inevitably snaps them, bodyboards are the norm. All spots break over severely shallow, sharp coral, characteristically hollow and lethal. Luc learned to surf in such waves, excelling now when injury looms.

"Ahhh, but this?" he exhaled, raising his eyebrows and opening a hand toward the sea. "My son never surf here. My son live on Aitutaki and surf those north atolls. This possible with the cargo ship: Pukapuka, Suwarrow, Penrhyn, Manihiki, Rakahanga...you should see. Taste the coconut crab and wear the black pearl. You *never* forget these places, my friend."

DAY SIX OF my Rarotonga visit, a convenient hop from French Polynesia. After floating the preceding two weeks away sniffing elite lineups in the Tuamotus, I was free from francs and French attitude. Rarotonga's authenticity blew life into a wavering psyche.

Rarotonga is the heart of the 15-island archipelago, scattered like lost stars over the massive Pacific Plate, a critical tectonic realm at the bottom of the ocean. Hustling west at 10 centimeters per year, the plate directly affects all of the region's volcanic landforms; youngest of the group, Rarotonga is the archipelago's one truly mountainous, volcanic island. Seductively lush and green, it is often called the "mini Tahiti."

Deplaning from Papeete depressed and scatterbrained, the Cooks were the cure.

"This is where the Maoris and the Hawaiians came from. Look up in the skies and see the Southern Cross. Crosby, Stills, and Nash wrote a song about it when they sailed down there in a schooner. Pick up shark stories, if there are any.

"The spirit of old Polynesia is there. The Hawaiians only wish for their lost heritage of old Rarotonga, like the Tahitians. You are in for a real treat that you will never forget."

—John Elwell

THROUGH A FRIEND at Air Rarotonga, Piri arranged the journey. Cruising solely with backpack and surfboard, I exited the hotel and taxied to the domestic terminal where I waited an extra hour for the flight's departure. Then, the 15-passenger turbo-prop dropped me onto Aitutaki Atoll's airstrip laid by U.S. forces during World War II, a long asphalt vein capable of receiving huge aircraft.

Luc is a cook at Aitutaki's Pearl Beach Resort on Akitua motu, a groomed five-star layout of verdant garden suites and over-water bungalows exemplifying all that is tropically luxe. Administered from Papeete as a unit of French Polynesia's Pearl Resorts chain, its grounds are the honeymooner's dream: a sumptuous, careless fantasia of South Pacific eden, hammocks strewn between coconutless palms shorn by grinning native workers all oblivious to the opulence.

Philippe, the resort's newly imported manager, was there to meet me. Conspicuously Parisian and forcibly polite, galaxies distant from Chanel and Jacques Chirac, Philippe appeared boiled and effete, his mustached face shining like ripe French cheese—a homebody complexion more at ease among wrought iron lampposts, fine wines, and narrow, cobblestone alleyways.

He walked me to my garden bungalow, an exotic hardwood dwelling so saturated with romance that its welcome packet contained an envelope addressed to 'Mr. and Mrs. Kew.' Spouseless, I puzzled Philippe. "You have no woman?"

"No, I'm single…here on business. Certainly a nice place to bring a girl, though, eh?"

With that, he nodded and wished me a pleasant stay. The sliding glass door closed with a soft, expensive click, denying natural dankness outside, sealing me into a microclimatic bulb of dry, air-conditioned coolness. A basket of fresh papaya, mango, carambola, coconut, and passionfruit, glistening under the window's afternoon sun rays, lured me to the king-size bed. Its crisp, white cotton sheets smelled of lush flora and fabric softener—ah, if there was a Mrs. Kew, then, yes, this would definitely do the trick, even if for only one night.

After a coconut-soap-and-shampoo rainwater shower, I went looking for Luc. He toiled in the kitchen behind the bar of the resort's restaurant, sweating over a grill of fried fish, vegetables, and whatever else. I sat on a barstool, made eye contact, and identified myself with a friendly wave; he returned the gesture with a huge smile and shaka. Symmetrically handsome, dark, lean and fit at age 24, Luc had to be one of Aitutaki's most desired bachelors—a short supply on an island/atoll of 2,300. A harem of native maidens and the odd expat-Kiwi's daughter was surely at his fingertips.

He signaled the bartender to hand me a bowl of *ika mata*, the Cooks' version of *poisson cru*, prepared for one of the restaurant's honeymooning diners but instead given to me. To my left was a boisterous trio of businessmen, aggressively British and likely on some sort of male-bonding holiday, abandoning their wives to the misery of England's winter. Schlock-floral masking sunburned potbellies, rounds of Steinlager flowed freely as their talk spiraled in volume and excitement.

"Those new Rovers have sure got a good block under the hood...."

"We'll get the bastard to sign the deal next week, no problem...."

Their gold-card voices conflicted with the hushed, sentimental tones of the tabled couple behind me, holding hands and sipping wine, gazing into each other's eyes, swallowed by the glossy, Westernized conception of what a proper honeymoon is and should be. Between them and the Brits, I was the odd man out with my solitary bowl of raw fish. But not for long.

"Michael!" Luc stood to my right, grinning enthusiastically. "Welcome to Aitutaki. Have you checked in?"

We shook hands—two strangers paired by his father—and the intent, conceived by Luc, was clear: we were to surf Manihiki, where

Piri's brother lived. Luc and I were booked on tomorrow's flight from Rarotonga, stopping here then continuing north to Manihiki and Penrhyn; Piri felt I should arrive a day early to spend a night on Aitutaki and, judging from my luxuriant quarters, it was a good call.

I finished the *ika mata* and started in on one of the mugs of Steinlager Luc brought from the tap. His shift ended and social hour commenced; despite his father's claim, Luc had never surfed Manihiki, so this was to be a fresh adventure for both of us. "Tonight," he said, "we'll have a few beers downtown, meet some girls, talk about tomorrow...."

Two hours later, we lounged wharfside around a small table at the open-air Blue Nun Café inside the Orongo Centre complex in Arutanga, watching a live band stumble through Bob Marley covers. At our table, the flow was dense cheeseburgers and salty fries accented with can after can of Lion Red lager; Luc flirted heavily with a few young ladies and went home with one. Wildly drunk, I caught a late-night ride from the band's bass player back to the bungalow and crashed fast on its sexless bed. Silence reigned with visions of the Southern Cross, a bold moon bleeding through curtained windows.

HOT AND CHEMICAL, the mid-morning cabin air was nauseating—small airplanes always seem microscopic when the hangover burns. Air Rarotonga's Saab 340 lifted us from Aitutaki, northbound for Manihiki Atoll, three hours and three hundred dollars away.

Time passed quickly with sleep. Repressing vertigo through the rough descent, I peered through the porthole at the ring of land below. A phalanx of coconut palms enduring heavy tradewinds offered visual solace: soon, we would again be on firm ground.

Idyll aside, atoll life can be harsh. The Cook Islands' northern group is infertile, unlike the green volcanic islands to the south, which flourish with fruits, flowers, livestock, and vegetables. On atolls, where soil quality is poor and the winds constant, low vegetation and coconut palms predominate.

For atoll residents, the palm is the tree of life. Coconut water is sterile and the safest thing to drink in potable water-deprived environs.

Coconut flesh, squeezed for coconut oil and milk, is also a valued food; matured and dried, it produces copra, an important Cook Islands export. Coconut husks are used for rope when green; mature, brown husks provide fuel and charcoal. Coconut wood is used for carving and lumber, the fronds for thatch, rope, and baskets. Ultimately, the tree has allowed humans to survive for centuries on extremely remote and barren strips of Pacific land.

The Saab lurched and sputtered as it hit the runway. The impact stirred Luc, asleep since our ascent. The plane taxied briefly and came around to the terminal building. Luc's uncle stood on the tarmac; even from inside the airplane, I could see his genteel face was a skin of cracked licorice, his pigment working overtime against a lifetime of tropic sun. A gap-toothed grin greeted both of us, followed by an earnest handshake, baggage retrieval, and a transfer to his waterfront residence. The thatched pandanus-roof home, with a floor of straw mats and walls of palm fronds supported by coconut trunks, smelled of must and desertion despite Tuanu's obvious long-term tenancy. We entered and slumped immediately onto the colorful pareu plastering his cushiony bamboo-frame couch.

Tuanu stood in the doorway and pointed out to the lagoon. "Tomorrow, we go across to find the waves." I squinted through the palms to see that, beneath a searing late afternoon sun, the water was bright and fiercely corrugated by the trades. Tuanu assured us the wind would die through the night and morning would bring sheet glass.

"But today," he smiled, eyes widening, "we have feast and homebrew!"

I looked out the window above our heads. The fading sky was huge, its only blemish a distant jet trail. Darkness fell swiftly at 6 p.m. and the lagoon became a blustery wash of ink. We huddled inside Tuanu's spartan front room, sitting cross-legged on mats, the scene lit by gimbaled oil lamps which looked to have been salvaged from one of the area's many shipwrecks.

Joined by Kauraka, a friend from Rarotonga now living here, Luc and I watched Tuanu ladle homebrewed beer from a deep, wide plastic bowl into a coconut-shell cup, then gulp the milky brew with aplomb. He refilled the cup with beer and passed it to me. Its taste was horrid and bitterly alcoholic; Tuanu's proud grin and laugh augmented the sensation.

"Good, eh, Michael? Luc next!"

Meanwhile, somebody had prepared a mound of coconut crabs on the firepit outside. Hunted by night under the coral rubble, then roasted on a bed of hot stones, the crabs are sweet and delicious—an esoteric Cook Islands delicacy for us, subsistance for the Maoris. While the crabs sizzled whole in their shells, the four of us drained the bowl through the next hour, growing fairly intoxicated by this weird, stomach-torturing liquor. Soon, the succulent coconut crab, chased with Bacardi shots and baked breadfruit, was consumed with zest.

Accompanying our good cheer, spasms of discontent filtered up through the palm fronds. "When I was a child in school on Rarotonga, if you got caught not speaking English, you were punished." Kauraka said, radiant with rum. "But today we are starting to relearn our own language—the Maori language. We were losing our tongue. If you spoke Maori at school, they hit you. They wouldn't stand for it."

The wind ceased late. Lulled by moonrise in thick, tropical silence, I slept thinly on a narrow bed—a son's bed. In an organically prim home edging one of Earth's bluest lagoons, I'd never known a privacy so deep and self-contained as this. Tuanu retired early and Kauraka and Luc had passed out in the front room's floor; this unoccupied nook was in the house's rear quarters and, seizing an introspective segue, I made it mine for the night.

MORNING…PALMS AFLAME at dawn. Climbed a tree and yanked off a green coconut, cracked it on the trunk and poured the water into my parched mouth. In the distance, to the atoll's opposite side, a dense green tangle rose from a long, low shore of coral and pale sand. It led into what was left of the sunrise; a few low cloud banks smeared with mauve and ocher. North Pacific swells are abundant in February, and Manihiki's windward coast was bound to embrace the energy—where, exactly, was unknown to us, but Tuanu swore he'd seen "the big breaking waves over there." Whether they'd actually been surfed was also unknown but unlikely.

The morning sun was hard and bright, the water a bold powder-blue. In Tuanu's longboat, we skimmed five miles from the village to the atoll's uninhabited northeast rib. Along the way, seeding houses flecked the lagoon, perched tipsily on coral heads, serving as platforms for the diving, cleaning, and harvesting of pearl oysters.

On Rarotonga, I was told that far more Cook Islanders live abroad than in the Cooks themselves. Twenty thousand people live on all 15 of the Cook Islands combined, yet 100,000 Cook Islanders live in New Zealand and Australia—a fact not lost on those carrying national pride and economic sustainability, like Tuanu.

"It was ridiculous," he said above the drone of the outboard motor. "About 10 years ago, our economy collapsed from mismanagement of the government—wasting money, traveling, overpaying themselves. Suddenly, there no more money in the safe. Two thousand public servants had no choice and left for New Zealand and Australia because our government could not afford to pay the people, or to create enough jobs in the private sector."

Still, Tuanu was an exemplary figure of self-reliance, industry, and business acumen who profited by farming black pearls, the Cook Islands' most lucrative and internationally famous export. Cultivated in the lagoon, the pearls—a Cook Islands specialty—are Manihiki's economic mainstay, and Tuanu was a harvester of legend, routinely freediving between 80 and 120 feet.

He was a creature of nature and luck. Apparently, Luc and I weren't: the wind, sideshore and stiff, shredded the atoll's opposite coast. This was clear as we docked the boat lagoonside and strolled through the palm forest to the open ocean, expectations dimmed, and drew our virgin glimpse of Manihiki's surfing potential.

What appeared as a tattered, seamless line of barrier reef whitewater soon revealed a wave of considerable shape. The tide was far too low and the scene—a mess of boils and wretched reef-suck—lacked temptation. Rideable, yes, but with deeper water and preferred wind. Viewed through binoculars, we could see the shelf being stripped raw with each surge ebb, the coral promoting its doom: football-sized urchins abetting fierce spires, mushrooms, chasms, and ledges.

Accessing the wave would require a precise death-schlepp, inch by inch, while leering at this wave which was so close yet so distant. Once immersed, the surfer would pursue survival-mode tactics for an inevitable airdrop into a dry tube, followed by a hard spit spray and beserk adrenaline rush. Could be good.

...for Luc, that is. Weaned on identical waves throughout the Cook Islands and French Polynesia (his mother lives on Tahiti), my softcock life of thin-lipped Santa Barbara pointbreaks was comical compared to Luc's perspective. To him, this wave was routine, merely something to surf. He'd never explored Manihiki and was exultant at the chance to taste a new bump on his archipelagic periphery. Another day, another wind....

PORK AND PAPAYA earned rave reviews that night. Kauraka, a keen carnivore cook, expounded on the pig's virtues, professing an acute appreciation for its flesh: "This pig here, he eat so many fruit and coconut—must be why he taste so sweet. I *love* the pig."

Envisioning a spell of uncle-nephew bondage after our wave reconnaissance, Tuanu and Luc retreated to Tuanu's place, leaving me with Kauraka at day's end; again I was treated to impressive, traditional Cook Islands cuisine and relentless hospitality.

Evidence of a Polynesian bachelor's life peppered Kauraka's tiny house, two doors down from Tuanu's. Thumbtacked to the kitchen wall was an olive-skinned *Playboy* centerfold of Hawaiian blood, mimicking the postcards of nude island girls I'd seen in Papeete tourist shops. Kauraka pointed to the picture: "This girl...you like?"

"Mmmm....not bad."

An index finger shoots up. "Wait here!"

He left the house, returning several minutes later with a fragrantly intoxicating maiden—Kauraka's child—who sauntered over and presented me a garland of pink frangipani, fresh from her mother's yard. Flattered, and then...ah, I knew the tune: Clearly a dangerous yet classic fairytale scheme, this paternal offering of a child, lost in the romantic fiction of running away to a developed country—a Western hall pass, beelining to college, jobs, nightclubs, an engagement ring, a house with a garden, refrigerator, spin-dryer...a white wedding with a providing husband wistfully agreeing to the Polynesian Love Dream. A newer, exposed life unregimented by copra, the coconut tree, or the black pearl.

It is the heartache of Manihiki, one of Polynesia's loneliest outposts: New Zealand's government offers free schooling on Rarotonga, and Manihiki's youth, if they can afford the airfare, continue with scholarships for tertiary education in New Zealand. Emigration far exceeds immigration. "The grass always greener, you know?" Kauraka said. "My two sons left for university in New Zealand. I want a different life for my daughter; she deserves the big world of America. But when our young people go, everything will go. Who will there be to learn to weave the coconut frond in our style? Who will learn to fish our way? All custom and all tradition will die."

Direct from a South Pacific romance novel, the stuff of any white man's fantasy, Kauraka's daughter was the sexiest, most beautiful island girl I'd ever seen. Age 19, flawless teak skin, balanced face, emerald eyes, classy smile, thick brown hair to lower back, ornate black pearl-and-shell jewelry. Bikini-topped and well-endowed, her hourglass figure drew my eyes and imagination from her face down to her smooth brown dancer's belly, down to her sarong-draped hips, hairless legs, and manicured toes. Textbook features—most girls long for them, many work for them, some create them, and others are born with them. If Hugh Hefner ever needs another Polynesian Playmate....

To me, her fragrances were epiphanic: This girl *was* the Cook Islands, the Polynesia of old and new—astonishing natural beauty, clean, culturally rich, humble, a phenomenal dancer oozing with tradition and subtle suggestiveness. The islands *are* sexy, and their traditional dances exist in deference to Tangaroa, god of sea and fertility. Hawaiians and Tahitians of yore shared the religion featuring Tangaroa, hence the resembling dance style, and, akin to Hawaiians and Tahitians, the Cook Islanders believe they came from the mystic ancestral homeland of Avaiki.

Taken very seriously, dance is the preeminent artform here. Rhythmic drumming on the paté and wild, sensuous movements of both genders allow Cook Islands teams to repeatedly triumph in all major Pacific dance festivals. The Hawaiian hula and the Tahitian tamuré are more widely recognized, crediting vast publicity through the past century, but the Cook Islands hura is considerably more erotic and fierce. Dubbing these atolls "detached parts of the Earth," Captain James Cook left a curious take in 1777:

> *Motions and gestures beyond imagination wanton, in the practice of which they are brought up from their earliest childhood, accompanied by words, which, if it were possible, would more explicitly convey the same idea…(the women) swing their hips and walk in a provocative way, and assume postural attitudes which are highly charged with sex.*

I COULD SEE those hips, dressed in frond skirt, gyrating to native rhythm at the weekly 'Island Night' feast/dance at Aitutaki's Pearl Beach Resort. Her fleshy temptation gnawed through me, a natural and unattached slave to carnal desire. So sultry was she, so accessible, so nubile, so…addicting.

We spent the night together. Nuances of an instant, ready-made romance loomed as our warmths converged. No nudity but plenty of touch—a harmless, innocent encounter as the lagoon shone brilliantly under a waxing gibbous moon. The ambience withdrew me to the double-stuffed pillows in my Pearl Beach bungalow—I could take her there and fade into sublime content. Harsh heartbreak cast by my ex-girlfriend would be stalled indefinitely.

Yet it was not to be. Too innocent, too pure, too…inconvenient: She had no passport, no money for airfare, and, roofless in Santa Barbara, I had no place to take her once off the jet in Los Angeles. The scope of responsibility was much too broad for my own internal struggle.

A GROOMED STORYBOOK peak lifts onto the abrupt shelf and spews both ways, tapering dreamlike into the dual channels. Quality windswell, richly turquoise and poster-ready, this is not a tired hallucination. Contrarily, it is a manifestation of my home's relatively poor surf quality that rose much too vividly.

Eyebrows raised, Tuanu turns to me: "Good? This what you looking for?"

Instantly, I ached to be a part of his exotic diaspora. To surf here, love here, live here, die here. With a one-way ticket, I could leave the wetsuit in California, sell my boat, cancel the phone, abandon everything in storage, and bid a fond farewell. Already homeless and jobless, ties were few in America, and seeding a new life on Manihiki with the atoll's goddess and a perfect wave catered to all prior fantasies I'd conceived.

But with so many dreams, there was an ugly twist to the idyll: Our wave, riddled with black-tipped sharks and deadly reef, required picking a careful line across the lagoon over severe coral heavily infested with black urchins armed with six-inch spines. One misstep would incur bloodshed and extreme discomfort.

Tuanu took shade beneath a palm as we waded out over soft sand, which quickly deteriorated to coral, the lagoon's placid surface masking the ragged bottom. Stepping carefully and clumsily, then paddling, then stepping again, we neared the barrier reef, the water surface here warbled with backwash. From this close vantage, our spot's treachery grew painfully lucid.

Affording rich opportunities for injury, the wave's character was bad but interesting. From the depths, it drew onto the reef and dredged below sea level, subverting and choking over the same urchin-caked coral in two to four feet of water. One botched take-off could likely be your last. Was a spot reserved for the advanced and/or ill surfer—nice to watch, evil to ride. A pseudo-surfable wave, yes, but much too fate-tempting, and the Cooks are unfortunately littered with them.

I hesitated but Luc pressed on, cropping up onto the barrier reef in ankle-deep water, then committing himself with a well-timed leap into the keyhole. Underqualified, I turned back, my slice of heroic adventure swiftly vanishing with each reclaimed yard. Safely sandside with a camera, I watched Luc's natural prowess, his session lasting two waves, 13 minutes apart. Not that it was inconsistent: most waves were severe and, in the case of the lefts, unrideable.

That night, we toasted our find—however flawed—with Tuanu's potent homebrew. The week was a fast memory and our Rarotonga-bound flight departs tomorrow; one night there...before reality loomed.

> *"...an island is much more than a principate. It is the ultimate refuge...."*
>
> *—Paul Theroux*

FLAT IN BED, eyes agape. Staring up, I see nothing—this world is a black, frightening place. In resignation to circumstance, I ponder realities of being alone, of private dereliction, of living without love. Outside, cornstalk rustle of Rarotonga's 3 a.m. surf accompanies brooding of near-future California uncertainties: The girlfriend...painfully missed...by now, she's dating somebody else. Who do I have to come home to? And what will I do for income? How will I pay for food, bills, gas? When will I find a place to live? Where will I park to sleep in my car following arrival at LAX?

Desperate thoughts ignore paradise. Depression is a strange bedfellow in Polynesia.

Next day. In the airport, I sit near two pale, chainsmoking British girls here on round-the-world tickets, both appearing quite relieved with their exit. "This place is so boring," yawned the short one. "We can't wait to get out of here...I like big cities like London and Paris, you know? We're back to Tahiti for a couple of days, then on to Auckland and Sydney, which is where we really want to go on this trip. These islands are pretty and that, but—"

"—there's just nothing here to do," her friend assures. "And it's *so* hot.

I shrug and put headphones on to suffocate all airport ambiance. Click and suddenly Sade sings, first withdrawing me to the smile of a girlfriend from five years back, then to Manihiki and its surreal, starry nights. Yes, two women had vanished from this life—now leaving one in the Cooks, returning to another in California...but not really. With both, it was a peaceful sail until the wind blew us apart; I'd shipwrecked severely in Santa Barbara, and now, a month later, am fleeing an impossible scheme in the South Pacific.

Our Air New Zealand 767 lands from Papeete. Shortly, I stand at the check-in counter, toting soiled baggage and a heavy heart. Lounge forty minutes later in seat 36A…behind me, the British girls gab about nightlife in Amsterdam and Ibiza, noses deep in *Maxim* and *Vogue.* Easing the seat, I again relax with Sade, preparing to soon face the rough sea of home.

PART

III

Scandinavia

9

DISTILLING THE VODKA COAST

2001

THICK SILENCE AND drips of twilight dew. Mushrooms and moss below as we step lightly through undergrowth, toppled trees and twigs, pancake rocks and the cherished hush that is Scandinavian wood.

This boreal forest…still, lucid. She leads me along the needle dirt trail to a vast lake so mirror-like, I pause to reconsider. Fiberglass summer boats strewn along the grass shore, a damp Finnish hour reserved for all humans present—me, the girl. Calm wind. Realm of the reindeer, sauna, woodsmoke and juniper tea.

Slow-growing and slender, conifers reach toward starlight. Forest is a muted rainbow of greens, oranges, reds, blacks and browns. Lake assumes cooling hue of green beer bottle. Silhouettes of birch and pine trees prick a darkening sky. Easing onto a downed log, we adjust with the mood of twilight.

[SVERIGE]

"You'd better not meet any Swedish women, or you might not leave."

THURSDAY, 8 A.M.

Hangover.

Renowned commercial lensman Binge Eliasson opens the door and flicks the room light. Inquires whether I'm ready for my first Swedish surf.

"Yeah, sure…(cough)…of course," I mumble through the blanket, wincing from sudden, shocking fluorescent glare. Eyelids crusted together, mouth a stew of beer and late-night grease. Sticky, dried booze sweat adheres the T-shirt to my skin. Reeking of cigarettes. Nauseous and wholly exhausted from the prior comical eve of drinking in downtown Stockholm with a gang of professional Scandinavian skateboarders now residing in the United States. Their homecoming was part of an informal exhibition tour—rather a "drinking tour," as one of them quipped.

I'd watched these skaters—a sport invented in America—blow minds at the indoor Stockholm Skate Park as the sound system blasted American heavy metal. Most everyone wore American clothing and shoes; American skate company stickers were plastered on the walls; huge posters advertised Adidas and Pepsi.

Around town, many signs are written in English; everybody speaks English and American music is all over the radio. American franchises like 7-11 and McDonald's and Shell are ubiquitous. ATMs, cars, traffic lights, neon, fashion, supermarkets, gas stations, televisions, telephones, washing machines, soda, fast food, computers, baseball caps. The list goes on.

Many Swedes are weaned on American product, dialect and ideology. Arriving back at Binge's one night, I noticed his wife was watching "Friends" followed by "Ally McBeal" and some basketball flick starring Whoopi Goldberg. Last night, they watched "ER," "Boston Public," "Frasier" and "The Conan O'Brien Show." This family knows more about American television than I do. Disney, Hollywood and Harry Potter are nationally huge.

"Sweden is like America with German organization," Binge says during the Jeep commute from Stockholm to Torö Beach, Sweden's surf hub.

Eventually emerging from the cocoon of heated leather seats, we view the blustery Baltic Sea. Mobile phone rings; Australian expat Lee on the other end.

"Is it big? Like one or two feet?" he jokes.

"It looks horrible."

"Oh, that means it's good."

Hands in pockets, we observe. Eternally optimistic Binge senses invisible greatness from the waist-high windslop.

"This is warm," he grins as I shiver in the 20-knot onshores. "There's hardly any wind. Usually it's completely gale-force when the surf's really pumping. You should be here when it's raining or snowing in mid-winter. When you walk out to the beach and find you can't stand up—that's when it's windy. You have to lean forward (laughs). Once, when it was like that while we were surfing, a friend said to me, Wow, this is just like a really strong offshore wind, only it's the other way around!" (laughs)

Rewind 36 hours. Peter Klang huddled on Torö's dusky cobblestone beach, squinting into the gale, fingers numb, calculating a score for a contestant's wave in the annual Swedish Surfing Championship. Sky was a uniform wash-gray, not a blotch in sight, draped low over distant islets. Baltic was tarnished silver, its ragged head-high windswell forlorn.

Yet the stoke was high. Pale faces grinned and conversed, bodies burdened heavily with winter clothing on this, a desolate, inhospitable nook of pines and rock peppered with modern surfboards and contest jerseys. Here was an event, after all. Nowhere else would 40 surfers greet a bitter dawn at a stormy freshwater beach, amping to get wet.

"Nothing comes easy here, and we don't expect it to," Klang says. "We have a hard climate to live in…it teaches us to be more appreciative of what we get. We have low expectations of our surf. Travel is essential to progress—no matter how much effort you put into surfing Sweden, you're only going to get inches ahead. You ache to go miles, but you're only going to go inches."

President of the Swedish Surfing Association, Klang's is a voice relating realities of environment for one of Earth's most surf-jazzed yet vastly surf-deprived landscapes. His 17-year-old Association proffers activity and identity for Swedes through times of bad and good—routinely freezing, smallish and whitecapped, necessitating stone-faced patience, dedication, luck and gallons of petrol. Besides stoke, Klang spearheads the aforementioned yearly contest, various expression sessions, surf movie nights, a Web site, beach clean-ups and assorted parties.

"I feel like if I don't (act as its president), the Association might die, and I don't want that to happen. You have to be someone who is willing to do this without any financial compensation whatsoever. That is difficult in Sweden. People are not really into doing things for free here. I do it because I like it…People are having fun. To me, that's a great satisfaction and is why I keep doing it."

Klang skateboarded professionally through the late 1970s and early 1980s before suffering a severe foot injury. His first taste of surfing came in 1979 via the Canary Islands, yet the bait was swallowed 1981-1987 during his tenure in San Diego, California. Has since returned to Sweden and surfs regularly.

"I can't really explain the feeling of surfing in Sweden for the first time. It was so exotic. I grew up here, and I never thought I ever would be able to surf in this country. To find something in your own backyard that you thought you had to travel across the world for, well…it was mind-blowing.

"I definitely knew it was different. Took several years before I started to get used to the fact that surfing is actually a normal thing you can do here."

[SUOMI]

"Only the Finns can live in Finland."

SCOPE OF A thousand pristine lakes, silent forests of pine and birch and spicy juniper, soothing sauna, potent booze and milky human skin. Finland. Tans are unheard of, as is surfing—almost.

Journeyed today west from Helsinki to Hangö, a dot of a town at the end of a small peninsula, to seek waves. Instead found a tranquil Gulf of Finland. Reputedly, diving and windsurfing are the watersports here. Surfing reigns novelty yet occasionally doable.

Finnish surfers sport six-millimeter fullsuits. Residents swim nude in the icy lakes of autumn or assume a pool of their own with sweat in the sauna. Most Finns have a sauna in their home. In her Vantaa lair with Sade on the stereo, ladyfriend Pipsa introduces me to the sauna concept, an ancient Finnish tradition where one sits or lies in a small pine-walled room with a heater and bucket of water containing fresh birch branches. Finns whack themselves with the branches during sauna. Gets hot in there. Thermometer reaches 85°C when I partake, which is something like 220°F or more. The sweat beads and drips as if you'd stepped from a shower. Beautiful to cleanse in such a simple manner.

Finnish is bizarre. Words are long, containing multiple same letters, often ending with 'en' or a vowel. I am a sanomalehtimiesnainen (journalist) and my hair is vaaleaverikkö (blond).

"Finnish isn't a language," claimed Klang the Swede. "It's a *noise*."

Pipsa has been on an airplane twice in her 26 years, once to see Los Angeles and Disneyland, home to Donald Duck, one of her favorite collectibles. She's studying to become a *viheralueidenhoitaja* (gardener), and her windowpanes are lined with plants. She usually chooses to wear boots and black leather, and her two black dogs are large, friendly and smelly. Black is a fitting color for winter Finland.

"I have no desire to live anywhere else," Pipsa says as we motor toward a McDonald's lunch. "Here we have it simple and clean, and Finns like it that way. We like to be left alone."

High noon in a Scandinavian winter looks like dusk. Many residents resort to vodka. Lack of natural light is unhealthy for humans—sleep problems, lethargism, indecisiveness, body soreness and serious depression are symptoms of Seasonal Affective Disorder (SAD), endured by many, some remedied with daily doses of bright light therapy.

"If we are very lucky, we skid straight into winter proper, skipping that phase of autumn when the first snow melts to slush and the days grow short and drab," said Teemu, a surfer friend of Pipsa's. "Many face their toughest psychological test now. Survival is absolutely a question of attitude."

And surfing is a question of storms, none too common for the dedicated.

[NORGE]

"It is a stern land, ruthless to weakness."

KONRAD HOISTS HIS canned Carlsberg to mine and we quaff in unison.

"Bottoms up, mate!"

No stranger to booze, the witty, whiskered Scot is a welcomed seatmate during this white-knuckled puddle-jump aboard a tiny, twin-prop unit of the Widerøe Airlines fleet. Its pilot had somehow executed lift-off under a storm sky and heavy wind back on the mainland, and we were now bouncing northwestward above majestic, windpocked fjords and ice-capped peaks.

Fast-forward to bone-jarring touchdown, rain, smiling blonde women, gales, rented Volkswagen van, serpentine road and…suddenly, we were there.

Spenskon Cape, Arctic Circle. Swells pile in from the west as we claw for the horizon. Slurred speech, benumbed extremities, lungs aching from the purest air on Earth. Wind gusts render the sea a streaky white as we scratch over the swell, a freak set from the rawest ocean we'd ever seen.

A white-tailed eagle drifts high in the valley gust, 25 bitter knots of air whipped seaward from a low-pressure bulb to the southwest...raptor complimenting a leaky sky...ominous and gritty, unyielding and oppressive. Fifty shades of gray.

Shivering, I gaze at the elements atop a flat boulder following a woolly introduction to arctic surfing—a humbling reminder of how distant my California homeland really was.

At my back and ripe for shearing, dozens of sheep gnaw on wet grasses festering through a soil of gravel, quartz, moss and boulders; a bucolic tundra spiked with fir thickets, wild berries and dizzying autumnal hues. To the west, a dreary sea lays ribbed with a fresh swell, offshores spinning immense white fans of spray out the back. One gargantuan black seal slithers beneath.

'Twas a sketchy idea-cum-reality cobbled together by a film crew during a spell of rainy October hours down Hossegor way: fire north and hope for something—anything—worth surfing. "North" meant somewhere between Iceland and the North Pole.

I and photographer Ted Grambeau enlisted two days before departure. In tote talent-wise were British professionals Sam Lamiroy and Spencer Hargraves, armed each with five-millimeter fullsuits and a cache of heavy winter clothing. Both were keen for some novelty surf, though nobody aboard expected to hit arctic pay dirt.

"The notion of coming up here to find waves was just bizarre," said Lamiroy, "but when we arrived, it was odd because we found perfect waves. The quality rivals anything that you can hope to get anywhere."

Fast and loose, Lamiroy lanced lips and stalled into countless bowl sections heaved open by the wind, emerging more often than not. A Newcastle bloke, he existed relatively unfazed by the arctic nip, reveling within the Kirra-esque sections at a set-up which Grambeau dubbed akin to his own Burleigh Heads motherland.

A certified Newquay rail-gouger and veritable land comic, Hargraves found the windswept barrels quite suitable to his wild disposition, even surfing sans booties for a few sessions. If nothing else, the scene sparked hints of wintertime Fistral.

"This is about as far north as I've ever been, and it's absolutely amazing," he beamed. "I was expecting to just try and come and surf and find some sort of peak, but we found some waves where we were actually getting world-class *barrels*, mate. Absolutely brilliant."

At 66° 30' North latitude, it is a fictitious line puncturing the innards of northern Russia and Scandinavia. A scope of continuous cold encompassing several seas and thousands of islands, the European Arctic pegs the edge of a realm where the sun remains above the horizon one or more days per year. The sun never sets on the longest day of summer, usually around June 21, and the sun never rises on the shortest day of winter, usually around December 21.

Man long believed the Arctic to be humanely uninhabitable, a notion swiftly dismissed after scientists discovered that, besides Greenland, nine-tenths of all arctic lands lack snow and ice during summer. Flowers, vegetables and berries flourish sporadically. Sun is omnipresent. Birds chirp and residents take long walks to goose the muscles before a painfully long, dark winter.

The area has always boasted exceptional significance for mankind. Valuable arctic weather station data feeds the forecast monitors of weather professionals worldwide, including those at NBC and the Weather Channel. European nations like Russia have erected military installations in the Arctic to safeguard trade routes and frontiers—engineers devised methods of building houses atop the permanently frozen soil (a.k.a. permafrost), while scientists scrutinized animal and plant life to discern how humans could survive.

You can surf up here, too. Good waves. Cold. Fickle. Lonely. Cold. Desolate. Pointbreaks, river mouths, beachbreaks, reefs…all available to those with money, tenacity and thick rubber. Bring a hooded 5-mil, bulky surfboards, surf wax (no surf shops), heavy clothing, wads of currency and plenty of Scotch whisky. Match horsepower with horsepower.

Wheeling atop immaculately maintained roads in a sparkling new rented van after dining in a quality eatery with stunning blonde waitresses in the middle of an obscure, weather-beaten landscape, I marvel at the fruits of a well-heeled nation as the bucolic scenery races past the tinted windows.

"We have a high standard of living," said Norwegian prime minister Jens Stoltenberg. "A waiter makes more money in Oslo than in most other places. There are differences in income, but consider this: in Norway, we've tripled our income since 1970. In the rest of western Europe, income has 'merely' doubled."

Swollen Norwegian wallets can be attributed to the gargantuan oil and gas deposits discovered below the North Sea circa 1966, and the nationalistic wealth surplus is evidenced virtually anywhere pavement exists. Scribe Ben Marcus coined the economic cream for *Surfer* magazine in 1998: "Just about everything touched by man in Norway is first-rate, clean, modern, sensible and in fully working order."

Humans have lived near Spenskon Cape since the latter Stone Age, sometime between 9,000 and 6,000 B.C. The beach is flanked by serrated mountain spines; ancient black rock suffocated with ice until 5,000 years ago. It is remote, primeval landscape blanketed with snow from October to May, replete with lakes and volcanic mountains aged 600 million years—the world's oldest land formations.

"Eerily beautiful," quipped Grambeau.

We saw the Northern Lights. Slugs of green aurora borealis phantom clouds twisted and rippled between the stars following a late rain, rallying hoots from the crew. Surreal, dreamlike. Fitting for a woodsy arctic eve after a few town hours wolfing pints and funky pizza.

The aurora fascinates. Frightens. Oft-regarded as supernatural. Poetry….nature's light show. A challenge to scientists; many secrets yet to be probed. Quantum leaps in the oxygen atom. Elementary particle physics, superstition, mythology and folklore.

More exact explanations of the phenomenon could not be given until modern particle physics were developed, and knowledge about details in the Earth's magnetosphere has been based on measurements from satellites.

Light is emitted when charged particles from the sun are guided by Earth's magnetic field into the atmosphere near the magnetic poles. When these particles collide with atmospheric molecules—primarily oxygen and nitrogen—at 60 to 185 miles high, some of the energy in these collisions transforms to visible light. Northern light.

Until the 18th century, the aurora was viewed with fear and reverence, related to contemporary concepts of heaven and hell. In Norse mythology, a bridge named Bifrost connected Earth and Åsgard, the home of gods, likely modeled after rainbows or the Northern Lights and guarded by the god Heimdal. Popular belief in Scandinavia linked the aurora to dead women, particularly to dead virgins.

Weather-wise, we'd been lucky. No snow, no drift ice, no fog, few gales, scant rain, morsels of sunlight. Over marinated whale meat and beers in the pub, a commercial fisherman reckoned the current climate was of the mildest he'd seen through a lifetime of heavy-duty seasons. Inebriated, he slipped me a small, hand-made fishing knife for the equivalent of US$10 and demonstrated the proper techniques for utilizing it as a killing tool...on humans.

All told, arctic Norway fared us well. Silent, alien country with spectacular surf is difficult to translate.

The final afternoon, somebody claimed snow was on the way, spawning unreal brain images of desolate barrels blasting onto a frozen white fairytale beach with cobblestone lining...barrels for no one...barrels left for the seal and the sheep and the eagle and the Northern Lights.

Perhaps that's the best way.

THIRD MORN WITH the girl. Another boreal forest stroll, this one aside the Baltic. Clouds shift. Tree branches sway and the sea embraces a whitecapped persona. Air crisp as ice; flocks of birds hustle from the storm and we don layer upon layer of clothing—boots, scarves, gloves, wool caps, heavy jackets, thermal underwear. Late-autumnal Scandinavia is a grand aura.

Abruptly, the breeze dies. Drizzling now. Eleven a.m. landscape is dulled, almost black-and-white. Winter knocks. Days are brief spurts of light twixt hours and hours of dark.

Our pace relaxes further. Noses ooze profusely, fingers icicles. Slate-gray Baltic sulks mute under an inky sky, blending with clouds and knotty pines at water's edge. Beach is bone-hued cobblestone, littered with quaint pine cones and random bird feathers.

I stop and she—a pure Scandinavian blonde—wanders ahead without a backglance; Baltic headland at my front, woods at rear. A glassy succession of perfect one-foot rights wind down the rock ledge, ideal for a surfer six inches tall. Behold a Finnish pointbreak occasionally occupied on better days—stormier, colder, bigger days. Such will suffice for the hardy souls I'd encountered, each face exemplifying a recalled quote, that of a Swede paddling and duckdiving amidst snowfall and sloppy 36°F waves:

"Surfing here is like living in a refrigerator. It preserves you."

10

ON DANISH SURF

2003

AH, DENMARK. SAGAS of Viking occupation and brutal, brilliant conquest lie dormant beneath immaculate farmlands, sweeping heathlands, and prim village lanes. Needle rows of sod and corn, acres of cattle and sheep and horses…windmills whirling above cyclists battling the breeze rifling in from the North Sea. Here, from Aalborg, points due west mark our zone.

Today? Northern Jutland…Thy, to be exact. Goat cheese, salami, rolls, and cheap merlot are purchased from the Spar corner market in Thisted. Fresh into civilization from a surfless quest through South Greenland, a collective flash of relief softens my face as we motor from Aalborg to seaside Klitmøller, cityscape relaxing into soothed tracts of green and grain, then miles of bogs, heath and dunes. Denmark's national surf champion, 28-year-old Asbjørn, had seen it all before.

Out on the remote beach we conversed, shared a few laughs, sipped the wine, chewed salami and bread and cheese, snapped a few sunset photographs and marveled at Viking lore.

We hadn't eyed them on the way in. Perhaps they'd littered a separate scope of the vast roadside pasture, or perhaps we'd been distracted by the moonrise's luminary orb and its effect on corrugated sea. But there they were, five in all off the fenceless south side of the street, tails and manes rippling in the wind. Asbjørn stopped the car and we exited, slightly buzzed with wine, enamored by these animals in the lee of night.

The stallion ambled near, equine curiosity prevailing...ears perked, his Icelandic fur a coat of primitive luxury. We connected: breath on my skin, muzzle decoding human scent. It was an unhurried and friendly encounter, typical of Denmark. Asbjørn fed wet grass to the smallest horse.

"We don't really have any poor people in Denmark," he said. "Here, someone is always looking out for you: we've got a system that takes care of everybody. You have to decide to be a bum or a homeless person. You can tell the state you have no money, and the state will give you money or a job.

"Danish people like to say that we don't have this or that, but when it comes down to it, we're satisfied and feel protected here. We'll always be able to live well because of our government, which is good, but it also has a lot of negative aspects: it can make people lazy. Still, even if you have a simple job, you get paid pretty well, so Danes can travel for good waves."

Come dawn, all travel was forgotten: the surf was good.

DENMARK IS NOT known for its waves, but, as any Copenhagen stroll or disco evening will confirm, its women are world-class.

"Oh, yes, our beers are cold and our women are hot," Mikkel Spellerberg smiled as he yanked beach tents from his van, staging a rare Danish surf contest at the decayed Klitmøller bunkers. That afternoon, over cold Økologisk Thy Pilsners at Mikkel's rented beach house, I questioned two other surfers—Copenhagen's Asbjørn and his friend Keld, from Fyn—about this life.

"In Denmark, we might not have the best waves or the best scenery, but we definitely have the best-looking women," Asbjørn said. "Danish surfing—at least around the Copenhagen area—is pretty international with all the different people coming in and getting Danish girlfriends. You're in the lineup and you have a black surfer, a Hispanic surfer, an Italian surfer...all because of our women."

Alas, the historic and classic Viking female: tall, textbook beauty features, independent, intelligent, stylish, sexy, worldly. Viking men were brutally ruthless, sure, but what about their mates? Cycling in Copenhagen from Point A (home) to Point B (work or school), flaxen hair flowing in the morning breeze, dressed to the nines in tasteful Scandinavian garb, these gene-blessed vixens would likely be quite detrimental to my peripatetic-but-home-loving lifestyle. None could steal me from California.

"Sometimes when you're surfing here," Asbjørn continues, "there can be a crowd of 20 surfers but half of them are from other parts of the world. A Danish woman will travel and meet some guy on the beach and bring him back home, so we have guys from Ecuador, the Caribbean, Australia, New Zealand...everywhere. We have contacts around the world, and when we go visit their homes, all of their friends become our friends."

Another beer and Asbjørn adjourns to the sauna; Keld, Steve, and I head back to the beach for a twilight surf check, viewed from the concrete bunkers half-buried in sand. Sullen and depleted, the swell had sunk into the tide, remnants of the morning greatness gracing Mikkel's event. Now was a gray mood with a wide horizon in drizzly soft focus—one could almost smell the Germans loitering in these bunkers during their World War II occupation.

Standing against colorful graffiti, Keld takes in the scene as darkness accrues. His relaxed expression hid a mindful of intensely frozen winter days at this beach, when North Atlantic groundswells wove southeast, beneath Norway, to detonate here as desolate, magic beachbreak barrels.

"During summer, you can feel the energy we get from the all the light," he said. "The sun goes down at 11 p.m. and is back up again at 3 a.m. But in winter, although it's dark most of the time, you should bring your 6'4" and give it a go, because our winter surf gets *incredible*."

MORNING. THIS COUCH, stern and narrow, irks my spine and jacks my neck. Early-morning dreams, however lucid, belie the whipping flag and sand flurries outside. Sky is blue but the cold gale shreds the sea—gusting too hard for windsurfing and, following our weeks in Greenland, this was not a tired hallucination: unsurfable oceans, whitecaps, parkas, wool sweaters, thermal underwear, dry wetsuits.

The Løkken hotel was a vacant base for a few speculative days of Danish surfing. A thick off-season country silence pressed through the walls, heavy architecture fine-tuned for whims of North Sea chaos—treachery for commercial fishermen, inconvenience for us. So we sit, read, and view subtitled television while the weather runs past.

Steve's hangover from last night's run earned him ample sack time in lee of today's drab light and leaden windslop. Contrarily, my 6'5" Patagonia Rocket Sled was unveiled and the 6/5/4mm hooded fullsuit (brought for Greenland but never used) was donned. Our Løkken beachbreak was gutless and surfing it was a stretch, yet the act unfolded, followed by a rustic toast of fiery Aalborg *akvavit*, never more apropos in its appearance on the coffee table. Chased with pilsner, *akvavit* is a "water of life" commonly enjoyed with traditional Danish fare like herring or *smørrebrød* (buttered bread.). I learned of its potent merits from a gruff fisherman in Greenland, once a Denmark resident, now living and working in Qaqortoq.

The 6-mil wetsuit, pliant and zipperless, boiled in September's mild North Sea. Sweaty and stiff from a three-week absence of daily movement, I duck-dove dozens of small, frail whitewater lines before discerning a potential sandbank out the back. There in the chop I sat, bobbing like a cork, a curious spectacle for the lingering German tourists in their cars on the vast, stark beach. Steve slept on the hire-car's hood. Clearly, this was not one for the annals of epic surfdom.

But then again, yes, it was—we'd surfed Denmark. Twice.

11

A CHIMERICAL FABRIC— SURREALITY IN THE FAROE ISLANDS

2007

ICELAND WAS UNKIND. The weather was wicked, the surf flat, and gas was seven euros per gallon, which was quite a lot considering I spent several days driving around the island to find the wind onshore everywhere. I got flat tires, I got hangovers, I got sick, I got lost—fortune was astray in that land of fire and ice.

Escape arrived by way of a complimentary Atlantic Airways ticket from Reykjavík to Vágar, international gateway of the Faroe Islands, an interesting little windswept country halfway between Iceland and Norway. It was one of those obscure places I had always wanted to visit; the free one-hour flight was a boon. It was mid-April, so I figured there would be some residual North Atlantic swell to surf in a place the surf world knew nothing about.

"You are going to Faroes?" asked a wide-eyed Icelandic brunette in the Reykjavík airport. "Well, I have story. Two years ago my husband and I took ferry to there. We were there for one night and he met a girl while we dancing in Tórshavn. He has sex with her next day. Five times! So I tell him he can stay in those fucking Faroe Islands."

She threw up her hands. "Asshole!"

"You left him there?"

"Of course! He is living there now. But I have new husband. He is from Shetland, and he only fuck *me!*"

"As far as you know."

At Vágar the plane landed in snowfall, which was interesting because as one of the world's rainiest places, the Faroes rarely freeze. The Gulf Stream runs right through the 18 islands, causing relatively mild year-round air temperatures (45°F), and in a land where rain falls 280 days annually, snow is a treat.

"You got lucky," the stewardess said to me, peering out the plane window as we taxied on the tarmac. "It's never cold here."

"After Iceland, I could use some good luck."

You'd need luck, too. Ideally positioned between Scotland, Norway, and Iceland—a trinity of North Atlantic surf havens—the Faroes are full of swell but bereft of surf spots. The coast is mostly steep and inaccessible and surfable beaches are few, typically on the islands' south and east coasts, sheltered from the prevailing west swells. East swells are rare and usually plagued with onshore wind. Sheepshit-scented offshores are anomalous but do occur.

And these are the islands of sheep—Føroyar—so named by 9th-century Norsemen who found the place crawling with sheep left by 6th-century Irish monks who, searching for an uninhabited, religion-free eden, sailed to the Faroes from Scotland. The monks were the first humans on Faroese soil, but nobody really knows what they did there, because, historically, what happened in the Faroe Islands before the 14th century remains a mystery.

Mystery and mystic are apt words for a place that uses its remoteness to retain itself, a green treeless archipelago of rocky, waterfall-laced isles far removed from the 21st century that penetrates the rest of Scandinavia. Tórshavn, the Faroese capital on Streymoy ("island of currents") and Europe's smallest capital, is home to 40 percent of the country's 48,000 people. The other 60 percent are scattered throughout the islands in dozens of tiny medieval grass-roofed settlements, some so old and weather-beaten as to forever resist change, their daily winds resonant with isolation.

GUNNAR, THE FRIENDLY blond manager of my Tórshavn hostel, leaned back in his desk chair and watched the morning rain patter onto his office's double-paned window.

"Here you get all seasons in one hour," he said.

The wind shrieked. Black clouds arched over the town. Twenty minutes prior there was a snow flurry; forty minutes prior there was blue sky.

"It's warming up now," he said. "It should be a fine day."

"I was thinking of taking a drive," I said.

"Better to wait for the rain to stop. Here, let's have some coffee."

He led me to the hostel's small, cluttered kitchen, and with pride he showed me his new high-tech French-made espresso maker. "This is the future of espresso. I am going to sell these machines. The people here, they will thank me!"

I hadn't had caffeine in nine months, but something about the Faroese weather condoned it, so I sank a few cups of espresso while chatting with Gunnar.

"The tourist season, it is changing now," he said. "There was an article in *National Geographic*...."

He was referring to the November/December 2007 issue of *National Geographic Traveler*, which ranked the Faroes number one out of 111 islands in the magazine's "report card for the world's islands," saying this: "Remote and cool, and thus safe from overcrowding, the autonomous archipelago...earns high marks from panelists for preservation of nature, historic architecture, and local pride...Lovely unspoiled islands—a delight to the traveler."

If there was any harbinger for a boost in Faroese tourism, that was it.

"Millions of people in the world saw that article," Gunnar said ruefully, "and many of them are wanting to visit a new place."

"Why would tourists come here instead of going to Iceland or Sweden?"

"Because we are more isolated, of course. People think we live in caves, but you come here and see that it's a modern society. Culturally it's probably more original, if you can say that. We have preserved a lot of the old rituals that disappeared with Christianity coming to the other countries. We have the old chain-formation dance and the grindadrap, our traditional whale-killing ritual; the national sport is rowing with traditional boats that look like Viking boats. We have all those things. We are different and smaller than Iceland and Sweden."

"More quaint," I said.

"Yes. But maybe tourism is the only way many Faroese people will realize that they aren't living in a—what do you call it—in a bubble. They think their village has the perfect society. They're very hostile toward foreigners—not hostile, really, but they think that everything else outside of their village is crap, you know? We usually say, like a joke, that they're very local. Very local. Everything is great. Everything that comes out of their village is just fabulous, and Tórshavn is the capital of sin."

"But you Faroese are preservation-minded, right? I would think that alone would prohibit excessive tourism and keep things low-key here."

"That's the idea," Gunnar said.

For 60 years the Faroes, like Greenland, have been an autonomous appendage of Denmark, though the Faroese shun the European Union and the Danish language and general bustle of Copenhagen, 1,200 miles away.

"Denmark is Denmark—we are Faroese," a large chain-smoking man named Fridtjof in a Klaksvík pub told me. He was thickly white-bearded and looked like Santa Claus. "We speak our own language, we have our own parliament and our own flag. The Danes can never take these things from us." He pulled his wallet from a coat pocket and set some Faroese currency on the bar. "Look, we even have our own money!"

"What if Denmark stopped subsidizing you?"

"This is not possible. All we can export are wool and fish."

"Perhaps you could export this beer, too." I was on my fifth bottle of Klaksvík-brewed Green Islands Stout. "It's quite good, and it's getting me buzzed."

"Beer is from the Vikings, you know, so people drink a lot more here," Fridtjof said. "For example, they drink twice as much in Denmark as they do in other countries. It's like a world record. You can drink a lot of alcohol without having a problem."

The following afternoon I emptied several bottles of a different kind of local beer (Föroya Bjór Pilsnar) with David, a tall, thin, pale man who had recently become the first native Faroese surfer. A visit from some American and French pro surfers in 2007 inspired him to start surfing, and we'd met randomly this sunny spring day on a grassy coastal bluff on Sandoy, the relatively flat "island of sand" which had the country's best surf potential. I was shooting photos of sheep and he was looking for something to ride on his dark blue SurfTech 7'3" egg that he'd just bought in Norway for $1,000 ("I think I got ripped off."). The swell was up and the wind was right, but the waves were funky at best, ruined by jagged bathymetry and hideous rock mazes.

David was highly educated and friendly and spoke with a powerful voice, extolling his beloved Faroes, even if the islands weren't endowed with Raglans and Jeffreys Bays or even a decent beachbreak.

"Those Americans, they surfed up there," he said, pointing north to a crude A-frame peak blasting into an exposed shelf of boulders and seaweed. "They said it was okay."

Born in Tórshavn, David lived in Denmark for one year as a child before returning to Tórshavn until he was 16. He attended high school in Denmark, then at age 18 he traveled around Scandinavia looking for a job in precision mechanics. He found one in southern Denmark, did research and development there but eventually grew weary of it, so again he returned to Tórshavn and, with his parents, started the first Faroese aquarium.

"We are a fishery nation, so we figured we should at least have an aquarium," he said. "That was the argument for getting the funding."

"How about some artificial reefs for surfing?" I asked.

"Ha! That will never happen. The Faroese are familiar with only two things associated with the sea: you are either fishing in it, or you are dying in it."

Speaking of death-by-sea, I questioned David about the infamous Faroese ritual, the *grindadrap*, something that has come under international fire in recent years and is certainly unfavorable with animal rights activists and sealife-loving folks like surfers. Anyway, was *grindadrap* indeed cruel and evil?

"I can definitely understand peoples' reactions when they see the bloody pictures," he said, "just like with surf pictures where you never see what happens before or after the picture is taken."

"What's the process?" I asked.

"Basically, a guy in a fishing boat stumbles upon a pod of whales. Then he calls the police, usually, and then they contact these guys who are appointed to be the head guys to organize the killings. Everybody who wants to participate goes down to the harbor, takes their boat, and sails out to the whales. On the boats, you bring a lot of people because then you get more shares of the whales. Depending on the wind or the daytime or the sea current or the tide, then you decide where to go with the grind. This can take hours and hours and hours. You just leave the whales there. You don't push them or anything. You just keep an eye on them. And then slowly you form a line of boats and you make a wall. Whales naturally will move away from these boats, so you slowly drive the boats toward a beach—like herding sheep, you see. If the tide is right, you start pushing the whales by accelerating the boats, so they'll start swimming faster, and when you're close to shore, the whales have gained so much speed that they create a wake behind them. So they end up just floating up onto the beach—they beach themselves. And then all these guys are standing on the beach, waiting with a hook attached to a big rope, so they hook each whale and pull it up onto the beach. But instead of a normal hook, we use a hook that you put into the blowhole, and you pull it by the blowhole. The whale doesn't feel any pain. One guy has a big knife and he'll cut the whales' throats. You can kill 200 whales in 20 minutes. It's really fast. There are hundreds of people on the beach with their knives. It's very organized."

Last November there was a posting on Surfersvillage.com called "Pilot Whale Slaughters in Faroe Islands Raise Protests" featuring gruesome photos of the whales being killed at Faroese beaches, the sea blood-red, with pasty men raising knives to the shiny black cetaceans.

"While it may seem incredible," the posting read, "even today this custom continues in the Faroe Islands (Denmark). A country supposedly 'civilized' and an EU country at that. It is absolutely atrocious...This protest message...calls on Denmark, of which the Faroe Islands is a part, to stop the slaughter and urges recipients to pass on the message in order to raise awareness of the issue."

As the Faroes were not a surf destination, the appearance of a *grindadrap* protest piece on a surfing website confused me, but I agreed with British scribe Alex Wade, who, two days later, wrote his own online story called "The Faroe Isles Surf Trip Is Off."

"Perhaps the Faroese should be allowed to carry on with (*grindadrap*), for, as they argue, it's been a part of their culture for centuries?" Wade wrote. "Perhaps, too, hardline Somali Muslims should be allowed to stone women to death, for this, too, has long been a part of their culture? Likewise, shouldn't we repeal the ban on fox hunting, because, for centuries, this was an embedded part of the fabric of English country life?"

But on that windswept Sandoy beach, David refused foreign fury.

"That Canadian guy from Sea Shepherd, Paul Watson, he used very aggressive tactics to expose *grindadrap*. He can't see it from our point of view. He should be sailing his vessel into slaughterhouses where the chickens and cows are. They're having terrible lives, and then they're slaughtered. Our whales are having a great life until they are slaughtered. It's 100 percent ecological."

"What's the cultural significance of it?" I asked.

"It's a huge part of our diet. Some say that 25 percent of protein consumption in the Faroes comes from those whales, but it varies, also. You get some years without a single whale, and you get some years with a lot of whales."

Wildlife advocates and potential surf tourists like Wade might be pleased to know that recently, perhaps in a move to quell naysayers and stop the grindadrap altogether, the Danish government declared the whales to be unfit for human consumption, citing their high levels of mercury.

Which unfortunately did nothing to improve the surf. Yet to me none of this meant anything but a shade of inconvenience. Where there was swell, there was surfing.

THE ROAD WAS smooth and perfectly maintained, tracing scenic fjords where fishermen worked lines and sailed toward the open sea for the day's work. I passed villages—most looked identical—where laundry flapped in the breeze, chickens and geese scurried, young girls rode horses; sheep were all over the road in many places, and I wondered if there was a statistic somewhere saying how many sheep were hit by cars each year in the Faroe Islands.

Bore through hillsides were several tunnels, essential for such a small, mountainous country. The new tunnels were wide and bright and highly economical; the older tunnels were low and narrow and drippy and very dark, some of them dating back to the 1960s. Without the tunnels, the route would be painfully long and slow and precipitous and from Tórshavn it would take hours to reach Oyrarbakki and its Shell station, which played Beethoven at the pumps. While I filled up, an attractive young blonde in the car behind me noticed the surfboard in my van.

"What is that?" she asked.

"A surfboard."

She rolled her eyes. "Oh, dear. What is wrong with you?"

"I'm a surfer."

Sheep shit and piss covered the roads in the villages, which seemed deserted. I saw very few people—either they were in Tórshavn working, or they were holed up inside, or they were simply gone. Occasionally I saw a person walking along the road, exercising in the freshest of sea air.

In the town of Eiði was a beach with strong potential—reefs galore. It appeared to receive large swell, because there were boulders and logs washed over into the adjacent lagoon, and the road's pavement had been ripped off, also pushed into the lagoon. Loitering on the beach were shaggy sheep with their ears tagged, all spraypainted for identification: green foreheads, pink butts.

In Elduvík I waved at a boy riding a go-cart; he glowered back. Sheep baaahhed as I drove past, the road ending at a pretty bay ribbed with swell; unfortunately the bay was too deep for it to break, except to rise up and crash straight onto the rocky beach. Tiny Elduvík, population 102, would never host a Faroese surf spot, which goes for 99.9 percent of the 693 miles of Faroese coastline.

Yet eventually a thin lane led me to a small cluster of colorful cottages at the back of a narrow fjord, the homes surrounded by a natural mountain amphitheater, the rim topped with snow, the slopes full of grazing sheep and waterfalls. Approaching the town from the west, behind the beach, I could look directly down into the sea all the way up to the shoreline, and what I took to be rocks on the seafloor was actually black sand mixed with white. The wind was slightly onshore, the tide low, and as I pulled up to view the misty cove straight on, small lines—perhaps knee-high—crumbled toward the mouth of a snowmelt stream.

Tired of driving, I decided to sit and wait for the tide to turn; a few bottles of Green Islands Stout were uncapped. Only Jesus music came through on the radio, so I switched it off and eased the seat back, listening to the muffled silence of the waves and skua birds squawking above. For two hours I saw no one, and, literally at the end of the road, the village seemed empty. Eventually I fell asleep.

It could have been the beer, or the fact I was in a fairytale setting, but when I opened my eyes I was shocked—the wind had swung lightly offshore, the tide was higher, the sun was out, and in the south corner of the cove, a very clean and fun-looking chest-high right peeled down a sandbar. As I slept the place had transformed into a little Faroese fantasy nook, the sun sparkling off the waves, each one exactly the same as the last, with orderly four-wave sets every few minutes. Groggy and buzzed from the beers—it didn't matter, and my 6'6" Andreini quad was unsheathed.

As I was getting into my wetsuit, a large, tough-looking man on a motorcycle pulled up to my car. He was dressed in black leather and, judging from his posture when he stood, he looked pissed. Apparently he had something to say.

"What are you doing?" he asked, voice muffled inside his helmet.

"I'm going to go surfing here."

"Surfing?"

He removed his helmet, revealing a wide grin. He shook my hand. "I am Oli. Welcome to the Faroes. You are from—?"

"United States. I come from California."

"Ah! Lots of surfing in California, yes? That is true. I have always wanted to go to California."

"Where did you come from today, Oli?"

"I live on Vágar. Do you know Vágar? Where the airport is? I am just taking a little day trip around."

"What do you do here in the Faroes?"

"I am a fisherman. I am an engineer on the boat. I have just returned from Newfoundland, fishing for black halibut. I have been doing it for four years. When the fishing is good, I make good money. Last year I made 800,000 kroner." (Nearly $170,000.)

"Which helped buy your new motorcycle," I said.

"Yes!" he said. "It is my favorite way to get around."

I waxed the Andreini. "Maybe you can buy a surfboard next. I have a friend in Tórshavn—he's the first Faroese surfer. Maybe you could be the second?"

"I did not know surfing was ever possible in the Faroe Islands," he said, looking at the waves.

"It hardly is. But it looks like I have some good luck, because the waves look nice today. I'm hoping it's like this again tomorrow."

"Hope has a place," he said. "Things here often aren't what they seem."

[Postscript]

Three months after my Faroe Islands visit, I received this email from David: "The waves have been okay, and I'm getting better and better. But I am starting to feel the urge to go on a surf trip somewhere where the waves are better. I need to try to surf some real surf waves.

PART

IV

Indian Ocean

12

CREOLE MOSAIC

2009

I WASN'T ON Mauritius to surf Tamarin Bay—a biased regularfoot, I rarely traveled for lefts—but it was mandatory to check the spot if there was enough swell. Like any surfer who'd seen 1974's *Forgotten Island of Santosha*, Tamarin looked elite and irresistible, and I was keen to surf the blazing-fast left over its perfectly contoured kaleidoscope coral, channeling Joey Cabell, streaking toward the iconic black stone of Montagne Du Rempart.

But Tamarin was flat. Other spots like Souillac and One Eyes were fun and consistent, but with Mauritius's large population of locals and visitors, the island was too busy for me. Relief arose via the quiet, volcanic isle of Rodrigues, 400 miles to the northeast, an isolated place with a large, beautiful lagoon and barrier reef. Excluding the Cargados Carajos shoals, Rodrigues was the smallest (11 miles by five) of the Mascarene Islands and a dependency of Mauritius but with no Indian influence, unlike the mainland, which had so many Indians (Creoles called them "Hindis"), that to me it was almost like being in India.

French colonialists were smitten when they sighted Rodrigues in 1691, but it wasn't until 1735 that they made a permanent mark on the island, one of the Indian Ocean's most-endowed for swell that, had geological evolution permitted, might have its own Tamarin Bay—perhaps more than one—plus a thriving surf community, surf shops, and even a groovy surf film attached to it, because throughout the austral winter Rodrigues's western reef was bombarded with swell trains groomed by the southeasterly tradewind.

When I arrived it was a sustained 40 knots. "Is it this windy every day?" I asked Mervin as he drove us from Sir Gaëtan Duval Airport to tidy little Mourouk Ebony Hotel on the island's windward south coast, which overlooked a deep pass and the wide, shallow lagoon that was somewhat famous for kitesurfing. "Oh no," he said sarcastically. "Wind on Rodrigues? Never!"

Mervin was a middle-aged Creole man with taut, shiny skin, black hair, squinty eyes, and a slight build. He wore sandals, blue jeans, and a black Marlboro racing jacket. He was employed by Mourouk Ebony and he was born and raised on Rodrigues. The extent of his travels was to a 1991 futbol match on nearby Réunion.

We passed two barefoot men jogging on the potholed asphalt road. "That is very good," Mervin said, pointing at them. "Good for health."

"Do you run?" I asked.

"Yes, at 6 a.m. every two days. I run because I sit in the car so much."

Eroded by grazing and deforestation, the scenery was stark, unlike Mauritius, with gray clouds fading the deep blues of the lagoon. There was a palpably relaxed outer-island speed to Rodrigues, a bit somnolent too, distanced from the mainland bustle. It was a rich soil to people who were proudly non-Indian and non-French—they were of the African diaspora, they were devout Roman Catholics, and they cherished their serene backwater lifestyle. Rodrigues was a Creole haven, a speck on the 20th parallel, an oasis of tradition in a heavily touristed sea.

After breakfast my first morning I took a stairway to the beach fronting my hotel. All night the wind had howled—it woke me several times. On the beach was Osmosis Club, a small business catering to foreign kitesurfers for whom Rodrigues was a sort of utopia, the Bali or Oahu of their sport. But Osmosis also offered sailing, mountain-biking, and occasional day-trips for surfing.

I fell into conversation with a friendly 39-year-old Frenchman named Jerome; Osmosis was his business and he had owned it for 12 years. He was wed to a Rodriguan woman and bore two children with her. Originally a competitive sailor and windsurfer from Brittany, Jerome was stocky, tanned, bald, energetic, and he wore a blue T-shirt with a kitesurfing logo on the front.

"Windy place, eh?" I asked him.

He grinned. "Yes, mostly. Are you a kiter?"

"I'm hoping to do some surfing."

"No waves today," he said. "We have been having some professional kitesurfers here and we have been going over there, to the pass, and there is nothing." He stuck out his tongue and made a thumbs-down gesture. "But in the next few days they say the wind may not be more than 10 knots, so maybe we can go."

"What about that south reef pass?" I had studied it through binoculars; it looked like it could possibly have a left and, on a windless day, possibly be good with its tapered wrap into the lagoon.

"It rarely is surfable," Jerome said, "and the currents are very strong because it is the main pass for this part of the lagoon. It is always windy, but sometimes there can be a right that bowls at first, then becomes a burger. It is also very sharky—gray reef sharks, tigers, very territorial. I have seen them all on dives."

I asked him about perhaps trying a little kiting, something I'd never done, but noting my injured shoulder (drunken wrestling), I thought it could be risky. He frowned and said, "Yes, and I am starting to have a shoulder problem myself."

"Why did you quit windsurfing?"

"Windsurfing has so much gear to travel with—three boards, five sails. Wow, what a nightmare! But in kiting you can bring one board, two sails, and do everything."

"What makes Rodrigues so good for kiting?"

"The size of the lagoon. You are not stressed too much. Kitesurfing is already a stressing sport, but here you can practice every kind of kitesurfing in a really peaceful state of mind because it's a massive lagoon with no obstacles, constant wind, and shallow water, so you can always see the bottom. The lagoon is full of islets so you can cruise around, and you can do down-winders of more than three hours. In the east we got the small reforming waves up there, we got flat on the west, on the sandbank, for doing some speed kitesurfing and also just cruising on flat surface. We got good freestyle area, and we got waves in the west, where we sometimes go surfing."

THROUGH THE HOTEL I arranged for an island tour, driven by Curtis. He was soft-spoken, tall and slender, married and had two kids, ages 9 and 6. He lived in Port Mathurin, the island's capital (population 6,000). I asked him what he thought of Mauritius. "Mauritius very busy," he said. "I don't like."

I mentioned that, culturally, being in Mauritius was almost akin to being in India.

"Yes," he said. "Here we are just Creole, 95 percent Roman Catholic, other five percent are Hindi, Muslim. The Hindis are money-minded. Very few of them here."

He drove slowly—perhaps 15 mph—the entire time, never shifting gears, lugging the engine up hills. At the low cement crossing of Rivieré Baleine he pointed to the planted mangroves and said they were used to control soil erosion, but by the bare look of the hillsides, little more could be eroded. The damage initially occurred after settlers felled trees for houses, wood, and furniture, and now much of the island's landscape had a stony, grassy, flaxen appearance, like a tropical Scotland, dotted with low aluminum houses, goats, and cattle, leading to pretty vistas of the lagoon and distant reef, which I scanned for defined whitewater lines.

Near Pointe Raffin several fishermen walked in from their boats. "Good catch," Curtis said—the men carried reef fish, octopus, lobster. Aside the road some women harvested peanuts and toiled in fields of young corn, stalks bent in the breeze. We admired an overview of Rivieré Pistache then wound our way east to Port Mathurin, a colorful little town where most everyone was cheerful and traffic was nonexistent. I saw no tourists but several handicraft shops selling woven baskets and hats. It was a pleasurable place in which to walk and shop, snap photos, talk to locals, eat and relax, with no flyblown drunks or beggars, no litter, no police sirens or parking tickets, no gummy sidewalks, the whole place unpretentious and unspoiled by the outside world.

The island's east coast was lush—banana trees and coconut palms alternated with cacti and verdant ravines, and greeny-yellow grasses rippled in the wind. Facing the village of St. François was a sandy beach and roiling reef pass, another possible surf spot on a calm day, and along the road people walked, waving as we passed. Near 3 p.m. the route grew crowded with uniformed schoolchildren, laughing and smiling along the narrow street, which was mostly well-paved, flanked by weathered road signs and green stepped hillsides.

Curtis said he was puzzled about why I'd come to Rodrigues. Mauritius, he said, was where all the surfers were.

"That is what I'm avoiding," I said.

"Why?"

"Your island speaks for itself."

The next morning was windy with rain looming from the southeast, but after breakfast I saw blue sky. It would be a fine day. Sipping strong Mauritian coffee, I decided that Rodrigues could be to today's kiters what Tamarin was to yesteryear's surfers—an exotic Mascarene isle unspoiled by tourism, malls, junk food, high-speed motorways, luxury hotels hogging the best beaches, a majority population of Indians and the clear racial tension. Kiters could make a special Santosha-esque film, and still viewers would be mystified by the locale, much like *FIOS*'s were before Tamarin Fever infected the entire surf world. Yet Tamarin was never cheap nor easy—the wave hardly broke, and Mauritius was inconvenient. Today, for international kiters accustomed to expensive travels, Rodrigues was cheap and easy, its wind howling most days from the same direction, at the same speed, rattling my hotel's glass doors and whooshing over its red metal roof. The climate was visceral. But the roar of onshore wind and trashed surf was constant, the south coast constantly unsurfable, and my time was limited, which is why at last I had to look away.

IN A NORTH coast cove I met Annabelle, a docent who was to show me a coralline sand cay islet—a nature preserve—three miles out in the lagoon. We stepped aboard a fiberglass skiff driven by a middle-aged fisherman who spoke no English; he told her he was confused by my surfboard—nobody surfed this place. Annabelle agreed. Short, smiley, and enthusiastic about her island, she worked for Rodrigues Discover, a non-profit conservancy group that started in 2007. She was 27 and from Port Mathurin; she'd spent four years as a pharmacist on Mauritius, commuting daily from Beau Bassin to Port Louis, but missed Rodrigues so much that she returned and vowed never to again live on the mainland which, to the average Rodriguan, was alien. "Mauritius is too fast," Annabelle said. "Here we take time to live."

By air it was expensive for Rodriguans to visit the mainland, so most went by sea aboard the *Mauritius Pride*. The crossing took 24 hours, 36 on the return. "It's not so comfortable, but we prefer it," she said. "Everybody gets seasick."

As we headed out on the shallow lagoon, the boat driver line-fished but caught nothing. We passed Pointe Fouche, which was treeless and bone-dry. Cattle drowsed on the beach. "Here, rain is precious," Annabelle said. "This part of the island, the animals here, they drink saltwater. They drink the sea. When we eat them, there is no need to add salt because the meat is already salted."

We skimmed across the water, passing waving fishermen, and since the tide was out we went slowly—the hull scraped sand a few times.

I asked Annabelle if she'd brought lunch. "Only for you," she said. "I don't eat on Tuesdays and Fridays—not every week, but sometimes—to pray to my god. Are you Catholic?"

"No. For me, nature is God."

She worshiped at the Apostolic Vicariate, a Roman Catholic church in Port Mathurin. "No smoking, no alcohol," she said. "I prefer purity." I told her I was slightly hungover.

The islet's leeward side offered a bright whitesand beach sheltered from the wind, a private paradise, the kind where a honeymoon resort could exist. Instead there was a shack with a resident warden and thousands of birds—terns and noddies squawked and flew at us as we stepped ashore.

Casuarina trees provided shade from the sun. The leeward air was remarkably hot and still, but out along the edge of the lagoon, amid mild spindrift, the surf looked sublime. Perhaps head-high and symmetrical, the swells bent along a curve in the reef, creating a mellow left-hander that was ideal for the 5'6" Andreini stubbie I'd brought.

Wearing reef booties I walked a kilometer across the sandy shallows of the lagoon, avoiding urchins and bits of sharp coral, and paddled through a thin gap in the reef. Under small swell the setup was benign, devoid of current; each wave broke in the same place and peeled along the reef for 50 yards before expiring in deep water. It was sectiony with an almondy tube and a thin, high-line lip. The sets were consistent and from a steep southwest angle, hitting the reef properly. I doubted the spot could hold any larger, but Jerome later said a friend of his had kitesurfed there on a much bigger, slabbier day, prompting the name L'Etape, French for "The Step."

But at head-high the wave was user-friendly, something C-grade that you might find in the Maldives or on a small day at One Eyes. Its sea was alive with baitballs and diving birds and flying fish chased by barracuda; L'Etape was undoubtedly sharky and volatile and inherently risky as it was a long way from help. It was a wild wave that I enjoyed surfing, and it was unlikely to host another surfer for a long time.

Back beneath the shade of the casuarinas, Annabelle asked me if I had ever seen snow, and if California had beaches like this.

"Yes, and no," I said.

"But I thought California was like a paradise place."

"It's far from tropical. And it's very crowded and expensive."

"The snow is so cold, yes? How do you live in it?"

"It never snows where I live. Snow is in the mountains, far away."

"Are there many birds, like here?"

"Yes, but they are much more skittish and wary of humans."

We walked to the eastern windward side of the island, which was doused with litter. Annabelle said there was a man who comes specifically to remove it. Terns and noddies soared around and swooped at us—a few nearly landed on my head—and they were both curious and territorial since the islet was their breeding ground. Human presence was a massive intrusion.

EVENTUALLY THE WIND fell slack, so I paid Mervin to drive me to Port Mathurin, where I hired a boatman to motor me out to the reef pass that Jerome and Erwan Simon, another French friend of mine, had ridden. It was Rodrigues's main surf spot, a shallow, fast left and an even shallower, faster right, surfable only when small and high tide. Any wave bigger than two meters would flood the pass.

"There is a very big swell coming," Jerome told me at breakfast. "Today might be your only chance for the pass, eh? Tomorrow will be very big at Tamarin. You are leaving tomorrow?"

"Yes, on the first flight."

My boatman spoke no English but he knew where to go—he had used the pass countless times to access open ocean. I applied sunscreen and he line-fished on the way out, hooking a number of small, white fish, which he tossed onto the floor of the boat. They looked too small to eat, so I assumed he used them to make stew.

An hour later we faced the pass—belly- to shoulder- high waves sparkled in the midday sun, wrapping around both sides of the reef. Just outside, a whale spouted. The wind blew lightly offshore; it was a pretty scene.

The left looked bigger and longer, so I tried it first and caught several walls that challenged my speed ability while keeping an eye on the reef. As one who seldom surfs backside, I pretended I was training for Tamarin Bay.

Then I paddled over to the right, which was far too shallow—barely thigh-deep at the takeoff spot—so I caught one wave. The reef met my fins, snapping one of them. End of session.

Driving back to my hotel, Mervin turned the car radio up; Michael Jackson was singing "Beat It," his 1983 hit.

"He died today," Mervin said.

"Who did?"

"Michael Jackson. Heart attack in Los Angeles."

I was never a Jackson fan but the news surprised me. He was only 50 and poised to launch a series of live concerts, his first since 1997. A tortured man, it seemed a bit sad that he had passed.

"He sold more than 750 million albums," Mervin said. "I liked Michael Jackson, not how he was later, but his earlier albums like Thriller and Bad were really good."

"Yeah, I've got some fun memories of his old songs," I said, at age eight first hearing Jackson say *Just beat it, beat it*, which is exactly what I did the next morning, Tamarin-bound, by stepping aboard Air Mauritius flight 121.

13

INDIAN OCEAN PASS

2009

MAURITIUS COULD ACTUALLY be Las Vegas.

Tamarin Bay, the tropical island's marquee spot, is so rare but so good that a typical Mauritius surf trip is like lounging and blowing cash at Cheetah's or Déjà Vu—please look and spend, sir, but you will not touch the girls. In Tamarin's case, it's usually: Please look and spend, bro, but you will not surf the world-class wave you came for.

For the traveler, it requires luck. Amid an Indian Ocean island-hop, my timing was perfect. Poised to meet sunshine and a large southwest swell—ideal for Tamarin—I arrived from the neighboring isle of Rodrigues and found a seaside bungalow in Mahébourg, a quiet town on Mauritius's southeast coast. My guidebook said the place carried "an old-fashioned charm" and provided "a pleasant introduction" to the island.

But I was itchy. Véronique, the bungalow's jovial Creole owner, gasped when she saw the dozens of insect bites on my skin. "Be very careful," she said. "Do not scratch them. How are you feeling? Tired or cold? Because there is dengue fever around."

"I am tired, actually. But I got these bites in Madagascar, not Rodrigues."

"Oh, that is much worse. There is lots of malaria in Madagascar. Where did you stay?"

"The northeast."

"Mister Michael, cerebral malaria is there! Are you dizzy? You must see a doctor."

I was reading her restaurant's menu—I had eaten nothing since breakfast on Rodrigues that morning.

"Can I order something to eat?"

Véronique laughed. "Dinner? I am on strike." She phoned a longhaired, soft-spoken Indian named Parwayze ("like Patrick Swayze"), head cook and manager of a small restaurant a few blocks away. He drove me there and created an excellent fish curry in coconut milk, which I washed down with three cold Phoenix beers. Then he returned me to the bungalow, where we sat in his car for a few minutes, chatting about Mahébourg.

"Is not big, strange place," he said, sipping from a bottle of orange Fanta. "Is good for family. My whole family live here. No many tourist, no big hotel, but sometime I make my restaurant into discothèque for a night of fun."

"What else do you do?"

"Sometime I organize fishing tour from Blue Bay, or I make tour to Curepipe for day to party. I am social worker—I do all these things for free."

"What's good about Mahébourg?"

"Is not wrecked by big resort and rich tourist villa."

"What's bad?"

"I think nothing."

For a surfer, the windswept- and barrier-reefed town's tragedy was its lack of surf spots, which is why locals and visitors congregated around Le Morne and Tamarin, the island's best surf zones. But I loathed mass surfer-congregation.

The next morning, after a deep sleep, I admired a psychedelic sunrise over Île aux Aigrettes, the silhouetted nature reserve just offshore. Outside my window, with long wooden sticks, fishermen pushed their small boats out of the low-tide lagoon. Others walked on the flat reef, scanning and slapping the water, grabbing whatever it was they preyed upon.

Seeking coffee, I went for a stroll down a leafy road adjacent to the hotel. Very few people were around—a few walked to work, a few waited for a bus. Many birds twittered and flew. The early air was warm and still, the lagoon glittery, and within minutes I found a tiny café where Pierre, a smiling Creole from the town of Quatre Bornes, had just ordered a steaming cup of espresso.

"I have always wanted to go to California," he said after asking of my origin. "Is beautiful, yes?"

"I'd say so."

We sat at a small red plastic table on the café's waterfront patio. It offered a fine view of the lagoon and the steep wilds of Lion Mountain, looming to the north. Pierre had the day off from working in Mahébourg's branch of Mauritius Commercial Bank; he'd been a clerk there for six years. Before that he manned the reception desk of Lémuria Resort on Praslin in Seychelles, where I was headed, tracking the swell north, after I'd surfed Tamarin Bay.

"Going to Praslin is like going back in time," he said, lighting a cigarette. "People still think differently there. I love the beaches, and the girls are very nice."

His passion was *futbol*—he'd played for Lémuria's team. "Many of the hotels have their own teams. We had a winning record—the best record in Seychelles."

"What's your favorite big team?"

"I like Manchester United. Also South Africa."

"Where else have you traveled?"

"For playing football I have also been to Nosy Be in Madagascar, Réunion, and Rodrigues. I want to go to South Africa for the 2010 World Cup, but it is very too expensive for me."

He asked me what I did for work.

"Ah! I met many journalists before. Russian ones are bad. They think the world still has slavery, like slaves here in the cane fields. I think it funny because we have no slaves now. Not for long time. Tourism is main industry. Ten years ago it was only sugar and textiles, but tourism make much more money for Mauritius."

In a week-old newspaper from the next table I skimmed a report that said Mauritius's tourism, which averaged half a million visitors annually—mostly European, quite a lot for a remote, 781-square-mile island—had declined in the first six months of 2009, nearly a 10-percent drop from the same period in 2008. I showed the story to Pierre.

"*Oui.* It is the economy, you see? So bad. It is affecting everybody. But whatever happens, we Mauritians will always have Mauritius. Sort of like you and your California, eh?"

"I suppose, but California is already bankrupt."

Back in the bungalow I drowsed then studied a Mauritius map, looking for the south coast's most swell-prone spot. I chose Macondé, a short lefthander at Baie du Cap on the southwest side of the island, and rang for a taxi at half-past noon.

Harry was a large, wheezy Indian man, fleshy-faced, 62, good-natured, with a murky accent. He seemed to like surfers and carried soft racks in the trunk of his brown Mercedes sedan. "Sometimes from the airport I drive surfers to hotels," he said, strapping my board to the roof. "Usually to Tamarin, Le Morne, sometimes to Flic en Flac. But never in Mahébourg. You are first surfer I drive in Mahébourg."

He lived in the small town of Chemin Grenier, between Mahébourg and Baie du Cap. "It's a good place. Quiet. Not so busy. My wife and me, we live peaceful."

Heading west, we drove past miles of sugarcane fields. "Is harvest time now," Harry said, gesturing toward the tall green rows flanking the road. "Most of the cane is cut by hand, some by machine. I worked in the cane fields when I was young."

I asked him where the cane was exported. "Europe. But today sugar has a very low price. The government also wants to make it into ethanol."

"Can you eat raw sugarcane?"

"Yes, of course!" Immediately he stopped aside a field, exited the car, and ripped off a green, woody 18-inch piece. Then, while driving, he showed me how to eat it: "Bite it like this to take the bark off, then you bite and chew, like this." He gnawed a chunk off, chewed it, then spat the wad out the window. He handed the cane to me, and I did the same. It tasted just like....sugar, but crunchy and fibrous.

"How long did you work in the fields?"

"About 14 to 27. Thirteen years, in my younger time. Very hard, very hard. I never forget my bad time in my life. And the women did not like field workers. You get old very fast, eh? At 50 you look 60. Ten years more old. When I was 27, I look like I was 37. (laughs) People say I looked horrible. They say, 'When you are awake, you look half died.' At 27 years! Hands so rough, face rough, eyes burned with sun, skin cuts from cane and tools. So I did not marry until I was 33 years old. Is late for a Mauritian man to marry. I meet my wife, 27, and I 33. Good match, six years difference. I married her and got two daughters and one son. Now I live like a king compared to when I was field worker."

"What was the process?"

"Cut and load. You fill the basket about four or five times a day. And then I get 20 rupees for pay. What is this—nothing? This for working seven or eight hours. Well, in this time, things were cheaper. Pound of rice was one rupee. But when I started taxi, first day I work for 150 rupees. Seven time more than the field work. Then, second day, I make 250-300 rupees, and it just go from there. For fuel, in 1975-'76, one gallon was six rupees and 10 cents. Gallon, eh? That is about four liters. Now one liter is 45 rupees. Every day I get full tank and I drive, drive. Local people, eh? People to work, to school, to cinema, to market. Sometime they miss bus, so I have to drive these people to the next village or town."

"How many Mauritians work in the cane fields?"

"About half—50 percent in fields, 25 percent in government office, and 25 percent in hotels, or builders, building house. But before, it was nothing else but sugar and fishing. No hotels in this time. No tourists, nothing. We did not know about tourists."

Along the way Harry pointed out the various large hotels and luxury freehold villas being built, carrying names like Villas Valriche and Emerald Heights. "They are the new thing," he said. "There are about 10 big projects happening now, all very expensive."

"Who buys them?"

"Strangers. France, England, South Africa, some Germans. No Mauritians, really. I cannot live in places like these. These are high-class. I am low-class."

"Maybe some famous actors or rock stars will move here," I said.

He asked me if I had heard of Michael Jackson's death two days prior.

"Yes, I was on Rodrigues when it happened. Heart attack, eh? He was only 50."

"Very sad news," Harry said. "People are crying in India!"

At Macondé he left me on the side of the road, fronting the hollow, shallow left that was a 10-minute paddle offshore. Nobody was surfing. The waves looked to be about chest-high and clean.

"My friend will come and get you in two hours, okay? I call him. Just stand here in two hours and he will take you back to Mahébourg."

"Lovely. Thank you." I paid the fare and shook his hand, then he drove away, probably to his home in Chemin Grenier.

The waves were in fact chest-high and fairly consistent with the high tide, offering a decent cushion over the sharp coral reef. The cool water felt good on my bug bites. Surfing backside, the punchy lefts were challenging, also quite fun, and it was sublime to surf a foreign wave alone at the edge of the Indian Ocean, wide open, with only the Kerguelen Islands between me and Antarctica.

Later, at the agreed time, I was collected by a Dakshesh, a fat 46-year-old Indian who was a fifth-generation resident of Pointe aux Piments, a town in the island's northwest. His ancestors had arrived as slaves to the British. He was friendly and chatty, spoke excellent English, and had driven taxis for 27 years.

"Many people here have no work," Dakshesh said. "Is global economic crisis, you see? But I thank gods every day. I lucky—very lucky."

It was Saturday, just before sundown, with lovely orangey-hued views, some rain squalls, but general clarity in the darkening sky. Trailing smelly, diesel fume-spewing trucks, we retraced the route to Mahébourg, across wide verdant spaces and through the cane fields and several small towns. Indians were everywhere—working in shops, walking or cycling on the road, idling in doorways, fishing from rocks, drinking beer beneath palm trees. I saw no tourists. Once back in Mahébourg, Dakshesh stopped for me to buy bottled water and a case of cold Phoenix beer; he then deposited me at my bungalow.

"You come from California," he said. "I know there is snow there."

"Only in the mountains. I live at the beach."

"I want to see a cold place. Maybe go to see the snow for one week, just to see what it is like. Is my dream."

"My dream is to surf Tamarin Bay."

"You want go to Tamarin tomorrow?" He handed me his business card. "Call. I take you."

Hours later, after dinner and several beers, I clicked through television channels and found a "breaking news report" about a high-surf advisory, something about the waves at Flic en Flac—a beach near Tamarin—being "unusually high today" and that "such waves aren't abnormal during the winter months." Authorities had advised the public to avoid the ocean.

This new swell was from a powerful anticyclone beneath Madagascar: four to five meters at 15-second intervals, heading straight to Tamarin. It was a nice predicament. Because tomorrow on Mauritius, like Dakshesh, I too would be lucky—Vegas lucky.

14

TRIBAL SCENERY

2009

THE CITY'S ABATTOIR attracted them, he said. It pumped fresh blood straight into the Indian Ocean.

"I see *many* shark here. Many big shark, small shark. Tiger, hammerhead, zambezi. Dis place, we have most shark in Madagascar."

He was Rija, a slight fisherman, 61 and ancient for a man from an island where humans mostly missed the twilight of their 50s. He was equally rare in his English-speaking ability since he had never left Madagascar—he'd spent his entire life fishing offshore in the vicinity of Toamasina, the island's largest port, a place so full of sharks, ocean swimming had been banned. A bloody seashore was no place to surf, either, which is why after deplaning from Réunion I immediately exited Toamasina, the former French colonial resort city, and vanished into the bush.

I'd met Rija on the sand a few dozen yards from the door of my wooden beach bungalow; the sunrise was blinding and already the day was hot. He was cheerful and barefoot and color-coordinated in his tattered beige cap that said New York, an orangey Oriental-patterned collared shirt, and threadbare beige shorts. He and his friend, wearing a gray V-necked women's sweater and white bucket hat, had just beached their dugout wood lakana (pirogues) and were plucking shiny gray hand-size reef fish from tangled green nets; the men's' day had begun at 3:30 that morning, launching their pirogues beneath starlight.

Rija made stew with the small fish. "Very little meat. Not good like langouste or captain."

"Do you fish each day?" I asked.

"Oui, but not in weather bad, like cyclone. Then not possible."

"Who do you fish for?"

"For family. Also for hotel and market. Sometimes I make big money to buy something new, like bicycle." He smiled, his teeth made whiter by the intense low sunlight. I mentioned that all hotels I'd seen here looked empty, I hadn't encountered a single tourist, and I was the sole guest at this collection of rustic bungalows managed by a beatific young Frenchman named Jason. Like everyone else's, his business was dead.

"*Oui*, za crisis!" Rija said, referring to the political violence 140 miles away in Antananarivo, Madagascar's capital. Anti-government protests had started in January, and by June, when I visited, 135 people had been killed and the conflict remained. Initially the protests were directed at then-president Marc Ravalomanana and were organized by Antananarivo's then-mayor, Andry Rajoelina, who in March declared himself to be Madagascar's new president after Ravalomanana's forced resignation. Because of the turmoil, foreign countries advised their citizens to avoid the island, and tourist revenue plunged 80 percent.

One hundred and sixty million years ago, Madagascar split from Africa and became a complex eden home to 5 percent of Earth's plant and animal species—more than 80 percent were endemic to the island. It was a haven for naturalists, but culturally Madagascar was in bad shape. The United Nations declared it to be the world's poorest and one of its least-developed countries. There was the low life-expectancy, rapid population growth, frail infrastructure, poor health care, famine, and high infant mortality. Just 5 percent of the land was arable—vanilla, coffee, and cloves were the main exports—and although Madagascar was a big island in the Indian Ocean, commercial fishing was nonexistent. More than 85 percent of its 20 million people survived on less than $1 a day, and food insecurity and malnutrition were chronic, especially in the east and drought-prone south, which was loaded with swell and setups but plagued by strong onshore tradewinds and lack of access. Flights were costly, roads were terrible, and it was generally mandatory that you spoke French or, better yet, Malagasy.

Despite the island's 3,000 miles of coast, tiny Anakao in the southwest was where 99 percent of foreign surfers went because surf camps existed there and the waves had proven themselves. The southern villages of Lavanono and Fort Dauphin were the other two zones visiting surfers sought but, overall, Madagascar was one large, unsurfed wilderness.

Rija didn't surf, though a few of his kin did. They were all of the tribe Betsimisaraka, which meant "numerous and inseparable," and traditionally they were fishers, seafarers, and traders—simple, peaceful—who thrived galaxies from the feuds and strife of the teeming capital. The 2009 political mess was a spectacle and somewhat trite compared to the fierce cyclones that had recently thrashed the Betsimisaraka coast. Rija's life orbited around nature, and in the bush he was wholly self-sufficient, surviving off land and sea—tourism cash was a bonus, not crucial. In 2004 his wife died in her sleep, but he had a brood of relatives scattered in and around Toamasina; 11 years ago he lost a nephew to a tiger shark in three feet of water, an incident that sent schisms through Rija's dirt-and-thatch village. So he moved away, not far, but far enough to numb the pain and blur visions of that mutilated 8-year-old boy.

Rija's beach was an alcove of tranquility, enough so to attract the soft-spoken Frenchman Jason and his spartan brand of leisure—his bungalows were clean and functional, well-built from local wood and clay. He didn't surf but knew of the shallow gems offshore, particularly the Malagasy Velzyland in the crosshairs of my front window.

Jason was pale and thin with tawny shoulder-lengthed hair; he was unflappable, 23, and had recently worked as an upscale pastry chef in Nice, serving millionaires who paid $70 for soufflé. When I met him he had been in Madagascar for seven months, inheriting the bungalow business from his father, who had been on the island for 22 years. "I never thought you would be coming here with a surfboard," Jason said when I arrived toting a 5'6" Andreini 2+1 stubbie. "My friend Bruce, when he was out surfing here last week, the waves were twice as tall as him!"

Bruce was en route to take me to a sheltered, sandy right point down the coast. Jason and I were lounging at a wooden table beneath coconut palms, drinking cold Three Horses Beer, which was preferred over the local water. "Don't drink our water unless you want to poo for three days," he told me. Using a small portable radio we listened to a cassette of Ballack, maestro of the *valiha*, Madagascar's national instrument, a bamboo tube zither I'd first seen being played by a Creole boy in the film Forgotten Island of Santosha. "We wandered through valleys," the narrator said, "hearing the exotic melodies of the valiha ringing out from mountain to mountain."

The music was delicate and mesmerizing, floaty and fluid with the din of surf and southeasterly trades that rustled the green fronds above. It was a cooling wind, respite from the searing midday heat that kept fishermen like Rija on land until late afternoon, when the trades eased and fishing could resume. Daily the wind wailed, wrecking the hollow left and sectiony right that flanked the reef pass the fisherman used to reach the open sea. For them it was perfect geography—a defined pass, an inner lagoon, a protected white-sand beach, a safe place to store their pirogues, unspoiled reefs, and a good fishery in the immediate vicinity. When he had guests to feed, Jason patronized the men for their various catches—prawns, lobster, meaty whitefish like captain—and synchronicity of place withdrew him from the worries of the world.

Surfing there was worrisome for me. The trades blew sideshore/offshore at the Velzylandish right, and usually it was the only spot to ride. It was also the most consistent, taking any southern swell—windswell or ground—and warping it into a clean barrel within spitting distance of black urchins and bare pink coral. The waves were uncatchable anywhere but on the initial bowl—shoulder-hopping was impossible—and if you fell, you hit reef. The nearest hospital was two hours away via rough dirt roads, and the wave broke a kilometer from shore, requiring a sketchy paddle over deep, murky water alongside a reef where fishermen set traps and nets. Once in the lineup sitting on my board, I couldn't see my feet and felt like bait—out of all my time surfing alone at sharky surf spots worldwide, nothing rivaled the spookiness of Madagascar.

But Jason's friend Bruce lived unfazed. It was his home, and if he held fear he would never surf. He appeared at our table just as I finished my drink; he was smiling and excited to get wet—for him business was nil, too, so he had spare time. He was 40, Madagascar-born, had moved to Marseilles when he was five, then at age 16 he moved to shark-riddled Réunion and lived there for two decades before permanently resettling on the Cyclone Coast in 2002. He was a keen surfer and, regularfooted, he enjoyed the selection of right-handers at his doorstep.

"Where you come from?" he asked. His accent was thick and he spoke fast.

"America."

"You like Barack Obama?"

"I didn't vote for him."

"Where in USA you from?"

"Santa Barbara, California."

"Ah! Tom Curren! My favorite surfer. I see him surfing Saint-Leu and Trois Bassins—he come to La Réunion many time. He like the big waves there."

I wondered what happened when a big swell hit the Malagasy Velzyland out front.

"You can drive big truck through it!" Bruce held his arms out. "You can stand in tube like this!"

I asked him if anyone had been badly injured on the reef. "Oui, everyone get cut and bleeding," he said. For being the spot's most frequent surfer, Bruce remained unscathed. "I very lucky guy, eh?"

With him came 19-year-old Lucien, who only spoke Malagasy. Related to Rija, Lucien lived in the village and had been surfing here for the last few years, using Bruce's battered boards. Bruce told me that

Lucien was the area's best surfer out of perhaps a dozen, most of them teenagers, and we would see some of them at the remote sand point we intended to surf that day. He said it was fairly mushy spot that broke on the leeward side of a long forested headland, so it was reliable and user-friendly.

I bid *au revoir* to Jason and got into Bruce's blue pickup; Lucien rode with our boards in the bed. We bumped and rattled our way out to the main road, which for a hundred yards was lined with colorful stalls and their sellers of things like fruit and hot tea. From a young girl Bruce bought bananas, lycees, and deep-fried bread. "Energy!" he said as he wolfed a banana, then bit open a lycee. He handed one to me. "These very special. Special Mada lycee. You like?"

"Tangy but sweet," I said. "*Trés délicieux*."

It was a pleasant drive atop the thin muddy road, badly potholed, bisecting leafy green rain forests and plantations of corn and coconut, brown fields of black cattle and cloves, all beneath a deep blue sky. It felt like a warm summer day in southern California. "This is winter," Bruce said. "Is cold. Summer *trés chaud*—Sahara! 45 degrees!"

We passed many idle people, kids gawking and shouting, skinny men and women walking slowly, some with baskets of produce atop their heads, men on bikes towing makeshift trailers full of twigs or bundles of bananas. At the beach junction the road narrowed and became sand/rock/mud with frail wooden bridges spanning creeks and gullies. Bruce talked about surfing here and about how he was born in Antananarivo in 1969 to a family that had been in Madagascar for 200 years. After life on Réunion, the Cyclone Coast return was indeed a homecoming. "Is easy for me here," he said, steering with his elbow while peeling another banana. "Is natural. I like the Malagasy. We are same people."

A small clearing revealed the top of the point; Bruce parked the truck and we stepped out for a look. Five local kids were surfing in the chest-high windswell, but it was clean, with pretty jade-green water color. The backdrop was lush, the wind tearing at the treetops.

"No good, eh?" Bruce said. "No barrel today. You are not seeing it the best."

"Looks fun to me," I said. Lucien was back at the truck, waxing his board. He was yelling excitedly back and forth with his friends in the water.

The three of us paddled out off the reef at the top of the point, which was flat and padded with seaweed, a nice change from the treacherous Velzyland wave. But with eight guys out it seemed crowded, though the vibe was of stoke and innocence, the kids hooting at each other's waves. All rode old yellowed thrusters, hand-me-downs from Bruce, who bought his surf gear in Réunion, a 90-minute flight east.

The session was good but I soon tired from the hot sun and paddling against the strong current after each wave. So we left, retracing the jungle route back toward town, first stopping at Bruce's property, a beautiful 5,000-square-meter spread behind a tall wooden fence with two tourist bungalows and an onsite pizza joint that he ran for income. His last guests, a Catholic church group from Toamasina, came three weeks ago.

"No profit now," Bruce said. "All my money go out, not in. Government crisis!"

His pretty 25-year-old Malagasy wife Enaino brought us bottles of Three Horses Beer and took orders for pizza, which she relayed to Lucien, who went into the kitchen and prepared the dough. Above him, large spiders rested in webs strung from the wood rafters. We sat at a table and Bruce strummed a guitar, asking me what classic rock bands I liked. He told shark tales from Réunion. He offered me a shot of homemade lycee liquor which, after seeing the jar it came from, I declined. He showed me a kilo of fresh vanilla, moist leathery black spears that he kept in a plastic bag—he stuck his nose into it and inhaled deeply. "Ah, *le parfum*!" He wanted to sell me some but exporting vanilla in my luggage was illegal. When the pizzas arrived from the oven I went to wash my hands in one of his two bungalows—brown water poured from the tap. "Special for you, eh?" Bruce said, laughing.

Enaino joined us with a bowl of zebu and rice and a pot of tea. She found amusement in the "Romance" section of my French phrasebook:

sentences like *Je ne suis qu'un objet sexuel pour toi* ("You're just using me for sex") and *C'est un con* ("He is a prick") made her giggle. She spoke no English. Upon finishing my pizza I looked at Lucien and said, "*Mes compliments au chef*" ("My compliments to the chef"), which Bruce translated into Malagasy. Lucien smiled, gave me a thumbs-up, and took my empty plate.

The afternoon waned swiftly and we made plans to surf the next day, so I left my gear in Bruce's truck. An outdoors Madagascar dusk was no place to avoid bug bites, however, especially from malarial mosquitoes, so I thanked Bruce and Lucien and Enaino and walked back toward Jason's bungalows. Omnipresent was the smell of burning leaves, and amid the serene rural mosaic came sounds of roosters crowing, chickens clucking, geese screeching, children laughing. Through the village was a rubbly dirt lane with tea stands and men in yards repairing fishing nets, women washing clothes and dishes and, to nobody, small girls peddling trinkets like pink corals, white shells, and intricate shell necklaces. A young dreadlocked man asked me if I wanted to smoke marijuana with him. Seconds later a cheery old lady with a large nose wart asked me my age (33), which I wrote in the dirt. She too wrote her age (57 but she looked 75) in the dirt fronting her home, a thatched hut where another woman was washing dishes on the ground, a small fire nearby boiling water for tea, chickens amok. The old lady pushed her granddaughter at me and I took photos of them together, showing the woman the photos on the back of my camera. "*Ooh-la-la!*" she said with a grin. Her husband was amazed I spoke English. "*Anglais! Il parle l'anglais!*" he shouted to somebody in a neighboring hut. Despite the language barrier I could see that these people were happy, friendly, and though dirt-poor, they were content with their simple slice of life. Goodness knows it was shelter from the political storm.

Back on the beach I smoked a kretek while watching a psychedelic pastel-pink sunset fade into the silhouetted western landscape. The tradewind blew and the swell remained, but for the Velzyland wave the tide was dangerously low, each barrel draining the reef and spitting below sea level—it was perfect, scenic, a fringe of wilderness, something a surfer would return to. Sounds were the wind and surf, chirping crickets, distant birdsong, and fishermen at their beached pirogues, the men laughing and yakking, picking fish from green mesh nets. Fifty yards up the beach I saw Rija in his New York cap and orangey shirt, dragging his boat from the water; he waved urgently at me, pointing down at his pirogue. "Come! Come! Look!"

I ran over to him. In his pirogue lay a dead tiger shark, about four feet long, slightly bleeding from a wound near its left eye. Rija ran his finger down the slick finned torpedo body, which was badly scratched—he'd found the lifeless shark on the lagoon's reef in a foot of water. Strangely it had died on its own—recently, too—and Rija was going to eat it. "I have to thanks gods for ziss!" he said.

A small crowd gathered 'round the toothy spectre, children and women and fellow fishermen gibbering in Malagasy, much laughing and hooting, hand-gesturing and pointing, as if they were discussing who would get what. "I keep jaw," Rija told me, smiling.

Moments later a heavy squall swept in from the south, scattering the people and drowning the roar of the surf. Drenched, I jogged back to my bungalow and took a cold shower while drinking a large, unchilled bottle of beer. Then, amid candlelight on the bed beneath a white mosquito net, I read a *Vanity Fair* article about Johnny Depp and his private 45-acre Bahamian island, to where he sailed aboard his 156-foot luxury yacht, the *S/V Vajoliroja*. "Money doesn't buy you happiness," Depp told the author, "but it buys you a big enough yacht to sail right up to it."

Or in Madagascar you could fell a native hardwood tree like the arofy or soarafo, dig it out, and make a pirogue. You could launch it aside Rija before dawn the next day, plot a course and set lines and nets, float with the breeze, and admire your coast with no concept of time. Then, before the sun rose high and its heat seared your skin, you could collect your lines and nets and row back to shore, carefully avoiding the bad currents and roiling surf. Your fellow Betsimisaraka tribe fishermen and their children could be on the beach, gauging the morning's catch, cleaning the boats, intoning of affairs that never drifted beyond this rural nook of tropical idyll. Because on Rija's beach, happiness came for free.

15

ISLANDS OF THE MOON

2007

"We anchored in a channel with surf breaking over a reef on each side, and it didn't take long to get the board unloaded. While I clicked away with my camera, Geoff made it through several tight tubes, turning on with head dips. The whole routine really stoked a native crowd gathered on the shore… so stoked they gave Geoff a ride back to the yacht in the head man's outrigger canoe. Upping anchor, we motored the yacht into the small settlement of Dzaoudzi over glassy water with the smell of flowers heavy in the air."

—Ron Perrott, Surfer *magazine, November 1967*

THE UNEXPECTED OCCURRED a month from Durban. Yet the unexpected too was a "help wanted" note tacked to a bulletin board inside the smoky bar of an old South African yacht club, where two Australians were downing beer, looking for something to do, someplace new to go. Their escape flashed on the scrap of paper.

And so August 1967 saw writer/photographer Ron Perrott and surfer Geoff White volunteering to crew on the Kyalami, a 46-foot trimaran bound for Greece via the Red Sea, Seychelles, and the East African coast. But first came the Mozambique Channel, a thousand miles of turbulent blue dotted with atolls and volcanic isles. Four of these—Grande Comore (locally known as Ngazidja), Moheli (Mwali), Anjouan (Ndzuani), and Mayotte (Maore)—comprised the French colony of Comoros, one of the most remote and mysterious places on Earth, a routine port of call for boats cruising across the channel's north entrance. It was off Mayotte where, after four weeks of sailing, Perrott and White stumbled upon waves—good waves, clean waves, virgin reef-pass waves that exactly 40 years later I could see clearly through the window of a Boeing 737.

Still a French territory, Mayotte was a quick stop en route to Grande Comore and its ancient slum of Moroni, where I rendezvoused with France's Erwan Simon, Italy's Emiliano Cataldi, Hawaii's Randy Rarick, and Singapore's John Callahan, who, after Perrott, would become the second person ever to photograph surfing in Comoros, perfumed isles of immense beauty, complex culture, violent politics, and—as the two Australians found—watery spells of sweet surprise.

> *"The Comoros islands, scattered like pebbles in the ocean to the northwest of Madagascar, are just about as far off the world's radar as it's possible to be."*
>
> *—Lonely Planet*

RAIN ALL NIGHT, rain all morning. Hot and humid. No water in the hotel, no toilet, no shower. No matter: "Be careful," Simon said from the dim foyer. "I was talking to this French guy who works for the Red Cross here, and he said there's a major outbreak of cholera. There are more than 800 cases, and 14 people have died."

Malaria, crumbling sewage systems, lack of potable water, streets strewn with trash—sanitation is a big problem in Moroni, once the seat of a powerful sultanate, a bustling nexus of Swahili commerce home to 12 sultans. In the 15th and 16th centuries Comoros prospered; Oman and nearby Zanzibar were favored partners. Slaves and spices were the goods of choice, drawing immigrants from Persia, Madagascar, Asia, Africa, and the Arab desert to these palmy volcanic shores, injecting Islam into the heart of an otherwise eclectic diaspora.

"My people come from many people," said a white-robed Comorian man sitting on the steps of the harborside Friday mosque. He was one of the rare locals who spoke English. "But we are one, you see. Allah-u-Akbar—God is great. This do you know? There is no god but God. God is great."

"Yes," I said, "God is great. Where is the ferry office?"

Priority, aside from enjoying a grim Moroni day, was obtaining boat tickets to leave town promptly because Grande Comore lacked waves and because the planes of Comores Aviation were too small for surfboards. A 70-kilometer sail to the southeast, lush Anjouan was the archipelago's promised land, home to the varied reef pass and the black-sand beachbreak, the slabby point and the wind-sheltered cove, the nearest surfer thousands of miles away.

"Do not go to Anjouan," the man warned, raising his left index finger at me. "Not safe there. Many problem with election, people angry, the president is bad. Fighting can happen. Better to stay here in Moroni, where you and your friends are welcomed."

"We have no choice," I said. "Unlike here, there are waves on Anjouan."

From within the mosque the muezzin began, summoning dozens of people from the streets, a sea of white robes and skullcaps over dark faces walking toward us. Greeting the prayers, the man stood to enter the building.

"God is great."

Our ferry was scheduled to leave Moroni at 5 p.m., arriving at the Anjouan port of Mutsamudu several hours later. Simon, our trusted French translator, secured the tickets and arranged our visas, because despite Anjouan, Mohéli, and Grande Comore being in the same country, politically they are worlds apart—foreigners need a different visa for each island because each has its own unique breed of dysfunctional government.

One of the world's poorest countries, L'Union des Comores has weathered more than 19 coups or attempted coups, assassinations, and mercenary invasions since it gained independence from France in 1975. France backed the early coups but now supports African Union mediation, and Colonel Bob Denard, the widely hated French mercenary involved in four of the coups, was recently imprisoned and has Alzheimer's disease, no longer able to plot political mayhem. But with such a history, Comoros is infamous for instability and inter-island squabbling. Of course, French-controlled Mayotte is immune to all of this.

Back at the hotel I went for a fish sandwich and fell into conversation with the restaurant's waitress, a middle-aged French woman wearing dirty brown eyeglasses and a brown threadbare dress. She had horribly brown and bucked front teeth, wild and wiry gray hair, a narrow face with warts and a crooked nose and pointy chin—witchlike. But she was quite friendly and chatty, and had recently returned from Mayotte.

I said, "It's basically a piece of France in the Mozambique Channel, isn't it?"

"Mayotte for lazy French people," she said, setting a small glass of ginger tea on the table. "It just a big holiday for them. They work little, make lot of money, live in nice island. Many of them hate Comorians, who are much nicer people than the French. I am French and even I think the French on Mayotte are not nice!"

"So you prefer Moroni?"

"Oh yes. I am from Chamonix, but Moroni is where my husband from. He worked on Anjouan many years ago but came back to Grande Comore because it is better. Here we have bank, Internet, airplanes, shops, cinema, anything we need. Anjouan is bare."

"We're taking a boat to Anjouan this evening."

At this she looked concerned, leaning in toward me and lowering her voice. "Some people there don't like white people because they are scared of mercenaries. You need to declare that you are an American sportsman. Keep identification on you at all times to show you are American, not French or South African. I don't want to afraid you about Anjouan, though."

After a violent conflict in 1997, Anjouan and Mohéli seceded from Grande Comore and the whole concept of L'Union des Comores. In 2001 the country reunited with itself when voters established a new constitution keeping the three islands as one country, granting greater autonomy to each. For several years there prevailed a semblance of order, and 2006's presidential election was Comoros' first peaceful transition of power in 31 years.

The tranquility came to a screeching halt shortly before our visit. In May 2007, Mohamed Bacar, who was elected president of Anjouan in 2002, was asked to step down by the constitutional court because he had served his five-year term; the court then nominated an interim president to head Anjouan's government until the elections were held. But seeking island independence, Bacar refused to leave, instead printing his own ballot papers and staging his own election in June despite a statement from the African Union and Comorian government saying Bacar's poll was bullshit. Still, Bacar claimed a landslide victory of 90 percent for his "liberation" regime, and at least two people were killed in subsequent tiffs between the national army and Anjouan police. The island's airport and harbor closed, military presence increased, and tensions soared. Knowing this, we seriously began to wonder if we'd be safe on Anjouan after all.

"SACHET, MONSIEUR! SACHET! Sachet, s'il vous plaît!" People—mostly children—began vomiting within an hour out from Moroni's harbor, frantically screaming for the blue plastic bags (*sachets*) that a man darting around the deck was dispersing, trying to reach people before they puked onto the ship or someone next to them. Instead of just vomiting over the gunwales and into the sea, a Comorian would stick his or her head into a bag, spew, then pass the bag to anyone in vicinity who was also ill, assuming they hadn't expelled onto the deck already. When a bag was deemed full, the sachet man would grab it, tie it shut, and toss it overboard.

Initially since it was dark and since we couldn't really see what was happening, Emiliano and I thought it was a game. Simon corrected us. "It's disgusting," he said. Rarick, who was sitting on the deck amongst several seasick locals, caught the brunt of it, narrowly avoiding random sprays of chunky white vomit.

"Looks like they all ate the same thing," Callahan said.

"Cassava," I said.

"Nice, isn't it?" Cataldi said, grinning.

We'd left an hour before sunset—babies crying, strong wind, whale spouts, clearing skies—and when darkness fell, reality set in.

"Welcome to the Hell Ship," Callahan said, lighting a cigarette. "We're in for a long night."

The Anjouan-registered *Shissiwani-II* was an old 120-foot Norwegian trawler, a sad and filthy hunk of rusted iron, topping maybe four knots at full throttle, overloaded with cargo and smelly Comorians. The ship had no toilets, no food, no lights, no shelter, nowhere to sleep, only a few dirty plastic chairs to sit on. The crossing was to consume 14 hours: 10 hours of sailing followed by four hours on the boat outside Mutsamudu's harbor, waiting for the Anjouan customs office to open.

The lower decks were littered with garbage, bits of rope and wire, dirt, plastic bags, bald tires, goats, ratty chickens running amok. Up on the top deck, where we were crammed in with the other passengers, were lines of the crew's drying clothes, flapping in the wind—not much else except a few crates of bottles and chunky rice sacks of dubious contents. The air smelled of shit, diesel smoke, sweat, and vomit.

Eventually the crowd fell silent. Immense darkness at sea, a sliver of moon, countless stars and the Southern Cross. Judging from the rough sea, there was plenty of swell. I tried to doze partially supine on some chunky bags, but a man soon scolded me—"Fragile!" People were jammed into corners and in the corridors, sleeping almost on top of each other. The deck was layered with spew. I put my iPod on and tried to zone out for the duration, but its battery died as we neared Anjouan, which was sighted at 1:45 a.m.

IT WAS INDEPENDENCE Day on this hilly isle of green. President Bacar had just declared sovereignty from L'Union des Comores, and, theoretically, as of August 3, 2007, Anjouan was on its own. Yet alone without tourism or any real cash-generating export, Anjouan would stay adrift and terribly poor, poised for peril, an ugly reality in a very beautiful place—so beautiful, in fact, that Anjouan could easily be one of the world's finest holiday islands.

"We have the sea and nothing else," an old bearded man on the ferry said as we waited to disembark in Mutsamudu's port. Smoke rose from villages along the luxuriant shoreline, shadowed by steamy, mountainous rain forest and fronted by a calm blue sea and sweaty fishermen in dugout canoes, setting out in the shimmering morning heat.

"What about spices?" I asked.

"Clove not enough. We have nothing."

"Ylang-ylang?"

"Yes, we have the ylang-ylang, but this has not made us rich. Only the president is rich, and he does not grow ylang-ylang."

Anjouan once supplied about 90 percent of the world's ylang-ylang, a wispy yellow flower that produces an essential oil used in expensive French perfumes. Transplanted from Asia to Comoros by French colonialists, the flowers enhanced both the air and the Comorian economy for more than a century, and the islands enjoyed a bit of worldly importance. But this is no more—demand has plunged as most French perfume manufacturers have turned to synthetic essence, and because ylang-ylang was introduced by the French as a cash crop intended for French markets, it has no traditional value in Comorian society.

"At least Anjouan should smell good," Rarick said.

Vanilla, the Comoros' other main export, has seen a recent collapse in price due to marketplace speculation and oversupply. Seafood exports are nil. So today, to make ends meet, most Anjounais rely heavily on foreign aid and remittances sent home from expat relatives living in Marseilles.

Once entry was cleared we stuffed our bags into the black Toyota truck of Moustali, our jovial Anjounais guide, who drove us across the island to our destination, a village on the windward southwest coast. Along the way were square brown roadside patches of cloves drying in the sun, their heated scent wafting through the truck's open windows. At the breezy village of Sima, two armed military men on motorcycles sidled up to us and asked Moustali, "Who are these people, where are they from, and when are they leaving?"

Our serpentine route wound through thick forests of breadfruit and coconut palm; past tangled plantations of banana, ylang-ylang, coffee, nutmeg, cassava, vanilla, taro, avocado, cinnamon, jasmine, mango; alongside rocky creeks and gushing waterfalls; through small villages of mud huts, chickens scrambling across the road, goats munching on grass, wide-eyed children who screamed "Bonjour!" as we rumbled past.

"These people seem blissfully unaware that they're independent," Rarick said.

Men sat beneath palm trees, some playing games of dominoes, many gazing at nothing. Colorfully veiled women had faces coated with yellowish sandalwood paste, affording them a ghoulish look in the shade of the loads of wood atop their heads. Everyone smiled and waved at this truckload of mzungus (white people), a rare sight for Comorians, and soon we were skirting sublime vistas of the swell-laced Anjouan coast.

ENORMOUS FRUIT BATS swooped and soared in the dusk sky above our hotel's outdoor eating area, a few plastic tables arranged on a cement floor. Known as Livingstone's flying foxes, the bats are endemic to Anjouan and are critically endangered, one of the world's rarest, with wing spans of nearly two meters.

Directly out in front of us were two or three potentially epic reefbreaks if the elements ever came together (they didn't). Each day we were forced to ring Moustali for a ride elsewhere, and it didn't take long for us to suss the island, because with the wind continually blowing from the same direction, only a few spots were surfable. If only the wind would die was repeated numerous times, because without wind, Anjouan's south coast offers at least a dozen high-quality waves.

"Out front could be the spot—with no wind," Callahan said. "Someone needs to train the fishermen so they can take surfers out and know where to anchor."

"Nobody's going to come here," I said. "It's too difficult."

"It's not easy or cheap," Callahan agreed, "or else it would have been surfed and colonized by South Africans or French guys a long time ago."

For dinner all five of us ordered lobster, a delicious local specialty which actually was fairly cheap. Cold beers were cracked, candles were lit—the hotel generator was broken and the nearest electricity was in Domoni, an hour away, which is where we had bought the beer, a tough find in Islamic Comoros.

The full August moon rose from the sea, illuminating lines of new swell. Earlier that day we had found real waves—the first of the trip—at a rocky headland up the coast, a hollow right-hander near a village full of kids who clearly had nothing to do. Mobs of them stood and watched as Cataldi, Rarick, and Simon negotiated the funky, shallow coral shelf that Simon named La Droite des Pecheurs Morts (Dead Fishermen Right). Apparently the rough water surrounding the point was a death zone for fishermen in dugout canoes, and several had died there over the years.

"I got pounded on a couple of sets," Cataldi said. "It goes from super deep to super shallow—the front of the wave slows down and the back of the wave throws over the shelf. There's just one entry point, and if you miss that, the lip is going to project you straight onto the reef. We probably bailed more waves than we took off on. It's a proper slab."

Rarick concurred.

"With the right conditions," he said, "that wave could almost be considered a classic. It's a really good setup."

Traveling to an Indian Ocean island during peak swell season is always a gamble as usually it coincides with stiff onshore southeast trade winds. Even if the wind lays low for an hour or two, the tide could be wrong or the swell direction skewed, or it could be impossible to access the spot. For the first several days of our trip, this was precisely the case. But things change.

THREE-THIRTY A.M. was not prime time to awaken each day. We had no choice. Near our hotel were two mosques with dueling muezzins, both vying for the same people, and apparently 3:30 a.m. was the perfect time to summon them. Strange, as most muezzins elsewhere sound no earlier than 6 a.m. Equally irritating were the 24/7 howling onshores at all the best-looking surf spots. We spent several days confronting this. The waves were hideous, setups numerous.

Dead Fishermen Right proved worthy only once more during our stay, and the bulk of our surf sessions occurred north of Domoni, a pleasant old town on Anjouan's east coast. There we found a sectiony right point and a semi-sheltered black-sand beachbreak that was quite peaky and punchy and consistent, even hollow at times. John suggested we call it Goat Wash because of children on the beach scrubbing their goats with seawater. The beach itself was covered in black stones and bordered by a narrow dirt track, coconut palms, a banana plantation, rows of cassava, stray garbage (sandals, plastic water bottles). Near sunset we had an audience of giggling children and discreetly dressed woman, their bodies covered in colorful shiromani.

Twilight to starlight. From the lineup we could hear the muezzin from a mosque in Domoni, Anjouan's original capital, a historic medina of mosques and tall minarets, large stone dwellings, elaborately carved Swahili doors, and narrow shaded alleyways. In the 15th century Domoni was a major trading center for Arabian, African, Indian, and Persian boats traveling between Asia and Africa. For us it was the place to buy booze and risk food poisoning.

For South African ichthyologist Dr. JLB Smith, Domoni held a special place in history. Predating dinosaurs by millions of years was a large, strange fish called the coelacanth, a fleshy-finned, steel-blue creature with hard scales and iridescent white spots, lurking inside caves at the bottom of the Indian Ocean. With its limb-like fins, the coelacanth was a cousin of Eusthenopteron, the fish once credited with developing legs and walking ashore 360 million years ago—a possible "missing link" between water and land animals.

Based on fossil records, the coelacanth was thought to have become extinct at the end of the Cretaceous Period some 70 million years ago. In 1938, however, the theory was smashed after a living coelacanth appeared in the net of an East London trawler. Smith: "That first sight hit me like a white-hot blast and made me feel shaky and queer, my body tingled. I stood as if stricken to stone."

Shockingly, in 1952 another coelacanth was hooked off Domoni, directly offshore from the beachbreak we had been surfing. The fisherman, Ahmed Hussein, received a £100 reward from Smith for his epic catch, and ichthyologists and evolutionists alike were whipped into a frenzy about Comoros. "My heart was filled with fierce deep content, for I had shed the worry and responsibility of the coelacanth," Smith wrote in 1956. "One of the greatest ambitions of my life, to find the home of the coelacanth, had been fulfilled."

Affording a similar vibe was an unexpectedly good left-hand point, one that to us had also looked extinct, at least in August. Multiple drive-bys confirmed the spot's potential, but severe winds and radical tides veered us away. Yet true to surf-trip cliché, the point revealed itself in the fading hours of our final day on Anjouan, a slack-wind period allowing groomed lines to peel along the point's bouldered curves.

"We knew it couldn't get any worse, eh?" Cataldi said, marveling at our good fortune.

As with two intrepid Australians 40 years prior, the perfumed Comorian mystique had drifted into our collective consciousness—beneath stars and moonlight we too had sailed there, albeit roughly. The romance was not lost. We had surfed waves in tropical idyll, found some of the globe's nicest people, and inserted ourselves deeply into an extremely exotic and convoluted country. Yet with societal isolation comes magic; with magic comes a very special place. Politically, economically, we'd hoped things would improve.

16

L'OCÉAN INDIEN FLARE/FLAIR

2009

I HOPED TO not need blood on Réunion. Sharks there take plenty.

But it's always interesting to land on an island amid a gala you know nothing about. For me, in St-Denis, it was the Globule Festival:

> *The festival is to celebrate life. Goal is to celebrate around this simple, generous and supportive as blood donation. A gesture that allows to treat each year in France more than a million patients. While the need for blood products increases faster than the number of gifts, come to discover or extend your knowledge on the wonderful world of blood donation.*

I CIRCUMNAVIGATED. MARVELED at the lava flows in the southeast. Acres of sugarcane, pampas grass. East-northeast was sparse, lush, less trafficky. South was congested and not nearly as pretty.

Near sunset there appeared lush scenery on the Plaine d'Affouches, behind La Possession. Coconut plantations below. Stark white homes on the green hillside.

Few people spoke English. For dinner I walked to a snack bar at La Prachois in St-Denis; used my phrasebook to order a *jambon* (fries

+ ketchup + cheese melted on top) for 3 euros, plus three Bourbon beers.

I was struck by the fact that France (5,700 miles northwest) instilled this. The architecture, the language, et al. If Réunion was never a French colony, it might be like, what?—it's hard to say, because most islands nearby were all French colonies, from Madagascar to Comoros to Rodrigues.

Next day. Early. Sunny. Breakfasted on strong espresso and croisstants, fresh pineapple, yogurt, pineapple juice, cheese, baguettes.

The surf was pumping, the weather perfect—blue sky, light wind, not muggy, not hot.

The sets were inconsistent—a 15-second swell from the southwest. The lineup was not pedestrian. One guy was truly ripping; from afar, I figured he was another Réunionnaise star like Boris le Texier or Jeremy Flores.

"Man, that guy can *really* surf," I thought.

Turns out he was some guy filming on site for the "Modern Collective" film, which I learned this morning after randomly browsing *Surfing* magazine's website.

Some guy named Jordy Smith.

17

EDEN ISLANDS—A SURF GENESIS

2010

ONE O'CLOCK IN the afternoon, the first Sunday in July. It's winter, the surf season, but there's no surf today, unsurprising since there's no surf most days here in the Seychelles archipelago.

Hot and muggy, Indian Ocean tropic, 1,200 miles east of Africa, relative humidity at 90 percent. Gerard Albert lounges loosely and open-armed on a white plastic lawn chair in the yard of his boyhood home, at Anse aux Poules Bleues (Cove of Blue Hens) on Mahé Island's southwest coast, where Simone, Gerard's widowed mother, lives. Gerard was born here on October 25, 1951.

It is Creole and colonial, a plantation home, two-storied, large and square. It looks like an overgrown tool shed. Its outside walls are covered with rectangular sheets of corrugated aluminum that are painted lime green; the hinged plank doors are tall and narrow, painted fire-brick red. Its second story was an add-on, Gerard says.

His father, Joe Albert, was one of the Indian Ocean's chief exporters of spices, mostly selling cinnamon oil and cinnamon bark to France and England. Working thousands of acres on Mahé and nearby Praslin, Joe was also Seychelles's largest employer, providing paydays for hundreds of laborers. During World War II he made a fortune by distilling and exporting the oil of patchouli; the French military used it to paint camouflage on aircraft.

"After the war," Gerard says, "everybody was poor. But my father was rich!"

There's a marvel in Gerard's speech, like he can't believe his life's luck. His voice is raspy, a smoker's voice, but Gerard doesn't smoke. His accent is thick and sandy. Six decades of equatorial sun has boiled the skin on his forearms and face.

In 1993 his father died while sitting in a rocking chair in the home's parlor, downstairs, on the tile floor. He was 84. "He was a genius," Gerard says, eyes widening, shoulders pushed forward. "A very, very smart man. He knew Latin, all the physics, chemistry, everything. And before he died, he would beat us in chemistry, eh? He would remember all these formulas, eh? Even when he was 80!"

Joe was also the largest private landowner in Seychelles.

"Back then, the properties were for the white people," Gerard says, "but most of the white people were getting old, and for all their children, Africa was the place to go. Because Seychelles was backward—it was still in the dark. So the children all went to Kenya. The English were there, you know? Nairobi was the place. You went to Nairobi because there you had a better social life, and there were more prospects. There were factories!"

When Gerard smiles there is a dark hole where his upper right canine and a molar once lived. He's an islander's smile. His eyes are milky green. He wears white boardshorts and a black T-shirt that says Seychelles Team over a busy painting of a raptor hovering over a coco de mer nut.

In the jungle behind us, doves coo. Huh-whoooo. Huh-whoooo. We are surrounded by pandanus, coconut, and breadfruit trees. As with all tropical places, the air is filled with the vaguely acrid scent of mildew.

"So a father would ask his children, 'Well, what are you going to do with our property? I'm getting too old.' The children would say, 'Dad, sell it. We are not coming back to Seychelles. Seychelles is too backward for us.' But what my father did instead was rent government property and he bought peoples' unwanted properties, which were very cheap."

One such property was this, Anse aux Poules Bleues, where we sit. It's 70 acres, a gem on a broad turquoise bay, its shoreline thick with coconut palms and sheltered from the southeast tradewind. There is also a shapely but rare lefthand reef wave out front. This is where Joe and Simone raised their seven children.

Simone is in the kitchen today making custard for her sons, daughters, grandchildren, nieces, nephews. On Sundays, occasionally, the Albert family gathers on the sandy beach that is her front yard.

"We grew up right here on the sea," Gerard said, gesturing toward the bay. "But our father was not very happy for us to go far out because he was scared we were too small to go in the sea. For permission, we had to go and ask the property manager. If the manager say it okay, then we took a piece of timber and made a surfboard—like a bellyboard, you see? We got the local timber, like balsa, and we used to make planks. I was still very small. But when I was 15, I remember my father told me there's a surfer who's come from Australia with his surfboard! I was so excited." He clenches a fist and smiles hugely, eyes clearing with the memory.

Simone, 84, in a pink blouse and white capris, brings us the homemade custard in small orange bowls. It is warm and delicious.

GEOFF WHITE'S MOTHER is 95. Fifty years ago she was a keen bodysurfer who introduced her boy to the beachbreak of Austinmer, a nice place outside the north Wollongong suburbs.

"As kids growing up anywhere on the coast in Australia, you just end up in the surf," Geoff says by telephone from his place outside Austinmer. He lives on 75 acres there. His voice is friendly and agreeable, almost inquisitive. "Everyone on the beach rode some type of surfcraft. You know those rubber surf mats? Pop-up surf mats? Every beach would have someone hiring those out, so a lot of the young kids would hire them, and that's how most kids—myself included—started surfing."

White graduates to a hollow 10'6" malibu, followed by a proper balsa board, and he begins combing the New South Wales coast once cars and teen freedom appear. Empty Lennox and Byron are routine.

In 1961 he becomes a lab tech for the New South Wales Department of Main Roads. His office is beneath the Sydney Harbour Bridge. But 18-year-old White hates Sydney, so he quickly transfers closer to Wollongong. On the off days, he surfs.

One day he volunteers to do publicity—the poster run—for Bob Evans's surf films. "I can't remember how I made the contact with Bob," White says, "but it was something to do and it put me into contact with the surf world and some people who were quite interesting." Folks like Nat Young, Bob McTavish, and Paul Witzig, for whom White also voluteers to do film-poster distribution.

In 1962 Witzig captures Australian footage for Bruce Brown's The Endless Summer; Witzig screens the film around Sydney in 1966. The young White, who's never left Australia, views it in a Wollongong theater. "Once I saw that movie, I thought, 'That's me. That's it—I'm out of here.'"

In February 1967, with a clean 9'6" Gordon Woods spoon, White walks onto a passenger liner to sail 14,000 miles from Sydney to Durban, South Africa. Three friends join him. White is 23. "Let's just say it was a pretty wild trip," he tells me with a laugh. "The ship's crew wasn't going to let us off in Durban."

The foursome feasts on empty Durban beachbreak and earns a few rands by shunting freight trains cars in the city port. It's dangerous work but things go well. And it's not long before the men save enough cash to buy a kombi to get them out of town and into the South African countryside.

Famed Australian surf photographer Ron Perrott is in Durban, too. He just returned from a road trip to Cape Town and has great things to say about it. Fellow photographer John Thorton, who arrived on White's boat from Sydney, hears of Perrott's jaunt and seeks to replicate same, so he enlists White and his three friends and set off in their newly purchased kombi. Naturally their first Endless Summer-inspired stop is Cape St. Francis.

"We did surf it, and it was quite special," White says, "so that was a bit of a stoke for us. But by then Jeffrey's Bay was the place to hang, so we went back there and surfed some fantastic waves. Nobody was around. We just camped in the back of our car."

Later they cruise and surf the Garden Route and hit Cape Town, where they meet John Whitmore of Endless Summer fame. He sends the boys to Elands Bay, one of the surf spots he'd pioneered. "Cold, cold water, but really hot on land," White says. "We loved it."

Eventually the men ditch the kombi and drift their separate ways. White hitchhikes through the center of South Africa ("A story in itself…."), up through Johannesburg and Rhodesia (now Zimbabwe), where he admires Victoria Falls before reversing course and plunging through Mozambique, back down to Durban for a dose of serendipity.

TRUE IS A popular American men's magazine. In late July 1967 a copy floats through the hands of the small Durban surf crew. In the magazine is an article about erotically shaped nuts and phallic inflorescence of the coco de mer palm that was endemic to Seychelles. Some of the photos reveal vague backgrounds of whitewater.

"Then word goes out that there is surf in Seychelles," White tells me, "and suddenly there's this advertisement somewhere requesting deckhands. A guy in Durban wants to sail a trimaran via Mauritius up to Seychelles and up through the Red Sea. He was going to do charters up in the Greek islands, see."

White doesn't like boats much—he's prone to seasickness. Yet he signs on. Same with Ron Perrott, a quiet and inconspicuous man who's eight years older than White and known for his iconic Australian surf photography.

"I'd seen Ron around Durban," White says. "Somehow we got together and I said, 'Look, I'll go on that yacht if you want to go and do an article.' Ron had written to John Severson and I think John said that, yes, yachties had called in and he had heard there was surf in Seychelles."

The *Kyalami* is a luxurious 46-foot trimaran the captain rented. He is recently divorced and wants adventure—a new life. "He was a funny guy," White says. "A mild-mannered, cravat-wearing wannabe yachtie."

The captain's first mate is an American who tends to jump from yacht to yacht and has ample sea experience. But the captain has none. Nice guy, though. A few others, including an economics teacher from Rhodesia, complete the eclectic crew. White is the only surfer.

The *Kyalami* leaves Durban in early August 1967 and traces the desolate Mozambique coast. The crew makes a few stops: Inhambane, Beira, Angoche. It is not smooth sailing—there are several close calls. "It was actually our knowledge of the surf that saved us a several times," White says. Occasionally the captain will tack too close to shore, or he grounds the boat on coral reef, or at night he anchors in the middle of a surf zone.

White wakesurfs behind the boat in the Mozambique Channel. This is a very sketchy piece of water. Tiger sharks trail the boat. Most days the crew dive off for a swim, only to be chased out. "We did a few risky things," White tells me.

The pretty Comorian isle of Mayotte is next. For the French, Mayotte is a perfume producer—ylang-ylang flowers scent the air. White noserides and head-dips in small windswell at a reef pass near the village of Pamandzi. Aside from wakesurfing, this is White's first surf session since leaving Durban one month ago. Soon the Indian Ocean trade winds howl at full strength, and from Mayotte it's a straight shot northeast to Seychelles.

"As soon as we left, we hit the trades, and that was fantastic," White says. "We ended up surfing these beautiful swells. We went so fast that we ripped the sails."

The *Kyalami* skims past the Glorieuses and the Seychelles atoll groups of Aldabra, Farquhar, Alphonse, Amirantes—archipelagos of idyll, aliases of fantasy. Places to dream about, shimmering sands to cast minds adrift. Because once the boat snags a fortnight of doldrums, there's a lot of time to think. Each day, the crew motors a few miles, just for something to do.

At last the winds resumed. "How we found Seychelles, I'll never know," White said. "The captain really wasn't a navigator or sailor. But we finally found the place, and all I can remember was seeing this magnificent island sticking up with a golf ball on the top of it." (laughs)

The island is Mahé and the "golf ball" is the geodesic dome that houses the satellite-tracking antenna for the U.S. Air Force Tracking Station atop La Misère. Seventy Americans work there. In the heart of Mahé's central mountains, the antenna bleeps with geosynchronous satellites over the Indian Ocean. A fresh addition to the island, it's a beguiling sight for the weary *Kyalami* crew.

"ANOTHER WORLD" IS the motto of the Seychelles Tourism Board, which, by the end of 2011, expects 170,000 tourists to deplane at Seychelles International Airport. That's a lot of people for a small country. But tourists bring money. Seychelles needs money.

Seychelles had no airport before 1972. Until then, aside from sailors off sporadic yachts and freighters, tourism was nil. Before their commercialism and mass marketing of the late 20th century, the 155 islands and atolls across 530,500 square miles of the western Indian Ocean were a broad breezy sweep of idyll, dreamlike and edenic in their natural endowments. Today most of the isles are exclusive retreats frequented by the rich and famous and the honeymooning, lured by the turquoise lagoons and exotic diaspora, the world-class fishing, the lush green mountains and palmy white beaches.

"Some earthly paradise" was John Jourdain's view in 1609. Jourdain was a pensive British sailor who'd arrived in the Seychelles aboard the East India Company's creaky ship Ascension, which, loaded with trade goods, was bound for India from Africa. A storm forced the stopover, heralding the archiplego's first recorded landing. The ship's salty crew had no clue the islands existed. Few did.

Among the archipelago's inner islands the men found a trove of fruit, fish, tortoises, coconuts, birds, and sunshine. Coming from England, it was paradise. But after 10 days, the Ascension raised anchor and never returned. For the next 133 years, Seychelles was unvisited.

In 1742 two French ships slid into a small bay off the largest and tallest Seychelles isle. This too was an unplanned stop. Commanded by Lazare Picault, who named the place L'Île d'Abondance (The Island of Abundance), the ships were a thousand miles off-course while reconnoitering for Mahé de La Bourdonnais, the fearless Parisian who governed the French colonies of Bourbon (now called Réunion) and Isle de France (now Mauritius). Once the ships returned home, La Bourdonnais expressed great interest in this L'Île d'Abondance, so in 1744 he dispatched another ship directed by Picault, who named the first anchorage after himself (Baie Lazare) and renamed the island Mahé in honor of his boss, though La Bourdonnais never sailed there and made no effort to populate it.

By 1756 Isle de France had a new governor who thought Mahé and its neighboring islands were worth another look. Colonially speaking, he wanted to usurp the British, so he sent another ship (*Le Cerf*) and quickly named the islands after France's Jean Moreau de Séchelles, King Louis XV's finance minister.

That same year, François Albert boarded a large wooden boat in his native Nantes, a grimy city in France's northwest that was the national slave-trading capital. Pre-Suez Canal, he sailed south aside West Africa, hooked left at Cape Agulhas, and steamed northeast to Bourbon and Isle de France, collecting slaves from Madagascar en route. Albert became involved in the oceanic trading of goods between the French colonies and India and East Africa before eventually settling on Mahé.

Proper colonization of Seychelles occurred in the 1770s—citizens fled political turmoil and economic hardship in France. Conversely the Indian Ocean islands were rich and tranquil. They hadn't been soured by war or strife. And if François Albert hadn't left Nantes in 1756, the birth of Seychelles surfing would've been a much different tale.

SEPTEMBER 1967. THE shortboard revolution. Worldwide, longboards suffer. But in Seychelles, Geoff White has a 9'6" Gordon Woods, and in Seychelles, that's good.

It's been a parched run. Little surfing accomplished, nothing memorable nor photogenic. Unbeknownst to Geoff White, Mahé isn't a swell magnet, even now, mid-winter, when the rest of the Indian Ocean is ribbed with Roaring Forties juice. He manages to ride small fin-scraping lefts at coral-reefed Anse Gaulettes, not really a surf spot, but it sits just off the main road. Any possible wave on the the island's east coast is trashed by the tradewind, which never truly eases. Yet freed from the *Kyalami*, White's having a splendid time with his rented motorscooter exploring the Mahé from his rented beach bungalow base at Beau Vallon, a lovely tropical crescent.

Ron Perrott revels, too. His famous Nikon cameras remain mostly idle. He meets a dark local woman and, with her, seems content to while the downtime away. She gets to know Perrott as an inconspicuous moon-faced wanderer, a quiet observer of Australian surfing as it was in the '50s and '60s, living and photographing life in and around Sydney. He regales her with stories from the last two years, when he traveled throughout the United Kingdom, France, and Spain before reverting south and digging into the South African circuit.

While the tradewinds rustle the palm fronds outside her rural shack, and perhaps while consuming a tin or two of evaporated milk, he relives the six-week sail on the luxury yacht from Durban, little details, things like the first mate's peanut butter addiction, how the man disliked Australians, how White had guided the captain through terrible seas off Mozambique. The close calls, the groundings, the sharky wake-surfing, the claustrophobic comfort of the mens' stern stateroom. The woman is impressed with Perrott's worldiness. With her, he becomes unconcerned with the Seychelles surf factor.

From his home's porch, 15-year-old Gerard Albert is a regular observer of Seychelles surf, what little there is. Just offshore, behind the rock with the dollhouse atop it, there is a shapely lefthand reef that breaks rarely, and only in winter. It requires a massive south or southwest swell, something with enough power to fold itself 180° around the granite promontory at Anse Soleil and punch its way into the wind, into the wide, shallow bay at Anse aux Poules Bleues.

By road, Anse aux Poules Bleues is a fair distance from Beau Vallon, and the old open-air public bus won't take White's big surfboard. He's outfitted his motorscooter with a rudimentary side surfboard rack, but the going's a bit dangerous on Mahé's narrow, bumpy, mountainous lanes. Anse aux Poules Bleues lies along the main road, in plain view. White and Perrott pass it several times, and there are never any waves breaking inside the bay. There is a small green cottage with a slanted aluminum roof about halfway between the beach and the outside point. There is a reef in front of the house. One day, there is whitewater unfurling across it.

KEW: What do you remember about the wave?
WHITE: It was great. There were quite a few coral heads, but it was just a really fun wave, especially on a malibu. And I had better days than what was shown in the *Surfer* article. Ron might've been with me on the first day, but I went over a couple of times by myself and had better surf than that day. Then one day Ron decided to come over and do a shoot, and that was the day he took the pictures you see in the article.
K: Do you remember your first encounter with the Albert family?
W: Not really. I remember there was this family there that was really friendly, and they put the table out and offered some Coke and stuff, but that's basically all I can remember. I mean, I was just surfing the wave in front of their house.
K: And you stashed your board there so you didn't have to take it on the bus from Beau Vallon, right?
W: I can't remember.
K: Gerard told me you'd left it with his father.
W: Oh, then I might've, yeah.
K: Do you remember showing Gerard Albert how to surf?
W: I can't remember that, no.
K: Do you remember Gerard?
W: No.
K: He remembers you! (laughs)
W: (laughing)
K: Didn't you leave your surfboard at the Alberts' when you left Seychelles?
W: I can't remember.

A SURFBOARD RESTS on the soft chocolate soil beneath the coconut canopy in the sideyard. After his first session at Anse aux Poules Bleues, Geoff White leaves his fiberglassed 9'6" Gordon Woods with Mr. Joe Albert for safekeeping and convenience. Nobody there minds—Joseph's is a beach house, after all. But of the Albert family kids, only Gerard, 15, shows interest in riding the waves at his doorstep.

"That one afternoon I came home from school, and I saw Geoff White's board," Gerard tells me. "Dad said, 'Do not touch the board!' So as soon as my father went somewhere, I took the board and I paddled out on it!"

He laughs. Simone appears and takes our empty custard bowls to wash them. She is a strong, sweet lady.

"How was zee custard?"

"Delicious. Thank you."

Light breeze freshens a sweaty brow. Gerard dabs his with his T-shirt, sucks on his teeth, exhales, rakes his tan bare feet across the grass. Again he tells me about the wooden bellyboard he used.

"I had seen some yachties coming from Australia with board. I saw them but I never met them. They never went surfing here. That's why I try and make local board. I wanted board of my own so I could!"

His face beams with the thought.

"I made it about nine feet long. The wood—you see the trees there? It's a very light timber, like balsa. My father used to have a carpenter. I just told him to sharpen the piece of wood, to cut it, and to put a little skeg in the middle, like I had seen on the Australians' surfboards on the yacht. But it was a homemade board. It was heavy, you see? It would absorb water every time I used it!

"When my father saw me on my wooden board, catching waves easily, he was very happy. So when Geoff came back later to go surfing here, my father told Geoff that his son would like to try the board, but of course I already did!"

He winks one eye and laughs, crossing his arms over his chest.

"Geoff was very pleased to show me the tactics, you know? He said that I was a bit gifted, that I could use both feet—switchstance—and said to my father that I had an ability to become a good surfer. I could go on that side or go on this side; I could change position without problem. And I could stand up on the board very fast."

Gerard Albert is the first Seychellois surfer, a solitary satellite of the west Indian Ocean surf family that blooms in South Africa, where

Geoff White, the ad hoc catalyst, returns to by Indian cargo ship a few weeks later. Geoff and Gerard will not meet again.

APRIL 1970. INDEPENDENCE is six years off. Seychelles is a British crown colony and Joe Albert has been exporting loads of cinnamon oil to England. Around Easter he finds himself on a business trip in Newquay, at the rainy west end of Cornwall, a pastoral place immune to the shortboard revolution, but there's a surf shop somewhere. He buys a fat 9'6" for his boy, who, since Geoff White left Mahé three years prior, has had to surf on the homemade, waterlogged, splintery plank on the soft lefts of Anse aux Poules Bleues and in the dumpy beachbreak of Grande Anse, a few miles north.

But Gerard is gifted a fiberglass-and-foam surfboard—a "real" board. Its stringer is balsa and its fin blue. Gerard is 19. Whenever waves come, he surfs in front of his home and at a few other Mahé spots and occasionally some funky reefs on a scenic neighboring isle. When there is no surf, he works hard on his father's cinnamon and patchouli plantations and at the family's mountaintop oil distillery. None of his Seychellois friends are interested in surfing.

Gerard fraternizes with a few American military dudes who work at the tracking station. Later, a couple more of them—Californians, actually—arrive with surfboards. They are stoked to meet the sole Seychellois surfer and they take to him kindly, introducing Gerard to Hollywood films and imported beer and wine after hours in this sealed bubble of Americana.

Gerard and the men snorkel and dive and sail, exploring the pretty shores and aquamarine depths. When waves appear, the men surf Mahé. The Americans have jeeps, too, so Gerard is able to function as informal island guide. He finds new surf spots, places like Barbarons, Police Bay, Anse Royale. Using *Pasadena*, his father's 40-foot sailboat, there are weekend trips to Praslin, Bird, Denis, Silhouette. For scuba diving, mainly. There might be a few small waves here and there. Gerard is pleased to reveal his archipelago's sublimity. Besides visiting yachties, few outside have seen it.

GERARD YEARNS FOR real yachtsmanship. He's been on boats his entire life. But he's sick of landlocked labor. A vein to new waves, boats support surfing and for Gerard can also be funnels for natural-resource cash without having to toil at his father's oil distillery, or in his plantation fields—from one of them Gerard exports 20,000 bananas weekly, about five tons. Coconuts are another commodity. Also vanilla beans, cinnamon, patchouli oil. But his footing is stationary; his scenery, however lush, is static.

His father's boat spends most days at Port Victoria. It's a tranquil place, especially in summer, when the wind lays down. In summer there aren't any waves on Mahé. It's a great time to be away on the water, across the horizon. The *Pasadena* is a motorsailer and can move.

In 1971, with three black Seychellois for crew, Gerard leaves Mahé for three weeks. His father thinks his son is lost, but he's actually in the Amirantes, a remote outer group of 13 coral islands, cays, and atolls. They are much different from the Seychelles' high, granitic inner isles, like Praslin and Mahé, that Gerard knows so well.

One of the crewmembers, an old seafarer, as many Seychellois are wont to be, helps with the navigation. "All the bearing was in his head," Gerard tells me. "We have my card and my ruler and we get a bearing. But that man, he was…he didn't know how to swim, he didn't know how to read, he didn't know how to write, but he knew all this in his head. He tell me his bearing, and I recheck on my card, and every time he was right, eh? He could use the stars."

It takes the *Pasadena* 24 hours to reach Desroches, the first of the Amirantes. It is a fine place to make saltfish. "We go, we catch fish, we dry it, we salt it, to bring it back to Mahé." Gerard says. "Any fish, even sharks, you know? Everything we could catch!"

Poivre, D'Arros, and Remire are subsequent ports of call. If possible, Gerard surfs. For traction, he melts candles and drips the wax onto his board. The waves are sharky and not world-class, but Gerard doesn't know what a world-class wave is. It's unlikely Seychelles has one. If it does, it certainly is not on Mahé or Praslin. It would be in the remote, unihabited recesses of the archipelago. But it's not in the Amirantes.

INDIAN OCEAN ISLOLATION. The days are long and hot, full of fishing and sweaty work. Saltfish takes time. But through much of the 1970s, Gerard is freed from Mahé. He is surfing. He is seafaring. He is thriving. While first-surfs are occurring in the Maldives and Madagascar, and as Jeffrey's Bay, St. Leu, and Tamarin dazzle the cognoscenti abroad, Gerard is conducting his own private wave search.

His extended forays find him traversing the Seychelles' farthest reaches, into the Alphonse and Farquhar groups, all the way west to ham-shaped Aldabra, the world's largest raised coral atoll.

"One day I was surfing there (he points to the beach at Anse aux Poules Bleues) by myself," Gerard tells me. "It was a Sunday, like today. I saw two foreigners snorkeling. I start talking to them, and they say they are from America. They told me they were supposed to go to Aldabra in a yacht, that they made two attempts but had to come back because the sea was too rough. I said I have a boat in town, and if you want, we will bring it to Aldabra. So the next day, they went there, they saw the boat, and they were keen, and the next year, they charter us for research."

For the next six years he visits Aldabra 15 times while transporting scientists from the Smithsonian Institution. Untouched by humans, Aldabra is unique. The American and Japanese scientists are stunned. In 1982 the atoll is designated as a UNESCO World Heritage site. Gerard surfs there but the waves are poor and the currents fierce.

To accommodate his lively new charter business, he upgrades to the *Pasadena*, a 56-foot motor yacht, then in 1984 he switches to *El Gringo*, a 65-foot sailboat. He names his business Pasadena Unlimited and spends a lot of time in the Aldabra Group, a natural laboratory.

"I been to Astove, you know?" Gerard says, sipping from a glass of water. "Not good surf there. I remember I brought some German photographer to take pictures of sharks. They told me they been all around the world to take pictures of shark. I said, 'Well, there you have to be careful—we have some monsters there!' They say they not scared of any shark. I say, 'Okay.' We prepare bait for two days, we put it in a big drum like this. So we reached Astove. That's the reef, and it's a 6,000-foot dropoff, like a wall—you have to put your anchor on the reef, and you make sure the wind doesn't change, eh? So about 3 o'clock we started setting the bait everywhere, the photographers prepare their equipment about 5:30 to go down with their camera and the lights. After 15 minutes, there was this rush of them back to the surface! (laughs) Some lost their cameras. One guy from that day, he said he never want to dive again. It was a narrow escape—tiger sharks!"

Gerard's sea-charter lifestyle grinds to a halt in 1991, when Joe, his older brother, starts a construction business on Mahé. *El Gringo* is simulataneously shipwrecked on Bird Island by the French ambassador who'd hired the yacht for a private Bastille Day celebration. The Albert family is now without a boat, but on Mahé, things are happening. The construction business explodes. Gerard does 10 years of 12-hour days, seven days a week. His surfing ends.

VICTORIA HAS NO city blood in its veins. Housing 24,000 people, the Seychelles capital is rustic yet modern, a comely, clean place flanked by verdant mountains with views to the six green islands of Sainte Anne Marine National Park. There are some good Creole restaurants and a lively marketplace, and, because England took Seychelles from France in 1814, a small replica of the clocktower on London's Vauxhall Bridge stands in the center of town.

On weekdays Guillaume Albert, 32, lords over a cluttered desk inside a drab office in the industrial outskirts near Victoria Harbour. He is the deputy general manager for Creole Travel Services, his family's tourism company, and he's very busy. His phone chirps constantly. Gregarious and articulate and a bit hyper, Guillaume is a consummate salesman and marketeer, skilled in the rhetoric of the tourism trade. He is also Gerard Albert's nephew and the Albert family's only other surfer. (Guillaume's younger brother, Gregory, sporadically dabbles but does not consider himself a "surfer.")

Creole Travel Services is owned by Joe Albert, Guillaume's dad and Gerard's brother. Additionally, Joe owns United Concrete Products Seychelles, the nation's largest private company, instrumental in Mahé's building boom in the 1990s. Professionally, Joe has many assets for hire, including private islands, luxury resorts, yachts, and Cap Lazare, a beautiful 161-acre nature reserve that abuts Anse Gaulettes, where, in September 1967, Geoff White surfed Seychelles for the first time.

In 1988 Joe Albert bought Cap Lazare for a million Seychelles rupees—about $200,000. In 2007 some Belgian billionaires sought to buy Cap Lazare from Joe for 53,000,000 euros—about $72 million. Cap Lazare had become valuable. But Joe couldn't sell it.

"I had the whole thing planned," Joe tells me over lunch one day in the kitchen of his home in the hills above Victoria. "I was going to buy a home in Australia. I was going to retire. But first I was going to meet with those Belgians guys at a hotel in France and finalize everything."

One sunny day Joe was oceanfishing with Guillaume, Gregory, and Jean-Christophe, the eldest of his three sons. The bite was poor—lots of downtime as they trolled offshore Mahé's coast. In a quiet interlude, Guillaume addressed his father in the past-tense and said, "Cap Lazare was good, wasn't it?"

The words smack Joe. Then Gregory asked him if he really needed the money.

"I flew to Paris with Greg's and Guillaume's words in my head," Joe says to me, "and the night before my meeting, I was sitting there in my hotel room and I decided that I couldn't sell Cap Lazare. The next day, those Belgians would not believe me. They thought I was crazy!"

But $72 million is a nice chunk.

"Can you imagine? It would have changed our family forever," Guillaume tells me over a two-hour lunch another day at Marie-Antoinette, a traditional Creole restaurant in Victoria. "Now I would be flying all over the world, dating supermodels. Ha!"

We clear plates of fried parrotfish, eggplant fritters, rice, spicy fish stew, chicken curry, golden apple chutney, grilled red snapper, tuna steaks, and hot pimin chilis. We drink from sweating green bottles of SeyBrew, the local lager. An executive from Air Seychelles stops at our table; Guillaume tells her I'm a surfer from California. She regards me quizzically.

"Why are you in Seychelles? You cannot really do surfing here."

"I like a challenge."

"Oh, he's a bit stupid," Guillaume says to her, grinning and taking a sip of beer. He points to my blond head. "Look at his hair color!"

Guillaume looks a little pale in his blue polo shirt. He hasn't surfed in awhile. It's been flat most of this year, and during the small southeast windswells that did arrive, he was in Europe on business trips. His timing was bad.

But swell is coming. Maybe. It's always maybe.

"I really want to go back to the Maldives, man," Guillaume says. He puts his beer down and slowly leans back in his chair. He inhales deep through his nose, wipes the corners of his mouth, looks out the window. "You can get some really good waves, eh? We should go on a boat charter. Or maybe I should just move up there, to North Malé. Malé sounds like Mahé, eh? I could move there, convert to Islam, and surf every day. What do you think, man? Should I move?"

IF SEYCHELLES COULD simply move a thousand miles west and trade places with the Chagos Archipelago, we'd have a new Indian Ocean surf garden.

But this will never happen and the Republic of Seychelles will be forever funky. Its outer coral atolls will always be difficult and costly to reach and bereft of good waves. Its inner granitic islands will always be marginally surfable but really not worth the expense and wasted time and the very real prospect of longboarding knee-high wind slop.

It's not easy for Guillaume. He'd rather surf the Maldives daily. But Mahé was all fine for Geoff White and Gerard Albert back in 1967. They were longboarding.

"I remember going down the coast one day on the other side, down from Victoria, and there were some really beautiful glassy swells coming in on the outer reefs," White tells me by phone. "But of course with a longboard, you wouldn't have thought about surfing that. I remember a big lagoon and some really nice waves breaking on the outside, but they were closing out a lot. In those days you were always looking for the malibu-type of waves. You weren't looking for big waves."

Today White likes waves both big or small, mushy or hollow, and gets happy when east swells strike Sandon, his local right point. But usually the swells are fickle and sporadic, kind of like they are in

Seychelles, and that takes a patient sort of soul, which is usually expected from a mediation teacher. White leads Vipassanā courses worldwide. No, he isn't Buddhist. He's taught in Indonesia, Dubai, New Zealand, Turkey, Romania, Russia, and in Israel, his favorite. "Lovely people."

Like Geoff White, Gerard Albert remains a bachelor with an arcadian lifestyle firmly rooted in the rewards of widening his gaze at a young age. He has a 26-year-old daughter. He lives alone in a large home atop the green mountain behind us. "Swimming pool and everything. You can see 360 degrees. You can see everything, everywhere!"

KEW: When was the last time you surfed?
ALBERT: About 10 years ago (2000), here.
K: Do you want to surf again?
A: I'm going to lose weight, then I am sure I will be able to do it, because I have tried to waterski, on mono ski. I didn't do it for 10 years, then afterward I did, so some friends were doing it at Anse à la Mouche. I say, "Okay, let me see," but they said I am too old now. I said, "I'm not too old for it." I just was in my clothes and underwear, and the first time, I went up, that's what gave me confidence I will do surfing again. But I must take some weight off. I want to go somewhere like Madagascar, you know, surfing everywhere.
K: And retire?
A: Yeah. What's happening is, I might sell a property. There's a little piece, and someone wants to buy it. I will sell this for, like, 900,000 euros, and I will make this like a reserve money. That's my backup. (laughs)
K: And you'll just sail around?
A: Cruise around, yeah. And make sure, before I am finished, to go up to the Mediterranean and visit everywhere. Cruise everywhere. That's my last ambition. That's the last thing I want to do.
K: You want to die on a boat?
A: Yes! On the sea.

SIMONE BRINGS MORE custard to Gerard and me. There's plenty left, she says. It's in the bowl on the stove. Her other son, Joe, had asked her to make it this morning because custard tastes good on a tropical winter afternoon, with the light seabreeze slinking through the palm trees, the noddies and the terns squawking, the doves cooing. Huh-whoooo. Huh-whoooo.

There is no surf today. There will be no surf tomorrow, nor the next day, nor next week. But maybe next month—August. Maybe.

Always maybe.

18

THE FIVE PILLARS OF LAKSHADWEEP

2011

THIS ROOM IS moving. Trevor Gordon's eyes are open and glazed, his pupils wide. It is 5:04 a.m. He rubs his belly clockwise, breathes oddly, speaks flatly.

"Don't let me pass out, man. We've got to stick together."

Outside, pale moonlight glints off the warm Laccadive Sea. The 89-meter *M/V Lakshadweep Sea* sways from side to side, motoring east at nine knots while Chadd Konig, also in the room, is awakened by the lanky sleepwalker.

"I really need some fresh air," Gordon slurs.

The two step outside. Gordon's balance is off. On the bulwark he rests his elbows. His shoulders feel sore. So much surfing lately. So many great waves. With Konig he ponders the universe and watches the sea slide by.

Out there, beyond the horizon, Somali pirates prowl for big boats like this. The isolation of Lakshadweep's palmy atolls has lured the slitted eyes of East African predators who, armed with grenade launchers and Kalashnikov rifles, seek ransom for seized cargo. Can be any cargo, really. Freighters and oil tankers are preferred. Unfortunately the Lakshadweep Sea holds nothing but islanders and Indians, 260 of them, bound for the port city of Cochin. It's a 21-hour sail.

We've got to stick together!

For pirates, this is no comfort zone—Lakshadweep is 1,600 miles east of Somalia. But with hijacked ships, the Somalis have widened their gaze to cover 2.5 million square nautical miles. In 2010, across the northwest Indian Ocean, they seized 1,181 hostages and gained several millions of ransom dollars, about 30 percent of which were sent to al Shabaab, a Somalia terrorist group linked with al Qaeda.

In early 2011, Lakshadweep brushed with Somali piracy, some violent. The uninhabited of Lakshadweep's isles may offer sanctuary to pirates, drug smugglers, and Islamic terrorists. Last year, three were found on one of the atolls we surfed. Gordon and Konig are blissfully ignorant of this as dawn fills the sky.

Downstairs in a green-doored prayer room, a young Sunni Muslim man sits and ends his *fajr*, the first of five daily prayers included in the Five Pillars of Islam, which are: *shahada* (creed), *salāt* (prayer), *sawm* (fasting), *zakāt* (almsgiving), *hajj* (pilgrimage).

He turns his head to the right, then left. Assalamu alaikum wa rahmatullah—"Peace and blessings from Allah be upon you."

Elsewhere in the ship, Jones, Anderson, and Gibbens doze inside dreams. Peace for them. And for the past week, Allah's blessings came from blue skies and the southwest Indian Ocean—long-period swells that tonight ease the ship to and fro. Swells that rake the clean coral reefs of Lakshadweep, 12 atolls that geographically are sewn to the Maldives and the Chagos archipelago. It's a surfy zone, this.

Gordon's pupils shrink. He's awake now. The sea looks different—different from the warping blue guts of a Lakshadweep tube. Those are familiar to him. Konig concurs.

"Did that just happen?" Gordon asks, scratching his unwashed head. "Did we really get *that* barreled?"

Back on the atoll, between prayers and working in his father's sundry shop, the young Muslim man had watched the five surfers leap from the pier and repeatedly disappear in and emerge from waves. In Arabic, his father called them "water tunnels." With his friends and family and many of the passengers on this ship, the young Muslim man sat and stood on the white concrete railing, his dark face and beard catching the salt mist from big sets as they blasted through the pilings beneath him. The pier trembled.

The young Muslim man grew vexed at the government that poked this thing into the center of a surf zone. Boats can't dock to it. And since the reefs are environmentally sensitive, locals can't fish from it. The pier is useful only as an extension from the coconut confines of atoll life and to watch surfers, but nobody surfs in Lakshadweep. Yet. Konig left a Cossart alaia, Anderson left two snapped Hayden thrusters.

Today the young Muslim man feels fresh. He's going to see his younger brother and older sister. And the fajr is his favorite ritual because it connects him to Allah at dawn, his favorite time of day.

He walks upstairs and outside. The warm wind wipes his face as he inhales deeply. He waves at Konig and Gordon, up towards the ship's bow.

Cochin is near. It's his big-world downtown, a noisy, stinking, crowded sprawl of high-rises, a snake pit of sweat and slow traffic. It's his sister's temporary home while she attends Cochin University of Science & Technology. She wants to be a marine biologist.

The young Muslim man thinks that, next month, when he returns home, if pirates don't get to it first, he'd really like to try that alaia.

SHAHADA

The first wave spits. Craig Anderson sits.

"This place is on par with HTs," he says in Newcastle tongue.

Craig's on the concrete steps at the base of the pier. His black boardshorts drip. His moppy hair is damp and his shoulders ache.

"Except at HTs, you have five perfect waves in a set, whereas here you might only get one. Maybe."

He points at the lineup.

"But look at this!"

Brendon Gibbens bottom-turns full rail, stalls, disappears for six seconds. He emerges, digs a deep carnivorous gouge, exits the wave. Standard procedure. On the second wave, bearded/longhaired Chadd Konig styles and highlines into the tube, a picture straight from

Morning Of The Earth. Trevor Gordon, on an orange 6'7" Lovelace hull, blitzes through the third. The spit stings his back.

Swooosh.

Anderson smiles, nods, then sips sweet brown tea from a white paper cup. As they did daily, the boys from the hotel brought a Thermos to the beach.

Fresh from the long morning session, Daniel Jones walks up, sets his surfboard on the cement and helps himself. The tea's quite hot—not the best post-surf quench. The air is equally hot as the noon sun pegs the top of the sky. The air smells faintly of burning trash. Crows squawk and goats baahhh.

The tide is dropping and this wave is best at its shallowest, easing into a slow rise.

"That was a nice set," Jones says to Anderson. "Probably going to get better this afternoon, eh? This place is way better than those other two islands."

Anderson nods again, finishes his tea, crushes the cup in his hand. "We didn't think we were gonna get it this good," he says.

It's true. There could have been no swell—Lakshadweep is 4,000 miles from the Roaring Forties weather kitchen, with considerable swell-shadowing by Chagos and the Maldives. There could have been no real spots—on Google Earth, the atolls look bad for surfing. There could have been clouds and rain and onshore wind because, annually, May sparks the southwest monsoon. The *M/V Arabian Sea*, which sailed the surfers to this atoll, could have sunk or failed or been hijacked by Somalis. The ship could have never left Cochin (it almost didn't), because the trip was booked through the government, because that's how foreigners can visit the atolls (most are off-limits), and because the government was prone to reschedule or simply cancel, even if you have the required entry permit. To surf Lakshadweep, the odds are stacked high against you.

SAWM

Good things happen to everyone. For Dakhil, being born here is one.

"Is cleaner and better in Lakshadweep islands," he tells me as I film the surfers down the beach. "India mainland too fast and dirty. Many trash. Many people, many cars. Is, like, crazy there."

We're standing between two large black plastic pipes on the atoll's new desalination pier. The glassy ocean shimmers in the morning heat. The sky is a hazy blue. The water is crystal clear and full of exotic fish. In a black collared shirt and blue jeans and sandals, Dakhil is serene and slight of build, sweaty-faced and bushy mustachioed like most men here. I too am sweating—no matter what time of day, if the sun shines in Lakshadweep, it sears.

A concrete pourer, Dakhil found well-paying work through Chennai's National Institute of Ocean Technology, the organization behind the plant's construction. On such a small atoll, this plant, which distills seawater, is a big deal.

"Thanks to Allah, now we have fresh water all the time for drinking and cooking and everything," Dakhil says as Trevor Gordon stalls for his twelfth tube of the morning. "The sea tastes very good."

A set stacks. After five days of mediocrity, the sea's swell is rising. It must be really good in the Maldives right now. Maybe in the Chagos Archipelago, too, but Chagos doesn't really have any setups. So, no, it's not good in Chagos.

"What water did you drink before?"

"We used to harvest and drink rain waters. Always problems with peoples getting sick. Sometime the water have diseases in it. And sometime there not enough water for everybody on the island. But now is fixed."

"How much water can this plant make?"

"I think 10 million liters per day."

"How long has it been running?"

"Inauguration was about two weeks ago. But is still not 100 percent finished. We still making things on the outside"—he points to some rebar outside the main building—"so I still can work some more."

"What will you do when the plant is 100 percent finished?"

"I do coconuts again." He tilts his back slightly and looks at the trees along the beach. "Lakshadweep coconut is *best* coconut in India." He winks at me.

Behind us, a dense forest of palm fills the shore, a ribbon of white sand littered with brown coral boulders, three wooden canoes, a stack of rusty metal, a few old tractor tires. The nearby mosque's white minaret pokes above the trees. That's where Dakhil worships Allah five times daily.

Women wearing colorful jilbab walk slowly on the green grass between the palms, raking stray bits of trash into small mounds, soon to be burned. Large black crows skitter amongst the fronds, squawking loudly above the women and scavenging chickens and bony goats behind them that are unfazed when a man on a motorcycle buzzes by on the white coral track. He stops to talk with another man who, standing atop a rock at water's edge, fishes with a simple handline. None of the women or men notice Daniel Jones's deep backside barrel.

"You want to taste the water?" Dakhil asks me.

"Of course."

He hooks a brown index finger at me.

"Follow."

Fronting the plant is a small spigot for public use. I fill my stainless steel bottle and drink deeply.

"Good, eh?"

Dakhil's eyebrows lift. His face brightens. I grin. The Laccadive Sea tastes like nectar.

SALAT

Osama bin Laden's corpse rots on the floor of the Arabian Sea. There it is cold and dark. It's much brighter and hotter where Brendon Gibbens chews a breakfast forkful of spicy fish curry. Curry and rice for each meal, each day, and the trip has just begun.

"Better get used to it, bru," Alan van Gysen tells Gibbens. The two live on the same Cape Town street. To a point, apparently, Alan likes curry.

Gibbens hates curry. At home he never orders Indian take-out. But this morning he's in a local's house and food options do not exist. We eat what the cook cooks. Sweet tea is dessert. Unfortunately for me, beer is banned in Lakshadweep. The nearest can of Kingfisher is 300 miles west.

Today the wind is wrong for yesterday's pier-side wave, a small, rampy left built for Craig Anderson's aerial elasticity. Jones rides Chadd Konig's alaia. "Did you see some of those drops I made?" he later asks me. "Steep!" He got some goods ones. Had the swell been bigger, the left would've chucked stand-up tubes.

The regularfooters lurk mostly at the right opposite the left opposite the thin channel. The right is mushy but sports a decent wall and some rebounds off the left. There are a few near-collisions 'twixt Anderson and Trevor Gordon. Konig bodysurfs and Gibbens boosts and it is a great way to shed the travel grime. We hadn't expected waves on this atoll.

Lakshadweep's coral would really benefit from dynamite. As winds generally blow from the west and northwest, blasting wide, tapering reef passes through the southeast and east sides of the atolls' barrier reefs would birth dreamy Maldivian-style perfection. It is odd that, as part of the same underwater mountain range, the Maldives evolved with dozens of world-class reef passes while Lakshadweep did not. A waste of land, you might say. The surf world can use another Maldives.

Jones: "Let's scope the island's top." He's finished his morning curry and tea. Yesterday's welcome-session waves were fun but not great. Google Earth be damned—there must be something else here.

We fill two black auto rickshaws and peel north along the atoll's narrow concrete road, the drivers honking constantly as we pass numerous shops, pieces of trash, goats, chickens, cats, homes, palm groves, water tanks, piles of coconut husks, men on bicycles, schoolgirls in black burqas, a mosque, a graveyard. At road's end we are presented with a possibly epic right reef/point if the swell was big and if the wind wasn't hacking the spot to death.

Konig: "Let's check the south. Wind's perfect for down there."

Back into the rickshaws and backtrack south for a few miles. Glimpses through the palms of curling lips along the western barrier reef. Lots of almost waves.

Conveniently the road ends in front of another possibly epic right-hander at a bend in the turquoise lagoon's barrier reef.

Almost.

Gordon: “This place could be a three-mile-long J-Bay if the swell angle was just so.”

Anderson: “Barreling forever!”

Almost.

The wave is photogenic but unmakeable so we think “south tip,” where the wind is straight offshore. Problem is we have to walk the beach for a mile to get there. And now, near noon, it’s blazingly hot.

Almost.

With surfboards as umbrellas, we sweat and walk on the fine white sand. The lagoon is used for refreshment. Groin rashes occur. The beach ends at a channel and there is an islet on the other side. As the wind cools our backs, we wonder what’s on the islet’s opposite shore.

A blue *dhoni* is docked on the islet’s beach. Jones and an Australian surfer named Louis ford the channel and ask the boat driver if he can give us all a lift across since most of us have cameras. The boatman obliges and soon we are walking across the rubbly islet and emerging from bushes to see Jones standing in a groomed left-hand pit.

HAJJ

Daniel Jones and Craig Anderson are fresh from Bali; Brendon Gibbens and photographer Alan van Gysen from Cape Town, South Africa; Gordon and Chadd Konig and I from Santa Barbara, California. Everyone had slept well. Spirits are high despite the low surf forecast. We have no choice, really. Cochin is the jumping-off point. We’re not mainlanding. We have to jump.

The *M/V Arabian Sea* is a big white passenger ship owned by the Indian government. It’s the only way to reach an atoll 300 miles out. We should get there—India’s Navy, the world’s sixth largest, just opened a base in Lakshadweep to boost coastal security to stop Somali piracy and Islamic terrorist strikes, like 2008’s mass coordinated shooting and bombing attacks in Mumbai, India’s largest city.

“Insh’Allah,” a small Lakshadweep man astern says. His name is Rafiq. We discuss bin Laden’s death. We watch the boiling wake emerge from the transom and lay a wide white line atop the sea. The sun sinks into the horizon. Slowly, Cochin dissolves in the distance.

Dressed in traditional white Muslim clothes, Rafiq is a copra seller heading home from Chennai, where he visited family. Today he seems relieved. Now that bin Laden is dead, Rafiq says, clasping his hands as if in prayer—God willing—al Qaeda's threat to India will now wane.

"India gets terror threats every day," Rafiq says, stroking his pointy beard, squinting. "These people are very bad Muslims, you see? They make us look bad. Do you think Muslim people are bad?"

"No."

"Okay. Well, these Muslims are very bad. They want kill everybody in India. Maybe some terrorists hide in Lakshadweep, maybe from Pakistan. Some Lakshadweep islands are uninhabited. So now we have make radar stations and Navy and Coast Guard bases in the islands. Terrorists have try to recruit people from Lakshadweep because we are Muslims. And the pirates come near now. Do you know Somalia?"

ZAKAT

Last night in Abbottabad, Pakistan, U.S. forces double-tapped Osama bin Laden with 5.56-millimeter bullets from a M4 carbine assault rifle. This killed him instantly and coated his floor red. It also exposed his brain's left frontal lobe to the subtropical Orash Valley air.

Last night in Cochin, India, Trevor Gordon and I occupied a clean air-conditioned room at Hotel Bright Heritage. This morning, before checking email and Buoyweather's seven-day chart for the Laccadive Sea, CNN sings of bin Laden's death.

"You think this is gonna change anything?" Gordon asks me.

"Like stop terrorism?"

"Yeah."

"Insh'Allah."

"What?"

"God willing. It's Arabic."

Buoyweather's chart looks bad: small (one meter) medium-period swell from the southwest, not the medium-to-large (two to three meters) long-period southern pulse we hope for. The wind will be offshore but....

"So," I posit, standing above my MacBook, wishing those blue

Buoyweather lines on the screen would grow. "Knee-high in Lakshadweep? Waist-high?"

Gordon smirks, pausing for effect.

"Insh'Allah."

19

THE FOUR PRINCES OF SERENDIP

2013

THE FIRST DAY: *THOUGHTS ON BUFFET FOOD, SELF-IMMOLATION, AND KYLE ALBERS' 9'11" TWIN-FIN*

TRUE STORY: A skinny 6'6" Kyle Albers is kneebound, puking water into the seaside bungalow's clogged, unflushing toilet on the opposite side of Earth.

"Hey, Kyle," someone says. "We're going for lunch. Should we get you some fish curry? Beef?"

Yesterday Albers' gastrointestinal tract was assaulted by the all-you-can-eat buffet on the ground floor of a Kuala Lumpur hotel. He had heaped his plate with assorted Asian fare. Some hot, some cold. Fish curry, rice, noodles, chutney, naan, mango, lychee.

Outside across the dusty dirt lane is a flyblown tin shed echoing with utterances of fishermen who all night were at sea, 15 kilometers out in small fiberglass boats, using torchlights to prep bait atop the black Bay of Bengal. It's a primitive and dangerous occupation. Two months ago, not far from here, 51 fishermen were swamped and slain by a midnight storm.

This morning the boats returned to the steep white-sand beach with skipjack, trevally, yellowfin, and mackerel, most to be sold to restaurants and hawked in the nearby Muslim town. Tonight some of the fish will be cooked and made into curry, a national dish. It's tasty.

Not for Albers.

Bleaaaarehhhh...(cough-cough)... clurrgh....

Echoing Albers' bilious gutturalism are the caws from a raucous gang of black crows near the bathroom's small window. The bathroom's pink tile walls amplify the loud birds.

Caa-caa-caaa!

Outside, directly above Albers, one juvenile and three adult tufted-gray langurs lounge on the moldy red-tile roof flecked white with crow guano. The leaf-eating monkeys are surrounded by blowsy acacias and fronds of coconut trees below a big blue sky typical of late summer. The palm fronds and acacia leaves are lightly puffed by an offshore wind which carries the universal tropic scent of burning trash directly into the small square bathroom window above Albers' longhaired head. The casual observer will notice his hair pulled back tight in a ponytail to avoid bile splash exposure.

Fish curry? No.

Beef?

Which, I learn whilst reading a two-month-old issue of *The Island* outside the room next to Albers', does not jive with the 70 Buddhist percentile of Serendip's 20 million humans—no killing of animals, which are sentient beings and human souls reborn from past misdeeds.

Cows too are sacred. So sacred that the newspaper's editorial that day discussed Bowatte Indarathana, a 29-year-old Buddhist monk who in May 2013 soaked his robe in gasoline and set himself on fire at a Buddhist festival in the nearby town of Kandy. This was to protest Serendip's slaughter of cattle for human consumption despite the fact that monks eat much meat. Indarathana belonged to a hardline Buddhist group that was campaigning against the Muslim halal method of killing animals (swift, deep incision with a sharp knife to the throat, cutting the jugular veins and carotid arteries of both sides but leaving the spinal cord intact). He had also been calling for an end to proselytizing by Muslims and Christians and followers of other faiths.

Hater? Perhaps.

Ninety percent of his body scorched, Indarathana died the next day. Suicide success. This led *The Island*'s editorialist to start his column with: "The biggest problem at this moment is not the Western encirclement (of Serendip) nor is it the holding of the northern provincial council election, but the phenomenon of out-of-control Buddhist monks on the streets…We did not come through 30 years of war to end up with anarchy and mob rule."

Albers cares not. He has food poisoning and the swell is up and he is unable to wax his current whip, a self-shaped 9'11" tri-hued keel twinnie he calls Megafish, which is exactly what it is—a fish identical to the keeled self-shaped (his 100th!) 5'3" he's also hauled to Serendip, but stretched 56 inches.

Near my old newspaper sits a copy of Kelsang Gyatso's *Introduction to Buddhism: An Explanation of the Buddhist Way of Life*. Simon Murdoch brought it. He's enrolled in religious studies at Santa Barbara City College. Skimming through the book I learn about sangha and karma and dharma and soon I am enlightened by the Four Noble Truths. So enlightened that I stand, walk into Albers's bathroom, and tell him that he is experiencing the first Truth stemming from the principle of dukkha, a concept central to Buddhist thought which deals with physical and mental suffering, that all sentient beings must endure some suffering and pain throughout their lives.

"Hey, Kyle. This might be you." Holding the book so he can see it, I tap page 29. "Do you have bad karma?"

Pale and irritated, he raises a slow glance up to me, away from the porcelain.

"Dude. Get out of here."

Aloud I read a passage: A MENTAL INTENTION THAT IS A DETERMINATION TO PERFORM AN ACTION IS A MENTAL ACTION OR MENTAL KARMA. THUS, BODILY KARMA IS BODILY ACTIVITY INITIATED BY A MENTAL ACTION.

"See? Your mind told you—a mental action—to eat that fish curry, and now you have bodily karma from eating the curry, because maybe you weren't supposed to eat that fish. Puking is a bodily activity. An action. Karma means 'action.' It's Sanskrit."

Albers looks at me again before lying flat on the cold concrete floor and shutting his eyes. "Maybe the fish was just rotten," he says feebly, resting his pale right forearm on his sweaty forehead. "Maybe the fish had bad karma."

"Possibly. Maybe the fish was a bad human in its previous life."

"Can you please close the door? I need to sleep."

Albers is below the toilet which was installed by a man who works here, a man who is part of Serendip's Theravāda branch of the Buddhist majority. This man built the walls too. Set the concrete floor. That little square window with the cackling crows. The shower and its hair-clogged drain. The thin wooden door and the cheap plastic towel rack. The too-small sink with its too-small faucet.

It is unlikely this Theravāda Buddhist man will set himself aflame to protest cow-killing (beef is served in his restaurant). But he feels safe and warmly at home on his small Indian Ocean island, with the sight of each Buddha temple and bodhisattva shrine along the road, deep in the rainforest or atop stony mountains or along gentle rivers or in the bustling center of town, decorated with candles, flowers, water bowls, and incense, venerating his moral code nearly 2,400 kilometers from where Siddhartha Gautama, the original Buddha, slid from the womb and inhaled Himalayan air circa 5th century BC.

This Theravāda Buddhist man makes a world-class fish curry. Would taste fine regurgitated.

Kyle?

THE SECOND WEEKEND: *THOUGHTS ON NATIONALISM, DEATH BY HACKING, AND JARED MELL'S 6'6" FINLESS*

WEDNESDAY NIGHT. Mundane machete murder. Chopped was a 69-year-old Hindu priest. Crime scene was a kovil (temple) in Kilinochchi,

350 kilometers north from us in Serendip's wooded tip. Likely Buddhist, no suspect was found, his motive likely religious re: the then-looming elections.

That was three days ago. Post-breakfast we will pierce the jungle and emerge onto a steep beige-sand beach fronting a handsome sand point. Civil unrest will not be present. No politicking or murderous freaks.

Today, four years from the doomed fall of the Tamil Tigers—four years of Serendip's longest peacetime in 30 years, four years after the isle's bloody, bitter civil war was spawned by ethnic tensions 'twixt the minority Tamil (Hindus) and the majority Sinhalese (Buddhists)—the island's heavily militarized north province held its first democratic elections for a semi-autonomous council. Winning with 78 percent of the vote was the Tamil National Alliance, once a political front for the Tigers who'd fought for their own state. Now, of Serendip's nine zones, the north is the sole pan-Tamil, freed from the island's Sinhalese ruling class.

"We want a settlement for the Tamils," an elderly woman told the BBC in an article I found online. "That's why we came to vote this time. We've been waiting so many years—now we want peace."

Hopefully it works. In our serene and mostly Muslim town, there was no election except the elect to depart. On this sunny Saturday morn, Newport Beach's Jared Mell leaves Serendip for one Indian Ocean island that is 85 percent Hindu among 17,508 islands in a country that is 88 percent Muslim.

"Time for some real waves, man," he says. He's neither Hindu nor Muslim. He was up late, drinking everything. No sleep till sunrise.

The charts tout a big non-denominational swell beelining for Bali, coinciding with Mell's first hungover step back onto the hot black tarmac of Ngurah Rai International Airport. A few days later, another 2,000 kilometers north, the rest of us here will reap the same swell, woefully stripped of size. Longitudinally screwed.

We'll call it the Tamil Tease.

Because, since colonially clipped from England in 1948, Serendip's south Sinhalese government birthed all sorts of things that greased them at the expense of the Tamils, widening the ethnic rift. These things weren't fair nor logical. For starters, the Indian Tamil tea plantation grunts, previously imported by the Brits, were barred citizenship. With help from an authoritarian government (which is still in place) of Sinhalese nationalism, a 'Sinhala-only' language law was passed. Tamils got mad. Tension and riots ensued. More than 100 were killed in widespread violence. Reverse anti-Tamil riots left hundreds dead and more than 25,000 Tamil refugees moved north.

In 1970 came the banning of Tamil media and literature importation followed by a new law that favored Sinhalese enrollees in universities, cutting the number of Tamil admissions. Later, Buddhism was deemed the country's religion, further oppressing and irking the Tamils. While assuring freedom of religion to all citizens, the 1978 Constitution offered "foremost place" to Buddhism and required "the duty of the State to protect and foster the Buddhist Sasana (broad teachings of the Buddha)." This led many young Tamils to push for a separate Tamil state called Eelam and the Liberation Tigers of Tamil Eelam group was born.

In June 1981 things really soured when a mob of Sinhalese police and government paramilitias launched two days of Tamil annihilation, destroying the Jaffna Public Library, one of Asia's biggest and most significant, housing nearly 98,000 irreplaceable manuscripts, scrolls, and books. The chaos was sparked by the killings of Sinhalese policemen at a Tamil-sponsored Jaffna rally.

Two years later came Black July, an anti-Tamil pogrom and riots as a response to a Tamil Tigers ambush that slew 13 Serendip Army soldiers. For a week, gangs of Sinhalese attacked Tamil targets—killing, looting, burning. Three thousand died, 150,000 became homeless. Throngs of Tamils fled the island. Of the youths who stayed, many joined militant clans and hence began the major civil war between the Tamil Tigers and Serendip's government that would not cease for 26 years.

When the dust settled, more than 100,000 people were dead from attacks that included massacres, bombings, robberies, military battles, and assassinations of civilian and military targets. The government and the Tigers were accused of human rights abuses throughout the war, with much focus on its final stages, when thousands of civilians were trapped in a thin strip of land in the north of Serendip.

The whole thing went against the grain. Religion is a silly reason to fight. It's contrary to natural inclination. Like a fish with no fins.

But, wait—what's that supposed to mean?

But, wait. Ellis Ericson, what's up with this board you made, the one Mell is stuffing into his tattered boardbag before he leaves us for Bukit bliss?

Technically it's not Mell's board. Technically inspired by Derek Hynd's finless theories, technically it belongs to Ericson, its creator who technically told me this in an email several weeks later: "It was a one-off, just an attempt at some of the friction-free boards I'd seen Derek riding. It kind of worked, but I'm still learning, so I'm sure his work better. I'm not making them for anyone—just myself. I want to be clear on that as Derek is making the best friction-free boards out there. So much R&D has gone into them and I have a lot of respect for his board-modification and building techniques."

Jared Mell in a Bali dispatch, also some weeks later, before he visited Rome and Istanbul: "Ellis' finless worked great. I had the best time going straight, sideways, backwards, diagonal, upside-down. Whatever which way I could think of. The board is similar to one of Derek's but it's more of an all-around version that can go right or left. Derek's boards seem to be focused on the one wave he is going to surf, which is great if you can get them made all the time."

The one wave we are going to surf today is waist-high and perfect, smashing onto the outermost promontory granite boulders before cleanly spooling along the point over a soft sand bottom, ending as a shorebreak closeout 300 yards north. It operates in close proximity to an Africanesque wildlife sanctuary which my guidebook says is "the Jungle Book brought to glorious life," home to 46 species of reptiles (including saltwater crocs), 44 species of mammals (including elephants and the world's highest concentration of leopards), and a lot of other things. At the beach, all we see are birds.

THE THIRD BEER: *THOUGHTS ON FLAGS, ETHNIC CLEANSING, AND CONNOR LYON'S 5'5" FINLESS*

THE LION STARES. Eyes wide, he seems rapt to roar. Like he's about to walk, lion to Lyon.

His lifted right paw rests on a brown knuckle of stone. His orange mane is big, his whiplike tail swayed right. Washing his body is a low gold light from a sunrise or sunset. Above his head is *1881* and below his paws are the words LION LAGER, odd since lions have never lived in Serendip. LEOPARD LAGER would be more apt. Or LITTLE EGRET LAGER. Or LESSER BANDICOOT RAT LAGER. Or whatever. At least the old Brits brought beer to the Indian Ocean.

Ceylon Brewery was Serendip's first, built in 1881 to install a boozy piece of home for the Brits while they gazed over their tea plantations in the hilly burg of Nuwara Eliya, 115 kilometers west of where Santa Barbara's lionish Connor Lyon had side-slipped on his self-modified, finless Spence displacement hull across his 26th wave of the afternoon session that had led to a chromatic dusk.

With its subtropical highland climate and spring water, Nuwara Eilya was a sweet spot for a brewery. Nicknamed "Little England," the town was an ark for the British civil servants and tea planters, an insular sanctuary where they could improvise Union Jack leisure like hunting, polo, golf, and cricket.

Not a big beer drinker, Lyon does like a good pint, generally of California craft beers. But those are on the other side of the world. Tonight in Serendip he's drank two large Lion Lagers before the one he's now holding, all three bought from the empty Rasta-themed bar down the lane, just past the empty beach and the empty tin fish shack. The carbonated yellow liquid in his brown glass bottle behind the big male lion label is lukewarm. Lyon thinks Lion is better than Bintang, the other Asian beer he's tried. At best, lukewarm Lion is "mildly refreshing," he says. At worst, I counter, it's another limp beer on another hot island. But that's a topic for another tale.

Seven p.m.—dark. Crickets with mosquitoes and other pests that bite our feet. Lyon is lounging on a white plastic chair in front of the room where Kyle Albers was once vomiting. Drinking the beer and thumbing through a copy of *Slide* magazine, Lyon's manelike hair remains damp from the late surf session. The hair covers his ears, clogged with saltwater, but he can hear the male muezzin reciting Salat al-'Isha, the Islamic early-night prayer, his Arabic words drifting from the speakers on the minaret atop the nearby mosque. We can't see the mosque; it's somewhere over the hill, south, in the dark.

The muezzin's voice is hypnotic, spooky. Soothing in a weird way. It's the fifth and final of the daily ritual Muslim prayers, starting with the first chapter of the Qur'ān, the core religious text of Islam, translated to:

> In The Name Of Allah, Most Gracious, Most Merciful. Praise Be To Allah, Lord Of The Worlds. Most Gracious, Most Merciful. Master Of The Day Of Judgment. Thee (Alone) We Worship And Thee (Alone) We Ask For Help. Show Us The Straight Path. The Path Of Those Whom Thou Hast Favored; Not The (Path) Of Those Who Earn Thine Anger Nor Of Those Who Go Astray.

Allah is Arabic for "God" who in Islam is the prophet Muhammad (full name: Abū al-Qāsim Muḥammad ibn 'Abd Allāh ibn 'Abd al-Muṭṭalib ibn Hāshim) from the Arabian hamlet of Mecca. He launched Islam 4,794 kilometers and 1,391 years from where Connor Lyon sits with his warm beer and wild hair and magazine and bugs and the small mosque summoning him through the darkness of twilight.

But like 91 percent of Serendipians, Lyon is not Muslim.

"I ain't religious, dog."

Serendip mosques seem a bit quaint, though Islam has existed here since the 8th century and is represented on the national flag, the one Lyon admired three hours ago as it flapped in the offshore breeze in front of a small roadside restaurant. (Its fish curry was superb.)

Called the Lion Flag (more lions!), the Sinhalese ethnicity is repped by a yellow lion clutching a sword over a red rectangular background with a fig leaf in each corner. Around the background is a yellow border and to its left are two vertical stripes—one orange, one green. The orange represents Tamils and the green represents Muslims, the majority ethnicity around the beaches we're surfing. To us, they're nice, friendly folks—fishermen, farmers, merchants, taxi drivers—but not everyone agrees.

Back in the late '80s, because Muslims were believed to back the Sinhalese government, the Tamil Tigers began attacking Muslim towns, forcing thousands from their homes, torching buildings and killing residents. In August 1990, during this very same Salat al-'Isha prayer that Lyon hears, the Tigers murdered 147 prostrating Muslims in attacks on four mosques in Kattankudi, 93 kilometers upcoast from where Lyon has just now sank his third Lion Lager of the evening. In October 1990 the Tigers expelled 95,000 Muslims from Serendip's north, calling it an "ethnic cleansing" to help reach the Tigers' goal of creating Eelam, their monoethnic state.

Perhaps they should've built a brewery up there and made Liberation Lager or Attack Ale. Something like that.

Me: "Should we go get more warm beer?"

Lyon: "Hell no. Shit tasted wack. Like, double wack."

Recently Sinhalese nationalists flipped their ire from Tamils to Muslims and, led by Buddhist monks, they're attacking mosques and Muslim-owned businesses plus churches and clergy.

Allah Ale? Islamic IPA?

No.

Buddha Beer? Sinhala Stout?

Connor Lyon would sink those. But he's not. He's going to bed with a lion-sized headache.

THE FOURTH SAND POINT: *THOUGHTS ON TENTS, GOTHIC WHIGS, AND SIMON MURDOCH'S 5'3" QUAD*

SMASHED UNCONSCIOUS AT CHURCH. Why not? It's what they do.

Throughout 2013, in a gambit to "protect" Serendip's Sinhalese and their Buddhist beliefs, two Buddhist-extremist groups terrorized

Catholic Christians with arson, church demolitions, mob attacks, and physical assaults. The Bodu Bala Sena ("Buddhist Power Force") and the Sinhala Ravaya ("Sinhalese Echo") led nearly 50 anti-Christian incidents, mostly on churches, though individual folks were also marked.

Before flying to Serendip I read an online news story containing a quote from a prominent Buddhist lawyer: "Such attacks show there is a political agenda that aims to unite the Buddhists. Everyone should have the freedom to change religion in this country. We Buddhists are the first to be harmed in our culture and religion from these petty actions. Whoever is behind (these incidents) should not be supported. As a Buddhist I feel embarrassed because real Buddhism is not about attacking and killing."

Awaiting my daily pre-dawn curry breakfast from the sweet Buddhist ladies in the guesthouse kitchen, I read a story in a new issue of *The Island*, my preferred Serendip newspaper. Out west last week, a Bodu Bala Sena monk and his four thugs stormed into a Catholic church and used a guitar to knock out the pastor who, along with his mother, required hospitalization. The Buddhists then trashed the sacred grounds and freaked everyone out. It was the year's 45th anti-Christian incident up to this quiet late-September morning which finds Simon Murdoch slowly stirring cane sugar into his ginger tea at the breakfast table while antisocially reading *Gyatso's Introduction to Buddhism: An Explanation of the Buddhist Way of Life.*

A fly lands in Murdoch's tea. Serendipity?

Serendipity, as manifested by the fly: death from drowning in delicious tea. Serendip is famous for its tea.

Serendipity, as defined in the Oxford English Dictionary: "The faculty of making happy and unexpected discoveries by accident."

Serendipity, as invented by England's effeminate Gothic fictionalist and Whig Party (liberal/anti-Catholic) politician Horace Walpole, the fourth and last Earl of Orford, the youngest son of British Prime Minister Sir Robert Walpole: in his letter to a friend on January 28, 1754, little Horace mentioned "The Three Princes of Serendip," a Persian fairytale in which the princes, he wrote, "were always making discoveries, by accidents and sagacity, of things they were not in quest of…this discovery, indeed, is almost of that kind which I call Serendipity, a very expressive word." The fairytale's location was indeed Serendip, the old Arabic name for Sri Lanka.

A chimney-sweeper by day, by night the friendly and mustachioed Murdoch, a Mormon, sleeps at his self-made Tent Palace on his parents' leafy property in Santa Barbara's Hidden Valley sect. The Palace is an impromptu and functional example of youth groove. It is cozy and colorful and festooned with sarongs and tapestries and floored with rugs, soon with one Murdoch purchased yesterday from a smiling roadside vendor who probably would have liked what Murdoch has got going on back at home.

His 12-person nylon tent is five kilometers from his beloved Sandspit, 73 kilometers from Supertubes and 14,902 kilometers from the hazardous wave he finds on our second-to-last day. It's a foul mix of those two California spots, though it breaks more often and with far fewer surfers in much warmer water and the residents nearby are Muslims with no cars or cash.

Serendipity, as shared by Murdoch: engaging the long view from a northern headland and, in the hazy south, seeing tubes spit. It is to be the fourth point we surf in the last two days, though geologically this place is a collection of brown boulders that ease shoreward into a sand-bottomed cove. The paddle-outs are simple but the wave, which French-kisses rock and pounds bare sand, is freakish. Each wave requires careful skill and cavalier risk.

This morning, Murdoch endangers a leashless 5'3" round-tail quad that 816 days prior was shaped for me by Ryan Lovelace. It is maroon with a splattered bluey-yellow-purple-red bottom, birthed in Gregg Tally's garage of White Owl Surfboards fame. The board was later ping-ponged between a few friends and countries, much like the way it ping-pongs through the boulders when Murdoch blows a take-off or gets pinched in a sand-sucking tube.

After one session the board is wrecked. Tomorrow, after a second session (this time with a leash), Murdoch will gift it to a stocky dark Serendip surfer of ding-fixing repute, prompting this letter from

Lovelace in California: "In the past year, Simon had definitely breathed some new life into that board, drawing his own lines and putting a fresh spin on a board I'd seen surfed a zillion times. Watching Simon surf it at home was a joy, and I was a bit heartbroken that it got left in Serendip, although why it was left and who with couldn't be any happier of a continuation for that board's life."

On the bottom of that board, in the center of Lovelace's yellow resin-dot logo, is a debossed half-inch-wide *om* symbol. Lovelace used a wooden stamp to do this—it is his last movement on each shaped blank. *Om* is a mystic syllable, considered the most sacred of Buddhist mantras, uttered at the start and end of most Sanskrit texts, prayers, and recitations. Lovelace does not say *om* before and after he shapes a board, and it is unlikely Buddhist and Hindu terrorists say *om* when they attack non-believers, like when insane Islamic terrorists yell the Takbīr, the Arabic term for the phrase *Allāhu Akbar* ("God is greatest").

Serendipity, after Simon Murdoch hoots through his 12th tube of the hour: ecstatic, he slides off the green shoulder and into the deep channel. He yells to the non-drunk Lyon and the non-food-poisoned Albers, both paddling frantically, each about to get kegged on the set's next two waves.

"Dudes! Why weren't we surfing here during the whole trip?"

Somewhere in Bali, the fourth prince smiles.

PART V

Melanesia

20

UN EDEN AUSTRAL

2003

ALONE, THE 12TH of May. Evening settles like song over tranquil lagoon, low tide, post-twilight. Clouds shift and the moon appears on the wet sand at my feet. In the distance, araucaria pine silhouettes block the barrier reef from this beach—untracked, unknown.

And fronting a right-hand coral bliss, unsurfed. Hours ago, standing chest-deep in the lagoon, late-day binocular viewing revealed a subtropical El Capitan. Now it is the muffled, singular sound: warm south swell expires in darkness. Tomorrow, New Caledonia will fade from the Aircalin glass. Perhaps another time, another voyage....

Another Number One lager, the resident *biere de qualite superieure*, and I'm out. Bizarre dreams unfold within a fitful sleep beneath the bungalow bed's mosquito tent. Unforecasted, hard rain stirs the wee hours' ambient lethargy. A gale ensues.

Withdrawals from dime-sized scopolamine patches—worn behind the ear for 10 days at sea, then removed on land—induce constant sharp headache and mild vertigo. I wake disoriented, brain pitching and yawing as if still aboard the *Téré*. Flip the light on and reach for *National Geographic*; tales of Sherpas and Mayan treasure soon engross.

Reading eventually blurs to weightless dozing, dozing to lucid mirages, and mirages to memories of impending seasickness, boredom, fishing, and shallow, flawless reef passes. Surreal it was not.

FEW THRILLS EQUAL the romantic, ageless breeze of South Seas sailing. The waves, the wind, the whitecaps...the catamaran flow. Pascal knows this yacht. A French expatriate, amiable and unflappable, he is quite possibly the finest non-surfing skipper one can hire down here.

"Most skippers drive the boat and do nothing else," guide Jonathon says. "Pascal does it all—he cleans, he cooks...."

Preceding the charter, a relaxing afternoon drive through the hills above Noumea, the nation's capital, brings us to a striking vista. Expounding civilization's great need for nickel ore, Jonathon stops the car and points to the monolithic Doniambo smelter below.

"Mate, Noumea exists because of *that*."

Flooded with rust-hued ore dust, the effluent-spewing fortress sprawls incongruously in verdant surroundings. Along with 200 swell-exposed reef passes, Grande Terre holds the world's largest nickel deposits, drawing 90 percent of the country's export profit.

In industrialized Western nations, nickel is a vital ingredient for the steel and armament industries, being both anticorrosive and heat-resistant. In New Caledonia, smelter employees endure an unhealthy, gritty work scenario while just across the way, an immaculate harbor cradling million-dollar yachts caters to folks like...us.

Minutes later, we arrive at Port Moselle, home of the *Téré*, 46 French-molded feet of fiberglass decency, our lair for 10 days. The others arrive from Brisbane tonight.

And it's a motley crew: Fresh from a big Pipe win is Hawaii's Jamie O'Brien, toting his videographer Ruben Tejada; aside affable lensman Andrew Shield, Australia is represented by Damon Harvey, Ryan Campbell, Clint Kimmins, and Ryan Hipwood—solid blokes with humor and consistent tuberiding panache.

Accessible only by boat, surfing New Caledonia is an oft-clandestine affair. Embarking beneath the stars, this junket begins. Grand Terre is gone and the mental pace slows, bound for a distant barrier reef pass spared from land-viewing by blackness and acres of lagoon.

These passes—deep underwater valleys, remnants of ancient riverbeds—fuel our voyage; swell cooperates, the wind generally does not. Hence the bane of a limited sea life.

CALEDONIA IS THE Roman word for Scotland. Upon sighting Grande Terre in 1774, the archipelago's main island, English explorer James Cook recalled the Scottish landscape, christening his new South Seas find New Caledonia in deference to. Later, fearing British occupation, France stepped in and annexed the place for use as a penal colony.

A massive variety of endemic plants ("You tell botanists you are coming here," botanist Pete Lowry told *National Geographic*, "and they will envy you and wish they could visit here once in their lifetime.") coats Grande Terre, New Caledonia's mountainous, cigar-shaped main island and the South Pacific's fourth-largest. Yet physically, the island is unversed with regard to breaking waves.

Splintered from Australia 80 million years ago, Grande Terre's barrier reef couldn't have formed much later. Enclosing the world's largest lagoon dotted with marine reserves, Grande Terre's western barrier reef is 370 miles long and wide open to swell and occasionally erratic weather from the Tasman and Coral seas.

As such, the biggest day dawns unseasonably dour and wind-beaten. We motor into the nearest pass for a pulse check and, realizing the intimate proximity of seething barrels on both sides of the boat, Captain Pascal quickly reverses course with a nervous grin.

"Hmmm....zees de big waves, *oui?*"

So we motor miles southward atop the sanity of the lagoon. Trolling three lines always lands something, except this morning. Eventually, no one cares: Inside the lagoon, a dredging mushroom of reef receives filtered swell. The lads rejoice, trading lures for surf wax.

> *"We are from here and nowhere else. You are from here but also from somewhere else."*
>
> *—message to French locals from Kanak chief Jean-Marie Tjibaou, 1983*

MORNING AND THE pre-booked departure time arrives. A loud telephone rings with a summoning from the concierge. The van awaits; I hop in with a bonjour. My driver, a middle-aged Kanak, begins easing down the road, then suddenly soliloquizes in perfect English.

The sins of France are many, he insists. Repressive colonialism. Penal camps, armed revolt. High costs. Racial tension and the Kanak peoples' widespread "backburner" status. Deforestation and pollutive cattle farming. Lucrative nickel mining—"scarring our mountains for the world's economy," are his words. This as we roll east toward a French airport in a French van atop flawless French pavement. His, an ancestor-worshiping Melanesian culture, was New Caledonia's first. He lights a cigarette and points to his chest.

"You cannot see the scars," he frowns, "but they are here."

What would independence bring?

"Our country…our life."

Noumea shrinks in the rearview mirror. Uniform European architecture, the yachts, the cleanliness and fashion, the manicured flora and the soothing ocean views—this is French Riviera, not South Pacific.

The driver hands me a warm chocolate pastry from his local *boulangerie*; I ponder what New Caledonia would be if Napoleon III hadn't ordered French annexation in 1853. Health services, education, transportation, and economics? Thank you, Paris. Culturally? The Kanaks have my vote. Leave France in France.

MOTORLESS, SLICING NORTH under full sail miles from land, none of this stuff seems to matter. Cruising outside the barrier reef, savoring the untouchability enjoyed on a boat, it is the vessel, the crew, the fish, and the sea.

In New Caledonia, a hollow left-hand mélange exists. Sheer potential and zero crowds. For variation, coral cays lend foothold respite from days adrift. The fishing, the snorkeling, the utter isolation, the barrels—bon voyage.

Finding it? Well….

21

ORCHID COAST

2005

> *"If I were a king, the worst punishment I could inflict on my enemies would be to banish them to the Solomons. On second thought, king or no king, I don't think I'd have the heart to do it."*
>
> —*Jack London,* The Cruise of the Snark

IN LATE 2003 I suggested a journey to the Solomon Islands to the editor of a monthly American surf magazine. He approved the trip; a photographer and pro surfers were enlisted, dates were set, accommodation and boats booked. Solomon Airlines agreed, via Australia, to sponsor round-trip airfare for me and the photographer, so immediately I went to Qantas's Web site and bought a ticket to Brisbane.

In the coming weeks, logistics of loading a dozen surfboards and us onto the tiny aircraft of Solomon Airlines grew painfully difficult, and coupled with the photographer's tight schedule, it effectively minimized our number of days in the Solomons, which was not economically justifiable for the magazine, the photographer, or the surfers' sponsors. Cancellation ensued.

Problem was, I had a non-refundable, non-transferable, $1,300 round-trip ticket to Australia, and I wasn't prepared to go alone, on my own dime. No problem, the editor said, we'll send you a reimbursement check.

No check for the next seven months (*Yes, Mike, the check is in the mail—*); then came August and, at my request, the editor rescheduled the trip for February 2005. Yet by November 2004 he was battling budget crunches, and paying my expenses became a long shot, if not impossible.

So in January, with the old ticket credit, I rebooked with Qantas, organized an entirely new solo trip, and landed in Brisbane the dawn of March 4, 2005, bound for my connecting flight to Honiara, capital of the Solomon Islands.

In Brisbane I was relieved to be alone, lacking the baggage of professional surfers and photographers and the attitudes and the palpable pressures of getting sun and swell and blueness to appease editors and advertising managers.

During dinner on the plane from Los Angeles I read an interview with Paul Theroux, who said: "Traveling with another person is not my idea of travel."

I agreed.

"YOU'LL NEVER GET waves there, mate—it never breaks, and good luck convincing the airline to take your boards."

"I didn't bring any boards," I said.

"Ah, because you know you won't find surf."

"I've arranged to borrow one. Have you been there?"

"No, but some mates of my mates traveled around there for a month or two during swell season, and they didn't surf once. I reckon there's a real reason the Solomons aren't a bloody surf destination. It's a two-hour flight from here, and if it was any good up there, it'd be bloody swarming with Aussies."

"Well, I'm going."

"Then I hope you're into fishing and diving," he said. "Got your spear gun?"

He was a thirty-something, gangly, gaunt Sunshine Coaster, with horribly blotched and sun-damaged skin, a head of kinky red hair, big bloodshot eyes, and an elaborate tattoo of his name, Caesar, down his left forearm. He was a stonemason by day and a drinker by night, and it was late at a quiet bar in Brisbane's airport where we'd met, awaiting our flights, killing time with peanuts and Victoria Bitter. He was off to Bali for a fortnight.

"Got a little 'exotic goods' shop in Mooloolaba," he said. "I go to Bali, buy the shit, and my wife sells it in our little shop at four times the cost. The tourists love it—right now is our high season, and we've just run out of goods, which is why I'm going up now to get more, before all the tourists go home."

Caesar was a longboarder whose local spots included Point Cartwright, Coolum Beach, and, further north, the famous Noosa Heads. Naturally, the soft, long rights of Tea Tree and First Point are a strong draw for any longboarder, and coincidentally, that weekend, the Noosa Festival of Surfing was ongoing in tiny, windblown slop. Caesar had been up there all day, which showed on his sunburned face.

"Might as well stay here, mate. Come on, at least you're guaranteed waves—"

"I think I can do better."

"—rent a car, stay in Noosa, surf the park—"

"I'd love to, but perhaps another time."

"—meet some girls, do a little hiking...."

"Nope."

"Don't say I didn't warn you then," he said, wagging a bony finger at me. "You're not going to get any waves in the Solomons, mate."

I thought about this statement four hours later while sitting in another airport, early in the morning in a dirty shack on a small island far from Noosa, waiting for the driver of my taxi boat to arrive. I would be spending time in a traditional thatched bungalow near what looked on the charts to be a good right-hander, in the Solomon hinterlands.

On the plane from Honiara I could see whitewater curling around every exposed island, atoll, and barrier reef, and the morning was sunny and windless. Contrary to Caesar's claim, things looked promising.

A grubby little fine-featured man approached me.

"You Michael?"

"I am."

"Motor broken," he said. "I call for other motor, but not here."

"Is it on its way?"

"Yiss. Wait some time. No problem. I know you here."

It evolved into a very long day, morning slowly becoming afternoon. The airport shack was deserted, the toilets were inoperable, there was nothing to eat or drink, there was no town nearby. All the passengers from my flight had vanished hours ago, same with the airport employees and the tiny plane which had dropped me here.

I had spent no time in Honiara because my flight connection there was strangely on-time. Besides, I'd heard bad things about the town, that it was a snakepit I could do without—its requisite beggars, the noise, the broken glass on dusty streets, bored men who try to mug or scam you because you are a white foreigner, and you must have money if you are in Honiara, perhaps a diplomat from Sydney or a banker from Auckland.

Instead, Theroux's initial take on Honiara in The Happy Isles of Oceania saw it for me. First, the town itself—

> *...a place so ramshackle, so poor, so scary, so unexpectedly filthy, that I began to understand the theory behind culture shock—something I had never truly experienced in its paralyzing and malignant form. The idea that this miserable-looking town could be regarded as a capital city seemed laughable.*

—then its residents:

> *...among the scariest-looking people I had ever seen in my life—wild hair, huge feet, ripped and ragged clothes, tattoos on their foreheads, ornamental scars all over their faces, wearing broken sunglasses. They loped along in large groups, or else idled near the stores that played American rap music and looked for al the world like rappers themselves.*

I FELT I was not missing anything, although there was nothing happening where I was, in that tiny airport building, which was on its own island—no one lived there, there were no stores of any kind, no roads, no chickens, few trees.

It was too hot and shadeless to sit outside, so I laid flat on a betel nut-spit-stained wooden bench under the room's only ceiling fan, which mercifully had been left on. I finished a book, Jack London's Martin Eden, and started another, Passage To Juneau by Jonathan Raban. I listened to music on my portable CD player until its batteries died. My stomach grumbled. I sweated, dozed, dreamt in bright color.

"Sir—"

A tap on my arm.

"Sir, motor here now."

It was the same little man, the boat driver. He was clutching my bag and looked eager to leave. His name was Abraham, and he was from the island of Rennell. I was dazed and dehydrated but glad to see him.

We walked a short distance to a makeshift dock and sped away atop the smooth, blue lagoon, passing dozens of small uninhabited islands and atolls, mere tufts of palm trees and green tangle; we passed families in dugout canoes, some with sails sewn from old yellow grain bags; we passed whole villages fronting turquoise waters, backdropped by jungle and dark, misty ridgetops.

"Dat one volcano," Abraham pointed out.

"Is it active?"

He shrugged. "Dunno."

The sun was low in the sky when we beached the skiff at the island where I'd rented a bungalow, maintained by a New Zealand expat named Sid who catered to Australian anglers and divers. Sid was in Wellington tonight, but he reputedly was somewhat of a surfer and had a few old boards laying around, used by two local boys.

Caesar: I hope you're into fishing and diving....

I had chosen this island/atoll as a base because of its remoteness, its lack of infrastructure, and its proximity to what on maps appeared to be likely surf spots. Surf tourism was unknown, so the natives were not tainted by the influence of Western surfers and their iPods, their laptops, porn magazines, complaints, profanity, drunkenness. I hated traveling with surfers, hated the mood swings and the surliness that arose from flat-spells or foul winds. Most surfers I met abroad were there for only a week or two, for their annual vacation. They'd worked hard all year, and if the surf was not blue and perfect each day, the world was an evil place and I had to hear it all, the too-thises and the too-thats, the should-haves and the could-haves:

This place is too expensive—

The food sucks—

I should have brought my girlfriend—

We could have gone to Indo—

Myopia and self-absorption were two of the foulest mental scabs one could find on any trip, in any country, and if your traveling companion was afflicted, you might prefer death to this living hell. Even worse was malaria, rife in the Solomons, and it actually did kill people—every day, in fact, and my little host island hosted thousands of infected mosquitoes. I had no preventative pills, no bug spray, pants, shoes, or long-sleeved shirts, and if, during a sudden onset of chills and sweating and head-pounding fever, I would worry. Dengue fever is part of Solomon life too, but it was primarily in urban places, near concrete human dwellings—Honiara, for example—and this island had neither. Its handful of thatched huts looked innocent enough.

Cannibals could be another source of traveler's stress, and I was a tad skeptical once I saw how remote this island was and how primitive its people looked. I was also concerned with theft of my cash and cameras, but Abraham comforted me. Realistically, he said, these people would not know what to do with a camera, credit cards were useless, and cash was not exchanged here—traditional bartering was still the go.

The island's population came out to greet us, all seventeen people, curious and wide-eyed, the children naked and giggly. The adults were sedated by betel nut. Nobody spoke English, so in Solomons Pijin Abraham translated to the adults: "He is Michael from America. He is staying here in a hut."

There were three bungalows for hire, and in one of them was a thin, unsmiling, balding, Jewish American name Zeke who was here researching exotic birds for his Ph.D. at New York's Syracuse University. He was twenty-six and originally from Newport Beach, California.

Together we ate dinner in the small communal area between bungalows—there was a cook on hand at all times.

"Syracuse sucks," Zeke confided. "When I left, there was two feet of snow on the ground. Don't go to New York."

"I've never really been there—only to the JFK airport," I said.

"That's where I flew from. Took three days to get here. The airline lost all my bags. I've been wearing this shit for ten days."

He wore black denim jeans, leather boots, and a black long-sleeved shirt. Even at night, the Solomons are very hot and sticky; it made me uncomfortable just looking at him.

"Luckily I had my laptop and binoculars and books and bird-trapping gear on the plane with me. Otherwise, I'd be screwed."

Since Zeke was from Newport, I figured he must have known something about surfing, so I asked him if he had seen any waves since his arrival.

"No, man, there's no waves here. I was in a boat all day yesterday and didn't see anything." He looked confused. "And you're here to surf?"

"Sort of. I can fish and snorkel, too."

Two shy young men approached our table. Zeke waved them over and they stood next to us.

"This is Ravia and Samy, the local surfers," he told me. "They knew you were coming."

Samy was thin but muscular, bashful, gentle, age fifteen, with kinky blond hair despite his Negro complexion. He spoke no English, but Ravia's was decent, with an accent resembling Jamaican patois—appropriate because he had the appearance of a Rastaman, dreadlocks and all, serene-faced, age twenty-five.

"I had one American girlfriend," Ravia said. "We were in Marshall Islands. She was volunteer teacher on Majuro."

Ravia and Samy were raised in the Western Province, their fathers employees in the tuna cannery at Noro. The boys were destined to be cannery workers, too, until Sid the Kiwi arrived and leased this land from the family of his Solomon wife. He hired local hands to build the bungalows, did no advertising, and relied on word-of-mouth for business.

"You and Zeke are first American guest," Ravia said.

"Ever?" I asked.

"Yes."

"Have any surfers been here?"

"No. Only fishermen and scuba divers."

The Solomons are a marquee dive destination, easternmost of the Pacific's Coral Triangle, which includes Irian Jaya to the west and the Great Barrier Reef to the south, all home to the world's highest levels of marine biodiversity. Still, the islands receive scant tourist traffic, and certainly no Mentawais-style surf tourism.

Information about surf in the Solomon Islands is scarce, limited to a vague edition of the Surf Report and a page or two in the *Stormrider Guide*. The Internet was even less helpful, which didn't surprise me—handfuls of secretive Australians had surfed the Solomons for years, making surgical strikes when cyclones twisted in the Coral Sea, ferreting swell directly into the south shores of these so-called "Happy Isles," which, if you considered the state of the economy, were scarcely happy at all.

After decades of domestic peace, a simmer of ethnic tension rose to a boil-over in 1998, spawning a law-and-order crisis, then a coup, then a five-year civil war between Guadalcanal and Malaita. Eventually the Solomons' prime minister implored Australia to renew domestic harmony; the result was the Australia-led Regional Assistance Mission to Solomon Islands, or RAMSI, which included military, police, and personnel from fellow South Pacific nations.

RAMSI restored a semblance of normalcy in the Solomons, improving stability and a fraction of the tourism, of which I saw no evidence in any Solomon Airlines plane I flew in. During the civil unrest, there were no international flights to the Solomons, and it was only recently that foreign aircraft could again land at Honiara's Henderson Airport.

An Australian travel agent supposedly sold surf packages to the Solomons, but I could not reach anyone who could confirm the authenticity of those packages, the Surf Report, or the *Stormrider Guide*. This suited me, because I did not wish to be guided. I did not need a book or a travel agent to tell me where the waves were, because I could find them with Samy and Ravia, both who had never read a guidebook or touched a computer.

The peripatetic Ted Grambeau once said that the more he traveled, the surf world became bigger, not smaller, and despite the cancer of signage and virtual hand-holding, anything remains possible. All it takes is money, time, and, most importantly, resistance to nuisance, because Third World travel is full of it.

The Solomons could become my little nirvana, I thought, sitting there with Ravia and Samy on a small thatched-roofed patio between clusters of coconut palms and orchids, the only sound that of a small generator, humming softly in the darkness, keeping the fridgeful of beer cold and the fans spinning.

But any surfer's nirvana requires waves, and I heard none.

"We have wave here," Ravia assured me. "Da wind blowing in da wrong direction for you to hear dem now. Dey are behind us, out dere"—he gestured into the night. "Wait to morning."

NEARLY ONE THOUSAND islands comprise the Solomons, making it the South Pacific's third largest archipelago. Only a third of those islands are inhabited, one or two surfed with any regularity. It is a pristine, lush nation, famous for its place in World War II history, its undisturbed coral and its fantastic diving, its earthquakes and bubbling volcanoes, its traditionalism and resistance to modernization, and, most fascinating to me, its head-hunting and cannibalism, both societal normalities until the 1940s.

It is possible that I could have been decapitated and eaten had I visited the Solomons in 1925 instead of 2005. I could have been a British missionary or a German trader; Ravia or Samy could have rejected my intentions and paleness, then killed me, later enjoying the flame-broiled taste of my thighs, huddling around a stone firepit in the jungle. All flesh would have been scraped from my head, and my skull would have been placed at a shrine for worship, clustered with chiefs' skulls and other foreign victims', like a contemporary big-game hunter's roomful of taxidermied moose and bear heads, trophies from his boozy hunting trips to remote Alaska and Montana.

I was in the Solomons wilderness, but there was a noticeable lack of animals to shoot, certainly no bears or moose. The island was tiny. A few chickens could live there, geckos, red ants, a wild pig or two, but nothing else in terms of good meaty protein. Still, there was fishing—the unmolested Solomon Sea is full of tuna and marlin—and Abraham the boatman impressed me with his large sailfish early the next day, while I sat in the same seat as the previous night, drinking coffee, waiting for Samy and Ravia. They lived in a hut on the back of island, and only they knew the trail through the jungle. Abraham hadn't seen them, but he offered to take me in his skiff for a surf-check as soon as he finished filleting his catch.

"Dere is surfing waves on dee island other side," he said, knifing the fish on a filthy little beachside table. Fish blood trickled over the sides, staining the white sand red. He threw the fish guts into the lagoon, quickly attracting several small sand sharks into a feeding frenzy in six inches of water.

I looked at the tops of the palm trees; the frond tips were rustling toward the lagoon—onshore wind.

"That side?" I asked, motioning behind us, toward the ocean.

"Yiss."

"I don't think the wind is right."

"We go see." His hands were covered in blood and entrails. "Ravia surfboard is dere"—Ravia had two in the kitchen, for some reason, an egg and a shortboard.

I finished my coffee and returned to the bungalow for boardshorts and sunscreen. Next door, Zeke was on his bungalow porch, gawking through his binoculars at something in the sky, something white and large and regal, like an egret.

"That's a Solomon sea eagle," he whispered. "The first I've seen."

The palm trees surrounding the bungalows were full of red lorikeets, chirping with a high squeaky song, fluttering about. I shooed a treeload of them away when I pissed out the window.

Of Ravia's two surfboards I chose the yellowed and thrashed 6'7" Hot Brewz thruster, which I nick-named "SolBrewz" in deference to the local beer, SolBrew. Abraham carefully set it on the bottom of the skiff and pull-started the ancient outboard motor. Ravia appeared out of the jungle and ran down to join us, carrying the egg, an 8'2" Becker.

"That my first ding repair," he said as we pulled away from the beach, pointing at the Hot Brewz's crooked left side-fin.

Five minutes later we were squinting at small rights, consistent and shapely but mushy, like Waikiki, tainted by the fifteen-knot onshores.

"This is where you can surf," Ravia said. "When it good, the wave breaks from there"—he made a sweeping arm gesture—"to there. Big. Barrels. Yeah."

The setup was epic. The surf was not. I vowed to surf regardless, so I rode the egg instead of the Hot Brewz, and Ravia and Abraham went trolling for dinner.

I sat in the warm, choppy lineup, admiring the colorful corals below my feet. Barracuda chased flying fish. An old man drifted past in his dugout canoe, palm frond for a sail, white shirt on his head, like a turban.

The waves were about as bad as waves get, but the sun was shining, the water was clean, clear, and eighty-eight degrees, and there was nobody out. At that moment, however, unbeknownst to me, the winter's biggest and cleanest west swell was pushing into Santa Barbara County, igniting the rare pointbreaks, all the coveted nooks. Up until March, southern California had had a lousy, wet winter, and I had no qualms about leaving my home at the end of it, especially considering the rank ocean pollution, which had left me bedridden in February.

I was equally ignorant of the Solomons' swell forecast, whether it would stay a blustery and gutless waist-high, or if things would improve. For three days the weather worsened, with heavy rain, fearsome skies, thunder and lightning, steady onshores, long hours hunkered in my soggy bungalow, because I too worsened, with a harsh cold: fever, sore throat, runny nose, itchy eyes, sneezing, coughing, lethargy, shortness of breath. My health and the weather were a perfect match.

Briefly I considered malaria, that I could have been bitten the first day or two of my visit.

"No," Ravia said. "If you get malaria, you not feel it until you home again."

"Guess that gives me something to look forward to."

I slept and scribbled notes and read books—Henry Miller's *The Air-Conditioned Nightmare*, Judy Mandell's *Book Editors Talk to Writers*, J. Maarten Troost's *The Sex Lives of Cannibals*. I read Sid's old wrinkled copies of *The New Yorker*, *NZ Business*, *Sport Diver*, *New Zealand Fishing World*. He even had a French edition of *Playboy* and a pamphlet from the South Pacific Tourism Organization, where a Nature Conservancy spokeswoman noted the five hundred coral species and one thousand species of reef fishes the Conservancy had found in a recent Solomons survey.

My little island began to flood, and soon flotsam like beetles and twigs and leaves and plastic bags floated in unison around the bungalow, swirling with the wind, like a shallow lagoon gone awry. My bedsheets were clammy; everything was damp but not smelly—not yet.

Zeke was unfazed by the weather, because the island's birds remained active regardless of storms and onshore wind. Each morning he trampled off into the jungle wearing his heavy black boots and jeans, which now served a purpose—he was not there to sunbathe.

At last feeling healthier one afternoon, I borrowed Sid's decrepit kayak and paddled around the island, wearing my snorkel mask because the rain was blinding, to catch a glimpse of the spot I'd surfed. From the island's semi-sheltered southeast corner I could see the wave in the distance, whitewater spanning its reef, but blown to shreds. Oddly enough, a clean one-foot right was breaking where I was, in the rubbly sandy shallows fronting a cluster of mangrove trees, and I managed to ride a few waves in the kayak—good fun until I impaled it on a freakishly sharp coral head.

Back at the bungalows, drinking SolBrew, awaiting dinner, Abraham appeared from the jungle. I told him about my silly surf-kayak session, wearing a snorkel mask.

"You see crocodiles?" he asked.

"No, but should I have?"

"One month ago, a kid was taken here. Crocodile had—how you say, dis part?—"

His tapped his chest and waistline.

"Torso," I said.

"—had torso in its mouth. I held da kid's leg. Was a girl. I could not hold on. Crocodile ate her."

"And you saw this happen?"

"Yiss. Very bad. I have bad dreams now."

"How big was the crocodile?"

"Maybe five, six meters long," he said.

From that night on, I too had bad dreams.

ONE OF WEATHER'S most perplexing nuances is how an intensely stormy evening can dawn clear and placid, the sky vast, the sea and lagoon plates of bluey-green glass; one of surfing's most painful realities is a quality surf spot during peak season with perfect conditions but no swell.

It was the first sunny day in a week, and the natural beauty of the Solomons shone brightly. I borrowed the kayak again and paddled around the island's opposite side. After assessing the reef and its absence of whitewater, I became giddy thinking of the scenic photographs I could snap that day. After breakfast, while focusing my macro lens on an orchid (the Solomons have two hundred and thirty varieties), Ravia approached and suggested we go look for surf.

"It looks dead-flat out there," I said.

"We go other island."

I trusted his intuition, and soon we were in the skiff with surfboards, Samy driving, bow pointed northeast, skimming across the lagoon in the opposite direction of the open ocean, the island shrinking behind us.

The sun was hot, the wind slight from the south. The weather was perfect. During the hour-long trip, I applied sunscreen three times to my face, shoulders, and calves. Ravia applied it to my back; I envied his skin color, extremely dark and impervious to sunburn.

The motor was loud—we had to yell to talk—so mostly we sat speechless, watching the Solomons go by. Profuse coconut palms, lush mountains, turquoise lagoons...it rivaled the Seychelles in terms of raw beauty. I had seen a few aerial photographs of the Solomons, but nothing had prepared me for this.

Samy veered the skiff into a small bay with a village tucked into its narrow oceanside headland. Behind it, whitewater was clearly visible. We were facing north, not south, with an entirely new set of variables: the swell was from the North Pacific, not the Coral Sea, and the light southerly breeze blew offshore, not onshore. As we motored past the village, I saw women washing clothes, machete-wielding men hacking at coconuts, nude kids singing and running about. As we headed toward the reef pass, it seemed as though something special was about to happen—a travel pinnacle.

"Waves big," Ravia said. He held the Hot Brewz. "I want all my boards big, for place like dis."

Again I thought of Caesar: "You're not going to get any waves in the Solomons, mate."

Ravia set the anchor; Samy had never surfed there. The waves were hollow and back-lit, cheddary orange, a left on the west side of the pass, a right on the east. Regularfoots, Samy and I surfed it; Ravia, a goofyfoot, surfed the left.

Two canoes full of boys from the village paddled out to us, smiling and giggling and flashing the 'thumbs-up'. They were happy to see us. And I was happy—very happy—to see them.

22

DEPARTURE

2002

"The long spear, inserted at the fundament, ran through the man's body, appearing again with the neck. As on a spit, he was slowly singed over a fire, in order that the entire cuticle and all the hair might be removed. The intestines were next taken out, washed in sea-water, wrapped up in singed banana leaves (a singed banana-leaf, like oil-silk, retains liquid), cooked and eaten, this being the invariable perquisite of those who prepared the feast. The body was cooked, as pigs now are, in an oven specially set apart; red-hot basaltic stones, wrapped in leaves, being placed inside to insure its being equally done. The best joint was the thigh."

—William Gill, missionary

TONIGHT, WE DINE on passionfruit and parrotfish. Dehydration, festering reef wounds, and a betelnut daze bolster the scenario.

Chewing the chalky, bitter kernel of this green nut stains teeth, reddens saliva, blurs brain. Kabau, my host and betelnut aficionado, ejects his spit with extraordinary force, accuracy, and aplomb.

"Human flesh is delicious and very sweet," he says. "It was like eating the cassowry bird."

My head spins. Oppressive heat, SP Lager, and two weeks of surf had taken a toll, but the betelnut buzz iced the cake. Known locally as *buai* and generally chewed with lime powder, it's one of the most wretched things I've ever tasted.

Melanesians crave the stuff. Down Port Moresby way, roughly 200,000 nuts are consumed daily. City pavement is splattered with crimson spit stains, as is the dirt floor we sit upon. Kabau invited me into his rickety plywood/aluminum home on the edge of a palm forest as I strolled with sunset, snapping photographs. He welcomed the company of a foreigner.

"First time I saw white man, I was confused. Was this a human? Was it a spirit of the dead coming back to life? I did not know."

He spits again. Twilight wind rustles the palms. Darkness gathers and a candle is lit on a small table beneath a large Bob Marley poster. Lacking electricity, Kabau embraces night through dim touch and sound, surrounded by absolute black until dawn.

Fatigue soon ensues; I opt for sleep. A final spit/rinse/beer swig, and I bid a warm farewell to this man.

"The shoreline will take you to your bed, my friend."

Outside, the ocean, insects, and breeze take me in. Sweet hibiscus fragrance is there; muted weight of thick, wet air presses into all senses. Walk to the sand and reflect on Kabau's solitary, single-flamed alcove on this microscopic island. Yes, island life perseveres—a throwback fragment on the edge of nowhere.

And its surf is good.

> *"…a paradise so unspoiled and sensuous that it could have flowed from the brush of Gauguin."*
>
> —National Geographic

I VISITED PAPUA New Guinea in my imagination before making the actual journey. Then, through the windows of Air Niugini, it presented itself.

The island of New Guinea sprawls like a vast prehistoric bird across the sea north of Australia, its accompanying isles arcing up just below the equator; Papua New Guinea comprises the eastern half of the island (its western half is the Indonesian territory of Irian Jaya), is the world's second-largest island nation after Greenland, and its shape, size, and rugged interior are all the upshot of a peculiar geological history. It is Melanesia's largest and most diverse country, possessing forests and freshwater wetlands equal in world biological importance to those of the Amazon and Congo basins. Seventy percent of the country is dense tropical forest.

Once considered a land of savages and headhunters holding meager value for the western commercial world, today Papua New Guinea is one of the world's conservation hotspots. Its rain forests are the storehouse for nearly five percent of the world's biodiversity, and its ocean and coral reefs harbor some of the world's richest, most diverse marine environments.

The fringe islands to the north lie in a region of important tectonic activity where the large Pacific, Australia and Caroline plates join, separated by a complex of microplates underlying the Bismarck and Solomon seas. Through eons, Australia drifted north, accumulating islands and bits of other continents along its leading edge, and, like debris swept together by a broom, the clutter evolved into a large, chaotic pile of landforms, confirming the resemblance of Papua New Guinea's flora and fauna to Australia's. Abutting southeast Asia, Papua New Guinea lacks rhinos, tigers, and elephants, but it does have endangered tree-dwelling kangaroos.

A pleasant boat ride from Kavieng unveils Nusalik Island, where a surly hornbill welcomes me with a loud squawk and a pair of threatening lunges. Apparently, these large birds aren't fond of humans, especially weird white ones toting cameras and a boardbag. Nonetheless, I locate my mattress unscathed and, drained by three days of near-sleepless travel, fall into a dense 15-hour slumber.

Gleeful voices of four tiny boys inaugurate the next morning. For fun, they ford the channel between Nusalik and Nusa islands, scale a tall overhanging palm tree, and leap from it, laughing, down into the water. Sterile young minds free from Playstations and MTV is a refreshing concept.

Rising with exotic birdsong in the early sun, I wave to the kids. With massive grins, they yell back across the channel.

"Hey, sir! What your name? What your name? Hey, sir! Wooohooo!"

The water, 30 degrees warmer than California's, feels grand. I swim over and step onto the tree, shaking hands with the boys—the happiest, friendliest children I've ever met.

"Surfer! You surfer? Look!"

One of them points excitedly across the channel out to the far shore of Nusalik, where a windpocked left crumbles into coral. I smile and hoot with the boys. One Love Spiritual Upliftment won't be long now.

> *"...the extremes of experience which are often so far removed from daily life elsewhere...."*
> *—David Kirkland*

DREAMING OF TOMORROW, missing today. Picture a delicate Pacific island culture rewound from...us. Our vastly material, monetary influence; our tired timecards and painfully brief lunchbreaks; our gridlocked highways and luxe SUVs; our immense network of communications; our world-altering trends and status quo; our saturated diet and rampant societal obesity; our gross consumerism. Picture this, then picture a licorice-skinned people, unspoilt, at the twilight of their innocence.

"The local crew, yeah...the whole mindset and peoples' values and their judgments, their headspace. Yeah, very primitive in many ways...."

Nick relays his view as we lounge in pitch-blackness beneath a rain-slammed bungalow awning, gazing out across the strait—at nothing, essentially. Nick, sharp and slight-statured, is proprietor of Nusa Island Retreat, a rustic accommodation outfit on the southeast corner of tiny Nusalik Island. Shedding Australian society, he has effectively created a harmonious existence here, with the bungalow retreat a business byproduct of his 1997 homecoming.

"My old man came up here from South Oz when he was young and started working on plantations. Myself, my brother, and my sister were all born just south of here, in Rabaul; we grew up there for 12 years. We didn't even grow up in town—we grew up in the bush, basically, in the jungle on a plantation. No roads. We went to Rabaul every two weeks by boat, stayed a night there, then went back. It was a few hours by boat to Rabaul. Out in the plantation, it was just our family and the local crew. We had neighboring plantations—expatriate guys—but there weren't many kids around, so it was just us three, and all of our friends were local crew, which is something that gave us good familiarity.

"Then we moved back to Australia, learned to surf there, and started living in Australia for quite a long time. Moved up to North Queensland and Victoria, then came back to Papua New Guinea five years ago on a see-the-family/surf trip. That's how we came across this place."

The rain intensifies, pounding the palm frond roof, gurgling in miniature waterfalls down to the sand. We take long pulls of cold beer and absorb the raw vibe of Papua New Guinea's wet season—high summer and the hottest, stickiest time of year, even at this late hour. Beer is consumed quickly, effortlessly. A two-inch-long black beetle lands suddenly from nowhere onto my leg, then flies away. Nick rolls a cigarette and the conversation resumes.

"I've traveled around a bit and I've seen other places in the world that are so-called 'exotic,' and I reckon Papua New Guinea offers that and more in terms of exoticness. Easily. It's better, I reckon, because it's more undeveloped and the local crew are more…just more basic, more traditional. It's not so modern as the rest of the world is. It's different; it's still got it's own thing going on…."

More beer is opened and our words fade. The squall continues; the earth steams. Warm rain, cool sweat, mustiness, mugginess. Thick, tropical darkness allows for olfactory awareness.

Nick nods good-night and leaves me with my thoughts. Two degrees below the equator, a long way from anywhere and surrounded by rain drops, a vision of World War II seeps from the stillness. Not far from here, the ocean floor hosts several famous relics of South Pacific warfare as it were: Loud fighter planes, sinking battleships, bullets, societal unrest, rampant death, unchecked destruction. The South

Pacific campaign of World War II set new standards for savagery in modern warfare when the U.S. Marines landed at Guadalcanal in the Solomon Islands and the Australians repulsed the Japanese advance across New Guinea.

None of this is happening tonight. Out here, in this sweltering 21st century rain forest scene, halcyon harmony of culture and nature embraces a great peace and naivety from the rest of the planet. Today is Sunday, and the islanders' lethargic stride of life slows further to a blithe crawl. It's a sensitive portrait.

> "...*the richest coral life on our planet. These submarine archipelagoes are bathed in the warmest of waters, and the designs of life are fashioned like tapestries.*"
>
> —National Geographic

MONDAY AFTERNOON. ROLLING darkly over the Kavieng coast, an ominous squall line sweeps in from the Bismarck Sea. Whiteout ensues and the session ceases. Was a delightful gig at Nago—chest-high waves working a spell on shallow razor coral. One duck-dive creates a line of shredded fiberglass and fins. Epoxy surfboards withstand great abuse, but the coral insists. Clearly, it's a no-win predicament.

Tuesday morning. Bright, windless, oppressively hot. Heat and humidity differ slightly: morning flows into the afternoon, the afternoon feels like the night and the night unravels to morning. And so on.

We launch the skiff and motor around the point. Out of the stuff of dreams, palms thrust from the white sand lining Nusa Island: their fronds of green, the source of Earth's tropical affiliation; their fantastic nuts, the legacy of these sustenance trees. As sunlight sears the mist, the dawn song of the Bird of Paradise echoes through the flora.

Stepping from the skiff, Pacific salt clears my skin. Instant therapy—stroke down and touch the coral, eye the sky, then reach for the surfboard leash. The beginning of another session sublime. Flawless, head-high lefts loop along the reef, expiring into coral heads on the inside. Melanesian waves induce fantasy, yet this is not. Life imitates postcard.

Papua New Guinea's natural cornucopia is of Oceania's most pristine. A maze of islands, reefs, mangroves, and passes, here lies a marine domain of dazzling fertility. Dangling from the eastern edge of southeast Asia's center of coral reef biodiversity, Papua New Guinea's waters are poorly surveyed, hosting thousands of uncharted of coral reefs—including fringing, barrier, and atoll formations—and is one of the world's most stunning marine habitats, exceeding species known to the Australian Great Barrier Reef, the Hawaiian islands, and the West Indies combined.

Before surfing above one today, I was told that because Kavieng's reefs lie at low latitude, they are hidden from the seasonal cyclone belt and, consequentially, the upper reef slope and reef crest are rarely impacted by extreme high seas. Largely untouched by human activities—a result of the country's low population and absence of material development—Papua New Guinea offers one of the world's few remaining opportunities for conservation of stellar coral reef zones.

A scuba mecca, the number of fish species recorded on single dives here is usually among the highest recorded during rapid ecological South Pacific surveys. Constantly swept with oceanic and tidal currents, Kavieng has a reputation for being the pelagic species capital of Papua New Guinea.

Sweating and scanning for sharks between sets, I sit on my surfboard and marvel at these facts. Several colorful species—staghorn corals, table corals, tree corals, brain corals—coat the ocean bottom, mere inches from my feet. Basslets, parrotfish, wrasses, groupers swarm. A coral Eden, they say, leading the globe in pure coral glory, but falling far short in native surfing population.

In fact, surfing islanders are scarce. Boat driver Stanley, 19, drops anchor and enters the mood. Rare is the small black figure on a thrashed surfboard atop turquoise translucence. This is not the modern Action Sports Retailer surf image. In Papua New Guinea, reality supplants time.

Stanley's people, likely migrants from the Indonesian archipelago, arrived here some 50,000 years ago. They flocked in several waves, and the islands sired a unique effect on cultural texture. Since the bulk of

Papua New Guinea's terrain is quite mountainous and rugged, the islanders evolved in virtual isolation, developing their own languages and tribal cultures, lending Papua New Guinea one of the planet's most diverse and intriguing island demographics. Most still reside in small villages, adhering to traditional tribal customs.

Before the arrival of aircraft, islanders were as isolated from the rest of Papua New Guinea as people living on other continents. Though English is lingua franca in government and schools, the islands feature 800 different pidgin-based dialects.

First contact between white men and the islanders occurred in the early 16th century, when Portuguese explorer Jorge de Meneses sighted the place, naming it Ilhas dos Papuas ("Land of the Fuzzy-Haired People"). However, it wasn't until the mid-1800s that traders and missionaries began settling. Throughout the following decades, Papua New Guinea was claimed by England, Germany, and Holland, finally succumbing to Australia after World War I.

The inland Highland area, thought to be too inhospitable for human habitation, wasn't explored until the 1930s. European gold-seekers instead found a million people living in fertile mountain valleys—cultures steadfast since the Stone Age. By the 1960s, a significant independence movement emerged, and, in 1975, after a brief period of internal autonomy, Papua New Guinea declared full independence.

Stanley realizes none of this. He does, however, realize his reef's charm and ideal symmetry. A regularfoot, lefts are not a problem, evident by his confidence and savvy positioning. Without a DVD or VHS machine for miles in either direction, surf videos are alien things; Stanley draws inspiration and technique from within and from sojourning surfers, mostly Australian. His is a realization of imported stoke, a life path forever altered by the gift of a surfboard.

Skimming fast above the reef, one eye on the horrific coral heads, my own realization of Fletcher's epoxy shaping genius unfolds. Later, wide-eyed Stanley is bequeathed the 6'0" Patagonia fish following his premier interview:

What did you do before you started surfing?

"Before I went out surfing I talk with God first, then I go out surfing."

What do you like most about surfing?

"I like surfing with people happy. We sing and make fun when the waves coming."

Does singing bring the waves?

"Yeah. Singing to make a waves getting bigger. We call it tolak."

Will you surf forever?

"Yeah. On and on."

EVENING SETTLES LIKE song over reef and lagoon. Flanked by palms and fallen coconuts, we sit on the white-sand pocket beach. Young Tim's dark features are aglow with twilight, eyes fixed on the break. Dim rights spin off unridden, unknown. Melanesian outpost. The calm ushers a fishing boat past Long Long, a class barrel that churns during large swell and slack wind.

"Burning Spear....yes, me like Burning Spear. Anthony B, Luciano, Sizzla, Lucky Dube. And Augustus Pablo...*yeesss*." A relaxed white grin.

Sony's Mega Bass speakers thrust deep reggae drum and bass into the Tim psyche. Apt sounds for a paradisical scene, acknowledgement of high Jamaican vibes courtesy a portable boombox. His Bob Marley "Redemption" T-shirt, torn and dirty, reflects Papua New Guinea's massive popularity and engrained faith of reggae music. Rasta tricolors (red, gold, green) are everywhere, and the locals—many dreadlocked—realize the message behind the music. This is Jamaica of the South Pacific.

Behind us, far beyond any road, a faint trail unravels into lush forest. Nightfall arrives and it is time to go. Tim leads the way. A warm, musky, moldy, earthy scent permeates all as we immerse.

Enter his primitive abode, light two candles, and sit on the dirt floor. The boombox chokes on its last batteries after Tim changes the tape; Ras Shiloh now, crooning of Jamaican repatriation to Africa. I explain this to Tim; he assesses the concept and responds.

"This is home. I not surf anywhere but here. We happy but no need go nowhere else. Not have to."

Next morning, Tim paddles out to Nago in his dugout canoe; beaten surfboard balanced on top, his cutoff jeans used for boardshorts. Minimum gear, maximum authenticity.

Essence of a Papuan surfer? Leave your coco palm-encompassed island shack with buai in mouth, untie the canoe line from the tree trunk, and stroke out to the reef unhurried. Anchor in the channel with a rope and stone, then paddle over. Kabau, Tim, and Stanley bring it all home for me: Beginning and ending with paradise, Papua New Guinea is a departure from the modern world.

23

CRATERS AND CARGO CULTS

2004

It was a theory of mine that former cannibals of Oceania now feasted on Spam because Spam came the nearest to approximating the porky taste of human flesh. "Long pig," as they called a cooked human being in much of Melanesia. It was a fact that the people-eaters of the Pacific had all evolved, or perhaps degenerated, into Spam-eaters. And in the absence of Spam they settled for corned beef, which also had a corpsy flavor.

—Paul Theroux, The Happy Isles of Oceania

I WAS EATING enough Spam to fill a coffin—mine, perhaps, if I kept eating it. But it was its pastel pinky mushiness, its greasy fattiness, its immense saltiness and cryptic shelf life that enticed me. Frying Spam in vegetable oil in a rusty griddle on an ancient barbecue outside a moldy bamboo hut with a leaky roof in the muddy middle of nowhere seemed, at the time, to be a rite of passage.

Pacific islanders worship the stuff, after all. I was in Tafea Province, Vanuatu, on the lung-shaped rock of Tanna, on the outskirts of White Grass Village—indeed, where Theroux himself had stayed—seeking surf and culture. A fattish Fijian man in Nadi assured me both existed here in great abundance.

But I was on the windward/wrong side of the island, and anything resembling a wave was torn to bits by the onshores. After four days of crappy food and nights spent in a damp bed, the two things actually in abundance here in July, I learned, were storms and cult fanaticism.

Late that dark fourth day, standing in the rain, preparing my Spam feast under the hut's narrow awning, I was approached by a type of comic infantry. Which in fact it was—an army to appease Jon Frum, the elusive American benefactor whom everybody thought to exist, yet nobody had actually seen. Frum was an anticipated messiah of material riches, essentially a relic from World War II, Tanna's first brush with Americans.

Initially the men startled me, dripping wet, rounding the bend on the grassy track, appearing from the bush. There were thirty of them, short and muscular, from the nearby "Jon Frum village" of Imanaka, marching silently north, past my hut, shirtless and barefoot, on the grass, all wearing either blue or white jeans with black belts, carrying faux bamboo "rifles" capped with bright red paint. The same paint was used to messily tattoo "U.S.A" across their chests and upper backs, smeared from the rain, oozing down to their waistline, like something from a horror film. I later learned that the red paint symbolized America's Red Cross organization, which provided aid to Tanna during the war.

Most folks in the village looked feral, but these men were conspicuously well-groomed—city slickers compared to my nude neighbors and everyone else I'd seen since deplaning from Port Vila, the nation's capital, on Efate Island. There I had also sought surf, with photographer Art Brewer and an official crew for *Surfer* magazine; surf we found, but had no way of riding it due to Air Vanuatu's incompetency, failing to fly our surfboards and clean clothes from Nadi to Vila, a journey of ninety minutes. For a week, our boards sat in Fiji, and we had no choice but to abort the mission.

"I've been wearing the same underwear for a week," Brewer politely confided to the unsmiling woman behind the airport's check-in counter. "Would you like to see it?"

After months of planning, our time on Efate was slated to be quite promising, with Brewer behind the lens and four professional surfers there to perform for him, making their sponsors and the magazine's advertisers happy. In the end, what was set to be a sun-kissed tube orgy in paradise degenerated into a windy, rainy, sedentary binge at the hotel bar.

"This place fuckin' sucks," whinged Brian Toth, the young Puerto Rican, sucking yet another beer down his throat, peering out into the inky rain-pelted misery of the lagoon. Vanuatu sucked so much, in fact, that Toth and accomplice John Robertson managed to evoke a bar brawl in Vila later that night—the trip's cherry-topper, you could say. Even I was having difficulty keeping aggravation subdued. Eventually we returned to Nadi ready to kill something.

But back to Tanna. I was shivering, even in this dusky humidity, flipping Spam slices, seasoning them with pepper. The marchers' faces were of proud conviction, all cleanly shaven, and their hair was not black but rust-colored, a classic symbol of Melanesia's rampant malnutrition.

Knowing their savior lives in the United States, the "Frummers" typically refuse cooperation with Vanuatu's government for fear of compromising fidelity to their enigma. Vast confidence in Frum's ability to replenish any food shortage once provoked the Frummers to corrupt Tanna's economy by practicing succinct pig genocide, eating all of Tanna's available food, and tossing any local currency into the ocean.

This was a quiet, organized procession. The men looked at me knowingly, like I was privy to their gig, but it was not until that evening when Patrick, a dark, young, fat, druggy-looking man from nearby Lenakel, tutored me about Frum and the marchers. I fell into conversation with Patrick as he had strolled past my hut, distracting me from my aimless twilight gaze into the bushes on the other side of the track. Miraculously, the rain had stopped, and I was sitting outside, next to the barbecue, evading the hut's rank mustiness, pondering my next move, which had to occur soon regardless of cost or concern. I had been in Vanuatu for two weeks and had not surfed once. There were waves here, somewhere.

We made eye contact. Recalling the Lonely Planet book's list of basic sayings in Bislama, the local tongue, I said, "Yu save tok tok long Inglis?"—Do you speak English?

He nodded "Halo" with a wide, gapped grin. His had an enormous Afro, like a bizarre black orb of steel wool.

"Dis a cannibal-free zone," he said immediately. This struck me as an odd fact with which to start a conversation with a perfect stranger. His choppy Australian-accented English was dense and difficult to understand, and he slurred thickly, drooling and swaying slightly as he stood next to me. For support, he put his hand on the back of my chair. He was close enough for me to smell his hot, moist, horrible breath.

I looked up at him. "Are you drunk?"

"Nah. 'Sa kava...I drink 'sa kava, yunno. You try? 'Sa kava is da good shit, mate. Yeah."

I said I had several tins of Spam, but none of the famed, narcotic Tanna kava.

"Spam? Feckin' hunks 'a dried lard, mate. Wouldn't eat dat shit if it was da last chuff on da feckin' planet, ay."

Patrick was a recent transplant from Vila, living on Tanna with his locally born wife and their two boys.

"Da kids don' drink 'sa kava yet, yunno. M' papa use to give 'sa kava to me, but I no give it t' da kids, yunno. Make crazy!" He pointed to his Afro and smiled wickedly.

Changing the subject, I asked, "What were those marchers all about a little while ago?"

He laughed, nearly losing his balance. "'Dose guys feckin' crazy, too! Hey! Dey walking f' Jon Frum. Yunno Jon Frum?"

"No. But let me get my notebook."

Patrick proceeded to paint a fairly rough picture of Frum and his followers, people he regarded as lost souls, stuck in the Stone Age. From what I could piece together, no one could agree on Frum's appearance: one man would say Frum was short and thin, with a bald head and no teeth. Another would say Frum was tall and fat, with a beard. It is not known whether he was black or white. Apparently, nobody knows what they are talking about.

"'Sa feckin' myth, yunno."

Some disciples consider Frum a gainful spirit; others see him as a deity on Earth, or the emperor of America. All believe Frum will one day appear to elicit a bounteous, carefree era of limitless "cargo"—pidgin for America's material goods. Anthropologists thusly refer to the Frum phenomenon as a "cargo cult," one of several throughout Melanesia.

Primitive livelihood exemplified Tanna, one of Vanuatu's eighty-three islands, when Captain Cook found it in 1774. Trading ships followed suit, offering trinkets and tools to the natives—gifts that surely came from heaven, they said. The Tannese believed the god who gave the white sailors knives and cloth could never neglect the local people. Many Tannese used Christianity as a hopeful conduit to the sailors' affluence, but the cargo never came.

Frustration festered, peaking in 1940 with creation of the Frum cult. Proselytizers forecasted Frum's arrival on Tanna, and, in 1942, World War II graced the island's volcanic shores. American troops descended onto adjacent islands, ushering food, jobs, weapons, pre-fabricated homes, and an armada of jeeps. To the islanders, Frum's day had arrived.

But with the war's end, military cargo evaporated, and the Tannese glumly resumed their quest. Some reverted to mock army exercises with the intent of seducing GIs and their cargo-packed boats back to Tanna.

Though Frum has failed to arrive within the past sixty-five years, his people remain loyal, often blaming his truancy on their own faults or Vila's governmental interference, which the Tannese abhor. They say their government's ploy to extinguish the cult only supports a dogma that European officials contend to keep the Tannese deprived of cargo. Frummers hence adhere to Frum, daydreaming of brighter lives, while their Western detractors view the cult as plunging steadily toward fictitious promises and an imminent, bitter letdown. I tend to agree. So does Patrick.

"So no Jon Frum since 'sa war, yunno?" he shrugged. "'Sa fake man. 'Dese Tanna people crazy, mate. Evr'one dem feckin' crazy!"

I gazed back across to the bushes on the other side of the track. Time was running out. Today was Tuesday. My return flight to Vila was Friday. I vowed to leave White Grass Village first thing the next day.

I DIDN'T GET far—via an overcrowded public minibus, to Tanna's opposite side—but at least it was leeward, and in the swell-blessed month of July, a surfable wave was bound to exist.

My seatmate during the bumpy drive east was Joseph, a remarkably filthy and pale Scot, who had traveled alone from Edinburgh to Tanna to witness the eruption of Mount Yasur, hyped in tourist brochures as the "world's most accessible volcano." He sucked on cigarette after cigarette, as if he would asphyxiate from inhaling oxygen, puffing his whiskery cheeks like a blowfish whenever he exhaled. The three infected-looking warts on his right cheek glared at me. His scary, bloodshot, deep-set eyes met mine.

"Y' wan' a fookin' ciggy, mate?"

"No thanks. I don't smoke."

"None a' ya fookin' Yanks smoke, eh." He raised an eyebrow. "Worried 'bout yer fookin' health, are ya?"

"Sure."

As luck would have it, the volcano was only a mile or two from my accommodation, the tidy Turtle Bay Inn at Sharks Bay. (Apparently there were just as many turtles as there were sharks in this secluded, pretty spot.) Considerably upscale from my rotten White Grass hut, this Francophile cluster of wooden bungalows, a relative splurge at thirty-five dollars per night, was a welcome relief from Spam and mold. Here I could sleep on dry sheets, insect-free, enjoy fine cuisine in the hotel restaurant, and avoid the neurotic Frummers. And however hard the wind was blowing, I knew it would be offshore at Yatana, described thusly in my Lonely Planet book:

> *Another path brings you onto a top surf beach starting at Yatana and running into Yankaren Para with deep heavy swells along 2.5km of white-sand beach. Surfing groups from Australia come here, and a surfing film was made in 2002.*

THE MINIBUS DEPOSITED me at my hotel; Joseph was staying just up the road, at the Port Resolution Yacht Club.

"I ain' no fookin' sailor, mind, but I cun fookin' bleddy well drink like u'n, eh."

"Sounds good," I said. The bus drove away.

I checked into my bungalow then went for a short walk to Yatana Beach. No one I queried along the way had heard of the mythical Australian surf film, and, when I found the beach, there certainly were no groups of Aussies occupying the lineup.

It was flat. Groomed by the light offshore wind, yes, but flat. Drenched in sweat, I went for a swim in the clear blue water, marveling at the schools of colorful fish and the sharp coral that would happily impale me should I fall on a wave; that is, if the waves came. I had waited this long—what's another day?

Besides, Port Resolution was idyllic, and the beach fronting my hotel was deserted. I could settle in for a gourmet French dinner, washed down with a few pints of ice-cold Tusker, Vanuatu's "premium export beer," and admire another psychedelic South Pacific sunset from the comfort of my hammock. Anything, really, was better than solemn Frummers and burnt Spam.

Soiling my most optimistic of assumptions, Jon Frum zealotry lingered in this corner of Tanna as well. Clearly, there was no respite but to vacate the island, which I was to do in forty-eight hours: back to Vila, then Nadi and LAX.

But I had to surf. Only once, damnit, now that I had my surfboards. All this time and money and travel couldn't amount strictly to hefty bar tabs and bizarre social conduct. Yatana, the island's "top surf beach," had to produce something surfable, right?

A hot sunrise, a cold breakfast, and another sweaty walk to Yatana revealed the Pacific to be...well, pacific. On tap was another ten hours of surfless daylight. I went for a restorative swim, yearning for a mask and snorkel—Tanna's sea was explicitly untouched, and I was pleased to be there.

PLAN B: A HIKE up the Mount Yasur volcano. The hotel offered a local guide to take me there, to witness Yasur's smoky throat and perhaps see it spew molten lava.

We left the hotel at noon, with no hats or sunscreen, in the searing heat. Russell, my stocky, impish guide, age thirty, was indifferent to this. His skin was noticeably darker than most Vanuatuans', like someone from central Africa, and sunscreen to him was useful only to sell at exorbitant prices to tourists like me. But today he had none to sell. Fortunately, I still had a white, long-sleeved shirt to again spare my tortured Caucasian pigment.

We drove his boxy, rusted green sedan up a serpentine track to the volcano's carpark, a barren field. As we walked up the rugged trail from the carpark to the volcano's rim, Russell disclosed the following: his forefathers had thought Mount Yasur to be a sanctuary for holy spirits (*yasur* is a local word for "God"). Nowadays, young Tannese like Russell firmly believe that Yasur's fiery depths host approximately five thousand Jon Frum soldiers, ready to blast into action should Frum ever actually appear.

Clearly, no place on Tanna was exempt from this guy. The Tannese truly believed in him, like an elusive saint from the obese consumer-land of SUVs and Wal-Mart. If American material items were sacred to the Tannese, Wal-Mart would undoubtedly be their house of worship. Thankfully, Wal-Mart has yet to find Vanuatu.

"You seen Jon Frum, Mister Michael?" Russell's face gleamed with sweat.

"No, but you will be the first to know if I do."

"He in United States. Where you have home. Maybe Jon Frum your neighbor?"

I explained that I lived on a farm and had few neighbors.

"Maybe he go to your church?"

I don't go to church. Doubtful Frum does, either.

The day grew hotter the higher we hiked, thanks to the volcano, and we had no drinking water. We were sweating. Not to worry: the summit—the stark ash rim—was upon us.

There, amidst immense guttural burps emitted from Yasur's scorching bowels, we stood and watched the foul-smelling sulfuric smoke and bubbling orange lava a dim half-mile down. This felt like the hottest moment in Earth's history. I was verging on heatstroke. Russell was unaffected.

"When Jon Frum come, nobody have to live down there any more."

"His men must be hot in this crater," I said, panting. "They must wear some sort of protective clothing." Russell nodded sagely.

Seeking a souvenir, I stooped and plucked a rough hunk of dried black lava, about the size of a marble. Russell prohibited me from pocketing the specimen; he said it possessed a potent magic, and every local shaman has a cache of these rocks, each labeled with a distinct usage, like painless healing, good harvests, and coercing favorable winds.

Speaking of favorable wind, it was still offshore. I advised Russell that I was very uncomfortable; he said we could leave at any time, as he had done this hike hundreds of times, often with tourists more unfit than I, and, frankly, he was sick of doing it.

"Why don't you quit, then?"

"I very like working outside."

"How about farming or fishing?"

"Make me too tired."

On the way back to my hotel, I asked him if we could stop at Yatana for a brief surf-check. He obliged, and we took to the wide trail.

"I try surfing one time," Russell said sullenly. "Was here at Yatana. I not like it. Reef very sharp. Wave too big." He held his hand over his head. I took this as a positive gesture.

"Do the waves get big very often?"

"Yes, many time. They big today!"

We soon faced a tranquil azure sea, begging for swell. The afternoon sun reflected brilliantly off the water, beaming straight into our burnt eyeballs. The beach was perfect, tropical, empty, serene—just like any beach without wave action. Lake Casitas came to mind.

"Mister Michael, maybe you go pray to Jon Frum for big wave?"

Not bloody well likely.

FINAL MORNING. DEFEATED, at wit's end, literally and figuratively, lounging in the bed of my pleasant air-conditioned bungalow. My unzipped boardbag sulked in the corner of the room. Rising for coffee, I considered the bright side: At least I won't have to repack it for the trip home.

I also considered Russell's advice, to implore Frum for waves. Now, I am not a religious man, and I rarely pray—especially to an imaginary, elderly American World War II veteran who is seen by an obscure people to be the god of junk. Goodness knows I didn't need more of that.

But waves are not junk. Nor are they material items, available in the bargain bin at your local Wal-Mart. So how could Jon Frum provide them? It was impossible.

In my pathetic state, I knelt in front of the coffee maker and prayed anyway.

And so went the walk to the trailhead leading to Yatana Beach. I brought my 6'0" fish board, just in case. Stepping closer to the beach, I heard a slight muffle noise, like waves breaking. The sound grew louder by the minute, the distinct cracking of lip onto trough, and then....

Frum must be real! He smiles upon Tanna. He is surely alive and well, living in America, possibly even in Santa Barbara, California.

How do I know? After my third dry frontside barrel (slight exaggeration) off of the A-frame peak, it became all too obvious: Jon Frum is a surfer. I had perhaps seen him at Rincon, riding a glossy eleven-foot board shaped by Skip Frye, with a large red cross painted on both sides of it. He had a mustache and wild gray hair, like Einstein, and he had dropped on me numerous times the previous winter. I couldn't forget someone like that.

So the next time you are surfing Rincon in a horrendous crowd—which it will be—look for the geezer on the huge red-crossed Frye. It may be Jon Frum, the guy you read about here. After he's snaked you four times, paddle up to him and ask: If I pray to you, Mr. Frum, will you make all of these surfers vanish and provide me swell for the rest of the year?

His reply?

Not bloody well likely.

PART

VI

Caribbean

24

HOW ARE YOU LOVING THE WAVES SO FAR?

2011

SPARKING A SPLIFF is tough while driving an open-windowed jeep. But we're being bumped slowly—Billy can light and puff and also steer with his left knee. The A4 is a prosaic mosaic of puddles and potholes.

"It's nice," he says, "for it being the main highway. Yunno?" He flicks ash out the window.

This narrow vein threads fragrant green fields of Jamaica's finest. It skirts the lush, brooding John Crow Mountains. It fords historic burgs like Yallahs and Golden Grove and their loose storefronts and tiny pubs, the barber shops, the gas stations, old slavery plantations. It fronts rusty jerk-meat grills and mounds of burning trash, miles of sugarcane, loud waterfalls, craggy cliffs, the blue Caribbean, fruit stands, idle people.

Often, like today, Billy rolls the A4 while listening to songs by Mystic Revealers, his old reggae band of global fame. He sings along with his recorded lyrics and, often, he's spotted by folks along the road—"Hey, Rastaman!" they shout. "Love, love, love!" In Jamaica, Billy is a star.

Slouched in the back seat with their iPods are Shane and his pal Ivah, Billy's youngest. They will say little during our two-hour, 60-mile-drive from the south coast's Bull Bay, where Billy lives, to the north coast. Today the south coast is lake-flat, but windswell from Tropical Storm Emily, a big rainmaker for Puerto Rico and Hispaniola, is jolting Jamaica's surf hub of Boston Beach.

"This is the flattest the sea has been in three years, mon," Billy says in Port Morant. He spells it out. "F-l-a-a-a-a-t. Normally you see whitewater all over the place."

"On flat days down here, where do you look for surf?"

"When it's this small, mon, we smoke weed and chill out and wait for swell. Or we go north."

The east of his isle is lush but broken. "Saint Thomas is a neglected parish," he says, blowing smoke from his nose. "No tourism or any industry over here. It used to be big for sugarcane, for banana, but not any more. And the Goodyear tire factory closed down. That's why surfing is embraced here. It's something Montego Bay *cannot* take away from us. Negril *cannot*. Ocho Rios *cannot*."

Ah, Jamaica's trio of tourist havens, deep with suave resorts and bright white sand. Tourism is the island's main revenue, after all—2010 saw two million visitors, virtually all to the three zones Billy named, and 2011 is projected to welcome three million land-based and cruise-ship souls. "If you fly into Montego Bay, you see loads of white people," he says. "But you flew into Kingston, yeah? The people there probably thought you picked the wrong airport."

I was the only surfer and the only non-black in the JetBlue plane and in Norman Manley International because, if they don't surf, white tourists avoid Jamaica's south and east coasts. The beaches are windy and rocky, crime abounds, the roads are bad, there are no swim-up bars nor golfing greens. And much of the beach zone has been thrashed by hurricanes—a bad place to build another Sandals (Jamaica has seven).

"Ever been in a hurricane?" Billy asks me.

"Nope. Don't want to."

"You have to experience one to really know what it's like. Imagine the wind blowing 160 miles an hour for four hours! Anything that isn't bolted down, moves. It crumples steel and cement like aluminum foil, mon. It destroys every'ting."

As the pavement smooths (Billy: "We're heading into the main tourist area—the road's good for them."), the A4 snakes inland around Innes Bay and past the turn-off for Reich Falls, past the fishing village of Manchioneal, and again it greets the Caribbean at Long Bay, a long fetch of mostly unsurfable coast. Facing northeast, however, it is ribbed by blue, tit-high windswell. Thank you, Emily.

There are some spots here and there, Billy says. "Usually nothing worth the drive."

This volcanic east fringe is wild and corrugated, known, among other things, for its sea caves and the spicy scent of jerk pork embedded in the breeze. Boston Beach, which suddenly pops into view off the road's right side, would be easy for another driver—a tourist, say—to miss its turquoise-hued, C-shaped cove flanked by steep, green bluffs.

Billy parks us in the small, littered cement lot at the base of the hill fronting the surf. There's a left off the north side and a right off the south. Occasionally they meet in the middle. They're bumpy and backwashy. Many closeouts. The left looks a bit longer and steeper, but, as regularfooters, Shane and I opt for the right.

"How are you loving the waves so far?" he asks me after I catch a few bad ones. "Good, eh?"

"Yes, irie. I'm loving it."

"It's so *good*, mon! We all getting some good ones, yeah?"

On a short orange thruster, Shane surfs with strength and fluidity. Most of his friends too are skilled—floaters, airs, carves, snaps. I am impressed. The performance level rivals any Orange County hotbed. Out killing the left-handers, Icah, Billy's oldest son, has been called "the Rob Machado of Jamaica."

It was Machado who, in 2004's *A Broke Down Melody*, said "the future of surfing is gonna come from places that you least expect." This is the same film that introduced many—including me—to Jamaican surf. On a map, the island's small encircling sea doesn't seem to ooze waves. And it doesn't, really. But it does. Enough to afford the annual Makka Pro surf contest and two national contest series; a Jamaican representation at the World Surfing Games, at the ISA World Junior Surfing Championships, and at the Pan American Surfing Games; a thriving Jamaican Surfing Association, a surf camp or two, surf lessons, surfboard rentals, high school surf programs, corporate surf sponsorships, surfboard shapers, and a lot of obsessed kids.

"See?" Billy says after my short session. We're standing in the shade by his jeep. "The youths are killing it, mon. This is the future right here."

The late-day sun behind us floods the cove with bright, photogenic color. Like he often does, Billy videos the kids. It's important for them.

He lights a spliff as a family of white Floridians approaches. They're staying at Sandals in Ocho Rios and drove to Boston to taste its famous jerk meat. The mother is shocked—she didn't know surfing was so popular in Jamaica. Her two young sons seem intrigued by Billy's joint—marijuana is illegal where they come from. Her husband, rotund and unathletic, asks about renting a board and having a surf lesson here.

"There's your man," Billy says, pointing to a young dreadlocked surfer doing push-ups on the cement. I'd seen him out ripping. The kid's got a spliff between his lips.

PART VII

Asia

25

ALL IS POSSIBLE, MY FRIEND

2007

TRANSSEXUALS, EARTHQUAKES, AND plane crashes rarely occur during surf trips. But then you visit Thailand and realize that it's really nothing you'd expected it to be.

Our plan was hatched amid boredom of seeing the 19,046th photo of perfect Mentawais, and certainly to us Bali and the rest of Indonesia were considered ancient news. So, seeking a bit of non-Indo Asian flair, a new place in which to surf-search, Burkard and I unfurled a map to see which countries had already been covered in surf magazines—Philippines? Check. Japan? Check. India-Sri Lanka-Maldives-Russia-Taiwan-Vietnam-China-Malaysia-Andamans-Nicobars? Check. Korea and Cambodia sucked, and we weren't about to try Borneo. We'd heard that some Christian dudes were planning a surf/missionary trip to Bangladesh, and even Burma had been done years before in *The Surfer's Journal*. Apparently the Asian bone had been picked clean.

But then I remembered the guy who did that Burma article, famed surf photographer John Callahan, and that once upon a time he'd spoken of a place called Phuket, a lush, mountainous island that was a province of Thailand, hovering above Sumatra in the Andaman Sea. Not known for surf, this so-called "Pearl of the Orient" was also Mega

Touristville, attracting millions of visitors annually to its palmy shores, offering every sort of outdoor pastime from diving to fishing to hiking to elephant riding. But surfing?

"Phuket definitely has waves," Callahan told me. "It's consistent during the southwest monsoon; September is the best time."

On my 2007 calendar, September was a blank slate. On the map a finger drifted slowly from Burma down to Phuket. "Dude," I said to Burkard, "here's where we're going."

"Thailand? My grandparents just went there," he said. "I saw their photos and, dude, the place looks sick!"

The game was set. Interested players were California's Warren Smith, Florida's Sterling Spencer, and Australia's Dion Atkinson, a strange but sober crew that was keen for an Asian gamble. Each landing from different time zones, we gathered in a resort at Surin Beach, a pretty cove on Phuket's northwest coast where smiley Thai women offered hour-long massages, where skinny Thai prostitutes told sob stories of poverty and lost love, where fat Western tourists sizzled on white sand beneath equatorial sun. Surin was a quiet pocket of paradise, its coconut palms leaning gently toward the warm turquoise ocean, the vacant beachbreak, the rocky, wooded headlands at each end of the cove offering epic backdrops for surf shots.

"This place is a frickin' studio," Burkard said our first day.

"We need swell," purple-haired Smith said. "Either that or a serious case of Thai food mud-butt."

Atkinson was hoping his luck would shift from bad to good in Thailand. Fresh from a WQS event in Portugal, where all his boards had been stolen, he'd been having some issues with his girlfriend, who happened to be on holiday in Phuket at the same time we were there. The jovial Aussie walked with a heavy heart.

And on our second night, poor Spencer became shackled to the toilet in his hotel room, victim to a food-borne parasite that forced things out both ends for 24 hours straight. Smith only dreamed of such luck.

OUR ARRIVAL COINCIDED with mild weather and a hideous flat spell. Being the height of monsoon season, the surf was a blustery six feet a day or two before we came, but after looking at online marine forecasts, it was determined that we were in for a lot of downtime, even if that meant perfect, windless, sunny days. The last thing we needed was calmness, though, because in Thailand you need wind to make waves, and we had vowed to prove the skeptics wrong. "Why Thailand?" they'd ask. "You can't surf there. Just go to Bali—it's been firing all season."

Burkard and I pointed out that Phuket had its own surf community, surf shops, even a pair of yearly surf contests. And if you looked online, you could find several photos of good Phuket waves—"good" being a relative term, but good enough for what we needed—so it was obvious that surfing is possible in Thailand, especially in September. Theoretically.

Meteorologically we were screwed. We needed wind and rain and thunderstorms, the kind of unsettled climate monsoons produce. One perfect morning at Kata Beach, a happy Thai man raised an arm above his head and said, "Two days ago, waves this big!" Kata was supposedly Phuket's best swell magnet, yet here it was, offering translucent knee-slappers in peak swell season.

I needn't bore you with the details of the ensuing week, a calculated exercise in time-killing, bane of all editorial surf trips: eating, sleeping, TV-watching, skimboarding, swimming, shopping, driving, sight-seeing, elephant rides, surfing one-foot dribble, and getting massages. Thailand is world-famous for its soft and talented hands, and female masseuses can be found at any beach or on any street in one of Phuket's countless massage parlors. At $9 a pop, you really can't go wrong, especially when they cost $90 at home, and especially when you're a wee stressed from spending time and money touristing dry in a land of fickle surf. In Phuket, time was money, and for success we really needed a bit more of both.

BUT NO TRIP to Phuket is complete without a Saturday night in Patong, the island's infamous hub of human excess and commerce, an overcrowded cluster of markets, tailor shops (*Two Suits For $90!*), massage parlors, nightclubs, convenience stores, and restaurants spanning two kilometers of beach. Halfway through the trip we needed some cultural fusion, and since Smith was interested in hiring a transsexual to hang with us, just for fun, the chances of finding one were guaranteed in Patong, land of ladyboys.

"We've got to get one and just have her hang out with us for a whole day," Smith said. "I mean, how killer would that be?"

"How do you know it would be a 'her'?" Spencer asked.

"Fifty bucks to find out," I said.

From Surin we caught a *tuk-tuk* taxi to Patong, a 30-minute ride south. First priority was dinner, which we ate street-side while being pestered constantly by passing hawkers, who sold everything from oversized lighters to funny masks to magic wallets to fake jewelry. It was all junk from China, stuff nobody needed, but one thing the sellers needed was money, and, the town crawling with tourists, goodness knows Patong was full of it this night.

The town became increasingly crowded as the hours wore on. We walked up and down the streets, past stores selling knives and sabers, brass knuckles and throwing stars, avoiding the Thais who pushed flyers in our faces. "Free show! My friend! Come! Naked girl! My friend!" Or: "What's up, friend? You follow me. I have special present to show you."

"I never knew I had some many friends in Thailand," Atkinson said as we thumbed through a massive selection of counterfeit T-shirts.

At all the bars were scandalous and scantily-dressed women, most of them pale and bony, either gawking at male passersby or entertaining the fat white man whose lap they were sitting on. Invariably these women were the men's companions for the night or the duration of their holiday, and a common sight in Phuket is a young Thai woman holding hands with an old, fat, ugly white guy who can't get a woman back home. She's getting her bills paid, he's getting laid, and everyone's happy. Or so it seemed.

Saturday night Patong stunk of vomit and incense, Thai food, spilt beer, cigarette smoke. Loud rap music pulsated from all angles. Every bar was packed with sweaty drunk people. Locals thought we were Australian, greeting us with, "How ya goin', mate?", but once they learned we (Atkinson exempted) were American, they'd say, "Yo, what's up, man?"

Hookers tried to get our attention, cooing at us when we passed by—to them, Five-White-Dudes-With-No-Girls was a delicious target. Of course, being the sober, religious, loyal group we were, we declined.

Giggly masseuse girls grabbed our shoulders—"Mista! You wan' massage now! Good price!"—at every corner. But it was getting late, and Burkard took a vote; four wanted to leave, I wanted to stay because my back hurt. So when they left, I walked to the nearest massage parlor where a cute girl outside pinched my arm, flashed a big smile, and asked, "You want massage?"

"Very much so."

She led me into a dingy back room of individual stalls, each enclosed by a blue curtain, with a dirty mattress on the cement floor. We went into one of the stalls and she asked me to strip; I laid on my stomach and she placed a small red towel over my rear. Mui was cute and petite, from northeast Thailand, and had only worked in crazy Patong for four days.

"How did you learn to do massage?" I asked as she applied oil to my back.

"I go to Wat Pho Massage School in Bangkok. Everybody know it. But some girl go to other school. I went to best one." Judging from her expert technique, she wasn't lying.

She asked how old I was; I asked her to guess. She said 27, I said 32. I asked her her age, guessing 18, to which she smiled and clapped her hands: "Yes, thank you!" Mui was 22.

A Chinese man entered the stall next to ours. He spoke demandingly to his masseuse: "Sex? No sex?" She said no.

"Chinese always talk so loud," Mui whispered. Then she poked my leg. "I want white skin. I don't want to be brown. Brown is not good."

"What? Brown skin is very good," I said.

She lived in an apartment in which her roommate—a hooker—regularly brought guys home. "No good there," Mui said. "And I pay for it!"

"How much?"

"I pay 3,000 baht for one month there."

Mui gave me two separate massages—one oil, one Thai. I was there for more than two hours, chatting while being rubbed and contorted. It felt good, but not as good as if the boys had bagged some surf shots earlier that day, or that week. It had been a dismal run thus far, but by the looks of it, not as dismal as Mui's daily reality. In the end I gave her 3,000 baht for her rent, plus 650 baht for the massages.

"You nice man," she said, handing me her phone number. "Hopefully you not lose this."

Better than losing my mind in Patong.

A FEW SURFLESS days later, when the wheels really fell off, we caved in and hired a jet ski. Wonder began about whether this would become a "tow-at" trip (perish the thought). Was this really happening? Were we paying some Thai dude a large amount of cash in an attempt to get some shots in knee-high waves? Dumb mistake.

"It's so hard to shoot," Burkard said after 20 minutes. "It's too small. We're over this."

As we packed up, four young bikinied women sauntered down and sat on some beach chairs beneath an umbrella. To attract our attention, one of them clapped her hands and pulled her top town, then made a pinching motion with her fingertips as if to ask whether we'd like to feel her breasts, which upon glance later, were clearly fake. At this point I thought they were girls, but a local man grinned and asked me, "You like ladyboys?"

"Those are all women?"

"Yes!"

"Are you sure?"

"If you do not believe me, you can find out!" He howled with laughter.

Another one of them suggestingly removed her sarong revealing a black bikini and very skinny legs (no hips). She strolled down to the water's edge and spun around so we could see "her" whole body, then she looked at us, smiled, and waved.

I asked the man, "Do they have dicks?"

"No, most get removed in surgery."

"They are all girls?"

He was laughing and nodding. "All girls!"

I looked closer and could see that their faces really were in fact masculine, but with gobs of makeup. I asked Smith to go talk to them so I could photograph the spectacle.

"Man, I just can't, dude. That shit's not right."

What was right was the darkening sky and the increasing wind. It appeared that soon all climatic hell would unleash, and that was good—we required waves, and we had only a few days left. Late that day the clear blue sky clogged itself with thick black clouds, hard rain fell, and the wind started to blow. And then the earth shook (or so we were told, because we felt nothing).

Apparently a quake registering 8.4 on the Richter scale had rumbled the sea floor off southern Sumatra, it and its aftershocks eventually killing 21 people and destroying buildings in Bengkulu. Tremors were felt in Phuket, so Prime Minister Surayud Chulanon issued a tsunami warning, but since Phuket was so sheltered by Sumatra, the precaution was futile. Still, people were panicking, telling us to stay out of the water, which was absurd since the quakes coincided with our trip's biggest waves. So we surfed, photographed, and got happy. Meanwhile there were mini-tsunamis elsewhere, deaths in Sumatra, and in coastal Indo, people ran for the hills.

The whole thing felt like Armageddon—earthquakes, fatalities, gales, blinding rain, thunder and lightning, black clouds—and it was all a bit stressful, but in the end it was what we needed because the storms directly affected the surf size. A Surin lifeguard even went as far to say we'd scored the best waves he'd ever seen at his beach.

For the ensuing few days the rain was nearly non-stop, but since it was so warm, nobody cared. Unfortunately it was too much for the pilot of a 24-year-old McDonnell Douglas MD-82 plane operated by One-Two-Go Airlines. On the afternoon of September 16, he had flown 123 passengers and seven crewmembers from Bangkok to Phuket. Landing in a thick squall, his plane skidded off the runway and burst into flames, killing 89 people, most of them foreigners. It was Thailand's deadliest aviation disaster in 10 years.

We were scheduled to leave Phuket two days later, but authorities had temporarily closed the airport. "What's next?" became our group's big question.

The next day we lunched in an Australian-owned restaurant/hotel, a place we'd eaten at several times. The owner, normally a friendly Sydneyite, looked quite glum this day, and rightly so. Several people killed in that plane crash were regular customers of his, often staying in his hotel, eating in his restaurant, and instead of checking into their rooms last night, they were locked in refrigerated containers at the airport.

"Last week you guys probably sat here and ate lunch next to some of them," he told us.

Authorities said that wind shear was the accident's likely cause, and it was that wind which made the waves we had enjoyed so much.

EQUALLY SOBERING WAS the sight of the plane wreckage as we took off from Phuket Airport. Our aircraft, a new and sturdy Boeing 737 flown by Thai Airways, gave us little relief as takeoff was rather rough, the plane shuddering and weaving as it penetrated the storm. It was a nail-biting ascent, but soon we were above the clouds, gliding weightlessly through stark blue, the problems of Phuket left miles behind.

My seatmate on the flight to Bangkok was an elderly Thai man who spoke good English. I told him about our journey. He had seen most of the world but always returned home, because to him Phuket was the end of the rainbow. During our days there, we could see why, but other realities of the place threw us for individual head spins. Two weeks prior we'd arrived on the island not knowing what to expect—ultimately we expected the unexpected, and that's what Thailand gave us.

"It sounds like you boys had an interesting trip." The man was adding salt to his beer. "In Thailand, all is possible, my friend."

Somewhere over Japan, we whipped out a laptop and looked at Burkard's photos.

26

REASONING RUSSIA

2009

"*NYET!*" THE FAT frizzy-haired customs wench wrinkled her nose and scowled behind the glass of her Vladivostok airport booth, raising the open passport of photographer Chris Burkard to eye level. "This not good!" she hissed at him, a long red fingernail pointing to the Entry From date on his $236 Russian Federation visa. Apparently the authorities back in America had misprinted the day Burkard was to arrive—technically he wasn't allowed into the Rossiyskaya Federatsiya for another two days.

Burkard was to be placed on the next flight back to Seoul, South Korea, leaving in 45 minutes. But after a futile two-hour hash with authorities upstairs, someone said, "It is time to go," and Burkard was pushed outside by three armed airport guards. The rainy sky was a darkening burnt gray, silhouetted with industrial smokestacks, whorls of brown mist, and pristine mountain ranges of the Primorsky Krai. The air was cool and a touch humid, the gale strong from the southeast, a wave-making wind.

"Zis big problem for you," the tallest guard said as he strong-armed the stout Amerikanski into the small holding cell near the airport, a converted hotel room with no fresh air or door handle but five deadbolts and a skeleton key used by a rude one-eyed bald policeman with teen-style face zits. The cell's toilet leaked and the cement floor was wet; there were bars on the cracked window and there would be no room service. The linens were stained and stinky. The cop locked the door and walked away.

Eight hours later, around 1 a.m., there came a knock. A guard opened the door and made a spooning pantomime up to his mouth. "*Eda?*"—food? "*Da,*" Burkard replied. he'd learned a few Russian words—*da* meant "yes"—from a friend back home. He'd also spent the past several hours adding $2,000 to his cell phone bill alternating between the U.S. embassy, Korean Airlines, and his frantic wife, who could do nothing from home in California. But finally they would feed him, and the guard banged a plate of tepid gut-scratching stew called *solyanka*, a cube of meat, and cold dried cucumbers onto the steel table next to the leaky toilet.

Still the rain fell.

In the afternoon Burkard exited the cell and was sent back to Seoul, where he overnighted at a sauna inside Incheon International Airport, returned to Vladivostok the following day, and concurrently missed the majority of waves of our two-week trip, thanks to a tiny visa-page date mistake.

Better late than never? *Nyet!*

> *"It had always been a city of delay and death, and now it was poverty-stricken as well, distant, out of touch."*
>
> —*Paul Theroux,* Ghost Train to the Eastern Star, 2007

PERHAPS VLADIVOSTOK COULD look strange in late summer—sunny, warm, windless, welcoming. Yet in February 2007, during his second visit amid wintry slush and soot and long lack of light, the hub of Russia's Far East turned a dour face to Mr. Theroux, the famous travel writer who had first passed Vladivostok in a train 33 years prior. In 2007 the city of 600,000 was still 6,000 miles from Moscow, but it was indeed a different Russia, a detached state, a distant culture that had barred tourists until 1992, the year the Soviet Union collapsed into independent nations, bleeding civil freedom from Cold War communist wounds. Theroux's second impressions, however, were not edifying.

For us in August and September 2009, amid this New Russia, with the world's biggest country enjoying the liberalizing reforms of ex-Soviet President Mikhail Gorbachev's *perestroika* ("reorganization") and *glasnost* ("openness"), Vladivostok looked as bright and prosperous as any cosmopolitan city, especially one that closely resembled California's San Francisco. There were the picturesque buildings, the graffiti, the crisscrossed trolley wires above the streets, loud motorcycles, people shouting, cars honking, the steep roads, wailing car alarms, scent of diesel, squawking seabirds, bird shit, techno music, dirty crowded public buses, the railway, the scenic vistas, leafy parks, gesticulating statues, the hills and harbor, the container ships and the naval fleet, the cold fog and the breezy surrounding saltwater bay. Geographically Asian, surrounded by China, Japan, and North Korea, Vladivostok showed little Asian influence, though few Asians walked its streets—Russia was vastly Caucasian. But there was plenty of cheap China-made junk for sale, Japan was good at blocking Pacific groundswells, and North Korea was just nasty, a nation of nuclear, the dusky horizon presence on a clear summer day.

Vladivostok was a sublime city you could explore and stay in awhile, necessary considering its outlying coast received swell only a handful of days yearly. By global standards, Russia's Far East was one of the most difficult places to find waves, and we were lucky to even get wet. Our first two (and sans-Burkard) days revealed myriad set-ups and potential galore—north of Vladivostok, the forested Primorsky Krai coast was old and so it was not sheer, its pretty white-sand beaches gently undulating out into flat, refined reefs, pointbreaks, quirky slabs, and chocolate-box beachbreaks. One of these provided an afternoon of offshore peaks, and it was pure chance that we happened to have stopped for lunch there—in 20 minutes the surf went from onshore slop to crisp head-high fun. A fleeting glimpse of what Russia could be but rarely is.

On our third day, at last with Burkard in tow, Californians Josh Mulcoy and Mike Losness studied the blue East Sea at the end of a bumpy dirt road. And they saw nothing. In the lee of Japan, the water had died. Japan's east coast was windy and pumping, but Internet promises of typhoon swells, southeast gales, rain, and short-period, two-meter pulses only amounted to the finest summertime holiday weather Russia could offer: lake-flat, oily glass, 80°F on the sand, topless women in thongs, barbecues, boats, children amok, cold beers for a dollar in the beachfront kiosks. We tanned and drank, partied with Andrey and the boys at the windsurfing school, had an impromtu soccer game (USA: 10, Russia: 9) on rustic island in the south.

One morning we drove far to the north, to a spot with excellent swell and wind exposure. En route we were nearly arrested for having breakfast in a military town. "And zere are no waves in zee forecast," our driver/friend said slowly while we sat in his car at the surfless but scenic cove that took six dirt-road hours to reach. "Zis is bad." He chuckled. He was serene Valera, Vladivostok's first surfer, excited to have witnessed Losness and Mulcoy surfing the previous day. They were the first foreigners to ride waves near his hometown. Excited too was the lovely blonde Olga, the city's first wahine, our trusty translator and overall fixer. More than anyone, though, Valera knew his zone's requirements for rideable swell, and throughout the rest of our trip there were enough false-start days to kill even the strongest optimism. The much-needed typhoon never happened. The wind blew lightly and the sun cooked, and Buoyweather.com lent no hope. When the East Sea went flat, it went f-l-a-t.

Warren Smith, CJ Kanuha, and Sam Hammer arrived later but could not wet a rail. Instead we killed time in Vladivostok, where we could dissolve and lose ourselves among oceans of cheap vodka, cigarettes, hookahs, end-at-8 a.m. nightclubs, new friends, good food and music, and—for the unmarried among us—the world's most beautiful women. "Let's drink vodka together" became a theme. Eventually time distorted itself and the city's soul was unveiled, yet Russia's subtle intelligence was no match for the stubborn East Sea. It was an act of restraint before the annual winter freeze.

Burkard was shattered. He'd flown all that way, endured detainment and deportation, was emotionally and financially drained, and, with us, he watched nearly a year of planning evaporate into the sunny Siberian sky. Russia was truly a tough place to ingest—huge, stoic, unpredictable. The East Sea's typhoon season was in premature hibernation, its gates sealed. We surrendered—the Soviet surf trip was done.

27

QUIETING THE SELF

2002

BACK TO NATURE. Divine the future, consult the past. Allure five senses with geographical isolation. Adapt to life in ancient, immortal lands oblivious to modern lifestyle, where an eastern Eden of culture taints any mirage of Western theory. Squint into the glare of an Indian Ocean sun, departing all mind, thought, homespun memory. And so on.

Early afternoon. A cooling sea of blues unwinds to vast, parched pastels of scrub, bush and palm as we dip and deplane into Waingapu. A rough overland bus journey follows, terminating at a desolate beach on the isle's southeast shore. At sunset, Captain Alwi extends his hand to mine in a cleansing dose of liberty in our ad hoc port of embarkment. Exit from the swell-flanked anchorage segues the halt of civilization into a compelling, introspective outpost sojourn.

Spice Islands. Irian Jaya. Timor. Roti. Bali. Nusa Lembongan. Lombok. Sumbawa. Sumba. Java. Panaitan. Sumatra. Asu. Bawa. Hinako. Nias. Mentawais. All names you've heard before. Yet the concept of combing clandestine Indonesian territory devoid of crowds and surf charter boats requires that you likely have not heard the names—hidden words printed in micro fonts on the map…or not at all.

Swell clairvoyance point our course, primarily at night. Settling into the stuffy bunk with soothing ironwood hull creaks, dreams ensue, disturbed only with anchorage beneath a sea of starlight leading to the cosmic dawn…good morning, starshine. Awakening to Indonesian idyll manifests essence of surf search.

Hence the voyage: Lesser Sundas and reefs between. Corals and sands. Rocks and cliffs. Harsh crossings and stark beaches. Reconnoitering favored yet unknown nooks aboard the *Indo Jiwa* is a savory affair—gunkholing along Nusa Tenggara's enchanted coasts scarcely viewed through blue eyes and rarely (if ever) surfed.

HISTORICALLY, INDONESIA'S ARCHIPELAGIC complex required that its denizens knew their way around boats. Many texts suggest the European Age of Exploration as the pinnacle of mankind's seaborne expansion, yet these tales must fade to those of southeast Asians, who colonized Indonesia 6,000 years ago. Likening our solitary passage to these ancient mariners' ideologies of seeking the new, Indo Jiwa serves its purpose.

Stone megaliths…where spirits dwell. Ritual objects. Tropical desert. Primordial mountain ranges alternate with classic white sand rimmed with palms and bush and turquoise lagoon. Far drier than Indonesia's more equatorial expanse, cool evening winds press heat from afternoon into the following mid-morning, mimicking the arid clime of northwest Australia.

The island is a rugged paradise—an exposed, remote slab of rock, where human life manages to blossom with greater success than on the more fertile islands nearby. Its earth is stony and barren, yet due to the lontar palm economy, the locals enjoy an organic scheme of health.

Buzzing shorebound from the mothership…an escape. Two fishermen with throw nets float near shore in a tattered wood canoe. Our Mercury-powered fiberglass skiff is dragged onto the scorching beach—utterly Arabian if not for gangled lontar palm fronds, Christian church, seaweed harvest, or Asian eye. In blinding midday sun, the beach is wide and perfect, littered with colored pebbles and bleached shards of coral.

Lore and romanticism saturate wooden boats. Retroglancing, *Indo Jiwa* looms strategically in the back bay between two reefs, imitating a pirate ship circa 1946; it is a traditional Buginese pinisi, zenith of the southern Sulawesi shipwrights—also infamous pirates. Built of ironwood, an increasingly limited resource found only in eastern Indonesia, she spans 110 feet bow to stern, allowing substantial elbow room and certain degrees of creature comforts found in several Indonesian surf charter boats.

A rough trail from the beach. We stroll into the village. Sweating profusely, foreheads lift when immersed in a palm forest—falling coconuts can harm. Further in, a pig ambushes our lethargic ensemble…coconuts drop inches away from point-blank cranium.

A clearing appears in the dense brush; a child cries, his sister grins. Sideways breeze folds her black hair while father scales a palm tree. Frail shacks surround a modest firepit/communal area soaked with betel nut spit. Sustenance, subsistence, survival…ah, this is a picture of an island maintaining a culture—a society on stilts, if you will, hovering beyond status quo and momentary awards, existing from and for the long-term. Primitive? Only to us.

The interpreter—*Indo Jiwa*'s chief mechanic—filters our intent to the puzzled villagers. Anomaly exists in pale skin: They are brown, we are white. They come from cloudless land, we come from sunless outer space. Invading in slaps and trunks, this is the sect of foreign diplomacy familiar to Captain James Cook, who sailed here in 1770—a milestone for westerners—visiting villages and assessing the ikat and lontar economies; here, the drought-resistant lontar palm provides everything from house-building fibers to syrup.

For several hundred years prior, the island shunned colonial interest with great simplicity. A 1676 Portuguese war expedition seeking slaves was slaughtered deftly by the natives; the Portuguese and Dutch kept their distance thereafter. Lucky for us, Cook made a good impression.

The islanders saw us coming—pondered the mothership offshore, anchored since Tuesday. Our interpreter initiates and, immediately, cold faces crack with handouts of lontar syrup, smooth as silk, offered as a formal welcome. Raw and boldly sweet, we chase it with coconut flesh and thank the natives with smiles and firm handshakes.

In the end, I wander off toward the chickens and pigs and piles of coconuts to feel the island sans humans...which remained cloaked from the outer world until 1860, when Christian missionaries arrived with smallpox, inadvertently killing nearly half of the population. The missionaries mustered meager success against a staunchly Islamic population; today, besides Christianity, many embrace animism: 1. Doctrine that the vital principle of organic development is immaterial spirit. 2. Attribution of conscious life to objects in and phenomena of nature or to inanimate objects. 3. Belief in the existence of spirits separable from bodies.

Tradition flourishes. We step into the hub of the island's animism—the kampung, or sacred house. Exposed to unwanted foreign magic, visitors were once exorcized by the kepala adat before being allowed inside.

Three sets of megaliths and a complex ritual structure, the place is bounded by taboos. A common vernal ritual has food and living animals shoved to sea bound in lontar palm boats, veiled in ikat as an offer to the gods. Puppies and premature goats are especially valued as they exemplify feeble victims who will suffer the penance of the gods in place of the villagers. When a priest dies, a fresh acolyte must quaff an elixir of the dead priest's blood blended with the venom of a poisonous fish. Those who survive are ordained; this last occurred in 1997.

OFF THE BEATEN track. Extreme isolation; flat, hot, mute. Random sessions in mysto lineups equate to a complacency found only in this sea. Here.

Another island comes into view, Indonesia's driest—even the lontar palm wilts. Reputed hub of local human ancestry and its spiritual passage from Asia to India. Home to what some famous folk consider to be the nation's best lefthander. On an island with no roads or airport, rarefied pleasures spawn with access: nearing sunset, we drop anchor and observe. Two paddle out. Four waves ridden, none conquered. Detonating top-to-bottom, bending below sea level—one false move and pay the price. A beast of a wave. "Ahhh, *yeahhh*, it's heavy out there, mate."

Isolation is equidistant from relaxation. Between? The wave: Indonesian exotica perfection, treacherously shallow. Unseen. Unsurfed.

This is where a realization of wild Indonesia raises its wings. Redoubt of cerebral peace exists on a trackless sea. Book a flight. Board a boat. But don't ever say it doesn't exist. Because it does.

PART

VIII

Micronesia

28

JEWEL OF PALM AND RAIN— A PACIFIC EPIPHANY

2004

IT WAS CALIFORNIA'S autumn equinox, with its earthy browns and yellows, its wind and its chill, on the cusp of solitude, that had sent me away. A shirtless late-afternoon bike ride across the farm, down the leafy corridor of Rincon Creek and out to the beach afforded goose bumps from a wan sun, with glassy, head-high waves wrapping around the famed point of Rincoñada del Mar.

The air was clear, the sky vast and cloudless. In the distance were the shadowy hills and gullies of the islands Santa Rosa and Santa Cruz; even Anacapa looked warmly near and familiar. In time, rain would fall there and here, and the beach sand would darken—the tourists were gone—but today, under the auspices of seagulls and hawks, autumn had arrived. This was Rincon in late October, a polyglot pointbreak returned to itself, to the locals and the afternoon low tides, the clean swells and sunburned eyes, squinting into the glare of a setting sun.

Rincon is a destination, a marquee on the world's surf map, an archetype of crowded precision and expensive beachfront homes, depositing human waste into the lineup, toxic following rainfall.

There was rain in sight mid-week, and for this I felt lucky, because there was an envelope in my mailbox holding a ticket to paradise. To Earth, rain is life, and the ticket was to an archipelago that annually receives thirty feet of it.

Santa Barbara is difficult to leave, especially at the start of winter, and when I had recently returned from Oceania. But Santa Barbara is also a paradise, and coming home is sometimes like flying away—my life exists between two utopias. One is static and familial, where my rent is paid, while the others are distant and humid, these bluey-green postcard places you read about in *Islands* and *National Geographic*. Indeed, all homecomings are jet-lagged fogs—my bank account drained, my health poisoned by a cold or flu from long flights on germy, sneezy airplanes.

I was afflicted from the last trip but again restless, uninspired, with writer's block, unable to rhapsodize about the journey I had just taken. Epiphanies of travel are rampant when one travels alone—this was a good reason for doing it, not because the epiphanies were random but because they also were holistically metaphoric. Living on a small farm a half-mile from a famous surf spot, it is easy to become insular, filling summers with work and women and boozy barbecues, neglecting the dormant ocean, your mind smug knowing the best has yet to come.

And here it was, this crisp afternoon, with a clean swell from the northwest, coining the onset of Rincon's celebrated winter surf season. At that moment it seemed wrong for me to leave again. Rincon Point, so sunny and serene, with its bubble of smiling folks and holiday homes and shady trees and smooth rocks, its pretty blonde surfer girls flirting with surfer boys along the point, in and out of the surf, its fathers and mothers and aunts and uncles shell-hunting with Frisbees and skittish leashed dogs, all within the drowsy calm of a fading autumn day—this was a reflection of Californian health and comfort. I felt happy here, and happiness had been a strain to achieve, years in the making.

But few things make me happier than travel, no matter how tiresome and inconvenient. Rincon's sea was cold and green—warm and blue was where my mind had been.

TWO YEARS BEFORE, facing a rubious sunset, Yvon Chouinard had told me about the place. We were yakking about travel, eating sashimi and drinking beer astern on a boat down in the Tuamotu Archipelago. As founder of apparel company Patagonia, Chouinard had seen much of the tropical world—surfing, sailing, exploring, bonefishing—but he hadn't made it to the islands we discussed, which surprised me.

"It's somewhere I've always wanted to see," he confided. "Untouched nature, good waves, lots of reef passes, no surfers. All you need is a local fisherman to take you out to them."

"Why haven't you been there?"

"Probably because there's no bonefish."

Chuck Corbett of Tabuaeran, to where Chouinard had once sailed from O'ahu, later confirmed the claim to me through email. A longtime merchantman and an expatriated Californian now on his own atoll of idyll, Corbett has seen and surfed more Pacific obscurity than anyone alive.

"Would you like an insiders tip?" he wrote. "Buy a small Jap truck for around a grand or less, then buy a ten-foot aluminum boat with a fifteen-horsepower outboard. Ship from San Francisco. You will find epic, world-class surf—up to giant sizes, too. When you're finished, you can sell the car and boat. Nobody knows the island sits with Tahiti in waves because the waves are a minimum of a few miles out, on a barrier reef."

I was there at three a.m. after four flights, with two bags, two surfboards, and zero expectations, not even for sunshine. Besides the hotel reservation, no other arrangements had been made.

The airport terminal was a dim concrete room with old flaky paint and an incredibly foul restroom, a small sign glued above the sink:

> *Please keep our airport environment clean and fit to work in, especially our restrooms.*

AT THE CURB outside was an old brown sedan, an orange light on its roof, which made me think it was a taxi. It was, though its dusky driver was asleep and drooling, as was the pregnant middle-aged woman in the back seat. Both of their jaws bulged with betel nut, a natural sedative enjoyed in great abundance along the equator.

I tapped on the driver's window, startling him.

"Taxi?"

I grinned, showing him five dollars. He was red-eyed and pickled but reasonably coherent, so I gave him the money, lowered the passenger seat for my surfboards, and squeezed into the back with the woman, who reeked of garlic and sweaty armpits.

She turned her head slowly and looked at me square, her flat face barely visible in the darkness.

"I am Gina Zanardi."

So much for exotic island names. I had hoped for complete sovereignty with little Westernization, but European whalers roamed these ports a hundred years ago, and Gina was likely an offspring from one of them. She was pregnant but fat nonetheless, with a pretty purple floral dress and an elaborate shell necklace. Her head was a mass of short, kinky black hair, her teeth tiny kernels of red.

"You want chew?"

"Betel nut?"

She nodded. "Yes. Betel nut."

"Sure, I'd love some."

She plucked three small green nuts from a pouch she kept in a hidden dress pocket and handed them to me with a wilted pepper leaf and a dirty vial of lime. Lime is baked coral, a fine white powder resembling cocaine, sprinkled on betel nut for an effect unknown to me; by trip's end, nobody else I asked knew why all their lives they put lime on their betel nut.

I was thirty minutes off the plane and already with a cheekful. In Melanesia we had used a slice of an actual lime fruit, which made the experience putrid and unforgettable.

The driver stared blankly through the windshield.

"Where you going?"

"Palm Hotel."

"Palm Hotel? OK, we go Palm Motel." And he started the car.

About a mile on, he pulled over in front of a small store festooned with cheery but faded beer posters (*Miller Lite—The Beer of the Islands!*) and food advertisements for the latest shipment from Hawai'i (*New York Steak just in!* and *Now Fresh California Iceberg Lettuce!*). I too was a U.S. import but was not feeling particularly fresh, or even cheery, and I wondered aloud why we were stopped here instead of at my hotel. The driver eyed me in his rearview mirror, his face sweaty and fretful, like he was going to faint.

"Sir, I stop here."

"Do you need to buy something? The store looks closed."

"No. But I not drive you to hotel." He put a finger on his cheek. "Very tired."

"So you're dropping me here?"

"Yes. I call new taxi."

"Fine."

We sat in the car and waited. I was too tired to care. At this hour of the night, who wasn't?

The road was dark. Nothing moved. The air was warm and thick and muggy. I was grimy. Gina snored softly, both hands on her round belly. The driver lowered his head and tilted the seat back, and fell asleep. It started to rain. I closed my eyes and listened to the crickets and creatures of night making their noise, in the rain, thinking: Two days ago I was wearing a parka and driving eighty miles an hour on a Los Angeles freeway.

Then came bizarre color visions of a rodeo I'd never seen, hicks I'd never met, hot cowgirls in tight jeans, bull-riding, steer wrestling, sunglasses, tobacco, bourbon, paper plates and fatty meat, pickup trucks, aluminum folding chairs, green hills, bright lights, dirty fingers clutching pink ticket stubs. So lucid and intense it all was, I shot upright and yelped when the driver slapped my left knee.

"Sir, you taxi here!" he cried.

An hour had passed. In a daze I loaded my bags into the other car, which was smellier, with damp seats. The driver made a futile attempt at conversation.

At last he deposited me in the rainy darkness outside my hotel, in the middle of the jungle, several miles from the airport and nearest town. The air here smelled of plumeria and moss, rain and ripe fruit. The silence was extraordinary. Eventually a clerk led me along a ferny path to my room—actually an old wooden bungalow, full of insects and geckos—where I showered and slept like a log until noon the next day, woken by an errant rooster and croaking toads.

BEING A SURFER in a land of non-surfers suited me, because nothing is more irksome than flying halfway around the world to a remote Third World island, only to find yourself in the immigration line behind a gaggle of Australians or Americans with surfboards. They came for the same reasons as you, alone or with their wives or girlfriends or rowdy peers, draining the airplane's booze stock all the way from Honolulu or Brisbane, later staying at your same hotel, hassling for your same waves, prowling at your same seedy pub for the same curious dark local girls and cheap beers and shabby billiard tables, the barstools, the peanuts, the juke box, the filthy urinal.

But, really, is this the spirit of surf travel? It occurs almost daily in Malé and San José, Denpasar and Padang, in Nadi and Papeete, which is why I avoid those places. The world is huge—thousands of warm waves are going unridden right now. Anyone with the money and moxie can find them, and those willing to endure great expense and hassle are often rewarded with lineups unlike the clogged ones they left at home.

I did not discover this unmolested island chain, and it had been surfed, but as far as I could tell, I was the only surfer there and could briefly claim it for myself, which is every surfer's dream.

The first five days produced small windswell and heavy rain. From the hotel's gazebo a reef pass was visible, perhaps three miles out, and on the first sunny day I rented a kayak and began paddling toward it, surfboard in tow, with water and food. Hiring a fisherman for transport was the normal thing to do, but also more expensive, and I needed exercise.

A small bald boy spearfishing around the mangroves at the launch ramp regarded me with glee, frantically waving me over with his skinny arms. He was naked except for a baggy white American Airlines shirt that said *Proud To Be An American* across the front of it. When I was closest to him he grinned and ogled at me through his mask, pointing an index finger.

"Ho, eh, mister! What you doing? What?—"

"Going surfing."

"Ho, sharks, eh? Ho, kill you!" He smiled and gnashed his brown teeth. "Eat!"

I paddled past him and flashed a shaka sign. "Enjoy your day, buddy."

The weather was perfect. Paddling was effortless, and the kayak sliced quickly across the plate-glass lagoon, the sky a sparkly mirror above acres of healthy, colorful corals, fluorescent blue holes, and brilliant white sand. It certainly was a spearfisherman's heaven, but aside from the boy back at the shore, the lagoon was mine. Nobody was fishing or diving or paddling or swimming. It was only the birds and the fish.

The land looked uninhabited and remarkably lush, like the nirvana it was, only it looked more so from this sea-level vantage. All week I had been peering out through the gray and rain; now I was being rewarded with this hallmark tropical island scenery.

The mountain silhouettes were soft and elegant, verdant ridges fading into the distance, steamy in the sunlight, like a pressure-easing thaw after endless rain, the way dew evaporates under warm sun on a California winter morning. This was an isolated corner of the island, so no human development was visible, which comforted me, because the land was dense and would remain pure for a long time, hopefully forever.

In the lagoon were several small islands, dense in coconut palms, with a few waterfront aluminum-roofed plywood shacks. These islands looked abandoned—nothing moved, there were no people. Clotheslines were strewn between trees, heavy with drying laundry. Each shack had a white panga—today's South Pacific standard—moored out front, with nets and oars resting on the gunwales. I'd seen men fishing in the mornings and evenings—now was midday and very hot, so most people wouldn't be active—this was the time for naps and betel nut, perhaps a few shells of kava or cans of beer.

I welcomed the sun directly overhead, because it lent light to the lagoon's psychedelic beauty, its textures and its fish, its dazzling corals. Other islands I had seen recently suffered badly from coral bleaching and dynamite fishing, but this ecosystem was incredibly alive and intact. I wondered how, in this age of packaged "adventure travel" and fashionable "ecotourism," it could not be overrun with sportfishing charters and wealthy scuba divers.

I also wondered how it could not be crawling with surfers and surf camps, because, two hours later, after reaching the pass, I was shocked: A translucent three-wave symmetry of head-high rights peeled around the reef, expiring into the channel. The lips were thin and the tubes almond-shaped, and the tide was rising, so the reef was non-threatening and there was no chance of me or the kayak getting sucked out to sea.

Ironically, the wave was identical to the Polynesian wave Yvon Chouinard and I had surfed the day he had mentioned this island to me, and here I was, only alone, miles from land, in nobody's sight, with a battered kayak instead of a big air-conditioned boat.

I leashed the kayak to a rusty channel marker and paddled into the lineup. The scene was blissful and brilliant, the waves playful and consistent. It was sheet glass, not an ounce of wind, the water clarity unrivaled. Waylon Jennings's "Luckenback, Texas" lyrics circulated in my head, so alien to this shimmering place.

The only two things in life that make it worth livin'
Is guitars tuned good and firm-feelin' women—
Let's go to Luckenback, Texas
With Waylon and Willie and the boys

This is why we surf and travel—to do both simultaneously, with a certain degree of risk and naivete, without irritation or guidance. And from everyone I'd spoken with, the island's people had no interest in surfing or catering to surfers, so it is conceivable that this obscure archipelago could remain so for your own personal discovery.

The sublime reef-pass right was one of mine, and by the time landfall was made, at dusk, I was ravenous. Dark clouds hid the sunset, and by the time I walked through the jungle and found my bungalow, it was blustery and raining hard. Despite the day's glory, it was virtually impossible to go a full twelve hours here without some form of precipitation, usually in the form of lengthy downpours.

An informative Ecotourism Travel Guide in the bungalow detailed the island's flora and fauna, its waterfalls, its culture, legends, history, and climate, expounding on the virtues of record-breaking annual rainfall, which, at the island's center, exceeds four hundred inches. That's more than thirty feet of rain, or thirteen inches per week. Judging from my time there, this seemed an accurate number.

One line in the guide caught my eye:

People here say rain is a welcome sign, so why not get out and take some pictures during the next shower!

EVERYTHING WAS DARK and wet and windy and my cameras were not waterproof, so I opted for food and a drink at the hotel bar, where I fell into conversation with a fattish, raspy, red-faced Swede-cum-Finn named Lars Linden. He was about sixty and here on business ("I could tell you what, but then I'd have to kill you."). He was raised in a Stockholm suburb but moved to Helsinki for a Finnish wife when he was twenty-two. They divorced last year.

He was articulate and spoke perfect English and looked like Santa Claus; he wore stained pants and a rugby shirt, and his white beard was soggy from the walk here from his bungalow.

I mentioned the rain.

"At least it keep things cool," he said.

"Sunshine is nice, too. Like today's."

"You can get sunshine anywhere in the damn world. Where are you from, man?"

"California."

"Ah! See?" He wagged a fat told you so! finger at me and took a long pull from his can of Victoria Bitter. "All you Californians care about is your fucking sunshine. What would you people do if the sun went away forever and all you had was clouds and snow and rain?"

"Like Helsinki?"

"Like Helsinki."

"Then I suppose we'd all die, Lars."

He wagged another finger. "Fucking right you would. Helsinki's a crap place. Another beer?"

Dinner was an excellent but small plate of pepper tuna and rice with broccoli and bread. The restaurant was perched above the lagoon, affording scenic daytime panoramas of the islands I had kayaked between, and, if you looked hard enough, whitewater at the pass I had surfed.

I said to the waiter, "You must never get tired of this great view."

He said, "I am very tired of it. That is why I'm facing away from it."

The rain stopped as I ate dessert (gooey chocolate ice cream). Back in the bungalow, a gecko clinging to the ceiling of my bed's mosquito net had regurgitated a cricket, nearly whole, now a shiny little brown sausage on my pillowcase.

Once supine, I fell asleep immediately, only to be soon disturbed by a strange barrage of 1950s-era Christmas carols, blared by someone's radio nearby, piercing the pregnant night silence of a tropical rain forest. Initially I thought it was a dream, as this was only the first week of November, and nobody celebrates Christmas this early.

Frosty the Snowman was a jolly happy soul
With a corncob pipe and a button nose

What?

Rudolph the red-nosed reindeer
(reindeer)
Had a very shiny nose
(like a light bulb)
And if you ever saw it
(saw it)
You would even say it glows
(like a flashlight!)

And then:

He's making a list,
And checking it twice;
Gonna find out who's naughty and nice.
Santa Claus is coming to town!

I shut my eyes again, thinking Santa was already here—he's a Swede/Finn named Lars Linden, and he was staying in Bungalow Seven.

ON A PACIFIC ISLAND surrounded by a bounteous fishery, it seemed odd how the locals would eat canned tuna from Thailand and frozen salmon from New Zealand. In the mornings and evenings I had seen men fishing both in and outside the lagoon, but there were few roadside fish markets, and no fresh fish in the grocers. I later read that most seafood caught here was sent to Asia and elsewhere for processing and consumption.

"Nobody fishes here," a woman said outside a dirty launderette flanked by huge breadfruit trees. "If a man wants to impress his girlfriend, maybe he go catch a fish. But nobody fish for other reason."

She had a ring on her wedding finger. I asked, "Does your husband fish to impress you?"

"No. No fishing. He left here." She waved her hand. "To Hawai'i."

"Why?"

"To work in pineapple fields." Her eyes narrowed and she lowered her voice, like she was about to tell me a great secret. "In 1993 I went to Hawai'i to see him—to Honolulu."

"What did you do there?"

"I walk and take bus and see all the things. Went to Diamond Head. Went to Pearl Harbor, for example. I stay at Waikiki."

"Did you try surfing at Waikiki?"

"No." She spat betel nut spit. "Surfing too dangerous."

"I'm surfing here."

Her brow tightened. "You should not go surfing. Maybe you go fishing. But I think there no fish here."

It's ironic, then, that afternoon when I met a bald, stocky Tasmanian expatriate named Matt at the harbor, we went out in his boat and within two hours had hooked a giant sailfish and three tuna.

"Mate, it's fine with me if nobody fishes here," he grinned, sucking on his fifth bottle of Miller Lite, blood and fish scales on his hands and tattooed forearms. He was forty-one, unshaven, sun-damaged, and looked like a fisherman or an outlaw biker, tough but gregarious. He was a salty Lars Linden.

We were trolling around the pass I had surfed a few days before.

"Why would anybody want to hassle with all of this boat shit when they can just go and buy it for a buck in the store?"

"Then why do you fish?"

"Gives me something to do. Plus, I've always been into the fishing, even back in bloody Hobart."

"Does it impress your wife?"

"Nah, mate, she's a bloody vegetarian."

He offered to take me out to another reef pass in the morning, on the island's opposite side, claiming there had been surfers there when the winds were calm, like today, he said.

"Mostly Peace Corps blokes, sometimes a few of those Seventh Day Adventist kids, or yachties passing through. It's good shit, you know? I'd bloody kill myself trying it, aye." And he downed another beer.

I caught a taxi from the harbor to the hotel. It was a wet Friday night, which meant payday and bars full of tipsy islanders. My driver was Nixon, about my age, and he was drinking something sugary and red. I correctly guessed it to be spiked Kool-Aid.

"So where's the nightlife here, Nixon?"

He smiled widely. My interest excited him. "You must go to The Club. Many girls, many cheap drinks. You blond white man, you get what you want." He laughed. "You will thank me later!"

We were passing a group of teenagers on a street corner, at night, in the rain, hawking carwashes for a dollar.

"Will you be there?" I asked.

"Of course!"

That night the weather remained, with ferocious downpours and stiff wind. I decided to forego the loud pubs of smoke and debauchery and spend a quiet night in.

Darkness seems to intensify any storm. The roof of my bungalow was pelted with breadfruits, twigs, coconuts; the wind blew in a lagoony scent of salt, like stagnant mangrove air whipped up and carried through the windows. The wind shooshed loudly through the jungle, cooling the room. The rain never stopped the crickets from chirping, or the moths and mosquitoes from skirting around my ears.

A storm in a tropical mountain rain forest is a unique sort of storm—wetter, denser, louder, longer than a valley storm, or an open-ocean storm. Certainly unlike a desert sandstorm or an arctic snowstorm or an Irish gale. Here this storm was encouraged and accepted—it didn't stop traffic or anything else. It was part of life. It drenched and cleansed. There are few places where the air is purer, the water cleaner. Islanders do not own umbrellas or raincoats, or backyard rain gauges. The rain is beautiful and a blessing, unlike in southern California, where rain is just terrible.

I worked through a six-pack of Chinese beer and read more from the Ecotourism Travel Guide, learning that there are nearly eight hundred kinds of plants here, three hundred of them endemic, with a hundred unique species. I also learned about waterfalls:

> *The rains gave birth to rivers, which cascaded down to the lowlands and made all life possible. Volcanic mountains erupted, changing the landscape until a waterfall was formed. Even today, the island's lifeblood flows from these rivers and tumbles over these waterfalls, sustaining life and helping to make this island a present-day Garden of Eden.*

APPARENTLY THE PLACE was loaded with waterfalls, and I had seen the biggest one a few days before, easily accessible by a twenty-minute jungle hike. It was shadowy and majestic and loud, as waterfalls often are, a craggy seventy-foot wall of square, black basalt stones, with a large pool at the base perfect for swimming.

Within a few minutes after reaching the falls, clouds coalesced above and threatened rain. I had a camera but no protection for it, and as soon as I realized this, a downpour began.

MORNING—A HEAVY CALM. The storm blew itself away overnight, and the six Chinese beers left a haze in my head.

Out of the harbor we blasted into the lagoon at full-throttle, the water surface free of rain and wind. The sky was clear and there was promise of clean swell, judging from the whitewater lacing the barrier reef. Our ride was smooth and fast, passing several huge rusty Asian purse seiners at anchor. There were no other boats in the lagoon.

"Basically they're just huge shitty floating freezers," Matt said, slurping coffee from a red plastic mug. "Can you imagine living on one of those things?"

The pass was ten minutes east of the harbor, and as soon as we were close enough, a gaping right, turquoise and glorious, spooled along the reef. Then another. And another. It was flawless. It was double-overhead. It was epic. Where were the pro surfers and photographers? Why wasn't anyone out?

There was. He rode a smaller wave, avoiding the tube, as Matt set our anchor. Five minutes prior, the surfer had been in a skiff with three other males and one female, all Seventh Day Adventist volunteers from the U.S.—Allison and Blake from Idaho, Ben from Wyoming, Andrew from West Virginia, Todd from Oregon. They were fit and flaxen, and they could have been related. They were all in their twenties and were borderline beginners who learned to surf here a year ago, which struck me as respectable, because powerful, shallow reef-pass barrels are harsh for that first timid take-off and whitewater hobble.

"Aren't you going to wear some sort of shirt? Or are you, like, a sun guy?"

I was waxing my board as Matt smeared sunscreen across my back. He was off coffee and onto beer. It was eight in the morning.

"This is my last day here," I said. "Might as well get some color."

A second kid paddled out, promptly bailing his board mid-face on a set and taking a fin through his left cheek, which removed him from the water but not the spirit.

"I just can't stop smiling!" he yelled to us, fumbling around his skiff for a bandage. "I mean, how often does it peel like this at home?"

I found my place in the lineup, which was easy. Ben, who rode the day's first wave, flashed me a thumbs-up and a huge giddy grin.

"It's so good out here, man. By the way, I'm Ben." He held out his hand.

Ben had a large shaved head and a thick brown goatee. He looked like a misplaced farm boy, which he was, from the wilds of Wyoming. He rode a boxy '80s-era thruster with a gaudy paint job and several unpatched dings. We chatted for a minute about where we were from, what we thought of this island, and why we were here. He was here for religion; I was here for…well, because travel was what I did for a living. He seemed disappointed when I said I was on the evening's flight back to Los Angeles.

"Aw, man, too bad you can't hang out. We'd be stoked to surf with you some more."

"The surf's just starting to get good where I live," I said.

A set came. Ben was in position for the first wave.

He smiled. "This one's all yours, man."

I smiled back. "Thanks."

The wave, a glittery wall of crystal blue, gently picked me up and eased me in. At that moment I knew why I had come. And after setting a line as the lip threw over, I knew that I was at last ready for the winter at home.

29

BOMBS NOT BOWLS

2008

> *"At the moment of detonation there was a flash. At that instant I was able to see straight through my hands. I could see the veins. I could see the blood, I could see all the skin tissue, I could see the bones and worst of all, I could see the flash itself. It was like looking into a white-hot diamond, a second sun."*
>
> —*Ken McGinley,* No Risk Involved

IN THE LATE '50s and early '60s, Kiritimati was a great place to blow up. But in '08, standing on a white coral beach amid the shriek of east wind within sight of a feathering blue north swell, you have no idea that Kiritimati was once a nuclear-weapon whore. This, the world's largest atoll, located less than two degrees above the equator in the Central Pacific, was so remote and pristine and unpopulated that militarized Yanks and Brits slapped each other on the back and said, "Hell, why not?" Both countries needed to test 34 hydrogen bombs, after all, and there was no better place to do so than on a tranquil slice of Micronesian paradise.

"Who gives a damn?" said Henry Kissinger when asked about Pacific islanders and resultant radioactivity from the tests. "There are only 90,000 people out there."

One of those people fathered Etuati Arao, a man living near one of Kiritimati's best surf spots, a fast right point that bowled and pinwheeled around the reef pass, eventually petering out in the deep lagoon. In 1958 Etuati's dad was living on his native island of Tarawa, 2,013 miles west of Kiritimati, when he was recruited by the British to work for their bomb tests.

"My father wanted to be off crowded Tarawa," Etuati said softly as we watched the surf one particularly blustery afternoon. "He come here and was happy until he see first bomb explode. It hurt his eyes, made hard for him to breathe. He saw so many bombs. And his skin looked bad forever. On Tarawa he said his skin looked good and he felt good. On Kiritimati he said he felt like he would die."

Die he did, at home back on Tarawa. Etuati moved to Kiritimati to work in the government's copra plantations, and also to flee Tarawa's clusterfuck. Still, nobody had bothered to inspect the bodies of the elderly who witnessed the H-bomb blasts 50 years prior. And so the same story went for the late author Ken McGinley, quoted above, a Scot who too was enlisted to assist the Brits with their toxic far-flung war play. Nuclear death? No one knows.

In mid-January Santa Cruz's Josh Mulcoy, Hawaii's Mikala and Daniel Jones, Central California's Nate Tyler, photographer Chris Burkard, and I visited Kiritimati searching for bombs of a different sort—never mind the mint-green clouds ("it's only the reflection off the lagoon"). Reaching the big claw-shaped atoll was a simple once-weekly three-hour flight from Honolulu, and nearing the airstrip we saw organized lines of whitewater looping around the northern half of the island. We had expected this. Two days before, 1,300 miles north, Waimea Bay was closed out. Oahu's North Shore is the barometer for gauging swells on Kiritimati, because when a swell hits the North Shore, it hits Kiritimati two days later at half the size, the waves groomed and long-period, sometimes achingly inconsistent but always clean as Kiritimati's prevailing wind is offshore.

Wind was our bitch, however. (Mulcoy: "Is there a hurricane blowing?") It blew hard non-stop from the minute we arrived until the minute we left, and undoubtedly is blowing right now. It rendered most spots unsurfable. But at least we got swell—in the weeks preceding our trip, the North Shore was about two feet; Kiritimati was micro, with the excessive La Niña-induced trade winds. Up until a few days before we left Honolulu, the Hawaiian winter had been slow, which meant Kiritimati had been pancake-flat.

"Flattest winter ever," said Chuck, our jovial American-expat guide whose boat we stayed on, anchored offshore in clear blue water fronting the scrappy hamlet of London. A few miles south of us was Paris, an abandoned copra plantation. Beyond Paris was Poland, a remote speck of a village. These settlements were named by an eccentric French priest named Emmanuel Rougier, who, for copra, leased the island from 1917 to 1939 and planted 800,000 coconut trees there. Eventually Rougier made a fortune and split for Tahiti; windblown and tattered, the trees remained.

> *"It is a dazzling place, an arid Eden that even H-bombs could not destroy, a giant bracelet of coral, dappled with the hardiest shrubs and a million coconut trees; a lagoon that is not only shaped like a palette, but a palette splashed with every shade of green and blue...."*
>
> *—Paul Theroux*

POLYNESIA (HAWAI'I INCLUDED) is 500 islands; Melanesia is 1,500. Micronesia is more than 2,000 and sprawls 4.5 million square miles across the Pacific, the world's biggest ocean, which theoretically would make Micronesia the world's most surf-rich fetch, with the largest number of reef passes, the most swell exposure, and the fewest surfers. Deplaning on Kiritimati in Micronesia's Republic of Kiribati (pronounced '*Kiribas*'), your boards are the only ones in the baggage carousel, a curious oddity in today's world of tropical island surf-siege.

Of Earth's 194 countries, only five are comprised entirely of atolls: Maldives, Marshall Islands, Tokelau, Tuvalu, and Kiribati, and aside from Tokelau, a dependent of New Zealand, they are all sovereign. In the United Nations system, the Maldives, Kiribati, and Tuvalu are on the official 'Least Developed Countries' list, but in terms of surfing, the

Maldives are largely colonized, while Tuvalu remains obscure, one of the 'Least Developed Countries' in the surf-travel genre, even if its surf potential is low. Tokelau has no waves, and the Marshall Islands were recently dissected by Martin Daly, who is running plush surf/fish/dive charters there between November and March.

But what of Kiribati? Really, only one guy knows. Our Kiritimati host Chuck has spent the last 30 of his 52 years probing the surf potential out amongst Kiribati's 33 atolls, themselves split into three groups—the Gilbert, the Phoenix, and the Line islands. Kiribati's total land mass is just 313 square miles, but its total sea area encompasses 1,370,656 square miles, straddling the equator for 2,010 miles. That's a lot of surf real estate for one man.

Of the 33 atolls, only Kiritimati and Tarawa have regular (i.e. once weekly) international air service. The others are reachable solely by private yacht, or, if you've got months to burn and a thirst for adventure, you could try one of the rusty inter-island freighters that come and go infrequently. Or you could do what Chuck did: move there, start an export business, start a family, and renounce your U.S. citizenship, all for the sake of surfing.

In 1992, after surf-searching in the Gilbert Islands for 12 years, Chuck made his first trip to Kiritimati. "I knew where the wave was," he said. "I actually put my motorcycle on the plane, got off with the bike and my board, and went straight down to the point. There was swell that day, and I wrote in my journal: 'Holy shit—I've been in the wrong islands for 12 years!'"

Unfortunately our timing was not as good. For our entire stay the wave Chuck mentioned was a shallow, hacked-up mess thanks to the strong trades and their open acceleration over the 30 miles of lagoon before bisecting the wave. Didn't matter if it was normally a good right point—for us it was useless.

To expand surf-spot options, one day we alighted with borrowed wheels to scout Kiritimati's east and south coasts, seeing what we could see. But scenery changed slowly—there was nothing but the palms and acres of low salt bush, particularly in the surreal recesses of the atoll, where it is possible to not see another human for weeks. Thousands of screeching birds twirl overhead in this vast windy emptiness, the sky an unchanging blue, the air an unchanging 90°F, the sea an unchanging fetch of whitecaps. Nights are black as pitch, days bright and hot as the sun itself. On Kiritimati, isolation is imminent, especially if you are surfing.

We found waves after a brief sail below London, but with inappropriate swell, what looked like heaven on Google Earth was a much harsher reality at sea level.

"Wait, what are those brown spots?" Nate asked as we approached the first spot. "What's up with all the coral heads?"

Along this three-mile stretch of coast, the Google Earth satellite image showed more than 15 surf spots, the whitewater lines at each tapered perfectly into lovely deep channels. It looked to be good to be true, and it was. Had the swell been a few feet bigger, the waves could've possibly avoided dry reef, but the swell was small, and we weren't surfing—again.

"We should sue Google Earth," Mikala said.

Luckily at the London anchorage we had our old standby, an expanse of wind-sheltered reef that behaved like a beachbreak—peaky, bowly, sectiony, and occasionally fast. Kiritimati was loaded with waves, no doubt, but also with a wind that made surfing nearly impossible, especially on the perpetually blown-out east side and the drydocked-coral head-fun zone to the south. Waves aplenty but flawed bathymetry are the bane of any surf trip in paradise.

"If I had access to explosives, the government would really enjoy that on some of the atolls up here," Chuck said at the end of the trip. "If we had access to the explosives, we could help the government put canoe passes in. We'd just go around and look to where there might be a wave, and we'd help that wave out a whole lot. It's not very hard to do. And since Kiritimati has no south swell spots, you could blast out a great wave on the south coast for about $30,000."

World-class waves instead of H-bomb madness? Shame the military never thought of that.

30

HOME ON THE ATOLL—KILLING TIME IN KIRIBATI

2010

TARAWA'S BATTLEFIELDS WERE cyan saltwater and white-sand beach.

Technically they weren't fields. Technically the place wasn't built for war. Technically Tarawa was a beautiful, palmy atoll with a large lagoon and 24 sea-level islets 81 miles north of the equator in the sunny Central Pacific, where the tradewinds blew steadily and the fish were profuse.

It was a cozy, isolated place. Its air was warm and damp. Its people were smiley and simple. Artillery was alien. But two years after Japan's Pearl Harbor attacks, Tarawa's fields lay crimson.

And it was a bad place for surfing.

November 20-23, 1943, are the dates people remember. Operation Galvanic, code name Longsuit, encompassed the brutal Battle of Tarawa. The atoll, one of the Gilbert Islands, was a strategically placed paradise in the Japan-U.S. Pacific theater of World War II. Via Pearl Harbor, Japan had enraged America and needed operable land—minimal in that part of the Pacific, just small islands and atolls and unending swaths of sea—to draw a long defensive line against Yankee vengeance.

The Yanks needed the Gilbert Islands because they needed to take the Mariana Islands because they needed to plant air bases across the Pacific to the Philippines and into Japan. Stepping stones from Oahu, basically. The Marianas were heavily defended by the Japs, and for the Yanks to win, land-based bombers were required. The nearest suitable base for the planes were the Marshall Islands, but the Marshall Islands were barred from U.S. communications with Oahu by a Japanese garrison on Tarawa.

In 1941 Japan seized the Gilberts from England. The Brits didn't really need them. The Japs took 20 months to extensively fortify Betio, a piece of coral three miles long and a half-mile wide, the southwesternmost of Tarawa's islets. They built an airstrip that was guarded by 4,500 troops in thick cement bunkers linked by tunnels and protected by mines, barbed wire, and major weaponry.

Betio was the world's most heavily defended scrap of land.

"A million men," commander Keiji Shibazaki said, "cannot take Tarawa in a hundred years."

No problem, the U.S. said—we'll do it in three hours. After all, its Tarawa invasion force was the largest ever assembled for a Pacific mission.

U.S. battleships, cruisers, and destroyers wrecked Betio in November 20's pre-dawn humidity. "There was a tremendous burst on the land," embedded war journalist Robert Sherrod wrote. "Betio began to glow brightly from the fires the bombardment pattern had started. That was only the beginning."

With daybreak came a ferocious stream of U.S. air strikes—torpedo bombers, dive bombers, fighter planes—that would segue to the foot-based troops deployed from warships into five landing crafts.

"If there were actually any Japs left on the island, which I doubted strongly," Sherrod wrote, "they would all be dead by now."

A tidebook would've helped. Instead of during a hoped-for high spring tide, the Marines' landing craft entered the lagoon amid a listless neap tide and were stopped by the shallows 500 yards from shore. The depth wouldn't change all day. The boats could go no further. The troops were forced to slog through waist-deep water toward the beach.

The Japs saw this and opened fire. *Ratta-tat-tat-tat-tat-tat.*

"*...they would all be dead by now.*"

For the remaining Japs, it was fish-in-a-barrel spree at 0900 hours. Most of the Americans were raked with ease. Eventually a few U.S. amtrac (amphibious tractors) clawed over the reef and up onto the beach. Bodies littered the sand. The warm air reeked of death and smoke. For both sides, it would be a long day.

The next morning, reinforcement U.S. troops made the same lagoon trudge, later with amtracs and artillery, allowing the Marines to penetrate Betio's narrow interior. By afternoon, they had annhiliated the Japanese and held the upper hand.

By dark on day three, the cost of victory was high for the U.S.: 1,177 soldiers never went home. Scores were wounded. The death toll was much greater for Japan—of its 4,500 troops, only 17 survived.

This set the stage for many more U.S. wins, and many more troops would die on Pacific islands before the war-ending A-bombs of '45. "Before 1945 we were militaristic," Japanese novelist Haruki Murakami told American novelist Paul Theroux. "After that, we were peace-loving and gentle."

Today, technically, Tarawa is the capital of Kiribati (pronounced KIRR-ee-bas), a nation that officially gelled in 1979. Technically it is peaceful. Technically it is still bad for surfing.

THE PRESIDENT WAS on my flight to Tarawa. Kiribati had no Air Force One. In economy class, Anote Tong sat amongst local folks, expat consultants, military contractors, and government types. I was the only tourist in the half-empty plane.

A thin, serious man with a mustache and Asiatic eyes, Tong was flying home via Fiji from Taiwan, where he'd met with President Ma Ying-jeou to bag a $15 million loan for an upgrade to Tarawa's Bonriki International Airport, which had no lights, no fence, no security, no modernity. It was the sort of airport you expect of such places. Its graffitti-laced runway was used for soccer matches and car races. Pigs and dogs ran amuk. It was broad public space unless an aircraft was using it, which wasn't often.

Like everything in Kiribati, the runway was at sea level—another concern of Tong's. He and many others believed the atolls were at grave risk from allegedly rising oceans, a much-disputed topic pinning scientific fact against fiction and political posturing from the so-called "green" movement. Carbon emissions from industrialized nations were being blamed for the much-theorized climate shift, melting the ice cap and flooding the oceans. Foreign guilt money has poured into the Pacific's atoll nations, though it's unclear where (or in whose pockets) that money actually lands, and there is a scheme to move all i-Kiribati to New Zealand or Australia before the atolls are submerged.

Before my trip I watched an online video interview of Tong, who said: "The sea-level rise is a product of the work of man. We, at the other end of the scale, are in fact paying the ultimate price for that. The question is, what should the international community do? How should they respond, particularly those countries which have benefitted and continue to benefit and continue to pollute. How should they respond to what they have caused?"

One evening I mentioned this to a stocky, friendly man named Karea. We stood in front of his small home, where he had had put me up for a night. It was a "homestay"—Karea's entire extended i-Kiribati family, from grandparents to grandchildren and five dogs, lived there. None of the dwellings had walls. Privacy was irrelevent. "You don't really need walls," he told me. "You want to get the maximum air flow through your house, and walls don't allow that. I like to tell visitors that it's like watching live panoramic television."

Karea wore only a purple sarong and spoke in a clear West Country England accent. His mother was a Brit who married an i-Kiribati; he was born in London and grew up at his parents' bed-and-breakfast in Devon. "I was supposed to get an engineering degree in the U.K.," he said, "but I came out here and one year became two, two became three, on and on, and here I am."

"Do you think Kiribati will eventually be underwater?"

Karea drew a line in the sand with his big toe. "This is sea level," he said ruefully, looking down. "It's not enough."

"But people have lived here for thousands of years," I said. "The coral grows and adjusts with the sea height."

"Ideally that would be true."

Ideally for Karea and President Tong and most other i-Kiribati, the world's industrialized nations would drop their carbon emissions and hand money to Kiribati, which, as Tong believed, was "paying the ultimate price." But in August 2010, the Science & Public Policy Institute issued compelling results of a comprehensive 17-year study. In South Pacific Sea Level: A Reassessment, Vincent Gray wrote: "In almost all cases the positive upward trends depend almost exclusively on the depression of the ocean in 1997 and 1998 caused by two tropical cyclones. If these and other similar disturbances are ignored, almost all of the islands have shown negligible change in sea level from 1993 to 2010."

Karea introduced me to his wife, Veronica, who was about 40, as she set her laptop computer on a white plastic table next to us. A young girl brought me a meal of battered emperor fish, rice, pumpkin, and boiled Chinese cabbage. From the darkness appeared a New Zealander named Bill, an electrical contractor working for Karea, who was building a new office near the airport. He'd just finished a 16-hour day on South Tarawa.

The girl brought us each a cold can of XXXX Bitter, a good Australian beer.

"Why the name XXXX?" I asked Bill.

"Because Aussies can't spell 'beer.'"

Incredibly, Veronica's laptop had wireless Internet in the middle of nowhere. I asked her where it was coming from.

"From heaven."

Heaven's ISP came at a price. For his private satellite dish, Karea's monthly bill was nearly $600.

Veronica and I talked about the traditional design of the open-walled kuikui (bungalow) I was to sleep in and how rain managed to stay out of it. She said Tarawa had seen very little rain in the past few years. I mentioned that it had rained the last few days.

"We have been praying for rain," she said. "This is last year's that never came, but it is here now because we are in El Niño. It is a blessing. I am from Butaritari, where it rains a lot. Compared to Butaritari, Tarawa is a desert."

I heard footsteps in the darkness, and smelled the spicy smoke coming from a kretek. Romain, a young Bordeauxian, appeared, kretek dangling from his lips. He operated a clam farm near Karea's property and had arrived for supper. He'd spent the last four years on Tarawa following aquaculture stints in French Polynesia and the Marshall Islands. When I met him, he had a job offer from his clam buyer in Germany to work on Mauritius.

"So next month I might just get up and go," Romain said.

"What about your wife and kids?"

"They follow." He sucked on the kretek, exhaled the fragrant smoke, then sniffed his nose. "Why are you here?"

"Doing a little surfing, having a look around."

Romain sniffed again. He said that, while recently fishing off another atoll, he'd seen waves at one of its passes.

"Not big, but quite beautiful, eh?" he said, holding his his hand at stomach level to indicate wave size.

Veronica mentioned the three feral Australians who came and surfed Tarawa before visiting another atoll, where they stayed three weeks. Coincidentally, perhaps luckily, I would be flying there the next day.

At dawn I was woken by three children who waded into the lagoon and were singing with sweet voices while dancing in the water. They splashed around with smiles and giggles. It was a happy sight. Soon the sun shimmered off the choppy water, the seabreeze a natural air-conditioner for my open-walled bungalow.

In Kiribati I'd hoped for a form of sea-level rise—swell—and before I left Tarawa I wanted to surf a reef of fair repute. It was windswept and a pain to reach, literally, via an hour-long, spine-jolting boat ride across the lagoon in an open aluminum skiff.

Takaatu and his wife Uaata took me there. They were a young couple; Takaatu was Veronica's brother. At full throttle, we bounced past palm forests that appeared to have sprouted from the water—no land was visible since it was too low. Other islets had a thin beige strip of land between the trees and the lagoon, brightly teal in the midday sun, the heat searing our backs, and a steady wind that was supposed to be good for the reef we were gunning toward.

The lagoon was alive with leaping barracuda, shiny schools of silver baitfish, large black rays that looked like apparitions on the shallow sand bottom. We passed wide sand flats—bonefishing grounds—and a few traditional canoe fishermen worked their lines and nets in the wind.

Over the noise of the outboard motor, Takaatu asked if I was married or had kids. I said no. He yelled, "I think that is a good idea!"

There was a bizarre triangular tattoo between his eyebrows. He got inked in New Zealand, where such a thing cost $150.

"But local ones here are $20!" He cackled with a toothy grin.

Barbed wire encircled his neck; there was a large eagle on his left forearm with the names of his father, mom, wife, and first born; on his right shoulder was a scorpion; his left shoulder had something fierce and tribal. He had an earring in each ear, and his hairstyle was a mohawk. Takaatu fit the type of i-Kiribati who got blind drunk on Fridays (payday) and started late-night fights in the seedy South Tarawa nightclubs like Midtown, which I visited with my friend Iataake, a local tourism official.

A couple of nights ago we'd sat at the scuffed Midtown bar and drank XXXX while overly loud dancehall music blared from distorted speakers behind us. The nightclub's walls were painted black and the room was empty except for the bartender, two of Iataake's friends, a fat white middle-aged drunk man, and an equally drunk i-Kiribati girl of about 17.

The fat man pointed a fat finger at me. "Hey, see this girl?" he shouted from 10 feet away. "Her legs are open! Take her!"

Laughing, he grabbed her by the arm and waddled over, pushing the girl at me. He leaned in, like he was going for a hug, pressing his sweaty chest onto my left arm. A fat wet arm landed on my shoulders and breath warmed my ear. He slurred and spat as he spoke.

"My friend!" he shouted. "Where you come from?"

"U.S.A."

He laughed. "U.S.A.! My friend, you really are friend! I been all over the world, a sailor, you see? Americans the best people! If if was not for you Americans, we might be Japanese people now! I love the Americans!"

The girl was having difficulty standing so she stumbled over to a bench and fell asleep. The fat man pointed at her and, referring to a condom, yelled into my ear, "My friend, she is yours! Wear a raincoat, even if it's not raining!"

The story amused Takaatu.

"Many girl in Tarawa," he said, laughing. "You can have many girlfriend here." He shrugged his shoulders. "Maybe you can make i-Kiribati child?"

On approach, it was clear the waves at our destination were small and shredded by a wind that was absent at Karea's place. Takaatu beached the boat inside the lagoon and Uaata and I walked onto the uneven reef fronting the wave; the coral extended much farther out than I'd expected. The spot, a long righthander, had potential for greatness.

Uaata touched wet white sand onto my cheeks.

"For your first time here," she said.

After securing the boat, Takaatu joined us.

"Surfing?" he asked me excitedly. "Waves good?"

"No good."

I looked around. It was a sublime place, this remote recess of an atoll in a remote archipelago, soundtracked by onshore wind and surf and rustling palms fronds. In the distance the canoe fishermen paddled in slow motion across the lagoon. To them, time meant nothing, and viewed through the hazy portal of history, Tarawa was detached from the 21st century. Standing at the edge of the atoll, far from its crowded south, I felt widely exposed to the world, an "open room," as the writer Theroux once said, stranded in the center of the Pacific, with no one to hear my silent cursing of the wave-fouling wind.

After 20 minutes of watching and wishing, it was time to go. Takaatu readied the skiff and soon we were speeding back to Karea's, through clear water over shallow sand flats. The tide was dropping fast, and the lagoon would be impassable at low, when the sand flats resembled a vast, white-hot desert trapped in the Central Pacific.

AIR KIRIBATI'S HARBIN Y-12 was a kind of high-winged jalopy. From outside, the white twin-engine turboprop looked nice with its freshly handpainted livery, but after sitting on one of the the plane's 17 small green seats, I noticed small holes in the cabin walls, patched with duct tape, and missing chunks of the ceiling.

The flight was delayed six hours. There were disctinct odors of armpit and raw fish. Dried chewing gum was stuck to my window; rust spots around it were numerous. My 6'10" boardbag, a safety hazard, was stowed on its rail in the narrow aisle. Some passengers used it for an armrest. Everyone except me was barefoot. The cabin door to my left me didn't appear to be air-tight based on the breeze that cooled my arm as the Y-12 rose from Tarawa, and while it was loud and flawed aesthetically, the old plane seemed functionally sound.

The smiling old man in a white Nebraska Cornhuskers T-shirt next to me had an unwrapped birthday cake on his lap. He looked pleased to be leaving Tarawa. Apparently the outer islands were nothing like the crowded capital.

"Going home?"

"Yes, going home," he said raspingly. I'd seen him on the tarmac, sucking on hand-rolled cigarettes of Gallaher, the only tobacco sold in Kiribati.

The man said that, to get the cake, he had flown to Tarawa on the morning's flight.

"My granddaughter's birthday today. She is nine years old."

"Tell her happy birthday from me."

"Okay!" He made a thumbs-up. "She will like. Happy birthday from *i-matang*." (*i-matang* was Gilbertese for "foreigner.")

For its size, the plane was surprisingly stable at 20,000 feet up, piercing clouds and affording long views. Behind us, receding at 150 mph, Tarawa shrank to a dark squiggle on the ocean, soon vanishing into the glare of the late-afternoon sun.

"What do you think of Tarawa?" I asked the man.

"Tarawa is like a crazy world for me," he said. "I prefer my island. It is much healthier. Outer islanders are better off on the outer islands, but many want to go to South Tarawa. On their islands, they don't work, but they have everything they need to survive and to be healthy and happy. They go to Tarawa looking for work, but there is none. Half the people don't work, even if they have skills. Tarawa has alcohol, and no jobs, but people come from outer islands thinking they will have a better life."

"That explains all the idle people I saw on the streets in South Tarawa."

"Yes. It is a big, big problem. The Kiribati government should make more of a positive effort to keep people on their outer home islands."

Quickly, we were diving toward one. Its airport was cloaked by a dark gray rain cloud, but the pilot steered the plane straight into it as if flying by Braille—I'd hoped he had GPS. It was a frightening approach, but soon we were on the dirt airstrip, which was freshly damp from the heavy squall.

"You brought the rain!" a tall, friendly mustachioed man said to me His name was Tokamai and he worked as an agricultural consultant for the island council. "It hadn't rained here for two weeks."

Tokamai had arranged for the atoll's council truck to take my luggage to the council guesthouse while he and I would ride old red mopeds there. It was a fair distance from the airport. Dusk had fallen but the bikes' headlights shone brightly, and there was no traffic on the dirt road, which was darkened by the surrounding palm forest. Wearing no helmet, falling coconuts were my main concern.

We stopped at a small aluminum-walled sundries shop. Tokamai bought a tin of tobacco and I asked the clerk for beer, unknowing that alcohol had recently been banned on the atoll. "So many problems have gone away," Tokamai said. "We had many drunks, and even the children were starting to drink. Things are better now."

Faced with a cruel beer-less reality, I set off with Tokamai leading into the darkness, avoiding puddles and palm debris and crabs scuttling across the road. The moon, a perfect crescent, hung from the black sky and silhouetted the treetops. Along the road a few people walked, and every so often a motorbike would pass us, heading the opposite direction.

After a few kilometers, Tokamai, who was ahead of me, stopped suddenly, dismounted his moped, and started tinkering with its fuel line.

"Broken," he said. "Petrol is going onto my leg instead of into the motor. You go ahead to the next village—my cousin lives there. I can borrow his motorbike. Wait for me there."

"Do you want to hop on the back of mine?"

"I cannot leave the motorbike here."

"Why not?"

"It could be stolen. I'll push it to my cousin's."

"Does he speak English?"

"A little."

The village was a 10-minute scoot away; Tokamai described his cousin's place as the thatched shack nearest the left side of the road, to the right of the big chicken coop and the solar panel, with a blue motorbike in front. Despite the dark night, I found it easily. Tokamai's cousin Kokoria was outside on his *buia*, a thatch-covered, raised platform of pandanus leaves and palm wood. It served as a living room, dining room, and bedroom.

Having just finished supper, Kokoria and two dark men were lounging in their sarongs, chainsmoking and coughing and drinking sour toddy next to two small sleeping boys and a dazed wild-haired woman. In front of them were six plates of chicken bones and leftover breadfruit chips. Only Kokoria spoke a bit of English.

An old television set was in the corner. I asked Kokoria if he had satellite TV. "No, only DVD," he said in his gruff smoker's voice. His TV and buia lightbulb were solar-powered, he said, as were many villages in Kiribati. Diesel generators had long proved inefficient, and the government planned to provide solar power for every village.

One man asked Kokoria what I was doing there. An *i-matang* was a rare sight. Kokoria translated, telling him that I was waiting for Tokamai, I was from California, and I was in Kiribati looking for waves to ride.

"He says the waves must be very big where you come from."

"Occasionally," I said.

Unsolicited, the man slid off the *buia* and fetched a green coconut; he hacked a hole into it with the tip of a sharp knife and handed it to me with a brown-toothed smile.

"*Ko rabwa*," I said—Gilbertese for "thank you"—and had a refreshing drink of cool sweet coconut water.

In Kokoria's yard were a few oinking pigs, sleeping cats, clucking chickens, drooling dogs. The dirt was littered with coconuts and husks. It was a comfortable, cozy, well-worn space. It had nothing to do with the 21st century.

"How long have you lived here?" I asked him.

"For my life."

From the darkness Tokamai appeared, his face shiny with sweat. He chatted in Gilbertese with the family for a few minutes, then off we went, into the moonlight, Tokamai on Kokoria's aging moped, accelerating and braking across the uneven coral roadway that wove through the palms between the choppy ocean and the glassy lagoon.

Tokamai left me at the beachfront council guesthouse, a spartan cinderblock box with three small rooms and an echoey dining area with no table or chairs. The beds sagged and the bathroom was mildewed, the toilet had no handle or seat and the shower was a trickle, but it was a decent and cheap place to settle into.

In the kitchen I found some leftover fried breadfruit and cold rice to eat while watching a brilliant midnight moonset over the ocean, my tired mind lulled by the low roar of the small surf and chirping crickets.

Morning was hot and sunny and windless, the air heavy, the ocean smooth and blue. I went for a walk, looking for surf, which I found 10 minutes later at the atoll's quasi port, a man-made cut in the reef that led to the beach. A small yellow supply boat was anchored outside, offloading yellow sacks of rice and white sacks of flour, sent to shore aboard two small skiffs. Women and children sat and watched while men carried the heavy sacks up to a storage shed. Off the right side of the pass was a shapely little right-hand wave, perhaps stomach-high and thin-lipped, peeling through the clear turquoise water over flat reef and into the channel.

I jogged back to the guesthouse, readied my gear, and within 20 minutes tiny fish were swimming 'round my feet as I waited for a set. The waves were inconsistent but fun, alternating between drivey pockets and boggy flat spots, though my board, a 6'9" Andreini quad, carried speed. The water temperature was about 80°F and smelled like a soft and saline *eau de toilette*, oceanic yet woody, perhaps something from Pure Nautica, freshly tropical and soothing to the senses, readymade for the Macy's fragrance display.

Before they stopped coming, I rode four waves. On the third, a large blue parrotfish swam alongside. The beach was a backdrop of thatched huts and coconut palms and white sand. The coral reef was shallow but forgiving. There was no chance of another surfer appearing. It was the consummate remote atoll surf experience.

But the dropping tide killed it, so I paddled in. A brown naked boy leapt onto my board, giggling as his friends watched. They crowded around me as I walked up the beach. The adults on the beach seemed inquisitive. None spoke English. The children shouted at me and grabbed at my surfboard while demanding my name and age. The adults watched with amusement.

"You are like an alien to them," Tokamai said behind me. "They never see white people."

I hadn't noticed him sitting in the shade of the beachfront storage shed.

"How was the surfing?"

"It was fun, but a bit small. Very pretty out there, but a bit of a tease."

"What do you mean?"

"Needs to be a bit bigger—more swell."

Next to him was a woman breast-feeding a baby and a man in a purple sarong who was weaving a mat from pandan leaves. "My cousin and his wife and child," Tokamai said, motioning toward them with his thumb.

A teen girl asked where my wife was. "No wife," I said. Her friend offered me a cigarette that looked like a brown party favor. A pregnant beige dog and a black pig were on the ground together. The pig nuzzled my wet ankles. It was roped to a pandanus tree. There was litter about and a rusted cage and a few beached boats, one outrigger, the rest aluminum skiffs, including the two used for offloading the cargo.

Back at the guesthouse I lunched on fried breadfruit, tuna dumplings, rice, and coconut meat prepared by a fat and friendly young woman in a red floral dress. A bulb-nosed man with frizzy gray hair and wraparound sunglasses was also in the kitchen; he asked me questions—how did I get here? why did I come? where did I come from? was this my first time in Kiribati?—as he made a pot of tea. His name was Tebau, he was 63, and he was born and raised on the atoll.

"Sorry for the questions," he said, "but I am the mayor of this island and I am just curious. Normally we do not get visitors."

"Why not?"

"I am not sure. Because the Kiribati people, I think they are the best people in the world because they love each other, they are peaceful people, and they want to live peacefully with many people of the world. No quarrel, no fighting, no war. Just want to live with an enjoyable life."

"That's reason for tourism?"

"Yes, yes! To see our standard of living and how the people enjoy themselves here our beautiful country. Please, come to our dance this evening. It will be nice for you to see."

After a four-hour nap in my room, there came a knock. "Mister Michael, it is time to go," Tebau said behind the door. The room was dark—night had fallen.

In the council truck we drove for 15 minutes down the bumpy dirt road to a large maneaba, a large and sturdy pavilion-style structure with a high A-frame roof, a cement floor, and no walls. Throughout Kiribati, maneabas were village community centers and general meeting areas where locals could hash out politics, get married, play bingo, sleep, or have traditional *kaimatoa* ("dance of strength") nights, like this one.

"Come," Tebau said motioning to a mat on the floor. "Please sit."

A crowd surrounded the outside of the building. Its floor was open but the perimeter was ringed with dozens of older people sitting and fanning themselves, chatting and eating. It was a boisterous, energized event. Most people smoked cigarettes. Several of the men wore red sarongs and white shirts. Small children sprawled asleep on the cement. "They do not need beds," Tebau told me. "They sleep anywhere."

An impromptu guest, I was asked to introduce myself to the crowd; Tebau translated for them. When he was finished, a bald elderly man in thick eyeglasses stood and sang "God Bless America," something he learned from the U.S. soldiers on Tarawa in 1943. Then in Gilbertese he said to me, "Many thanks to you Americans, or we might be part of Japan. Thank you for letting us keep our home."

A large amount of food was passed around the circle—plastic bowls of chicken, papaya, bananas, rice, breadfruit, crab, coconuts, whole grilled fish—and when the meal was finished, dozens of female dancers appeared, ornately dressed in green grass skirts, white tank-tops, garlands of flowers on their heads and across their torsos and down their arms. All were barefooted. Many wore face paint. The dancing started almost immediately, with simultaneous, loud chanting and singing from the male dancers, who remained seated, and the crowd whooped and yelped along.

Behind the women, several men were sitting around a wooden box and, using it for percussion, they pounded it rhythmically with their hands, hollering in baritone against the shrillness of the women and children. The dancing resembled hula, though its purpose seemed more ceremonial than entertaining. The sweating, unsmiling women gyrated with outstretched arms and sudden bird-like jerks of their heads, almost feverishly, and one of them eventually fainted into the arms of an old lady behind her.

"Black magic," Tebau said. "Ask me about it later."

After several songs, young male dancers appeared, shirtless, decorated florally, and did a form of sitting dance called bino while the women and crowd clapped and sang. Tebau said most of the songs centered on love, and based on the women who wept, it was highly emotive.

After two hours, the event was finished—the dancers and crowd, including me, were exhausted. The air was heavy with the cloying scent of body odor and leftover food, and my legs were sore from sitting cross-legged on the hard mat.

Tebau looked florid. “We go?”

We drove back under a magnificent celestial ceiling—shooting stars, clear moon falling into the ocean. The air temperature was perfect. We bumped along the dirt road through the palm forest, our truck’s lights illuminating the fronds above, like a palm tunnel.

I was curious about the dancer who had collapsed. “Black magic?” I asked Tebau.

“Yes. Here, there are old people who are experts and they know quite a lot of magic regarding the dance. Many of them on the island. And so when a young girl wants to dance for her first time, she has to learn to dance from this expert. After then, he will make you dance, perform the skills for him, and if he thinks you are quite ready to perform a dance during a festival or something like that, he is going to do the magic. This kind of magic is like a black magic, because he is going to give you a kind of magic that will give you strength, so you will be powerful during the dance. A kind of feeling that will make you feel strong, happy, delighted when you perform. During the dance, you scream and shake, because it is from the magic which the old expert dancer did to you.”

“How do they do it?”

“Very early in the morning, they give you a kind of drink.”

“What’s in it?”

“In our culture, it is forbidden for the magicians to share this. But basically it’s from the water of a young coconut, and they mix it with the young shoot of a non plant. The dancer will drink this, and the magic will live with her forever. Many local people die from this. They have the black magic inside of them and sometimes it comes out when they dance. Not every dancer experiences it.”

“But the girl who collapsed tonight, she did?”

“Yes.”

We were driving through a clearing that ran along the beach. The water sparkled beneath the sinking crescent moon. The ocean looked lifeless.

"No waves," I said.

"You did some surfing today?" Tebau asked. "At the harbor? Some Australians have surfed there but in a different time of year. Huge waves at full moon. And spring tide. Now it is neap tide and not full moon, so the waves are very small."

"I noticed."

What surf existed that morning had long vanished. The atoll's leeward Pacific became a lake, and two days later I ascended again, watching an atoll shrink in the distance through the scratched plastic of an Air Kiribati window, eventually landing on another atoll which from aloft looked skeletal and toothy, its beige reef serrated and contoured, split by 10 azure passes, arteries of the lagoon.

Most of them had high surf potential but were all ill-placed. Swell in the Gilberts normally arrived from the wrong side, the windward side, so good waves—and southwest swells—were rare.

But for three days, alone at two of the passes, while the boatman fished, I rode two perfect rights, engaging a private daydream that all surfers would desire. Both passes had a left opposite the channel. The rights were head-high and fast. The wind was offshore. The coral reef was kaleidoscopic. This place was nothing like home.

"GET THE GAFF ready, man!"

Mike, a laughing American, beseeched the i-Kiribati boat driver watching him crank the reel, teasing the trembling line from the depths. A large fish was on the other end. Mike's pale face was flushed red, his white shirt dimmed with sweat and saltwater, his veins adrenaline-fueled. The three of us were aboard a 33-foot panga a few hundred yards offshore, in sight of the waves I'd surfed, admiring the outer-atoll scenery, drinking XXXX beer, and we'd trolled for an hour before something else bit.

"Got it!" Mike wrestled the large dog-toothed tuna onto the deck, next to the long barracuda he'd hooked earlier. "Sashimi tonight, dudes?"

Not a fisherman, Mike was a friendly man with a serious mind. He was 41, tall and blue-eyed, a multi-tour combat veteran who spent nine years as a sergeant in the United States Marine Corps. He also spent four years as an infantry squad leader in the California Army National Guard. He was intelligent and thoughtful and unassuming. His blond hair was shaven and he spoke with a slight drawl. He voted Republican. He loved his country. He loved beer. He loved hunting and camping and riding BMW motorcycles under a big sky; he ran a motorcycle rental business with his wife in Montana, but confided to me that he was unhappily married. He dreamnt of being a park ranger someplace pretty. He hated cities. He missed the military but enjoyed his civilian freedom very much. He carried with him the solemnent weariness of a fighter who had seen the hell of war and humanity at its worst, the suffering and the drama, and he knew well the scent of death.

Like the Middle East, Mike was not in Kiribati for joy, but he'd wrested 24 R&R hours on the outer atoll we fished from. He was not a surfer nor a sailor and had never lived by an ocean—the Pacific was not his habitat. He preferred snowy mountains and open prairie. He'd learned of Kiribati from an article in the January 2010 issue of the USCM's *Leatherneck* magazine and had flown from Montana for one reason: the Battle of Tarawa.

In 2010, 67 years after World War II, 74,190 American soliders—nearly 20 percent of the war's casualties—were still listed as Missing In Action. They never returned to the country they fought to preserve. They died on obscure battlefields and were sunk in makeshift graves, but their bones were never retrieved. Mike knew of this. It irked him. The Leatherneck article smacked his solar plexus.

The story detailed Moore's Maurauders, a non-profit group of anthropologists, archeologists, doctors, scientists, educators, retired military generals and admirals, police officers, and soldiers who shared one mission of finding the remains of the Tarawa MIAs that the U.S. government deemed recoverable. Mike enrolled immediately and was tasked with recon and logistics.

"The lost men on Tarawa are a mystery and a well-kept secret by our military and government," he told me as we motored back to land, fresh fish on the dinner menu. "We've never lost the graves of so many who were killed. Technically they're MIA, but it's more accurate to say their graves were misplaced."

"Why search for them?" I asked.

"Closure is what this mission really is all about. There are many people who don't know what happened to their loved ones here. We want to bring closure and awareness of the tragedy and the truth about what really happened to those brave men. They were lost and forgotten and they deserve better from their country."

Soon after the three-day 1943 battle, the U.S. Navy and Army built buildings and repaired the Japanese runway. Original soldier burial sites were moved and grave markers went astray. During the construction activity, hundreds were lost.

"A total lack of training and procedural control," Mike said.

Between Army and Navy miscommunication, management of the ad hoc graves promptly failed after the Marines' Tarawa departure.

In 1946 the U.S. sent a recovery team and 1,100 coffins to Tarawa; just 500 bodies were found and placed in the interim Lone Palm Cemetery. That mission was followed by another to retrieve the bodies from Lone Palm and bring them home. The other 600-plus MIAs were not sought until August 2010, when an archeological team for the U.S. Joint POW/MIA Accounting Command set up shop.

"So far, remains have been found under buildings, in trash dumps, under pig pens," Mike said. "Everywhere."

"Why'd you get involved"

"I felt a personal obligation to help bring the story of these men to some kind of conclusion. I'd want someone to do it for my family if I were a MIA. And the courage of those men deserves to be honored properly. Generations of us never knew of the real failure on Tarawa. We never knew the whole sad story. Marines don't leave their brothers behind, but we did. I can honestly tell you that every last one of us wants to help make this right."

"Why haven't they been recovered?"

"That's the million-dollar question."

Hours later I laid sticky and wakeful in the muggy darkness of my small bungalow on that desolate isle, listening to the soft rustle of surf on the reef and the dozens of black noddies, cooing and chortling as they flew about. I could also hear the screams of soldiers and the searing din of fighter planes and the exploding grenades and bombs and the swarms of bullets and the hissing flamethrowers and the thud of a man hitting dirt, exhaling for his last time.

Ratta-tat-tat-tat-tat.

Ratta-tat-tat-tat-tat-tat.

And I thought: today, despite its fickleness, Kiribati might be a good place to go surfing.

31

DOUBLE RAINBOW
2004

—EAST—

WITH THE LIGHTS low, on a clear night, anyone in a thirty-mile radius of Lompoc, California, can witness the miracle of rocket science, spearing the wee-hour sky with white-hot intensity, thrusting up, then over and out, high across the Pacific.

One summer night several years ago, camped illegally on a remote beach of Vandenberg Air Force Base (*Welcome to Space Country*), I saw my first missile-launch as I rubbed my eyes, tentless and shivering next to rotting kelp at the base of a low, dusty bluff.

In deep sleep I heard the launch's muted rumble, an aural oddity blending with the south swell cracking off the reef I would surf come sunrise, risking military arrest. Coyotes howled at the thin, bright line arcing across black sky, addressing the disturbance along this otherwise serene and ultimately high-tech coastline.

I later learned that the missile was fired from a launch pad near Point Sal, twenty-five miles north. But where was that missile going, and why?

A week later, lunching in a sunny downtown bistro, I found a coffee-stained Santa Barbara News-Press dated from the day of the launch:

VANDENBERG AFB—An unarmed Minuteman III intercontinental ballistic missile (ICBM) was successfully launched from North Vandenberg at 1:03 a.m. PDT today.

The mission was part of the Force Development Evaluation Program, which tests the reliability and accuracy of the weapon system.

The missile's two unarmed re-entry vehicles traveled approximately 4,200 miles in about 30 minutes, hitting pre-determined targets at the Kwajalein Missile Range in the western chain of the Marshall Islands.

THAT EVENING, I fished online and found a comprehensive Web site for the U.S. Army's Ronald Reagan Ballistic Missile Defense Test Site on Kwajalein, the world's largest atoll, in the Marshall Islands, rented for $11 million annually by the U.S. for a very specific purpose:

The Reagan Test Site (RTS) is a premiere asset within the Department of Defense Major Range and Test Facility Base. The unquestioned value of RTS is based upon its strategic geographical location, unique instrumentation, and unsurpassed capability to support ballistic missile testing and space operations. With nearly 40 years of successful support, RTS provides a vital role in the research, development, test and evaluation effort of America's missile defense and space programs.

THE MARSHALL ISLANDS, in the middle of the equatorial Pacific, are a Micronesian republic of twenty-nine atolls and five individual islands, nearly all of them inhabited and swell-blessed. As far as I knew, the only surfers there were some Americans who worked for the U.S. government. Intelligence about Marshallese surf potential was scant, limited mainly to what the expats occasionally surfed on Kwajalein and Majuro atolls.

Months after my Vandenberg camping trip, on a breezy, rainbowy morning in paradise, my friend Lance deposited me curbside at Honolulu International Airport, the Marshall Islands a five-hour flight away.

There's gotta be waves, brah," Lance said before pulling away from the curb. "You might be the first to surf some reef pass."

Kwajalein Atoll eluded me ("Sorry, sir," drawled an official from the U.S. Army Space & Missile Defense Command headquarters in Alabama, "but journalists just ain't allowed on Kwajalein."), though my flight landed at the military base on Kwajalein Island, en route to Majuro, to offload a few government workers and contractors. The terminal was drab, unwelcoming, with rust and flaky paint—like a prison, not a gateway—with ominous armed guards prowling its perimeter, eyeing our jet.

Five weeks prior, within one minute of landing here, New Mexico-based documentarian Adam Horowitz was arrested ("It's a shame nobody got that on video," he said) for filming the terminal from the plane's stairway. He was revisiting the Marshalls to create a sequel to his "Home on the Range" documentary, aired several years ago on PBS, detailing the relocation of Marshallese from Kwajalein Island to adjacent Ebeye Island, referred in *National Geographic* as "the slum of the Pacific."

Wearing handcuffs while the jet full of Majuro-bound civilians sat on the tarmac, Horowitz argued with the base commander.

"What's your idea of good journalism?" Horowitz asked. "Fox News?"

"Fox News is good journalism."

"What about Oliver North?"

"Oliver North is a good American."

"He subverted the Constitution."

Red-faced, the commander finally protested, "You're not a journalist! You're a damned loaded gun!"

In "Home on the Range," Horowitz declassified Kwajalein Atoll's conversion into a top-secret U.S. missile and "Star Wars" test site, flecked with radar dishes, highlighting the squalor of Ebeye and its displaced population's mission to regain their Kwajalein Island turf.

Three thousand Americans live on nine-hundred-acre Kwajalein Island; twelve thousand Marshallese live on eighty-acre Ebeye, described in my guidebook as having "the harsh, parched look of a Sonoran desert barrio that was picked up and dropped here so that Kwaj could have a supply of cheap labor."

Horowitz, thin and pale, piercingly blue-eyed and hawkish, with a head of kinky black hair, was an archetype of his ilk, like a paparazzo or war correspondent—abrasive, edgy, focused, intelligent, cynical, stopping at nothing to gain what he needs to produce what some would define as controversial and unpatriotic. To the U.S. Army, of course, Horowitz is a parasite, out to expose impurities within the system.

"My first film made the military look pretty bad, which is easy to do," he confided over beers one night in the crowded restaurant above my Majuro hotel. "Americans took all the best land, and the native owners live in the slum next door. Yet on Kwajalein Island, you have swimming pools, playing fields, professional landscaping, a bowling alley, golf courses, a Safeway, fresh produce, fresh meat. I hope my films will help the Marshallese gain some of the justice and basic human rights denied them by the U.S. for the sake of its weapons programs. If the American public really knew what we have done, and are continuing to do over there, they'd be outraged and ashamed."

I said, "I've heard it described as a rich American suburb stuck in middle of the Pacific."

"That's exactly what it is."

Japan ruled Kwajalein after taking it from Germany in 1914, during World War I, heeding a 1920 mandate from the League of Nations to govern all of Micronesia. More than twenty years later, during World War II, the U.S. Navy seized Kwajalein from Japan, and in 1947 the Marshalls were added to the U.S.'s Trust Territory of the Pacific Islands, which ultimately led to America's infamous eleven-year nuclear testing program.

Until 1958, Kwajalein was used to support the tests, which, after sixty-six detonations, had ruined Bikini and Enewetak atolls, westernmost of the Marshalls, vaporizing various islands and irradiating natives. (Despite relocation of their residents and millions of dollars in decontamination efforts, both atolls remain somewhat radioactive; Bikini has become an elite dive destination, while Enewetak has a bomb crater full of radioactive waste, capped with two feet of cement.)

When 1963's Limited Test Ban Treaty banished open-air nuclear testing (France quickly took it underground in Polynesia's surf-rich Tuamotu Archipelago), the U.S. established the Pacific Missile Range on Kwajalein Atoll. Today, Kwajalein monitors satellites and is the blue-water catcher's mitt for measuring splashdown accuracy of rockets fired from Vandenberg Air Force Base, another militarized fetch of obscure waves, armed guards, and spooky white radar dishes.

I WENT DEEP-SEA fishing my first day on Majuro. Captain Darryl fired up his small boat, the *Wild Fire*, and we blasted out into the big blue, which was lake-calm.

"You won't find any waves this time of year," he said. "I have a few mates who surf at home and they know what they're talking about."

"What part of Australia are you from?"

"New Zealand."

"Do you surf?"

"Once in a while." I could tell he was bullshitting. "But there's no surf here, mate. You've come at the wrong time."

Darryl didn't know his ass from his elbow regarding swells and surf conditions, so I ignored him. Instead, I chatted with the guy driving the boat, Bacchus from Oregon, who assured me his parents really did name him after the Greek god of wine.

"What can I say? I love pinot noir."

He had skippered many dive boats in the Caribbean and Hawai'i, and today was his first day on the job in the Marshalls. He and his wife had arrived on my flight from Honolulu.

"Love this job, man," Bacchus grinned. His teeth were perfect. "What other gig lets you cruise the ocean all day, go diving, see unreal things, and get paid for doing it? Nothing else."

Turns out we both once lived in two of the same California towns, both attended the same colleges, and both knew the same people. Here we were, on a tiny boat off Majuro, the first day of his job and the first day of mine, with so much to talk about. Too much, actually—I was at the onset of a cold and my throat was sore by the time we motored back to port, fishless. Not a bite or snag. Darryl blamed it on the windless and utterly hot conditions.

"The fish don't bite when it's like this, mate. Better when it's overcast and a bit windy."

"Then why did we go out today?"

"What else is there to do?"

"Look for surf."

Later, Bacchus suggested I attend a lagoon 'booze cruise' come sunset on the large *Oleanda*, another of Darryl's boats. There would be free food and beer, he said, and likely a few keen women. Despite my impending illness, I agreed and met him onboard at five-thirty.

The ship smelled of decay and had chipped paint and blotchy wood—it looked like an abused ferry more than a pleasure boat. Previously it had been used as a mothership for expensive dive charters up at Rongelap Atoll, which was recently opened for tourism but too remote and too costly to operate from. The *Oleanda* sailed to Majuro for additional dive business, but tonight, with stale hors d'oeuvres and overpriced beer and Pink Floyd on the stereo, it slid slowly across the tranquil, incandescent lagoon, toward the orange setting sun.

From this vantage, Majuro was a spread of small, boxy buildings interspersed with uneven palm tufts and flat color. Majuro seemed to be one of the world's bypassed places, the kind with few natural resources, an inconvenient location, and a government leniency toward Asian countries raping the atoll's fishery at an astounding rate.

The air was soft and restorative—until a woman near me lit a cigarette. Everyone smoked. The stench revived memories of cramped pubs and loud parties, college nights in Arcata and Isla Vista, drinking in Swansea and Stockholm, hangovers, sweaty sleep, women, wasted days.

In the spacious open-air lounge I sat and watched the passengers mingle, an odd mix of mostly American expats, student volunteers, and unprofessional businessmen. Feeling antisocial, I scribbled in a notebook, pretending to be busy. My forehead was greasy and my underarms reeked; I felt lousy.

Consuming beer in a hot country never made sense—so dehydrating, so caloric—but no one seems to mind, especially expats with little else to do. The ship was full of these people.

At the next table, then, came Don from Marina del Rey, who was sure I had made a poor choice in coming to the Marshalls for surf. He was dog-faced and wore a red floral shirt and his hairstyle was an awful ponytailed mullet. He squinted at me, clutching a wet can of Miller Lite.

"It's too calm here, man. Why don't you just stick to Hawai'i?"

"Because that's not my job."

"What's your job?"

"I'm not sure."

And there was Denny, who wouldn't tell me where he was from, wearing a hideous red shirt that matched his skin. He was freckly and had bright orange hair and a weedy mustache. He was a wholesale distributor on Majuro, in his forties, and he was drunk. He swayed and slurred.

"I haven't slept with a white girl in twenty years, damnit. It was a hairy Peace Corps girl. You could say I'm converted now. Must've been my trips in Afghanistan and Pakistan. India, too. Dirty place!"

He handed me his business card then put his mouth close to my ear, as if he were about to disclose an unspeakable secret.

"Hey, no matter how small your question, call me, but I'll never been in the office. You'll find me with a nubile...*in a naked state*."

Saying this seemed to please him. I pitied any female human who would sleep with Denny.

Moments later the *Oleanda* motored past a Taiwanese purse seiner; deckhands stood idly astern, sucking on cigarettes, gazing at our Jolly Ship of Drunken Expats. The snobby young woman with smeared lipstick next to me sucked on her cigarette and said pensively, "Look at those poor fishermen, working so hard when we're all partying like rock stars."

She looked at me abruptly. "Have you been to New Zealand?"

"I was once fined two hundred dollars in Auckland's airport."

"For what?"

"For bringing a carrot and some plums from New Caledonia to Auckland. I was constipated. The fruits were actually grown in New Zealand."

"Isn't New Caledonia like France or something?"

"To a degree. The surf is very good there. The capital city is very Francophile."

She blew smoke toward the purse seiner. "I hate the French. Surfers are dumb."

These expats and the smokers and the noise and the sloppiness—this was not why I'd come. It can be unsettling how people you meet in distant places make you feel as if you're actually somewhere else. The modern conveniences are there but the soul of the place is not.

As soon as the ship docked, I hailed a taxi and thought of tomorrow, seeking surf and culture and the unsoiled splendor that was so close yet so removed from what I had just seen.

ROBERT LOUIS STEVENSON, visiting Majuro Atoll in 1889, called it the "Pearl of the Pacific," and rightly so, because in 1889 Majuro was but a palmy coral ring. There was no unsightly industry, or rusty beer cans, or junked cars, or broken glass, or graffiti, or plastic debris, or diesel exhaust, or bar fights, or Asian ships in the lagoon, or ugly seawalls and the flimsy tin shacks virtually everywhere you looked in 2004.

Throughout history, Westernization has tainted the tropics in a myriad fashion—tradition fizzles, alcoholism pervades, families split, teens kill themselves or become pregnant. Pollution accrues as non-biodegradable goods are imported, requiring landfills on islands three feet above sea level, with only porous, rubbly coral for soil, and a very shallow water table. Still, Majuro has no honeymoon resorts or Bora Bora beaches, or much tourism infrastructure to speak of, yet it retains a peculiar charm in the smiles and ease of its people.

Before leaving home, I received an e-mail from Ric, a globe-trotting American who was building a tiny eco-resort on a ten-acre island on neighboring Arno Atoll:

"I wouldn't go in the water at Majuro. Too much boat and people pollution. Surf Arno instead. Fully private, fun waves all to yourself. It is better than porno!"

Majuro, nine miles west of Arno, is the Marshalls' nerve center, home to the republic's primary government, most of the its business, and about half of its entire population, making it one of the most densely populated atolls on Earth.

Despite all of this, and the atoll's penchant for attracting stray swell, surfers are essentially unknown. The few on Majuro are expat white American teachers and Seventh Day Adventist volunteers who can barely wax a surfboard, let alone handle the sucky tubes at the Bridge, Majuro's marquee surf spot.

The bridge itself, built with Japanese yen in 1983, is twelve feet high, deeming it Majuro's highest point, spanning a narrow channel the Japs blasted here to spare small boats the hassle of entry/exit up at Calalen Channel, several miles from the lagoon anchorage. Oddly, my Moon guidebook made mention of the spot:

> *The bottom is a very hard reef that should not be surfed, and there are often dangerous currents in the channel as the tide goes out. This is not a place for anyone but experts.*

I'M NO EXPERT, but the Bridge was quite good, a tropical Little Drakes (of Hollister Ranch fame), sans surly locals, shallower, with a severely jagged coral reef and parrot fish instead of flat, seaweedy rock and pinnipeds.

Konou Smith is a pilot for Air Marshall Islands and, in his early thirties, is Majuro's only native surfer. We surfed the Bridge one evening, trading waves facing a pastel sunset. The air was windless, the dusk soft and silent.

Between sets, he peered at the colorful reef, about two feet below our toes.

"The last time I surfed here was 1999, after El Niño. The coral was dead. Lots more coral here now. That's a healthy sign, eh?"

Konou found his atoll-escape via aviation several years ago, educating himself in the U.S., flying in Hawai'i and northern California, living years without speaking Marshallese. A few weeks after I left, Konou was again on O'ahu, newly enlisted in the U.S. Coast Guard.

After the session, in the dark, we drifted under the bridge with the incoming current and stepped back into the large blue garbage truck he had borrowed for a few hours, which, straight from the job, reeked of rot and household filth.

On the way back to town, we stopped at a house Konou was helping to renovate. Four young men were inside, coiling power cords and finishing the work day. The house smelled of mold and sawdust.

"I might move in," Konou said. "Would be nice, don't you think?"

I nodded and noticed a small square chicken-wire cage on the floor in the room's far corner, with a large coconut crab in it.

"What's this?"

"We found it in a tree outside."

"How long have you had it?"

"Maybe one week. We had a baby crab in there, too. One afternoon, we noticed the baby was missing a claw. Next morning, the baby was gone. That crab ate it." He pointed to the hideous creature.

"How does it survive?"

"We just keep feeding chunks of coconut to it."

Outside, twilight was limbo, a sea of stars crowding into a waxing moon, with a rain cloud directly overhead. The downpour was quick and seemed to occur only on us. We lumbered off down the road, passing people sitting outside their houses or roadside markets, or walking up or down the street, past houses with dinner on the table, everyone moving very slowly. The streetlights reflected brightly in the puddles in the road and off to the side, and though dark, the place appeared rejuvenated from the day's scorching sun.

Back at the hotel I couldn't help but think that the poor coconut crab—in its cage, kept alive artificially, mercifully—was metaphoric of the Marshalls' own precarious survival, completely dependent on U.S. subsidies, namely the Compact of Free Association, developed in 1983 and renewed in 2003. The Compact allows for substantial payments from the U.S. to the Marshallese government until 2023; including its Kwajalein rent, the U.S. will pay fifty-four million dollars annually to the Marshall Islands, cutting to thirty-seven million annually in 2017.

But the cash isn't supposed to evaporate by then. The Compact's authors envisioned the creation of a wholesome trust fund, which would garner interest, aiding the Marshalls after the U.S. withdraws in 2023. Time will tell whether both countries can fulfill the dream of economic self-sufficiency via interest rates and calculated spending.

The 2004 U.S. presidential elections were two months off, and things were really heating up on the satellite news stations—CNN and BBC World News showcased endless, shameless mudslinging between George W. Bush and John Kerry, the republicans and the democrats.

Down at the hotel bar that night, I asked the man next to me, a short and fattish Marshallese senator, who he would vote for if he was a U.S. citizen. He pursed his lips and shrugged impishly.

"Whoever will give us more money. Does Bush give us a lot of money? I think yes, he does. We are improving our things. But we need more nuclear testing reparations. Will John Kerry give us that money? Nobody knows. You Americans spend so much money on new war and weapons, but you don't fix what you destroyed so many years ago. And I ask why? We all ask you why?" He opened his hands at me.

Suddenly I felt like the hard, hairy, faceless coconut crab, hiding in my shell in this dim corner of the room. No one was dropping me scraps of coconut to survive, but I couldn't help sense a personal pang of guilt from the U.S.'s occasional selfishly destructive history. And here I was, nursing a Jack Daniel's on ice, watching American football (New York Giants: 20, Washington Redskins: 14) on the big-screen TV, with ZZ Top blaring from the pub's stereo:

I'm shufflin' through the Texas sand
But my head's in Mississippi—
Last night I saw a naked cowgirl
She was floatin' across the ceilin'

THE DINNER SPECIAL was in fact coconut crab, served whole. I slurped soup and crept back to my nuclear-free room, to CNN and a clean bed.

TWO WEEKS BEFORE my trip, after a night of particular debauchery, I took an online quiz, twenty-four yes-or-no questions to gauge one's alcoholism, scored thusly: zero to three meant you were a "probable social drinker"; four meant you were "borderline"; five-plus meant "possible alcoholism"; nine-plus meant "probable alcoholism."

I scored twenty-one.

So I was thrilled to learn that booze was illegal in the Marshalls' outer atolls. I could detoxify and sunbathe, read and explore, surf and snorkel, liberated from morning-after nausea and unfounded aggression. The outer Marshallese were a dusky race of purity, curiosity, sweetness, and their environs were brightly sterile and surfy, with no thugs or thievery. If there is one place Alcoholics Anonymous should build a rehab center, it is there.

One morning Konou and I boarded an old Dornier 228 prop plane and buzzed north to Likiep Atoll, stopping on Wotje en route. We would spend an hour or so on Likiep and return to Majuro late that same day. Basically, it was a surf-recon flight.

The noisy nineteen-seater was tight but comfortable, flying smooth and low, affording fine vistas of the reef passes and bluey-green ribbons of land between vast expanses of sea.

"A new plane costs three million dollars," Konou said. "We can refurbish this one in New Zealand for a hundred and fifty thousand. I hope I get on that flight: Majuro to Tarawa to Tuvalu to Nadi to Nouméa to Norfolk Island to North Island to Christchurch."

"That's quite a trip."

He reconsidered. "Actually, I hope I don't get that flight. I can't be in this plane for that long."

At daybreak, Konou had piloted the Majuro-Jaluit-Kili-Majuro flight, and now was serving as my ad hoc guide to Likiep, an oblique, simple atoll of sixty-five islands and wide lagoon. Its quality-wave potential seemed high.

"Once, during takeoff here, I ran over a pig," Konou said. "We stopped and turned around, but by that time, some boys from the village had dragged the pig off somewhere—it was their family's dinner for the week."

With loud pops and bangs, we bounced along Likiep's dirt airstrip, soon convening with passengers at the "terminal," a small pale cinderblock room with a few benches out front, surrounded by what appeared to be Likiep's entire population. The weekly plane was a spectacle, like a cockfight, for virgin eyes in a place without electricity, telephones, television, gas stations, grocery stores, pavement, police, or alcohol.

We were greeted by iconic Likiep personality Joe deBrum, whose great-grandfather sailed here on a Portuguese whaling ship in the late 1800s, purchasing the atoll from its chief.

Joe was sixty-two, short and slight, with a receding hairline and white stubble on his mousy face. He had squinty eyes, large ears, slightly buck teeth, and the taut brown skin of his German-Portuguese heritage, unaffected by a lifetime of tropic sun. He wore a white T-shirt depicting a colorful nautical map of the Hawai'ian Islands, and blue shorts, no shoes. He was very friendly and smiled constantly.

I admired his shirt. "Have you been to Hawai'i?"

"Oh! Many time. I love Hawai'i, especially the Kaua'i." He waved his hand in the air. "But here is more really beautiful! Would you like to see my beach?"

Konou and I sat on cardboard in the dirty bed of his white pickup truck for a few bumpy miles through lush forest to a serene crescent of sand, veering out toward the pass, site of two potentially epic waves. But not today.

At the end of the track behind a white picket fence was Joe's hotel, the Plantation Haus, a quaint and spartan cluster of twelve rooms around a courtyard strewn with tools, nets, fuel drums, skiffs, and, in the center of it all, a long mesh table used for drying salted fish, thus becoming "salt fish," a local favorite.

A dusky man in a blue shirt laid on the mesh about fifty pink fillets of raw marlin, all soon layered with flies, left to dry under the sweltering sun. (*Why don't they use nets?*) It was this combination of flesh and flies that dissuaded me from trying salt fish. Konou ate a few pieces.

"We'll see how long it stays down," he said.

On the flight back to Majuro we made an unscheduled stop on Maloelap, where I, the only white person around, urinated behind a thin tree, unable to get out of sight of the watchful villagers. Maloelap was another beautiful little atoll, identical to Likiep and every other atoll I had seen in the world, and I thought: What must life be like with no mountains?

A bit later, above Aur Atoll, Konou looked at me and winced, hand on belly.

"My stomach is in knots," he said. "I'm beginning to feel that salt fish."

The next day I too felt lousy, not from rank seafood but from the common cold I had been fighting since my first day in Majuro. I was stuffy and sniffy, with a dull headache and general fatigue.

So I watched television. BBC World News reported that on the other side of the world, Hurricane Ivan (Category Five, winds approaching three hundred knots) had trashed Jamaica and was spinning toward Cuba and the Cayman Islands, where residents were understandably hysterical.

But Majuro was sunny and tranquil and its air was calm, and wasting the day inside my hotel room sounded pathetic, so I took a taxi to Delap, on Majuro's southeastern tip, which, according to Konou, had good surf. It did, so I photographed it, coughing and blowing my nose into the dirt.

Four roosters ran around, cackling and pecking feverishly. Dirty stray dogs ran amok. Fronting the wave was a corrugated aluminum box elevated two feet about the coral rubble by rotten wood and rusty nails. In it was a surly warthog doing circles, glaring at me, threatening to escape and maul me, but it never did. If it wanted to flee its home, I'm sure it would have long ago. The shack next to the warthog's had three women in nice sitting on the ground outside, wearing Sunday church clothes, backs to the wall, staring aimlessly ahead at nothing, likely bored out of their skulls.

Off in the distance I could see a faint smudge that was Arno, nine miles out, a virgin atoll untouched by the ills of modernity. Comparatively, Majuro was Manhattan, so at that moment I decided I wanted to leave it as soon as possible.

I WAS TOLD that a trip to Majuro couldn't be complete without an Arno visit, anyway, so I booked a berth on its ferry and left at noon the next day. The "ferry" was a smallish speedboat with few passengers, and there was nowhere to sit except on the coolers of food Francis Reimers had brought for the time we were to spend out there. He owned the cottage we were staying in, and would be staying there also.

"Eight years ago I bought eleven acres on Arno for fifteen thousand dollars," he said. "I pay good money for the land. Normally it is three hundred dollars an acre. I grow bananas, papaya, corn, cabbage, radish, potato, bell pepper, tomatoes, string beans, eggplant. I grow on Arno then sell it in my dad's store here on Majuro."

"Are there no stores on Arno?" I asked him.

"No, there is nothing like that. There is not even telephones or electricity!"

Francis was the godfather of Arno and Majuro. Heavyset, sixty-two, darkly German-looking, with connections to just about everybody everywhere. He was a reliable and friendly man, with a deep, husky voice and dirty T-shirts and squashed sandals. His eyes were bloodshot, his face fleshy, and his skin was clean. He weighed two hundred and forty-two pounds and somewhat resembled my uncle Steve, who lives in Utah.

Francis was powerful, widely respected, well-liked, and a successful businessman educated in Honolulu. His grandfather Robert sailed from Germany years ago and set up shop on Majuro, opening a store, a hotel, a dock, and establishing a sort of legacy in a place galaxies away from Frankfurt.

As we motored out of the Majuro lagoon, we passed a Protestant church. Francis mentioned he was devout Baha'i and was chairman of the Marshalls' national spiritual assembly. This surprised me, so I asked him about it.

"I used to be Catholic," he said. "Catholics are supposed to marry once. I have been married three times."

"Where is the religion from originally?"

"Iran. Nineteenth century."

"What took you from Catholicism to Bahaism?"

"A long time ago I learned about the unity teachings of one god. There should only be one religion, one god. Why are we having all these religions?"

"Everyone is different, I guess."

"We are here on Earth to develop our spiritual qualities with our kindness and justice. In the womb you have eyes, a nose, but you don't know what to do with them. You accept what you have and you grow and develop yourself. Those hands, the nose. When you're born into this world, it is the only place you can develop spiritual qualities."

"That may be true, unless you lived on the moon."

Joining us was Chris Leonard, a friendly and articulate twenty-nine-year-old business reporter from Fayatteville, Arkansas, who was wrapping a three-week assignment for the *Arkansas Democrat-Gazette*. He had never surfed, was a clean-cut sort, about my height, very intelligent and enlightening to chat with. He had sideburns and short brown hair, he swam in his boxer shorts, and he often wore plaid collared shirts, calling himself a "square," which I dismissed.

In 2002 he began researching the phenomenon of the many Marshallese who've migrated to Springdale, Arkansas, to work at Tyson Foods. Three thousand Marshallese live in Springdale, about five percent of the Marshalls' entire population, creating the largest collection of Marshallese outside the islands themselves.

In 2004 Chris received a World Affairs Journalism Fellowship through the *Arkansas Democrat-Gazette* to dissect the Marshallese immigration from Micronesia to Arkansas, and vice versa. Today, after visiting Majuro and Kwajalein's Ebeye Island, this journey to Arno was his last before heading home to greet the onset of the American Midwest winter.

I asked him how his trip had been thus far.

"I didn't get in the ocean for the first two weeks," he said, "because the crystal-clear lagoons of Majuro and Ebeye were filled with garbage from the city—diapers, cans, Styrofoam and plastic junk floating in the surf. Nasty."

"Seen that in poor island nations all over the South Pacific. It's sad."

"Yeah, the Marshalls' economic situation is terribly depressing, too, but in Majuro I was inspired by the government officials and economic developers who tackle their nation's problems with undying energy and optimism."

"What about Ebeye?"

"The people there are plagued by health problems and overcrowding, but I was amazed at their hospitality and generosity."

"Typical of people who have nothing."

"Yeah. And it wasn't uncommon to interview a family in their home for an hour before they finally asked: 'Now, who are you? What are you doing here?' I was a stranger asking personal questions, but they never failed to invite me in. Here I've met some of the best people I have ever encountered, and some of the worst."

To me traveling with Chris was a serendipitous encounter—two writers the same age, on the same boat to Arno, staying at the same house for the same number of days, here to write about the same place. We had even stayed in the same Majuro hotel. He was never without a reporter's notepad and a pen and had no camera or tape recorder—Chris was a reporter in the truest sense, and I respected him instantly. I had written for two newspapers in northern California and could relate to his quest of knowing the facts, of constant questions and purebred documentation. It was not for everyone, certainly not a weak soul, and Chris's certainly had something mine lacked.

Upon docking at Arno we were gathered in a rusted red pickup truck and driven to the cottage, but not before stopping at a ramshackle hut in a shady grove of coconut palms. There two women were boiling breadfruit in coconut milk, like a soup, eaten with any type of fried fish, in this case red snapper. We sampled some—it was excellent—then left.

It was a glorious afternoon, and on the way into the harbor I had noticed swell curling along the reefs. I was going surfing, damnit—the nearest surfer was Konou, nine miles away back on Majuro.

Problem was, the pickup truck we were in was one of three operational cars on the entire atoll, and I couldn't borrow it.

"You can use my bike," Francis said.

"How far is the beach from the cottage?"

"Oh, not far. Maybe a few minutes by bike. Longer if you walk, of course."

"Does your bike work?"

"As far as I know."

We arrived the cottage a few minutes later, a small red barn short on fashion but long on function, with no air conditioning. I saw the bike: both tires were flat.

"No problem," Francis said. "Just carry this bike pump with you."

So I rigged the pump to the handlebars with a decayed bungee cord, stuffed my gear into a backpack and, board underarm, set off down the road back toward the harbor, riding with one hand and barely missing several rocks, coconuts, and muddy potholes.

Dense forest hid the coast except at the harbor. Once there, I scanned the ocean. Whitewater was everywhere, but it looked bigger to the south, and I was determined to discover a wave no surfer had ever seen. The conditions were promising, so I continued south onto an increasingly narrow and rutted track through wild jungle—this part of the atoll was virtually uninhabited, so who needed a traversable road?

But the bike was a pathetic piece of shit, with weeds wrapped in its gears, and it wobbled horribly, likely because everything on it was loose. I was sweating madly. Both tires were flat again, so I stopped at a thin clearing. Here the land was so narrow that I was five feet on either side of water, the calm turquoise lagoon on my left, the sparkly and equally turquoise Pacific on my right...which had a perfect right-hand reef wave peeling into deep water not far offshore.

What?

No hallucination: Here was something special, and it looked too good to be true, which in fact was, because I had a squirmy 5'11" fish and the sets were a top-to-bottom double-overhead, boiling along a slab of shallow, healthy coral. Nothing I saw earlier was remotely this size—either the swell had suddenly jacked, or it was coming from a very particular angle that denied the rest of the atoll.

This Marshall Islands trip, a journey far from anywhere, full of downtime and delay, was the result of a dream to surf the equatorial unknown. And on this bright and sunny day it was in front of me, through a lush palm grove, tucked into a broken coral beach on a deserted coast. Nobody knew I was here. There were no fisherman about, no beachcombers or kids, no chickens or stray dogs. Other discoveries ensued—including a prime left-hander—but this one was the most private, and it is what remained with me when I left Arno—the essence of surf travel.

I paddled out with my water camera and snapped some photos, first from afar for casual perspective, then up-close for personal intimidation. On the beach, the coconut palm thicket glowed brightly green in the direct late-day sun, and it would have been a perfect postcard image had my camera continued to work—I shot half a roll, then it was done.

I attempted to shoulder-hop a few on the inside, but there was too much water moving around for my fish to function, notwithstanding the busted camera around my neck. So I paddled in. The bike was gone.

HIS NAME WAS Chuck Cook, he was fifty-two, he was from Costa Mesa, California, and he had been sleeping alone in a tent on the beach near our cottage for three weeks.

"I haven't been to heaven, man, but I've been here," he said.

We were shaking hands in the cottage's main doorway. Chuck had brought three fresh coconuts.

"I have a shortwave radio," he said. "Last night I heard about Bill Clinton's triple bypass surgery. Some people might say he deserves it, that bastard!" And he laughed hysterically.

Chuck wore blowsy leopard-print soccer shorts and various accoutrements—a stainless steel watch; stainless steel anklets and bracelets from Thailand; silver rings from India, Malaysia, and Mexico; two toe rings; a Marshallese shell necklace; a dragon necklace from Cambodia ("...because I was born in the year of the dragon...."); three ornate gem rings on each hand. His hair was combed neatly, like he'd just stepped from the shower, not a moldy tent on the beach.

What struck me immediately was his tan, which was so dark it looked painted-on; Chuck was Caucasian but looked like a Spaniard or a Brazilian. His skin was clear and undamaged, and he seemed healthy and literate. His eyes were chocolate-brown, his jaw square, and features classically handsome. He lived in a foster home from ages one to four, and was adopted when he was five. Today he was a happy man with no possessions and no real direction other than away from California's Orange County.

My binder of music CDs lay on the kitchen table. Chuck flipped through the pages, noticing the Sade, the Erykah Badu, the Keola Beamer.

"You like Julio Iglesias?" he asked.

"Not really."

"I've got every album he's ever made."

I eyed him for a moment. "Has anyone ever told you that you look like Julio Iglesias?"

He shrugged and handed me his business card:

Have Fun Will Travel
Sun Fun Inc.
Charles Cook
"Paladin of Tropical Beaches"

There was no phone number, only an e-mail address. He winked.

"I do a little bit of everything. I like working with the earth."

He ran a small landscaping outfit in Newport Beach called Bongo's Garden Service, catering to the same rich clients year after year. The way his life had evolved, landscaping was his income for perhaps a few months, then he hit the road—Mexico, Asia, South Pacific.

"I've never had a career. Society looks at you and sets the bar, especially in L.A.—what car you drive, where you live, where you work. I haven't had a car in twenty-five years. Say, have you heard the one about the antenna's wedding?"

"The what?" Chris asked.

"The antenna's wedding?"

"I don't know what you're talking about."

"Well, I heard it was boring, but the reception was great."

So began a litany of dry jokes he'd stolen from late-night comedians over the years:

"What do you call the part of the chicken where the egg comes out? The eggsit."

"Where do wasps go on vacation? Stingapore."

"What did the lawyer name his daughter? Sue."

"What's a mummy's favorite kind of music? Rap."

"What did the pirate pay for his earrings? A buck an ear."

"What did the dollar name his daughter? Penny."

"Why did the banker ditch his girlfriend? He was losing interest."

Chuck and I walked toward the beach, along the atoll's only road, lined with tin shacks and clotheslines. Pigs and chickens were everywhere. There seemed to be no one between the ages of thirteen and twenty. This was true as all Arno teenagers move to Majuro for high school.

Then we set off on an overgrown path through the jungle, which ended at a small beachfront shack in a wide clearing, facing what appeared to be a decent surf spot.

We stared at the glassy ocean. Without prompt, Chuck soliloquized:

"I'm rediscovering the art of human being. When I look at people in today's society, I see human doings and human thinkings, but the 'being' part—what is that? What is it to just be? I want to just 'unbecome,' because our whole life is spent because something like being a beautiful creature isn't enough."

"Do you think you are a beautiful creature?" I asked.

He laughed. "Maybe I'm just being lazy. Or I'm crazy. But when you strip everything down, to when you were a baby, we were just there—we were alive, we were existing. In every human, there is something from when they were a baby that is still inside their soul. I can't say I've achieved it one hundred percent, but I've had moments."

The surf was small but very clean, fairly mushy but shapely, and easily accessible. The clearing had a few small structures on it, all of rough tin and wood, and there were several small children gawking at us. The adults—only one was male—sat in the shade of the shacks doing nothing. The man strummed a beat-up guitar. We waved and they waved back, but we felt boldly intrusive, so we left.

When we returned to the cottage I wanted to lay down. The walk fatigued me, and my throat was still sore from the cold I had. Fish sizzled in a pan on the kitchen stove—Francis was drinking green tea and frying fresh snapper with breadfruit for no one in particular. I told him where Chuck and I had walked, and where I found waves.

"Ah, that's the Kalles homestead," he said. "I know that family. Nice family. They are Arno's first family to live on the ocean side. Most families live on the lagoon side."

"They must prefer the ocean, then."

"They love it."

"I feel crappy."

"Here, have some noni juice," he said, handing me a small white bottle. The juice looked like worcestershire sauce and had a tangy, bitter scent. "We make this stuff here. No additives or dilution. It is the purest noni juice! Good for anytime you are sick. Cures many ailments. High blood pressure, diarrhea. Headaches, for example. You constipated? You drink noni juice. Diabetes, too. Arthritis. Inflammations. Noni has been used as natural medicine for two thousand years."

"Where does it come from?"

"Over there, across the street! It is from the ripe fruit of the wild citrifolia tree."

I looked outside. A few frigate birds flitted high above the noni tree Francis pointed out.

"When those birds fly low, there is a storm coming," he said.

"What is that structure over there?" I asked, gesturing up the road.

"That's our coconut oil processing facility. We make copra there and sell it to Majuro and other places."

The bottle in my hand depicted a small round fruit mottled with black spots—the noni fruit.

"So how much do I take?"

"Oh, just a few spoonfuls or so. Then sleep a little while. I guarantee you will feel better."

Francis was a man of his word, so I sank a few spoonfuls. Then he left the kitchen and went outside with Chuck and started chatting near the window, so I eavesdropped from my bed.

"See, the beauty of America is, if someone messes with you, you just sue them—"

"Babies in Africa starve to death from the day they are born—"

"The Catholics don't have an answer for it—"

On the kitchen floor sat Kuzzi, age ten, a curious and wide-eyed local boy, flipping through the Islands magazine I'd brought from home. He gawked at the ruins of Isola Bella, the wildlife of Madagascar, the faces of Jamaica. He giggled at the underwater photos, the monkeys, white women swimming in bikinis—it was pornography to him. And he must have ended up taking the magazine because I never saw it again.

People commune more in a society lacking television, telephones, modern conveniences, traffic, cops, rules, or signs. Francis and four grubby men with mullet hairdos quietly entered the house; one of them wore a black and yellow football jersey that said "Los Angeles" on it. Francis went into the kitchen, made a pot of tea, and dished out the fish he had been cooking, which by now had to be burnt and leathery. The men were barefoot and relaxed, smiling constantly and laughing softly, like they were stoned. I had met them earlier and they were shy and polite; they embodied the discreet life of Arno.

I drifted off to the sound of their hushed voices, awakened later by a loud squall. The rain released the pungency of rotting noni and banana and breadfruit outside my window, and the sky was dark gray and ominous, the tree trunks smeared wet. The men left the house wearing black trash bags for raincoats.

Loko, who I met yesterday, began filleting a rainbow runner on a tree stump. He was one of the three people on Arno with a working car; he wore a torn black shirt that said *Buster's Tavern, Mankato, MN*, and his face had horrible acne. His car was the same noisy, creaky, red Nissan pickup with a plywood bed; it never was shifted out of first gear, and could only run after push-starting it.

After my nap I felt better—perhaps the noni juice worked—and the sky had cleared, so I walked through the jungle to check the surf at a different area of the island, a bit north of where the Kalleses lived.

Near this rubbly beach were two boys, the older one husking coconuts, impaling them onto a metal pole stuck in the ground; the younger one sat in a dirty red wheelbarrow. The older one wore a black Snoop Dogg shirt and L.A. Dodgers gym shorts. I said I lived near Los Angeles.

He looked at me, cocked his head, and asked in a challenging sort of way, “You play baseball?”

“Once in a while.”

“You good?”

“Nah. Too clumsy. Can’t catch or throw balls. No hand-eye coordination. I was always the last guy picked for teams in high school P.E. class.”

He looked disappointed by this, and said nothing, so I resumed walking.

The surf had increased during the day, but at dusk the tide was too low and the light was fading. The swell was strong and orderly, about six feet, but warbly atop the shallow coral heads.

On the way back I walked past the boys again; the older one waved me over.

He said, “Why you no play baseball, eh?”

“Not into it. But I surf.”

“What is surf?”

“Tomorrow morning, meet me here and I’ll show you.” I pointed at the ocean. “The waves at that beach are good for surfing.”

The stroll back through the jungle pacified me, as if Arno wasn’t calm enough. It was pleasant knowing I was the only surfer there, and that any wave would be surfed alone, over coral colors beneath a deep blue sky.

The sunset made the clouds crimson, the sky a canvas of orange and purply pastel. Nightfall was a womb of warm, wet air, geckos and chirping crickets, invisible within the dusky tangle of rain forest silhouettes. All was soft, windless, dripping, like stalled time.

The boys never showed in the morning, but the surf was better in front of the Kalles’ place, and that was what mattered, because the family witnessed surfing for its first time. Not good surfing, mind you, but I was standing on waves, however not before startling the wits out of two girls washing dishes, squatting under a small coconut palm. I had suddenly popped out of the jungle with my shock-white surfboard, wearing colorful boardshorts and smelly sunscreen, and they were the first to see me. I apologized but they spoke no English.

I paddled out assuming it the was entire Kalles family that had quickly gathered to watch. The children clapped and screamed after each wave. Francis later translated the adults' reaction, which included "How can this guy stand on the wave?" and "Why does he not drown?" and "Why is he so stupid?"

The wave was a fast and consistent head-high left, peeling over a kaleidoscope of coral color, eventually sputtering into deep nearshore water. The water's stunning clarity was convenient for spotting reef imperfections and ghastly coral heads: It would not be good if I fall right...*there.*

A few hours later I was back in Majuro, at the hospital, with an IV stuck in my arm. I had bonked a coral head with my own head and could not surf straight or paddle without pain afterward, so Francis had me immediately ferried to Majuro for inspection. It was a mild concussion.

"You should not go surfing for a long time," the doctor said.

"But I am flying to Palau."

"Oh, you are lucky because there is no surfing in Palau."

"Are you sure?"

"I am positive."

—WEST—

WILLIAM LIVES IN the Republic of Palau, westernmost of Micronesian isles, in the blue Philippine Sea. He moved from southern California to Palau in 1987 to work for two years as a government lawyer. But, like so many expats, he eventually wed a local woman, had kids, and set root.

I met William through photographer Art Brewer, who visited Palau twice on assignment for *Islands* magazine.

"Nice guy—saw him once," Art said. "Tell him hello for me."

So I did upon late arrival at busy Koror International Airport, where I had deplaned from Guam with the entire cast and crew of the reality television series "Survivor," filming their next series in the famed Rock Islands south of Koror. As such, large areas of the Rock Islands were closed to the public due to the 'confidential' nature of the filming.

This irked me, so I was happy to tell everyone I knew that "Survivor" was being filmed in Palau. And after viewing a few episodes filmed in Vanuatu, I hoped they could do better here. But how could they? It was all crap.

"Guess you'll just have to see the Rock Islands on television," William said.

He ended up showing them to me from his little boat one day, with his wife Tlau and daughter Barbie, dodging squalls, touring the maze of pretty green limestone mounds in their pretty warm turquoise lagoon. We lunched on a white beach, snorkeled at a few holes, and I even got to bodysurf with sharks at Blue Corner, Palau's premier scuba spot. The "Survivor" posse was invisible, and that pleased me. They could have their ridiculous reality and I could have mine, because Palau is ridiculously beautiful.

A RUBY SUNRISE and crowing roosters and twittering birds found my hotel, run by Filipinos, which was cheap, spartan, old but efficient—I was broke and alone, after all. It was on a secluded residential side street, ideally quiet and unassuming, which meant no screaming kids, no barking dogs, no loud juke boxes in a hotel bar, or bums, or hookers, or clanking dishes. Oh, but yes, there were birds and roosters and the irritatingly ancient air-conditioner, which made my throat sore, so I slept sticky and hot for the rest of the trip.

But none of this amounted to anything. I was the hotel's only guest, and its surroundings were the real draw: blue sky, warm sea, bananas, coconuts, betel nut, sago palms, fragrant flowers, ferns and vines. It seemed like it could be a touristy botanical garden in Singapore, or the atrium of a vogue Australian resort, or what you pay three hundred bucks a night for at Tavarua, but it wasn't. Of the Pacific islands, Palau immediately struck me as being of the most unique and one of the cheapest.

Which is not lost in the tourism office's glossy brochures or the smug grins of the local people, most of whom own cars. On my first morning I took a sweaty walk west of town and realized I was the only pedestrian—Koror is a settlement of the automobile. Everybody drives.

It harked of Majuro, and several times I came very close to being roadkill. Motorists honked and swerved and the air was exhausty and the gutters were trashy; people smoked cigarettes and ate Cheetos and drank Coke and were obese and illiterate; the sun was out and Koror was hotter than hell. But what did I care? I was a grubby white guy visiting from the great land of SUVs and Wal-Mart, I was minding my own business, here to surf and to look around, and, no, I wasn't part of that damn "Survivor" cast.

Around three in the afternoon I rendezvoused with William at his moored boat, a twenty-foot fiberglass panga with canopy, in a private harbor beneath the Japan-Palau Friendship Bridge aside a rusting hulk of a half-sunken ship.

(This modern suspension bridge joins Koror to Babeldaob, which is the second largest island in Micronesia [Guam is the first], and was built by Japan in 2002 after the original Koror-Babeldaob Bridge collapsed in 1996, killing two people.)

"Before, the ship was valuable and people argued about who owned it," he said. "After it started to sink, everyone forgot about it."

An hour later, miles from land off the coast of Babeldaob Island, William looked toward Koror and said, "Sometimes I just don't want to go back."

"You don't say."

We'd skimmed for a half-hour through squalls across the lagoon after William bailed early from work. He is an attorney and was very busy, but the swell was on its last legs.

The wave we were surfing was a long and fun right-hander reminiscent of Cojo Point, but there weren't fifteen boats in the channel and forty people out hassling each other in the middle of nowhere, and it was much warmer.

"Two few days before you arrived," he said, "this spot was as good as it gets."

"That's typical."

The next morning we surfed a reef pass on Babeldaob's opposite side, a punchy right William usually surfs alone. ("I surfed alone here for a long time, but not by preference.") It is one of Palau's few surf spots easily accessible from shore, and if it was in Hawai'i or Tahiti, it would be localized and ruined. In Palau, it was only us and nature.

A rain cloud hid the sun for most of the session, but split finally at day's end. Then, awash in pastel incandescence, the sea surface—stone glass, as William called it—mirrored the crazy orange sunset behind us, filtering down into the black mountain silhouettes.

Back in the lagoon, minutes upon nightfall, two boys floated and fished for snapper from a bamboo raft, an image straight from *National Geographic.*

"That's really cool," William said. "You don't see much of that these days."

Satiated from the serenity of empty warm tubes peeling over healthy coral, we left in darkness, stopping at a remote store which appeared to be part of someone's house. I bought beer and a small bag of carrots grown a hundred miles from my home in California.

The friendly cashier lady eyed my purchase with a suspect smirk.

"Nice combination," she said sarcastically.

"I live off of this."

"Whatever." And she waved me off.

Outside, a young girl ran across the street holding a crab with a pair of salad tongs. The crabs scuttled around town each dusk, usually in the rain, which meant fresh protein in the stews and stir-fries in the adjacent candle-lit huts and tin shacks. This was a tiny village, an absolute outpost, but its people were happy and well-fed. It was an inviting place, with two surf spots, and there were no tourists, which is probably why I liked it so much.

I didn't see tourists anywhere in Palau, really, except in Koror (cheap food, nightlife, Internet cafés) or the expensive resorts on Malakal and Arakabesan (fake beaches, bus tours, black-tie dinners), and out on the dive boats (harassed expat guides, bad lunches, orange life jackets), which were filled mostly with pale, awkward, timid-looking Asians.

Reaching the village from Koror took an hour of driving through wilderness on bumpy red-dirt roads, past rivers, creeks, dense forests, fields of taro and cassava, hilly countryside and epic vistas. William owned Japan's version of the Toyota 4Runner, called the "4X4 Off-Road Surf," which is exactly what we had just done. The rain pissed hard and the roads were muddy; we drank beer, and William drove fast.

"I'll sell this in a couple of years," he said. "Cars get pretty thrashed here."

I commented on the heavy machinery we were passing, parked along the road, here to create Palau's new fifty-six miles of U.S.-funded pavement encircling Babeldaob. It's a governmental scheme to attract Koror residents and more foreign visitors to an island which is/was one of the Pacific's largest without road access. This is why I enjoyed it so much. Things will likely change fast. William concurred without hesitation.

"A way of life that existed only twenty years ago is already gone," he said. "Back then, there was no electricity, phones, or indoor plumbing on Babeldaob, and it was all strictly boat access. Now, land values are rising and developers are sniffing around."

"Do you think it could become wrecked like Guam?"

"I doubt it. Babeldaob's impediment to development, from everyone's point of view, is that the island is ringed by mangroves, which are both the filter and the nursery for Palau's ecosystem. I think any major coastal development, really, would come with a high environmental price tag."

The road's completion was years behind schedule and tens of millions of dollars over-budget. At the time there was pending litigation on the project between Daewoo Corporation, the South Korean contractor, and the U.S. Army Corp of Engineers, the project's manager.

"Some theorize that the reason that the Corp doesn't push the Koreans harder is because the Corp civilian staff assigned to the project consider Palau to be a sweet assignment. They don't want to finish here and then have to go somewhere else with a much lower quality of life."

"Do you think the road will encourage more surfers?"

"Well, maybe I'm out of touch the realities of modern surf tourism and surfers' desperation for the unique and pure experience, but I can't see Palau ever getting crowded. There's a reasonable quantity of decent surf here for maybe half the year, but any traveler will get way more bang for his or her surf buck in a million other places. Once you arrive here on your overpriced airline ticket, you'll face the prospect of minimum $300/day boat charters and two-week flat spells even in season. And anything else that you may want to do will cost. Palau is not a particularly expensive place to live, but it's not cheap to visit.

"Anyway, that being said, my dealings with Palau's few visiting surfers have so far been overwhelmingly positive."

NEXT MORNING. WILLIAM and I revisited the pass fronting the outpost village, arriving at seven; already the air was oppressively hot.

A van with surf racks was parked on the roadside opposite the lagoon.

"That's Shima's car," William said. "He looks gnarly, but he's actually a real nice guy."

In the blinding glare we could just make out the tiny dark figure in the distance, paddling for an overhead wave. Once out, I discovered that Shima was indeed intimidating but very friendly. He was quite tan, muscular, with tattoos and a tapered mustache—he looked like a Japanese porn star. He could hardly speak English or surf, but, as one of Palau's only surfers, he was trying.

The waves were warbly and the tide was dropping fast; the onshore wind came and soon the session was tainted. It became too shallow and bumpy to surf safely, so we went in, leaving Shima on his own once again.

Vigorous exercise early in a tropical day can drain even the most energetic soul, and for the rest of the day, I slept like a log. The hotel was quiet and private; I woke just before sunset and stepped outside into the blast of muggy air and loud crickets in the marshy woods across the street. Then I watched CNN and its relentless, biased coverage of the U.S. presidential election—from their reportage, George W. Bush was an asshole and John Kerry walked on water. I didn't care, because Palau was in the midst of its own election, which was more interesting.

Posters reading *Please Elect Polycarp Basilius—Smart Choice!* and *Please Re-Elect Tommy Remengesau Jr. for President: Preserve The Best, Improve The Rest* were everywhere, but neither candidate seemed worthy, William said. It was the same deal as in all Third World nations, like the Marshall Islands, with shyster politicians masquerading as sentimental guardians of the people, when essentially it boiled down to money and material possessions, like luxury cars and Honolulu homes, which would accrue further for the victor. Public funds would be squandered and roads would remain potholed; the parliament would get drunk and tourists would see the same desperation and dereliction year after year. Nothing changes. But that's the way it goes, because no small Pacific island country is a viable economic entity. William knew this.

"Palau has done well for the past ten years under its Compact of Free Association with the U.S.," he said. "Economic aid under that treaty is front-end loaded with the object to promote self-sustaining economic development, which hasn't happened. Palau will have to continue to sell itself in one way or another in coming years to keep its head above water."

The night was young and the moon was full, lighting the puffy clouds' perimeters, and the visible stars winked as I walked through Koror to the nearest market for the important stuff: beer.

A Chinese man was watering a plant by the market's entrance. He looked ill.

"Hello! A nice night," he grinned.

"It is."

I made a purchase then walked back toward the hotel, in a dark alleyway paralleling the main road. A Palauan man in a wet white T-shirt rode past on a bike; he looked at me point-blank and said "Hello!", which startled me.

The air was wonderfully still, and it smelled sugary, the flower nectars cooling after another hot day. The night was perfect, and in it I slept soundly, after beers and more CNN.

WILLIAM HAD ARRANGED to spend the weekend on one of Palau's southern islands, so I rose early to catch the five-dollar/four-hour ferry.

The Filipino woman in the hotel restaurant greeted me enthusiastically. After all, I was the hotel's only guest.

"Eggs and toast again, Michael?"

"And coffee, please. Mango, too, if you have it."

In the empty restaurant sat a girl of perhaps seven, pigtails in her hair, wearing a brown school uniform, glumly eating rice and grits. On the radio was—

Take this job and shove it
I ain't working here no more!

—which is likely what the Filipino woman thought as she banged a plate of slimy eggs, stale white bread, and overripe mango in front of me. The coffee was tepid and flavorless, the orange juice watery and much too sweet. But the meal was free, so I ate with a smile.

I read a newspaper, the *Palau Horizon*, which said the Philippines are Palau's gateway to Asia. This was obvious. My hotel was run by Filipinos, and nearly every other employee in Koror's restaurants and shops were Filipino. They earned $2.50 an hour. I mentioned this to an elderly Palauan man at the Malakal ferry terminal.

"It is hard to get Palauans to come to work," he said. "We are not big on servicing other people, especially foreigners."

At that moment a heavy downpour began, so everyone rushed to fill the ferry, the *Regina IV*. Cargo littered the spacious deck—cardboard parcels, duffel bags, lumber, rebar, fuel drums, tires, bikes, tarps, fifty-pound bags of rice, coolers, a moped, a boat trailer. There was even a black Nissan Pathfinder parked at the bow. I scrambled from William's car to the ship and stepped aboard.

"Slippery!" said a bony shirtless man.

"Where can I put this?" I asked, holding up my bag.

"Inside!"

The ship had much more cargo than passengers (about thirty), some of whom sat amongst it; William and I were the only whites. The ferry was cramped and nearly everything was wet. Everything was dirty, too, and it stunk, and in many places it needed repair.

I slugged my wet bag onto the floor in the galley, which reeked of salami and mildew and had four bunk beds occupied with betel nut-dazed passengers. Some wore headphones and bobbed their heads to music. Others were boisterous, laughing, happy to flee Koror—it was a cheery and yakking assemblage as we rumbled loudly out of Malakal Harbor under a fearsome sky.

Despite the rain, the trip was windless and smooth. We sailed southwesterly at seven knots, and soon we were aside the Rock Islands, these fuzzy mounds of green-cum-gray, the storm bestowing a different look to Palau's celebrated verdancy.

The Rock Islands were treeless but bulbous and bushy, like tropical chaparral, and there were no beaches; pale limestone rimmed their bases. They looked similar, almost uniform, but different from than any islands I'd seen. The lagoon was placid; we passed a few dive boats. The Rock Islands became distant as we motored further south, toward blue sky and our destination, which materialized slowly as a black smudge on the horizon.

Two women lounged on the bed behind me; one wore a purple shirt and paper towels around her neck. Slowly she peeled a betel nut, inserted it into her mouth, and spit into a soda can. The other woman rolled a cigarette. A shirtless man snored in the top bunk above them, holding a basketball on his belly. On the wall was a small sign that read *Do Not Wear Shoes In This Cabin*, yet nobody was barefoot.

Most of these people lived or used to live on our destination island, so this trip was a sort of a weekend homecoming, or longer, and most of them were fat. All had ugly red teeth. They dressed lightly. They were dark. They were islanders who eschewed the cold, and I wondered how they would fare in, say, Greenland or Siberia.

Many ate throughout the four-hour trip. They had all kinds of provisions from Koror—beer, potato chips, cookies, wire, pots and pans, parcels of processed American food, rags, radios, toilet paper—stuff that was apparently impossible to buy elsewhere in Palau.

One of the few skinny people was Jay, who had been living on Guam for several years. He was bouncing around astern, clutching a can of Budweiser, setting four trolling lines. Each line had a soda can looped in it; when a fish is hooked, the line is yanked taut and the can is crushed, signaling a hooked fish or a piece of trash.

Jay was about thirty, bald, short and mischievous-looking, a loose cannon. He had a thin black goatee, a mustache, narrow sideburns, and beady black eyes. He wore a bone necklace and a white tank-top that said *Got Wasabi?*.

He approached me and asked, "Hey, you pull the line if we hook a fish?"

"Sure."

"Nothing to do but fish and drink on this ride. Ha!"

"What brings you here?"

"I live in Guam but it has been too long. I have to come back here. I am building a store."

"On the island?"

"Yes. It is where I from. What you going for?"

"To surf."

"Ah!" His eyes lit up. "We have surf spot!"

"That's what I've heard. Do you surf?"

"No way, man. That stuff crazy."

But Jay seemed a little crazy to me, perhaps from the five cans of beer he had already consumed, and it was only eleven in the morning.

Most of the men on the ferry drank for the trip's duration. One of them, an elderly white-bearded man, was slumped in the galley. When our eyes met he held out his hand. I shook it; it was hot and greasy. He sipped from a can of Budweiser and was dressed in loose white clothing and a gold necklace, wiry white chest hair poofing from his shirt's neck. He looked seedy, like a Palauan mafioso, with a round face and a serene complexion. He handed me a beer.

"What you doing here?"

"Just looking around. Doing a little surfing."

"Oh! You bring your surfboard?"

"Yes, it's on deck next to the Pathfinder. I hope that thing is secure."

"The car? It not moving. It okay."

He said nothing for the remainder of the voyage. The woman in the purple shirt peeled another betel nut and fingered lime powder onto it, which she kept in a small plastic orange pill container. The old man had a betel nut in his jaw, but he was drinking beer concurrently.

Outside, the ferry's crew members were soaked, dripping but happy and chatty. All of them chewed betel nut, too. Budweiser was everywhere. Only the captain remained sober, steering with his foot.

Behind him in the pilothouse sat an old Indonesian-looking man wearing sunglasses who had painted his bald head black to look like he had hair. He was some sort of pastor; he was reading *Spiritual Leadership* by J. Oswald Sanders when I walked up the stairs for a view. He wore a light striped collared shirt, gray shorts, and was barefoot.

"Are you here for 'Survivor'?" he asked.

We were sailing past a tiny but perfect left-hander peeling along the barrier reef.

"No, I'm just visiting."

"Where you from?"

"California."

"Ah! I know that place. I have been to Pasadena. My son lives in San Diego. He is always wanting me to come to San Diego. I went to UCLA for my doctorate and got my masters in anthropology and theology. Now I ask people to find their interests then connect them to a heavenly calling"

"Where are you from?"

"I'm from Melekeok State, so I come down here once in a while."

Next to him sat a fairly attractive woman about my age, in a baggy white shirt that read *Operation Iraq Freedom*, wearing headphones and a blue bandana, snapping her fingers to the music beat and flipping through a family photo album. Next to her sat a huge woman in a gray shirt that read *Love To Shop*. She too wore headphones and a pink bandana, and she was so fat and shapeless she seemed to be part of her gray seat.

The younger woman smiled at me.

"Are you with 'Survivor'?"

"No, just visiting."

"Your first time here?"

"Yes."

"Why do you come?"

"To surf and see Palau."

This confused her. "Aren't you scared of sharks?"

"No, sharks are fine."

"We have no surfing on the island."

"Yes you do. My friend William has surfed there."

She smiled. Her teeth were actually white. "I am Lolita."

"I'm Mike."

"What part of U.S. are you from? New York?"

"California."

She smiled again. "All the people in California surf, eh?"

"Too many."

"I have been to New Jersey."

"They have surfing there, too."

"I was there for three months working as a nurse, taking care of old people. But I not like New Jersey much because it was very cold. I don't like the snow."

She changed the CD (Billy Ray Cyrus) in her player and looked back up at me.

"Are you twenty-eight?" she asked.

"Twenty-nine. How old are you?"

"Guess."

"Twenty-eight?"

"Thirty-one. I look young. So I look twenty-eight?"

"No, you look about thirty."

The pastor tapped my shoulder, holding a piece of white bread in his other hand. "You like bread?"

"No thanks."

"I get so hungry on this trip down here."

"Why are you going to the island?"

"Because I am the international coordinator for a Christian fellowship—Saipan, Malaysia, China, Chuuk, Yap, Philippines. I come down here once a month. I keep people from getting confused about God."

"That's interesting."

He looked poised to start preaching, so I excused myself and went outside. We were motoring into a dark squall which eliminated all color from the island's appearance. The scene grew gray and reflective, almost metallic, the wavelets gone black.

We were now spitting distance from the island, ideal to assess its jagged topography, a speck of raised coral limestone with shore caves, blowholes, sedate coves, tangled vines, ironwood forest, Ixora flowers, feral monkeys and megapode birds, coconut crabs and purple fruit doves.

Waves sloshed onto the island and the backwash gently rocked our ship. Suddenly we were under the sun again; the air heated instantly. The sea sparkled lazily, warm and azure. Flying fish flitted past us. White-tailed tropicbirds swooped in circles above.

As we drew closer to the harbor, I walked to the bow for a glimpse of the swell, stepping over people sleeping on lumber, the deck littered with soda cans of betel nut spit. Frail lines of whitewater scraped across the island's barrier reef.

The sun was scorching; I was sweating profusely. Within minutes we were inside the harbor, and everything and everyone were offloaded quickly—the ship was headed right back to Koror.

William and I caught a ride to our rented cottage, which was about a half-mile from the harbor, and once we'd "moved in," we borrowed two bikes from our neighbors and immediately set out to seek rideable waves.

We rode for a mile along the shaded coral road to the island's southern tip, near a reef/point that William had once surfed. The swell was small but very clean, perfect orangy little back-lit rights wrapping gently into a secluded cove. The waves were fairly long and consistent, though we had the wrong boards, William with his 7'6" mini-gun, me with my 6'4" pintail.

The wave hinted of Refugio Beach, but not sandy or frigid; rather, with frightening coral heads and heart-shaped stones among a hideously craggy reef, enjoyed by exotic fish, surveyed by a vertical rainbow and a rising moon and a surreal sundown of pure Palauan hue. On the beach were ironwood and pandanus and baby coconut palms, our two bikes leaned against them, and nothing else. It was a private session, fitting for a private island unknown to ninety-nine percent of humanity, including the 'Survivor' crew.

Light soon faded so we did a blind rock-dance to the beach and reluctantly biked back into the steamy jungle, toward a semblance of civilization, which presented itself immediately upon arrival back at the cottage.

Fat shirtless men scuttled by on mopeds; invisible kids squealed and giggled; chickens pecked at the dirt in front of our porch; billiard balls clinked and music blared and people shouted from homes nearby. It was Saturday evening and the island's weekly beer ration had arrived on our ferry, so the folks must have been partying. Or something.

Around seven o'clock, with wasps buzzing around our heads, we feasted on bean burritos and Asahi beer, listening to the twilight ruckus caused by crickets and night bugs in the foliage surrounding the house. The air was heavy and damp, the island alive in every way. I had hoped to see a few coconut crabs, but none appeared.

What did appear was a very drunk man holding a can of Budweiser, who wandered off the road toward us and sat on the porch stairs, feebly looking up at us.

"I looking for my sister," he slurred.

"She's not here," I said. And he stumbled away.

Later, attempting sleep in my room, three geckos twirped for hours from the ceiling and walls around my bed. The rusty air-conditioning unit was abrasively loud and threatened to combust, so I shut it off around eleven; instantly the room became a sauna. So I opened the curtains and windows and let the full moon soothe my face into a deep sleep that didn't end until eight the next morning.

After breakfast, William went outside for a minute and returned smiling: We had wheels.

"We really scored with this truck," William said. "Otherwise, we'd have to ride bikes everywhere."

"Not like it's torture."

We drove atop pretty limestone bluffs to the island's northwest corner and parked at a spot William also had surfed before. It was an area of the island where, during World War II, the Japanese army held its final stance against the U.S. invasion, around the time of the Peleliu battle.

"This place gets epic," William said. "Surfed it absolutely magical, but I know it gets even better."

Today the surf was funky and jumbled from the high tide, bouncing off the cliff, the waves shapeless but about head-high and powerful. The water was as clear as water gets.

Facing the lineup was a small, ornate Shinto shrine (Shinto is a religion indigenous to Japan based on cultic worship of gods of nature) and a Buddhist memorial, littered with dead ironwood needles and small orange packets of rice crackers as offerings.

"I guess locals leave the cheap stuff," William said.

It was a strange sight, this craggy overgrown bluff-top in the middle of nowhere with a shrine and a memorial and a statue of the Virgin Mary a hundred yards away from them, built in 1954 to tranquilize rough seas for the islanders' safety.

"How do you get down to the water?" I asked.

"Carefully."

Instead we opted for the reef from the previous evening, accessed easily and likely fun with the increased swell and slack wind. Rumbling back down the road, William remarked how we were the only surfers on the island, and that we could surf anywhere we wanted to without paranoia of anyone else arriving to hassle us or give us the dreaded stink-eye.

The surf was a consistent and a fiercely blue head-high with occasionally larger sets. The spot today reminded me not of Refugio but an empty morning in the cove at El Capitan, which never happens, unless you rewind fifty years. Three hours of windless perfection is also anomalous, particularly on remote islands susceptible to even the slightest air disturbance, as was the case today when a fifteen-knot sideshore breeze and ebbing tide soundly soiled the ambiance.

But the reef was proof that discoveries remain if you know where to look, or even if you don't—we were sailing back to Koror that afternoon, and we had gotten lucky with two sessions at a nameless nook. Such windows of opportunity are glimpses into the halcyon past William tasted so youthfully in California, denied to me at birth and to all subsequent generations.

Reality today includes unprecedented crowds and Internet-hyped swells, polluted water and pathetic localism—reality it is, unless, of course, you lead an outpost life far from the maddening hordes, thug-free, accessing arcane waves with boats or bikes or boots, adhering to the motto of Central California's venerable Point Arguello Yacht Club:

If there's a parking lot in front of it, it ain't surf.

MOTORING BACK INTO Malakal Channel late that same day, I watched several dive boats buzz to and from distant dive spots, transporting pale, skinny Asians in life vests, all paying a hundred and fifty dollars a day to dive twice in close proximity to dozens of others also paying a hundred and fifty dollars a day. It was exactly like pre-tsunami surf tourism in the Maldives, or certain places in the South Pacific where boatloads of surfers pay good money to surf paradise with dozens of strangers who all wish that the other guy wasn't there. In places like Palau, with less-salable and incredibly rare surf, I felt safe but sad for the divers, who had no other choice.

Back at the Malakal dock, on Halloween night, I watched fattish red-teethed Palauans offload parcels of betel nut and sacks of coconut crabs, caught by kids the night before.

Later in a seedy pub I met Paul, twenty-five, from Missouri, who had already been in Koror for a month, mostly to scuba dive. He was tall and muscular and boyishly handsome, a good pick for the next Abercrombie & Fitch back-to-school catalog shoot.

"Basically, in organized diving, what you get is lunch and two tanks for the day," he said, chewing salty peanuts. "It's not really worth it."

"Then why do you do it?"

"Because this is fucking Palau, man. It's like Mecca for divers." He had a thin line of foam above his upper lip from his fresh pint of Guinness stout. "And you're here to surf?"

"To a degree."

"Is it any good?"

"It can be, but not usually."

"Then why are you here?"

"Because it's fucking *Palau*, man!"

Paul was soon headed to O'ahu for a month before returning home to St. Louis. He had recently finished serving six years at a desk job at the U.S.'s Aviano Air Base in Pordenone, Italy.

"I'll do this traveling for a bit before going home," he said. "Then I'll have to get a job, figure out what I'm going to do with my life—all that crap."

"I may be in Hawai'i next month," I said.

"We should meet up. I want to try surfing."

"Sure thing. I'll be in Honolulu. Where are you staying?"

"I have no idea."

"Go to Waikiki, then. Rent a board and paddle out there. I'll teach you. It's one of the world's best places to learn how to surf."

Someone programmed a heavy metal song in the juke box, which was screechingly obnoxious, so Paul and I had to start shouting at each other. The pub was echoey and dark and nearly empty, which made the music louder, and I was getting a headache from the beers and cigarette smoke.

I said, "I think I'm going to leave!"

"I'm going to have a few more!"

"Sounds good!" I scribbled my phone number on a napkin and handed it to him. "Here's my number! Call me when you're in Hawai'i!"

THE SURF DETERIORATED exponentially since I'd arrived in Palau, and the upcoming week's forecast was bad. I woke early the next day and phoned William from my hotel.

"Yep, looks shitty," he said. "Flat and onshore for a while."

So I borrowed a bike and rode around town—side streets, alleys, dirt tracks, the main road. The sun was intense and it seared my body, shirtless but sunscreened, and I was chased by several barking dogs and again was near-roadkill, but the sky was a deep blue and everything glistened—pretty flowers yawned into to sun, and I was happy to be feeling the wind in Palau, at rainbow's end.

It was a Monday, and no one seemed to have jobs to go to—kids ran around screaming, women did laundry, and men sat drinking beer in grassy front yards. It wasn't a holiday; this was Palauan life in 2004, and the local economy was ruled largely by Asian interests. I thought of the old man at the ferry dock—Palauans are not at all insular, perhaps by economic reliance, perhaps by nature:

> *The friendliness of Palau's people is unabashed and disarming, but it is their immense esteem for the islands' natural resources—a respect anchored in steep tradition—that has yielded broad conservation of nature's gifts. (Palau Visitors Authority nature guide)*

MOST HOMES HAD corrugated aluminum roofs and wood structuring. The homes were single-story, modest, small and colorful, like American suburb homes in the 1950s. Birds quibbled in the pandanus trees, ripe bananas and papayas and coconuts went unpicked. There were cars and chickens and betel nut trees out front for a steady chew supply; gardens were flowery and lush, and everyone had a satellite dish for two hundred television channels. Almost every person older than eight had been fattened by Western and Asian foods, heavy in salt and oil and butter, evidenced by discarded food packaging in the trash cans on driveways.

On one road I cycled slowly past a palmy residence with nine dark shirtless men, probably in their late twenties, sitting outside on coolers and rusted beach chairs, drinking cans of Budweiser. The ground at their feet was littered with crumpled cans. The men looked fierce and felonious, especially when I was five feet away, and all but one stopped and stared; he was absorbed by a well-thumbed copy of *Hustler*.

The nearest man cocked his head and said forcefully, "Ey, what's up, brah?" He was unsmiling and stern; the others glowered.

I smiled. "Oh, you know, just cruising around."

He raised his can and furrowed his brow. "Ho, need a beea', brah?"

His teeth were gapped and reddish. His hands were greasy and he was visibly intoxicated. It was nine in the morning.

"No thanks."

This confused the men. How could I refuse a beer? I too was their age, male, shirtless, unshaven, and I was alone on a bike in their hidden neighborhood.

"Wha—? Ey, brah, c'mon, you don't wanna beea'?"

Modern rap music (Tupac Shakur) blared from the house, and for a fleeting moment it felt like a very hot day in Guam or Hawai'i, where youth embraces this sort of thing—the restless testosterone, the aggressive gangster rap, the mid-morning beer quaffage, the tattooed/goateed machismo. It was a far cry from slack-key serenades and coconut subsistence, and I felt uneasy, so I flashed the men a shaka and rode quietly away.

But something I later read in my Moon guidebook offered hope:

> *Palauans appear to be the most Americanized of Micronesians. Don't expect to see native dress. Beneath the surface, though, they are extremely tradition-oriented.*

I WENT TO see the museum but it was closed. Kids screamed at me when I passed them; older people smiled and waved; girls honked; punks sneered. There were few white men around, none on bikes. Who was I, anyway? To the locals, I was either with the Peace Corps, because it disallowed volunteers to have cars, or with "Survivor," because I apparently fit the cast's demographic.

It was Election Day, and in America, George W. Bush had just won a second term. In Koror, street corners were occupied with political hopefuls and their smiling supporters, waving and flashing the 'thumbs-up,' holding cardboard signs emblazoned with a particular candidate's name and a sincere reason to vote for him (*Your Best Choice!* or *True Care for Palau's Future!*).

I was drenched in sweat, the sunscreen irritated my eyes, and I wasn't feeling the campaigners' enthusiasm, probably because I was dehydrated and up late the previous night drinking beer with Paul, later glued to CNN, watching Wolf Blitzer and Larry King verging on tears as Bush's victory became obvious. Or maybe it was the humidity. Or it was because, two days earlier, William said, "This country is a bunch of pretenders, anyway. Everyone knows the U.S. does all the work. The elected leaders are out of touch with reality, spending American money like drunken sailors."

Eighteen thousand people live in Palau, five thousand of them Filipino and another thousand of Asian origin. Five hundred are

American, whose motherland assists Palau to the tune of hundreds of millions of dollars, to be paid in yearly installments until 2015.

Again, my Moon guidebook:

> *These payments are a central feature of Palau's economy today, and as in the other Freely Associated States of Micronesia, they have been used to maintain a bloated bureaucracy...for its population, Palau is one of the most overgoverned places on earth.*

And:

> *Palau appears to be betting its future on tourism...by 2004 Palau may have as many as 2,000 hotel rooms. It is not clear whether tourism will...fill new hotel rooms...it is not clear whether Palau's limited infrastructure and fragile ecology will be able to bear it.*

THOUGH FAR FROM new, my hotel was vacant in 2004, as were many others. The "Survivor" team was in town, but they really were not tourists. More than likely, the Palauan government happily agreed—for a fee—to let this posse of narcissistic Australian and American "reality TV" pseudo-stars rent the precious Rock Islands, Palau's biggest draw, so peasants like myself could be denied the pleasure of seeing the land unmolested by wires and cameras and bright lights.

The touristing Koreans and Taiwanese and Chinese and Japanese seemed only to be in Palau for the diving, but how did that benefit the local economy? Most dive businesses were run exclusively by expats who spent profits elsewhere, or sent it home. And how could Palau, so pretty and pristine, maintain a balance should it become plagued with hordes of sight-seers, many of whom know nothing about delicate tropical archipelagos?

From Michael Parfit in *National Geographic*, March 2003:

> *(Palau) is a great crucible, a smithy of life, a place where you can still hear the clang of the hammer of evolution beating out new shapes on the anvil of the world.*

From Margie Cushing Falanruw, quoted in the same article:

> *The thing about islands is that you can see the connections. It's easy to understand the problems on a small island, and that's probably the value of small islands to the whole world.*

THE VALUE OF Palau's islands is their innocence, their purity. Unchecked numbers of foreigners seeking this will undoubtedly scar the place for eternity, and one only has to look as far as nearby Guam for assurance, which trails in second place, behind Hawai'i, for regularly receiving the highest number of tourists out of all other Pacific islands.

One problem I faced was Koror's lack of swimmable beaches. I had no car nor boat, there were no waves, I had bicycled all day beneath searing sun, and I required refreshment. Fringed with mangrove forests, beaches are unknown around Koror—that is, unless they are man-made, like the one at Palau Pacific Resort, an overpriced outfit on adjacent Arakabesan Island, catering mostly to wealthy Asians and others seeking Palau's finest accommodation, though at two hundred and twenty-five dollars a night, I'd beg to differ. All said, at that price, those folks better have their own beach.

Malakal Island is between Koror and Arakabesan, so I rode there first, seeking sandy beach. Instead I found cement and Palau's gritty industrial district, a clutter of dirty storefronts, cracked windows, stained and rubbly pavement, potholes, dingy pubs, karaoke bars, signs written in Taiwanese and Japanese and Palauan and English.

In the center of the road near the dock was a broken car fender surrounded by shattered pieces of plastic red car lights. A few people stood and stared at the fender, like it was an illusion, and no one I asked had seen a car accident that day.

On the left side of the road was a spur, a narrow dirt lane leading up a steep hill, apparently to Malakal's summit, which enticed me because of its likely vistas exploding with color this sunny day. The hibiscus-flanked lane was sheer and deeply rutted, so I walked the bike up past a sewage-treatment plant to a green clearing next to a huge white water tower. An ancient jeep was parked there, and I assumed it belonged to the plump elderly Palauan lady in a brown dress tending a small plantation of leafy greens. She hacked at the plants with a machete, removing dead branches and tossing them into a pile. She was lethargic and glistening and said she had been toiling since eight o'clock. It was now one.

"What is this?" I asked, pointing to some low plants. "Cassava?"

"No. Dis de Palauan sweet potato. Very good eat."

She pointed behind me, at the tall, gangly bushes with prickly branches.

"Dat is tapioca."

"Isn't it also called cassava?"

"Not cassava. Tapioca. You want?"

"I don't know how to cook it."

She grinned. "Ah, yes. Maybe you come back. I give you some."

"That would be very nice of you."

"You want taro?"

"I don't know how to cook that, either."

"Okay, you come back. I give you tapioca and taro."

I noticed a few long gray hairs growing from her chin.

"Is this a new crop?" I asked, gesturing at the taro.

"Dis three month old." She pointed behind me again. "Dat is nine month old. Sweet potato good at six month old. Tapioca good at nine month old. I harvest."

She raised her machete. "Maybe you come back when I harvest taro?"

"Sounds like a plan."

I descended roughly back to the main road and took a dip alongside a cement causeway between Malakal and Koror, in a kind of park with picnic tables, and black buoys in the middle of the narrow channel. Cars rumbled past and the rocks were slimy with moss, but the water was clean and warm, and nothing could have been more refreshing. An approaching clump of rain clouds encouraged rainbow formation; within ten minutes, I saw three.

The road from Malakal to western Arakabesan was lush, passing the latter's business district and winding uphill before dipping into a shady canyon, the picture of idyllic island life, the villages of Meyungs and Echol, past profuse gardens, friendly children, dogs, chickens, pigs, verdant vistas. A small boy lunged at me from the curb, yelling "Hey!" as I passed him; another yelled "Hey! What your name! What your name!"; another clapped his hands spasmodically and yelled "Hey! What your name! You have big muscle!" None of the adults seemed to notice me as they lounged in doorways, or swept their garage, or drank beer at three in the afternoon.

I was unsure of Palau Pacific Resort's location, but on Arakabesan, you can only go so far, and I knew the stream of large buses full of Taiwanese, their noses pressed against the windows, could only be going to one place.

Arakabesan's slippery seaplane ramp was easy to find, directly southwest of the resort; I swam next to it, with a few small fish in shallow water covering dead, rough coral heads. A rusted hulk of war debris—a tank? a ship?—protruded from the channel's center, and I briefly considered swimming out to it. Small dive boats whizzed past, customers neatly seated, headed down the channel back to dive shops near Koror. The afternoon was serene, the surrounding bushy green islands lighted perfectly by the orange sun.

After my swim I hiked up a thin dirt trail near the seaplane ramp, among pandanus and ironwood trees and skittish lizards, to a decrepit Japanese bunker, sixty years old. I stood in front of and admired the view; today, with Palau's idyll, it was difficult to imagine a roar of fighter planes and rounds of bullets being fired at American troops from this exact place.

It was late by the time I found the resort's fake beach, the sun dropping fast into the sea, chased by a black bulk of rain clouds. On the imported white sand, wearing only sandals and swim shorts, I looked like I could have appeared directly from a luxe air-conditioned suite, but I had no towel or woman, I was dirty and I was pushing a rusty bike. Not that anyone seemed to notice, which was typical, because this was Palau, not Nassau.

I swam and floated aside a small rock jetty at the beach's north end, away from the sunburned Australian loungers, the American drinkers, the Asians at the dive-boat dock. There was serenity here, even if it was a contrived setting. I had the sound of the breeze, clear warm water, soft white sand, pretty shells, and a picturesque sunset. Patrons snorkeled and strolled, threw Frisbees, sipped cocktails. They were enjoying this slice of paradise, and who could blame them?

On the beach near the jetty, resort staffers assembled an elegant dinner, seating for two, with flowers and candles, a stool for the personal guitarist, silk tablecloth, fancy silverware, fine wine—it was perfect and so romantic, soon to be spoiled by the imminent squall, perhaps even before the lovers were seated.

Later I rode slowly through the resort itself, along the covered pathways, passing a restaurant, two gift shops, a spa, and a cage holding a large white parakeet before approaching a mossy pond full of water lilies and koi. I had arrived just in time for the resort's daily five o'clock feeding display, whence a polite Filipino fish-feeder would attempt to lure the koi toward onlookers with his deft technique of food-sprinkling on the pond's surface. Eight resorters watched the feeder fail to attract the fish.

"They're not even coming close," a fat lady said. "Why are they avoiding us?"

I thought: Probably because of your perfume!

The resorters were dressed for dinner, shaven, showered; I was whiskery, wet, shirtless, sandy, on a bike. They eyed me with contempt, an freeloader, a trespasser. They were comfortable; it was a comfortable place, and I envied them for a moment. I thought of spending a week there. Then I rode in a downpour the four miles back to my hotel.

PALAU'S WEST SIDE was flat for ninety percent of my trip, so one rainy morning William, his Australian friend Craig, and I motored north into the wilds of eastern Babeldaob, an island without pavement or hotels or restaurants. From its high points we could see distant reef passes with potential for greatness, and on this, the windward coast, prone to northeast swell, consistent lines of whitewater wrapping into them, tauntingly.

Palau is a boater's surf country. The passes are far offshore and usually flat and fickle, but our map displayed a few swell-and-wind-exposed nooks where we possibly could pull up and just hop out of the car. This was a mission to find a new spot, someplace William had never surfed, accessible not by boat but with his "4X4 Off-Road Surf" car, as we were again traversing dirt lanes, soon to be paved.

"Palau's existing fifteen miles of paved road are a maintenance disaster," William said, downshifting into four-wheel-drive up a rutted hill. "There's no reason to think that they can do a better job with fifty-six more miles of road to maintain."

For five hours we scanned the coast from Airai to Chol, finding nothing but puny windswell, foul currents, and an onshore breeze that strengthened as the day progressed. The air temperature increased, too, and by three o'clock we were ripe, our greasy bare backs sticking to the car's upholstery.

Sometime mid-trip we found a bay with two surfy reefs, garnering interest until William mentioned its hidden population of saltwater crocodiles. Then we found the Ngatpang Waterfall, one of the known four on Babeldaob, and chose to have a quick rinse near four sensationally fat Pohnpeian women wallowing and eating in the pond below the falls. They wore sarongs and bras, and used their fingers to shove food into their mouths from three floating Tupperware containers. Their faces were attractive, as many Pohnpeian women are, but there were too many blubber rolls, too many stretch-marks, too many whiskers and saggy breasts to compensate for anything. It was just another testament to the West's culinary influence when combined with the average Micronesian's innate laziness.

We swam into an empty pool on the fall's opposite side. The water was cool and murky, mossy-smelling, over a floor of uneven, soggy wood and sharp rocks.

"I feel like an alligator," Craig said.

"There's probably a lot of eels in here," William said.

Then we ventured beneath the fall itself for a loud tube-riding rush. You could stand up straight, close your eyes, and pretend you were inside the biggest barrel in Palauan history.

"This is the deepest we'll get today!" William yelled above the roar.

In the end, it had been a scenic photo trip but a hoax for surf—the passes were ill-formed, or too narrow, or too deep, and it was too windy. What looked good on the map looked hideous in person, and we ended up groveling in chest-high slop back at the place our trip had started, the bowly right-hander we'd surfed before.

By four o'clock, the tide was uncomfortably low and still ebbing—our dangling toes brushed against coral heads—and the wind trashed the waves, sectiony and warbly and hard to ride. The sunset was blinding, the current was terrible, the sets were shifty, we were exhausted, and soon, reef poked through the surface. Before somebody got hurt, we called it a day.

Downing a cold beer as we set out for Koror, Craig raised the mood: "Well, boys, at least we got some good photos."

"Hope so," William said.

"I'm sure we did," I said. "But you never know."

"Did you have film in your camera?" Craig asked me.

"Of course."

"Then we got good photos. You can't take bad photos of this place. It's too pretty."

"That may be true."

William said, "The conditions are supposed to be like this for the rest of the week." It was Monday.

"That's fine, mate, 'cause I've got a bloody shitload of work to do," Craig said. He was here on business, consulting for something involving Palau's youth sport teams in their preparation for the next South Pacific Games, Oceania's version of the Olympics.

"I don't have anything to do," I said.

"There's always beer," Craig said, crushing an empty can in his fist.

There was always betel nut, too, which is what occupied me late the following afternoon, after a long, stormy, idle day indoors. I had been in Palau for two weeks, was leaving for Pohnpei in the morning, and I hadn't sampled Palau's fabled natural narcotic. So it was a stroke of luck when I happened upon a stout, betel nut-chewing man sitting on an aluminum chair at a wooden picnic table in front of my hotel. His teeth were red and rotten, he spoke excellent English. His name was Timmy, and he was calm, pudgy, mustached, about sixty, wearing a black cap that said *USS Peleliu* and a dark green shirt that said Samoan Pride.

"Are you Samoan?" I asked.

"Nah. Palauan all the way. But I been to Samoa many times. Many friends there. You from the States?"

"California."

"Ah." He grinned. "I live in San José for eight years. I study at San José State. Right now my daughter lives in Arizona."

He produced a small plastic bag from his pocket.

"You want a chew?"

"I'd love one."

With his grubby hands he cracked a betel nut, laced it with lime—a white cocaine-esque powder made from cooked coral—then wrapped it in a piece of pepper leaf and handed it to me. This was the second time I tried betel nut; the first was in Papua New Guinea, where the stuff was untolerably bitter, and I was drunk. This time I was sober.

"Chew for maybe five, ten minutes," Timmy said. Then he spat. "But don't swallow the spit."

"I wasn't planning to."

The nut was very mild, almost ineffective, but I did feel a tinge of light-headedness as I stood there. We chewed and spat and talked.

"Yap and Palau were first to chew betel nut," Timmy said. "Then other places chewed it—Chuuk, Pohnpei, Solomons, New Guinea, Marshalls, Kiribati. All over the Pacific."

"What about Indonesia?"

"Yes, they have betel nut there."

"What about Hawai'i?"

He sat upright in his chair. "I know of a Palauan lady on O'ahu who grows betel nut. She sold enough betel nut that she built a house!"

"The house that betel nut built."

"Yes! So it is in Hawai'i, too."

"Have you chewed all your life?"

"I started when I was a young man. Then I stopped for maybe two years, but I started again." He spit then coughed, nearly ejecting the nut from his cheek. "When I have maybe three beers, I have a chew. Then it makes me ready for three more!" And he laughed.

Dusk had fallen and the muggy air was still, punctuated by chirping crickets and an occasional bird. A cold beer sounded good. Timmy popped another nut into his mouth and put his feet on the table.

"Have you heard of Yap Day?" he asked.

"I've read about it."

Yap is known for its topless women, who all gather for a three-day celebration of dancing and sporting and feasting and hooting in Yap's capital village of Colonia. Men, especially those foreign, tend to perve.

Timmy's bloodshot eyes widened. "Never have I seen so many tits! Even the white Peace Corps girls have to dance topless." He chuckled and spat. "I go every year. I have already made my reservation for next year!"

"I'm going to Pohnpei tomorrow. Are girls topless there?"

"Oh, Pohnpei. No, not topless. Nice place. I spent lot of time there. The women are beautiful. You surfing there, too?"

"Doubt it."

My betel nut had become stagnant and impotent, my spit pink instead of red. Timmy noticed.

"Have another chew," he said, pushing the bag at me. I plucked one out and grinned at him.

"Are my teeth red yet?" I asked.

"Nah."

"I want teeth like yours."

He chuckled. "You have to chew more. How long you go to Pohnpei for?"

"A week."

"Okay, so you chew the whole time you in Pohnpei and your teeth will turn red."

"Are you sure?"

"Yes, I guarantee."

This coming from an old Palauan, I believed it. Later I learned he was Palau's secretary of state.

ON MY FINAL night in Palau I ordered sushi in a restaurant called Mingles, but I did no mingling because the place was empty. So I ate in peace; the food was inexpensive and good.

Walking back to my hotel I came upon a gaunt, blotchy, geriatric white man sitting in a folding chair on the corner of the road, in front of the Koror post office, smoking a cigar. He wore a blue floral shirt and beige shorts; his bare legs were skinny pale pins of veiny flesh, and his eyeglasses were a quarter-inch thick. Two pieces of luggage were at his side.

"Your cigar smells quite good," I said.

"Want one?"

"Oh, no thank you. I don't smoke."

"Good for you. You don't need it."

He was an eighty-six-year-old World War II veteran named Cecil. He was sitting there waiting for his ride to the airport to fly back to his retirement home in Kansas, a marathon red-eye route stopping in Guam, Honolulu, Houston, and finally Wichita.

"That seems like an awful lot of flying for a guy like you," I said.

He scoffed. "Hell, I can take it. I got here, didn't I?"

"Good point. What brings you to Koror?"

"Peleliu."

In World War II the Japanese shooed natives from Arakabesan Island and made it a seaplane base, its remnants remaining in the vicinity of Meyungs and Palau Pacific Resort. In 1914 Japan took Palau from Germany, Koror became Japan's Micronesian capital, and for decades dominated the innocuous little island nation. Then came World War II, and things changed.

Palau's bloodiest battle occurred in the autumn of 1944 on Peleliu Island, twenty-five miles south of Koror, when two thousand Americans and eleven thousand Japanese troops perished. Under the command of First Marine Division Commander General William H. Rupertus (killed in combat in 1945), the U.S. attempted to seize Peleliu from Japan with Operation Stalemate II, a move Rupertus claimed would take three days. It took three months.

Jim Moran in his book *Peleliu 1944: The Forgotten Corner of Hell*:

> *Equalling Tarawa, Iwo Jima and Okinawa in scale and ferocity...the Japanese fought a bloody battle of attrition from*

prepared positions, and in a struggle of unprecedented savagery a whole Marine Division was bled white.

"I CAME BACK for three days to see Peleliu," Cecil said. "Hadn't been there since '44. Took a boat on Friday. Came back yesterday. Place looked beautiful. Broke my goddamn heart. Cried more'n I ever had, tell you what."

"The war must have come back to you."

"It never left. Happened sixty years ago. I've thought about that damn island every day since."

"What did you do?"

He puffed on his cigar. "First Marine Division. The Old Breed. Fifth Marine Regiment, infantry, second battalion. We'd hit Guadalcanal and Rabaul in '42 and '43. MacArthur wanted the Philippines from the Japs, but we had to get them out of the region. So we went to Peleliu. Nimitz ordered us in."

"Then what?"

"Then all hell broke loose. 'Course most folks think we could've saved lives if we'd just hit the Japs from the air. Bombed their boats and planes. Would've saved thousands of people."

I looked around at the cars and people, the happy kids and their mothers, the innocence of the starry Koror evening. Across the street was the cheap delicatessen that doubled as an Internet café, used heavily by tourists and locals, and it was full of them tonight. I wondered if any of these people realized the bloodshed and struggle required to enable Palau's domestic freedom, so they could check their e-mail there, mail a letter here, or sip sake down at Mingles until midnight.

It was all very peaceful and harmonious and normal. Folks were happy, there were no guns or aggression. It was not Sudan or the Middle East. This was Palau—yes, Micronesia—in 2004. I had been quite free to fly here, sleep here, walk here, eat here, surf here, dive here, explore here. It had been deeply enlightening and soul-cleansing, a stirring sojourn to a sublime place. Coming alone was the only way.

I looked at Cecil, chewing on his cigar.

"Was this trip worth it for you?" I asked.

"Well—" He exhaled smoke. "—did you see much of Palau?"

"I did."

"Did you feel safe and happy?"

"Absolutely."

"There's your answer."

The old man was right.

32

THE TAKING OF POHNPEI

2009

THE VENUE

POHNPEI IS ONE of those primordial tropical islands you might see in action movies and adventure reality shows, except none have been filmed there—Hollywood can't find it on a map and probably never will. There are lots of pretty waterfalls and dense, misty jungles, but the island has no beaches, it's too damn far away, the weather is often terrible, and the locals are typically stoned off weed or *sakau*.

With its immaculate satellite atolls of Ant and Pakin, lush little Pohnpei (PON-pay), one of three Senyavin Islands within the 500 Caroline Islands, occupies a few thousand muggy acres of the West Pacific. It is the capital of the Federated States of Micronesia (FSM), a sovereign island nation that includes the states of Yap, Chuuk, and Kosrae, about seven degrees above the equator, east of Palau, north of New Guinea. Ringed with mangrove forest, its lagoon and healthy barrier reef are pierced with 21 passes. Only 13 miles wide, Pohnpei, which means "upon a stone altar," is the FSM's biggest, tallest (Nahnalaud is 2,595 feet), most developed, and most populated (34,500) island, a smaller, rainier (more than 300 inches annually), more remote but similarly verdant cousin of Tahiti, with good diving, fishing, and the flawless right-hand barrels of Palikir Pass, two miles off the island's northwest coast.

The winter of 2004-2005 saw a string of unusually good swell and sunshine that had many pros claim Palikir to be the best wave they'd ever surfed. Superlative-laced coverage included *Australia's Surfing Life* calling it "the world's most perfect wave," and on a cover featuring Andy Irons, *Surfing* magazine said "P-Pass" was "the world's best right." Palikir was a great barrel, true, but to call it the "world's best" was a bit of a stretch. Palikir is not one of the world's most consistent spots, and the northeast trade winds regularly make slop of what would be perfection. But when it's on, Palikir is a heavy, perfect, dry tube, pedal-to-the-metal with few performance sections, a fairly forgiving reef, and a nice, deep paddling channel. "It's like something off a computer game," Dylan Longbottom told *Surfing World*, "something you'd draw when you were a kid."

Palikir is never hugely epic like Cloudbreak or Teahupo'o because its reef is incapable. The biggest and best it ever holds is what we saw Shane Dorian, Mark Mathews, and Dan Ross ride the afternoon of March 5, 2007, during the strongest swell Pohnpei had seen in at least a decade. (Their six-hour session resulted in simultaneous cover stories for *Surfing* and *ASL*, whose cover blurb was "*Finally*, the best wave in the world makes good on the hype." The 22-page pictorial was titled "This Was...The Best Trip Ever," and photographer Ted Grambeau said it was the best session he'd had in 25 years of surf photography.) When Palikir Pass maxes, like it did that morning, the wave mutates and doubles up and becomes fairly suicidal and almost impossible to surf. Kelly Slater discovered this, too, in early December 2008: "The largest sets sucked up the entire channel, a grinding, unrideable mess of foam, chunk, and current," Evan Slater wrote in *Surfing*'s May 2009 issue.

Aside from drowning or hitting your surfboard (or, these days, another surfer), Palikir's dangers are few. If a swell is long-period—say, 12 seconds or more—tide is inconsequential concerning the reef. Dead low can pose a problem on the wave's inside section, but generally Palikir's tidal swings are mild and the wave is surfable at all hours. Its personality parallels El Niño and La Niña—there have been long periods of strong trade winds blowing from large high-pressure systems to the east, affording short-period east-northeast windswell which rarely has enough power to produce real Palikir barrels; there have also been periods nearing nine weeks during peak winter surf season…with no swell. The opposite occurs when Palikir fires for weeks on end, like it did that fateful winter of 2004-2005, when sublime, long-period northwest swells seemed everlasting.

THE ANTECEDENTS

THE AFFABLE MORT MCINTOSH, now 60, was one of the first. Unclear who, exactly, its *first* surfer was, but Pohnpei was cracked in the 1960s, possibly by someone from Guam, where surfing landed around the same time Kennedy defeated Nixon in the 1960 U.S. presidential election. Or it might've been a local. "There was a Pohnpeian guy who went to school in Hawaii, where he started surfing," McIntosh recently told me. "He went back to Pohnpei and was surfing there way before anybody. I never met the guy—I just heard about him when I was there."

For any Guam surfer like McIntosh, island-hopping was innate considering Continental Airline's schedule, and so in February 1971 he spent three weeks on Pohnpei, surfing daily. The swell never dropped below eight feet. "People were surfing Main Pass the day I arrived," McIntosh said. "I borrowed the hotel's binoculars and I could see two guys who'd gotten dropped off by a fisherman. There was a shipwreck on the inside, and when they were done surfing, they came in and sat on the shipwreck and waited for somebody to pick them up."

Years later he surfed Palikir. But in '71, McIntosh simply made the rounds east, sampling Main Pass, Lighthouse, Mwahnd Pass, and a special little wraparound left near the Nan Madol ruins, courtesy of windswell. For one guy, it was more than enough surf, and McIntosh credited a local for the lead. "This Pohnpeian who I went to school with here on Guam, he came out with me a couple of times and saw the waves and said, 'Oh, yeah, we've got waves like that on Pohnpei, but they're bigger and they're farther out on the reef.' So I did some research and got some charts that showed me what it looked like and where it was, and I said, 'Okay, I'm going.' I went down there, and he'd take me out and drop me off. I'd surf alone, he'd go spearfishing for two hours and catch all these giant fish, and we'd go in, eat, drink some *sakau*, and pass out."

In 1980 another Guam surfer I'll call "Chevy" surfed Pohnpei. He worked for Continental, so he'd seen the island's surf from aloft; McIntosh also gave him a little insight. Not wanting to be directly quoted here, Chevy told me he didn't surf Palikir but found good waves at what locals called "the old harbor," the right-hander known today as Lighthouse. He'd hired a fisherman to take him to Nan Madol; along the way, blown-out windswell crumbled into the various eastside passes. But on the way back, as they motored around the north end of the lagoon, the wind switched and blew offshore into the wave at Lighthouse, which was "peeling." The fisherman stopped, and Chevy scored.

Alan Hamilton grew up in Palos Verdes, California, and moved to Santa Barbara in 1967, when he was 17. In 1971, a few months after Mort McIntosh surfed Pohnpei, Hamilton and partner John Bradbury became the first owners of a parcel (#55) in California's famous Hollister Ranch, a secluded right-point dreamland where the regular-footed Hamilton surfed exclusively. A diehard sailor, he became a commercial fisherman, skippering *Alamo*, an old shrimp boat based in Santa Barbara Harbor, and in 1987 he hired an energetic Pohnpeian deckhand named Danny, who was in Santa Barbara illegally as an undocumented alien. "After Pohnpei and those other islands got their independence in 1986," Hamilton told me, "they hired this guy named Bill Bixler to go out and do a survey of the tuna. Bixler hired Danny, and when they were done surveying, they smuggled him back to Santa Barbara, and he started getting jobs on everybody's boats."

At Danny's urging, Hamilton visited Pohnpei in early April 1991. He brought two surfboards with him and stayed at Danny's house at the base of Sokehs Rock. "I got a map of Pohnpei and saw Palikir Pass on it," Hamilton said. "I thought it looked like a good setup for surf.

Danny was there with me, and he had a little boat, and I said, 'Danny, take me out to this pass.' We went out there, and it was just this *dynamite* wave." Palikir was offering glassy, head-high sets. It was Hamilton's second day on Pohnpei; he stayed two months.

One night Hamilton was in a smoky bar called Rumors, shooting pool with FSM president Bailey Olter. Olter offered Hamilton the job of skippering the 80-foot *Kocho*, a Japanese fishing boat seized while fishing illegally in Pohnpeian waters. Skippering sounded good, and he knew boats, so in June 1991 Hamilton returned to Santa Barbara and sold everything he owned, including *Alamo* and the Ranch parcel, in less than two weeks, because on Pohnpei, a new life of deep sea-fishing and Palikir-tuberiding awaited.

But not everything went according to plan. "The senator who was in charge of the project was from Mokil Atoll, like 100 miles from Pohnpei, and he had a store out there. I ended up just taking all of these sacks of rice and cigarettes and everything out to the senator's little store instead of going fishing, like I was supposed to. I was supposed to do all these fishing trips and stuff, but never did." Yet surfing was never far. Palikir was Hamilton's main wave, but he surfed around the island, in all seasons. And he was always alone except the few times he took a visiting marine biologist out, or when he surfed Palikir with Mark Hepner, a Kauaian diver who exported tropical fish.

On April 9, 1994, Hamilton almost lost his left hand and forearm to an 8-foot bull shark. He was surfing at Palikir; it was a foot overhead and perfect, with nobody in sight. Around 2 p.m., he kicked out of wave, and started paddling back out. On his second stroke—*BAM*! "The shark came up from behind super fast and it was like a grenade went off in my arm. It was going in too fast; it bit and then it slid down my arm. The shark yanked me off my board and then went backwards off my arm with its jaw clamped down, scraping my flesh off down to my fingertips. It took all the tendons and it broke my bones—and I was way out there by myself at Palikir. My panga was parked on the reef, so I just caught a dinky wave with my one arm and glided on in to the boat. I was bleeding like crazy. The only chance I had was to get into town as quickly as I could."

Hamilton's boat had a paltry 9-horsepower outboard; the trip to Palikir from Kolonia took nearly 30 minutes, longer than most. He managed to start the motor, untie the anchor, and head back toward town, but immense blood loss caused Hamilton to drift in and out of consciousness. "I went blind because all the blood went out of my head, so I laid down because I couldn't see anymore. I figured that, hell, I was going to die, but when I was laying down, my vision came back, so I just stayed down and drove with my feet." Hamilton's boat crashed into the *Micro Glory*, a docked freighter that was about to depart for Kapingamarangi. The crew looked down, grabbed him, and rushed him to Pohnpei Hospital in Kolonia, where he remained for six days, receiving rudimentary but adequate care. He flew to Honolulu for further treatment at Tripler Army Medical Center, but the hospital would not accept him. So he rang Santa Barbara's Cottage Hospital, which "couldn't wait" to get him in. "They treated me like I was Mick Jagger," he said. Cottage sought to specialize in orthopedic surgery, and Hamilton was a prime guinea pig; the hospital treated "the sharkbite guy" for free, and over the next four months he had four operations. The fingers of Hamilton's left hand no longer functioned but, permanently stuck in an outward closed formation, he could still paddle, and in February 1995 he started surfing again. Back on Pohnpei, his blood-stained surfboard was nailed to a wall in Rumors, a lively bar among the mangroves at Sokehs Harbor.

In late 1995 Hamilton bought a 30-foot fiberglass boat and sailed it from Hawaii to Tahiti, where he stayed three years, doing essentially nothing. Via Yvon Chouinard, a friend of Hamilton's, Chuck Corbett heard of him and invited him to Tarawa. The two sailed to Fanning Island in separate boats. It was the summer of 1999; Hamilton stayed for 18 months, surfing Whaler Anchorage and English Harbor. "He was 49 years old, smoking two packs a day, and surfing double-overhead waves alone," Corbett said. "To this day, he is the most stylish surfer I have ever surfed with." In 2001 Hamilton traded his small boat for a 40-foot sailboat and went to Hawaii. Today he collects disability checks and lives on the boat in Molokai's Kaunakakai Harbor.

In the early 1990s there was another surfer on Pohnpei, but Hamilton never met him—he didn't surf Palikir. Bruce "Whitey" Talley, a beatific tradesman and sarong-wearing hippie, lived near Wapar in the island's remote southeastern jungle. He was the stepson of a Pan American World Airways captain stationed in Germany and France, where Talley lived until he was 17. He returned to the United States to attend college. It didn't last, so Talley joined the Marines and ended up on Guam, where he met and married a Pohnpeian woman. A few years later he decided to meet her parents, so he took a week off from pipefitting and flew to Pohnpei on January 13, 1990. On tattered dirt roads it took nearly four hours to drive the 22 miles from the airport to Wapar, where her parents lived. Two days later his pregnant wife grew ill, so Talley stayed. He'd brought three windsurfboards and two surfboards "just to check it out," he said, because in the '70s, a guy he knew on Guam, Mort McIntosh, said Main Pass "really smoked."

Talley surfed the other side of the island, opposite Palikir, because that's where he lived. Having no boat, Talley rode waves he could paddle to. "Well, here I was—Pohnpei," he said about his first day on the island. "I go in her parents' backyard and look out, and there's smokin' waves, right side, left side. Okay! But, here's the big thing that people seem to forget: that fantasy about going out in the water, being the first one to go surf the place, and all that, that's a bunch of horseshit. The simple fact is, it's scarier than shit when you go out there. To be sitting out there and look down and see three sharks underneath you, let me tell you something, man, your heart goes *really* fast."

Talley heard of Hamilton but never saw him because he was a south coast guy with no car; Hamilton was a north coast guy. His spot was Palikir. "Unfortunately for him," Talley said, "when you're at Palikir and the birds come, you'd better get out of the water, because the birds means the school is coming right onto the reef, and that means the sharks are following right after. He didn't get out of the water, and he got nailed."

But Hamilton left in April 1994. "So it was back to me only," Talley said. "Never did get to find anybody to go surf with. Then there was the guy from Hawaii, he was a fisherman. He came over here, I guess he got mixed up with a local girl, too—big total nightmare, man." That was Mark Hepner, and from 1987 to 1997 he lived on Pohnpei, surfing

Palikir and exporting tropical fish. He was a stylish regularfoot, and he occasionally surfed with Hamilton; he was unreachable at the time of this writing. Today Talley, 64, lives in a shack among mangroves near Nett Point. If he walks a hundred yards west he can see the right-hander at Lighthouse directly. There are often waves there. Talley has no computer, television, or telephone. Life is sweet.

The Next Generation

Mike Sipos was a Californian-cum-Floridian who, in 1986, after a five-week stint teaching windsurfing at Club Med in the Dominican Republic, decided to practice law. He graduated from the University of Miami and in 1990 relocated to Los Angeles, where he worked eight years at Haight Brown & Bonesteel. Yet the chaos drained Sipos. Serendipity saved the day.

May 1998, nighttime, beachfront Santa Monica. Online Sipos saw an ad seeking a lawyer to serve as general counsel to the Supreme Court of the FSM. Exact location? The national capital complex in the town of Palikir on the isle of Pohnpei. Yet Sipos knew nothing of Pohnpei or the FSM. After scribbling the job contact information onto a napkin, he reconsidered and dismissed bailing the L.A. law career he'd worked so hard to get. Another hour passed. Sipos crumpled the napkin and threw it into the trash. Two days later, slogging through San Diego freeway traffic, looking at high-rises, the smog, the cars, the concrete, the frowns and the garish billboards, he had a daydream. Bailing the rat race for an exotic island sounded pretty good, didn't it? That night he went online and couldn't find the FSM ad; trash-can digging revealed the suddenly valuable napkin. In the end Sipos got the job, a one-year contract.

He landed on Pohnpei—another planet—in June 1998. The ocean was flat. Using the 17-foot Boston Whaler he'd shipped from Long Beach, Sipos explored the pristine reef passes, fishing and envisioning waves breaking where no crowds existed. By August he'd met one of the two other surfers on island. This was Weston Yap, a Hawaiian in the Peace Corps; he'd landed on Pohnpei in May 1997 but had yet to surf

Palikir. Sipos had Yap on standby for the first winter groundswell. But one day in early September, as Sipos boated out to hook tuna beyond Sokehs Pass, a flawless, head-high right rose and peeled sectionless over the length of reef, expiring into the channel. "I was blown away," he said. "I couldn't believe the waves could be that perfect without anyone knowing about them." The sun seared his shirtless shoulders. Sipos knew his days in Los Angeles were done. Excel in the outpost law position, surf good waves, land big fish, marry the pretty local girl, make children, live happily ever after in Pohnpeian zen. Sipos reversed course, found Yap, and the two surfed that clean two-day typhoon swell. Yet six miles to the southwest and superior to Sokehs, Palikir Pass remained empty.

By October Yap and Sipos had sampled the passes from Main down to the ruins of Nan Madol (translation: "Spaces Between"), an ancient and famous aquatic city of basalt logs. The two men rode small, clean waves at Mwahnd and Ohwa passes; later, Sipos encountered some Americans from Guam who'd arrived for a dive holiday. They experienced one dreamy session off the south end of the Madolenihmw harbor entrance at Napali.

A month later Sipos rode smallish Palikir Pass for his first time. With him were Yap and Mark Hepner, who had returned briefly to finalize his divorce from a local woman. Hepner had asked around, looking for someone to take him surfing. Sipos offered a board and a boat ride and in return Hepner introduced him to the glory of Palikir. "We pulled up to Palikir and it was solid, consistent, overhead and glassy—and *empty*," Yap told me. "It broke so far out and bowled in *so* hard. It was amazing. Afterwards we actually looked for other surfers on Pohnpei because it's creepy sitting solo in that lineup. The ocean has things jumping and swimming all around. But there was no one. It was just us."

Yap finished his Peace Corps stint and left mid-1999. Shaun Stratton, an English professor employed by the College of Micronesia, arrived in August. Six weeks later, after occasionally surfing the reef at Nan Madol, Stratton's colleagues said something about another surfer living on Pohnpei. Soon Stratton met Sipos in Rumors, the dingy waterfront pub.

"Like a Little Leaguer excited about getting a hit," Stratton said, "I described how fun my Nan Madol sessions had been. Mike listened impassively before interjecting. 'The real wave is Palikir,' he said, pointing northwest. 'When it breaks, it's world-class, and you and I are the only ones here to ride it.'" Sipos mentioned his Boston Whaler, "our taxi to the surf," and for eight months Stratton and Sipos were the sole full-time surfers on the island; they surfed Palikir Pass every time it broke. (Talley occasionally surfed only the south coast spots.) In May 2000 Stratton left after a cholera epidemic closed the college.

Looking to recruit a lawyer who surfed, Sipos sent an email to friends in California; he found Scott Dodd, who was living in Hawaii. Dodd arrived on Pohnpei in August 2000 and stayed three years, tripling his one-year contract with the FSM Supreme Court. "The first time I surfed Palikir was with Mike within a week of my arrival," Dodd said. "It was beautiful conditions, slightly overhead on the sets—it was pretty mellow, not the bombs you see pictures of now. I could see the incredible colors of the reef, the fish. And we were the only ones out. In fact, there were no other boats of any kind, no other people at all. I was in disbelief—I could not believe how good it was."

A year later, a skinny blond kid named Ben Schroer arrived from New Hampshire. He was a Seventh Day Adventist volunteer school teacher, not a surfer, but on Pohnpei he quickly became one, learning how to surf at windy, hollow Palikir Pass. It was nothing like Waikiki or San Onofre. Schroer progressed from blowing each drop to consistently pulling even the latest bombs—backside. For the first three to four years of his surfing life, he never once rode frontside; he got barreled backside before ever making a drop going left. He surfed Palikir consistently, usually alone or with Tyler, his buddy from the Peace Corps. Occasionally they would see Sipos out there, but their paths rarely crossed. "That's how Palikir was," Schroer said. "Our sanctuary. Those first two years, 19 times out of 20 we would be the only people in the water. The other one time out of 20, it would be Mike and one of his friends. One time Mick Fanning was out with us for a couple days. I asked him for some advice on how I could improve; his response was: 'Just go for the barrel, mate.' And that's what I did."

From 1999 to 2004, taking advantage of the Air Nauru flight straight from Guam, Ernie Nelson saw the world from Palikir's biggest barrels more than anyone. A pale, lean, organic type, Nelson was moody, somewhat selfish, and occasionally flaky, but he was heavily committed to charging Palikir's precision and made serious sacrifices to establish such a lifestyle. A Floridian landscaper initially hired to work at Leo Palace in Yona, Guam, Nelson met Sipos through Wade Olszewski, a Floridian friend of Sipos who in 1995 also moved to Guam. Nelson rang Sipos, and in March 1999 found himself deep inside Palikir Pass tube gluttony.

A civil engineer on Guam, Olszewski first saw the wave in 1996 during a panga tour of the lagoon with his girlfriend. He didn't know it was a legit spot, but there was enough swell to pique his interest. "After I learned Palikir was a real wave," he said, "it always amazed me that it wasn't more exploited since the regular dive tours flew right over it and used the pass. But I guess a lot of divers don't surf for fear of sharks. If you dove off the ledge at Palikir you'd see a bunch of grey suits down deep, but they're well-fed out there and don't need to come up for the surfers."

With Olszewski, Nelson returned to Pohnpei in December 1999, lucking into two successive large, clean swells. "We were amazed," Nelson said. "Then the rush was on for trying to score it as much as possible before the word got out. By that time, I'd done quite a bit of traveling, and I knew surfers would go anywhere there's a wave, and with an international airport sitting right on top of Palikir, I knew it was only a matter of time."

The Media

NEAR 2 P.M. ON February 19, 2000, Rob Gilley aimed his telephoto Canon lens off the bow of Mike Sipos's 17-foot Boston Whaler Montauk® called *Smell the Glove*. The vessel was named after a Spinal Tap song and the Pohnpeian practice of wearing a fish-stenched glove to pull lines from the water.

Click-click-click.

Gilley was photographing something special.

Click-click-click-click.

July—five months later. It was in every surf shop, bookstore, and Muzaked 7-11. "Dan Malloy in the secret South Pacific" was the tiny caption on the lower left corner of the cover of Surfer's annual oversized summer issue, 316 pages of "Epic Surf Adventure" crowned with Gilley's photograph of the California regularfoot gouging the back half of his surfboard into a tropical-blue right wall, the lip line behind him cradling a perfect tube. Inside the magazine was a 12-page feature called "Simple Procedure," written and shot by Gilley, showcasing the young Malloy and his Laguna Beach goofyfooted friend Mike Todd pulling into perfect overhead barrels alone at the same "secret" spot. Gilley, one of the best in the business, had woven a new dream for readers worldwide.

We wanted to know where the wave was. It was in the Pacific, but the almond-eyed islanders in Gilley's photos precluded the wave from being Melanesian. And the island was rugged—Gilley didn't visit an atoll, so that nixed Kiribati and the Marshall Islands. Polynesia? Perhaps. But Gilley said English was the island's national language, and that disqualified everywhere between New Caledonia and the Archipiélago Juan Fernández.

In the story Gilley wrote about going to Barnes & Noble, where he'd found just one travel book about "the area," so I too visited Barnes & Noble to view its Pacific titles. Only one was about Micronesia; English-speaking bits of Micronesia were the Republic of Palau, the Territory of Guam, the Commonwealth of the Northern Marianas, and the FSM. I knew Gilley's shots weren't of Guam, because Guam had an active surf population. Later, my friend in Palau confirmed no pro surfers had been there, and suggested Gilley's shots were likely from the FSM—Pohnpei, to be exact.

In March 2002 I was in the lunch room at *Surfer* awaiting a slide show by then-photo editor Jason Murray. Sam George and Ross Garrett were there chatting with *Surfer*'s then-associate editor Carl Friedmann about a solo trip he'd just taken, something about a perfect right-hand barrier reef pass bowl off a mysterious Micronesian isle. At a pause in the conversation, I asked: "Where'd you go, Carl?"

"Pohnpei."

"Good?"

"Yeah."

The lights dimmed and slide show began. Friedmann left midway through. That night I emailed Dan Malloy.

"It was Pohnpei," he replied. "The wind can be bad, but if you get it clean, you're in for a treat."

Shawn Shamlou, an environmental project manager from San Diego, flew to Pohnpei with his artist friend Michael Cassidy in February 2003. Their trip resulted in an eight-page *The Surfer's Journal* feature called "Meganesia" and it was the first media exposure of Palikir Pass since Gilley's in *Surfer* four years prior. "It doesn't matter where it is, though, even if I told you," Shamlou wrote. "Know why? Because you are not going there…(it's) one of those places that's too expensive to justify in light of other more dependable wave zones…Aussies won't come here; Indo is closer and tremendously cheaper, and more consistent."

Page 57 of Shamlou's article showed a photograph of Sokehs Rock, a famous Pohnpei landmark, widely recognized and fatal proof of the story's location. Also included were four photographs from Gilley's 2000 *Surfer* trip. But how did Shamlou find Palikir Pass? "I figured it out from a Nature Conservancy magazine," he said. "The airport, lagoon, and steep topography were big clues. Around the same time, Cassidy had been wanting to explore Micronesia, and we agreed Pohnpei would be worthy. Gilley's *Surfer* article confirmed it."

"Gilley was in a skiff he had hired, holding a camera, when Sean Stratton and I pulled up in my Whaler late one weekday afternoon," Sipos said. "Dan and Mike Todd were the only guys out. I yelled to Gilley that he was breaking my heart, and that his group was the first time I'd encountered other surfers in the water since my arrival almost two years before." Sipos paddled out and chatted amicably with Malloy and Todd; they and Gilley later dined with Sipos at his home near Kolonia. "I filled them in on the whole deal after Rob agreed that they would all keep it under wraps, which they did," Sipos said. "I showed them videos and stills, the whole shebang. Those guys embodied what surfing and surf travel should be about, and I was glad to share it with them."

Via Gilley, Shamlou contacted one of the Pohnpei surfers mentioned in *Surfer*: Mike Sipos, though Gilley did not write his last name in the article. In *TSJ* Shamlou referred to Sipos as "Jude," Sipos's middle name. I asked Shamlou for "Jude's" email address, and on the grounds of secrecy, Sipos said he would be happy to meet me and take me out to surf Palikir Pass; after all, he'd done the same for Shamlou and Gilley.

In the late 1990s Gilley was *Surfer*'s photo editor; he'd tracked the Pohnpei scent from inside the magazine's drafty gray San Juan Capistrano warehouse—all editions of the now-defunct *Surf Report* lay within. On lunch breaks Gilley ditched his light table for the steel shelves to lose himself in the printed-guide world of waves. Naturally he saw the *Surf Report*'s February 1998 issue about Pohnpei, written and photographed by a Kiwi named Russell Hill. Alas, Hill's spot descriptions were grossly inaccurate—he even named a spot after himself, one that Talley and others had been riding for years. He also claimed Pohnpei's best surf season was summer.

But south swells in Pohnpei are painfully rare—the Solomon Islands and Papua New Guinea stand in the way. The calmest months are August and September, when Pohnpei has light and variable wind patterns and plate-glass seas, unless tropical disturbances sweep by. Autumn is transitional, with intensifying rain, wind, and swells, which almost never arrive until Halloween. Winter is windy, with sustained trades from the east or northeast in the 20 mph range almost every afternoon. Unfortunately the windiest season coincides with the biggest swells; onshores for most spots are the norm, and the rainfall can be brutal.

And although the *Surf Report* described eight surfable reef passes, only one of them would be considered real. "The other spots," Sipos told me, "are either too far away, too windy, too inconsistent, too shallow, unmanageable because of tides, currents, and boat anchorage/access issues, or unworthy as to wave form. Whereas Palikir Pass is the gem from all angles and is so much better than every other spot, it *is* the magnet, and in reality is the *only* 'true' surf spot of Pohnpei."

Gilley knew this. Augmenting intel from a Tavarua boat driver who'd competed in a Pohnpei fishing tournament, there was the conversation with his Oceanside, California-based dentist. A diehard scuba enthusiast, Dr. Bridges had visited Pohnpei and to Gilley described the shapely waves he'd seen at Palikir Pass, an obscure diver's paradise with superior visibility and copious marine life, the pass itself more than a half-mile long and 135 feet deep at its center. The bottom was more than 300 feet deep on the outside, and the currents could be severe, especially during the large winter swell which transformed Palikir into a surfer's paradise.

"Pohnpei opened the world to me," Gilley said. "It made me realize that most surfers were sheep, and what you really wanted to be was a shepherd. To paraphrase Ted Grambeau, anybody who thinks that all the best waves in the world have been discovered hasn't been looking."

Grambeau first went to Pohnpei in the late 1990s—maybe 1998. He doesn't recall. But he was alone, just scouting the setups; he had many frequent-flyer points with Continental Airlines. "The surf was pretty good," he said, "but it rained the whole time I was there. I then studied rainfall patterns of the area and found it was one of the wettest places on Earth. I shelved any immediate plans for a full-scale surf trip."

Soon Grambeau saw Gilley's *Surfer* article. "Straight away I knew where it was despite no indication given in the article," he said. In January 2004 Grambeau photographed Mick Fanning surfing Palikir during a three-day trip suggested by swell models. "With Fanning, it was just a quick raid, deliberately keeping it low-profile as there were already regular surfers from Guam and Australia and the U.S. by that stage. There was absolutely no advantage for me to pinpoint its location." An eight-page feature called "Clean Getaway" graced Issue 189 (April 2004) of *ASL*; photo editor Lee Pegus and cagey Grambeau tried to stump readers by including a portrait of afro-haired Papua New Guineans and an aerial photo of Chuuk's thin barrier reef.

Five years earlier, another Australian surf magazine (*Tracks*?) had shown Pohnpei via photos of small waves shot in summer; the feature was unmemorable. And the sole prior surf-media mention of Pohnpei appeared in the April 1986 issue of *Surfer*—photographer Erik Aeder had island-hopped from Guam back to his home on Maui, spending a week on Pohnpei (in *Surfer* he called it "Ponape," the island's name until 1984). It was summer, so he saw no surf, though he had heard good things about it. In his mistitled article "Melanesia," Aeder mentioned the ruins of Nan Madol and included a photo of women and handicrafts in Pohnpei's Polynesian village of Pohrakiet. His surf photos were from a different island.

In the four-year gap between Gilley and Grambeau, besides Pohnpei residents, Mike Sipos estimated Palikir Pass hosted fewer than a dozen solo travelers, guys like Shamlou, Cassidy, Tony Pittar, Eric Havens, Friedmann and Fred Mendiola, in addition to the temporary expat resident surfers: Ryo Aoki and Koyo Matsudaira from Japan, plus Dodd, Schroer, Stratton, Shaun Simmons, Dennis Gearheart, and Tyler McAdam from America. "But I should clarify that none of the magazine exposure came about at my urging or insistence," Sipos said. "I didn't initiate any of it. The photographers, writers, and pro surfers came on their own and contacted me, not the other way around. It was called sharing stoke and spreading aloha, which is something I did for every visitor who came along including, most notably, Allois Malfitani."

The Brazilian

IT'S A SIMPLE ACT—the scenic flight over the Pacific and its myriad atolls. Continental's thrice-weekly service from Honolulu/Kosrae (or four times weekly from Guam/Chuuk) puts you at Pohnpei International Airport, three miles east of Palikir Pass. You get your passport stamped, retrieve your bags from the carousel, drive to a hotel, unpack, and hope for stand-up barrels by sundown. This basic mode of surf travel occurs daily in Hawaii, Australia, Indonesia, Mexico, wherever. But the world is huge, the oceans somewhat infinite. Each day, millions of tropical waves break unseen. Anyone with time, money, and moxie can find them, and those willing to endure risk are sometimes rewarded with sublime lineups unlike the banal beaches at home.

Allois Malfitani was well aware of that. In 1986 the jovial goofyfooter was 24, living in Florianópolis, Brazil, skateboarding the city streets and surfing the scenic adjacent beachbreaks. Days passed quickly—life was good, but he knew it could be better. Brazil was home but, surf-wise, it had limitations.

That October Malfitani was casually thumbing through the new issue of *National Geographic*; a large color photo on page 478 made him stop and stare. It was an aerial view of Kosrae's airport, lines of whitewater wrapping around its barrier reef, with three passes—and more whitewater—clearly visible to the southwest. Malfitani knew nothing of Kosrae or Micronesia. Yet the bait was set, and he sensed opportunity in the Pacific. Ascending from Brazil in 1992, Malfitani landed on Oahu, where, after obtaining his green card, he managed the front desk in Mark Foo's Backpackers hostel at Waimea Bay. The dusky Brazilian was gregarious and charming, an endearing host. Some said Malfitani was conniving, manipulative, and somewhat effeminate, but none of it mattered—he was a good guy to know.

Eight years passed. Good times. But eventually Malfitani realized there was more to life than surfing the crowded North Shore. That Kosrae photo from the '86 *National Geographic* was permanently etched into his brain. They were so enticing, really, those three reef passes and the rights bending around the pale coral encircling the island's tarmac, 3,000 miles from Oahu, and certainly emptier than Haleiwa. Conveniently, Honolulu International Airport was the eastern hub for the Continental island-hopper path—heading west from Honolulu, the first three stops were Majuro, Kwajalein, then Kosrae. Malfitani saw the route map and smiled.

Arriving on Kosrae in the summer of 2000, Malfitani met Dr. Ken Miklos, an expat Southern Californian dentist who for a few years had had the island's waves to himself. Miklos gave Malfitani a tour of Kosrae's fickle surf spots. Unfortunately the airport wave was flawed and not Kosrae's wave of choice; for Malfitani, it couldn't justify a long-term stay. But only 300 miles away, an easy one-hour flight, the next westbound stop on Continental's island-hopper ticket was Pohnpei. It was worth a look. But before he left, Miklos made Malfitani swear that, despite seeing nothing world-class, he would tell nobody—his North Shore friends, especially—about what he saw on Kosrae.

Once on Pohnpei, Malfitani asked around. Many Pohnpeians knew Sipos was a surfer, often seen trailering his boat with surfboards strapped to the bow rail; colleagues saw his office walls covered with surf photos. So Malfitani heard Sipos's name and opened the Pohnpei phonebook. He called Sipos at home. "I told him he'd come during the wrong time of the year and wasn't going to find surf," Sipos said. "I then gave him the details about when and where it breaks during the season, and he returned the following March. I took him out and showed him Palikir Pass. We surfed together quite a bit that season and the next."

Malfitani then befriended Dodd and stayed at his house for a nearly a month. Malfitani returned each year for three weeks, occasionally with friends. In 2002 he arrived alone; a married lady from Brazil flew to Pohnpei for a fling with him. In 2003 he went with two friends who had been installing cell phone towers around Hawaii. Throughout, Malfitani solemnly pledged to Sipos and others, like Miklos and Dodd, that he would not expose or exploit Palikir Pass. He said he intended to retire on Pohnpei and would shield the wave from the public eye.

The Seed

GEOGRAPHICAL ISOLATION, bad infrastructure, and cultural values emphasizing sociality over financial prosperity have all stunted Pohnpei's economic growth. For now, the island's economy revolves around commercial long-line tuna fishing by Asian fleets; each year, the FSM receives nearly $30 million for license fees from foreign vessels. Profuse rainfall and a mountainous landscape aren't conducive to large-scale agriculture, either, and Pohnpei's main source of revenue comes from—you guessed it—the United States. Since 1986, under its Compact of Free Association, America pays around $100 million annually to the FSM, about a quarter of that going to Pohnpei's government. There is potential for tourist industry, however.

On February 21, 2004, Allois Malfitani and Chris Groark, a tall, lanky, twentysomething Southern Californian, flew from Honolulu to

Pohnpei. It was Groark's first trip to Micronesia. Ben Schroer's parents were also inside the plane. Once on the ground, Schroer's father noticed Groark and Malfitani had surfboards, and was quick to introduce them to his son as soon as they exited the baggage claim. It was a beautiful, sunny day. Ben Schroer was stoked to see the surfers and said they could contact him should they need a free boat ride to Palikir Pass. Forty-eight hours later Malfitani rang Schroer and asked if they could catch a ride; Schroer was skippering a 29-foot fishing boat, so he said yes. En route to Palikir the trio talked about how good the wave was, but once they arrived, the wind was onshore and the swell was one foot.

While trolling for fish on the way back to port, Malfitani turned to Schroer and said, "Aren't you scared about the surf camp that Mike Sipos is going to start?" Schroer looked at him blankly. Malfitani mentioned Shamlou's then-recent "Meganesia" article in *TSJ*, and said it was printed to subtly expose Palikir to the surf world to incite awareness and publicity about a camp that Sipos was founding. Schroer assured Malfitani that he was wrong. "Allois then pushed further and asked me, 'Well, why wouldn't he? Wouldn't *you?*'" Schroer replied: "Obviously not. That would ruin it."

Sipos assumed Malfitani was acting preemptively to convince other Pohnpei surfers that a surf camp was inevitable—in other words, an excuse for why it was suitable for Malfitani to start one. "He was trying to temper opposition," Sipos told me. "Never did I say I intended to start a camp, nor did I ever plan to do so. Rather, in a conversation with him in 2001, when the subject of potential future commercial exploitation of Palikir Pass came up—as it occasionally did between all of us—I said that *if* it was going to happen, I ought to be the one to do it as I was best-equipped. It was during that same conversation when Malfitani first promised he'd never start a surf camp, keeping with his many subsequent assurances of not exposing Palikir. I had the time, resources, and experience to open a surf tourism business, but it wasn't something I ever wanted to see happen."

Schroer took Malfitani and Groark to Palikir thrice more before their time came to leave Pohnpei. During the final return boat ride,

Schroer desired clarity. "I knew Allois lived on the North Shore, so I said to him, 'You guys are never going to tell anyone about this, right? I mean, this is a secret you have forever. You have a free place to stay here, you have a boat to use, and as long as it stays a secret, the wave will always be a sanctuary." Malfitani and Groark quickly agreed, promising Palikir would "always stay a secret" and they would "do anything to protect it."

"That was all I needed to hear," Schroer said.

The three men exchanged email addresses and phone numbers, made plans for next time. Unbeknownst to both Schroer and Sipos and everyone else on Pohnpei, however, Malfitani was in the process of applying for a foreign investment permit (FIP), which he was granted on June 14, 2004, to start "a new adventure eco-tourism business." His permit was issued for something called Hi-Point Adventures, but he and Groark would be doing business as Pohnpei Surf Club (PSC), with one restrictive condition: "Grantee shall not manage, operate, and own hotel or similar facility in the State. Instead, it shall secure with the local providers place for the guests and tourists to stay." So he sublet rooms from the decaying Misko Beach Hotel on the mangroved shore of Sokehs Bay, aside the airport's runway. From Misko it was a 15-minute boat ride to Palikir Pass. Malfitani wanted to have a larger operation, but his permit was limited, so he had no choice.

"I couldn't believe these were the same two guys who vowed to keep Palikir a secret," Schroer said. "The same guys who had talked about coming back over the next decades and surfing perfect waves with a few friends. Chris told me, 'Dude, next year I'm going to call you ahead of time and plan. I'll crash at your pad and we'll just cruise with your boat.'"

For answers, Schroer rang Groark in late June. Fifty cents per minute to call the U.S.

Schroer: "Chris, it's Ben."

Groark: "Hey, dude, how's it?"

Schroer: "So, is it true? Are you guys really starting a camp?"

Groark: "Yeah, man. It's what we see as best, but we're going to do it real low-key and make sure that it never gets crowded—not more than six to eight guys, ever."

Schroer: "How can you do this, Chris? You have it all. You know where the spot is, you can come back the rest of your life and surf it perfect with your friends. How is that not enough?"

Groark: "Ben, you know (Palikir) is a goldmine, and we're not going to let anyone else get it before us."

Groark then tried to justify the reasons why and how he would manage the camp maturely and properly: by limiting the numbers. "He even tried to persuade me into thinking that if I had enough money to invest," Schroer said, "I would've done the same thing." He "bitterly and sadly" tried to persuade Groark that a surf camp was wrong, that it was a blatant exploitation of foreign resources. Then Schroer's 20-minute phone card expired.

Churning interest ahead of the camp's opening, GlobalSurfGuides.com detailed seven passes, claiming all of them to be of good quality—lefts, rights, multiple possibilities. "It was false advertising since *everyone* who had surfed Pohnpei knew there was *one* wave—Palikir Pass—that held the trade wind at bay," Schroer said. "Every other pass was onshore and horrible during the winter months, but (the camp) still advertised as if people would get this diversity of waves."

In an email to his Kosrae friend Ken Miklos on May 22, 2004, Malfitani wrote: "Come on, what are you thinking about all this? The camp in Pohnpei is happening for sure. It is going to be a small operation carefully catering for 6 to 10 guests. I could have media from all over coming out there for exposure of my business, but I am not. I have the high end clients ready to come."

To which Miklos replied: "I think you're going to destroy one of the last classic uncrowded surf locations…What, you've had enough uncrowded perfect days there that your ready to turn it into Hawaii style crowds where everybody is scrambling for just one wave to themselves? You're the last person I thought would do something like this. After all the things you said about keeping it pristine and secret. I think you're a stupid greedy bastard that, yes, will make some money initially on your lame exposure of our surf, but only initially. You can't own our resources above the reef. But you certainly can ruin them for a handful of locals, future visitors, and yourself. Allois, why don't you just shoot yourself in your foot? It makes the same amount of sense as starting your surf camp here. One doesn't shit where one eats, but that's what you're doing."

Malfitani's reply: "On the last 2 month there were 3 articles about the FSM on 3 different magazines. There are 5,000,000 surfers in the world. Lots of them are not stupid, and have a lot of money. It is going fast now Ken. How long do you think it will take for them to come? I would not give more than one season. Someone once told me, that if anyone was ever going to do this kind of business in Pohnpei, it was going to be he [Sipos], not me. It hurts to loose a great business opportunity, specially after so much time spend advertising, just in case you were never told of this side of the story. If there had not been all this exposure, I would never had done it. What would really hurt would be me not do it now, and see someone doing it 6 month down the road. This is what I know how to do. It is going to be a clean and organized operation. I won't need to make a article on a magazine for people to come because I already have my clients." Malfitani then suggested Miklos start a surf camp on Kosrae "before someone else does it."

In September 2004 I came into possession of copies of a lawsuit filed a month earlier with the FSM Supreme Court. Much of it was legal gobbledygook, but essentially it was Sipos suing Malfitani and Groark for "copyright infringement, conversion, fraud and deceit, breach of contract, tortious breach of the implied covenant of good faith and fair dealing, tortious interference with contractual relationships, defamation, and injunctive relief." The case settled under confidential terms in October, and Malfitani continued his business launch.

While writing this article I contacted Malfitani several times, requesting an interview, but was ignored.

The Grand Opening

On the sunny morning of Monday, November 8, 2004, after two weeks of exploring Palau, I sat in Guam's airport awaiting my Boeing 737 cruise to Pohnpei. Continental Airlines Flight 958 would depart

Guam at 10:20 a.m., with a 45-minute stopover at the Weno airport on Chuuk, 600 miles southeast.

In the previous months I exchanged emails with Sipos, who suggested I stay at the rustic hilltop Village Hotel. Its expat owner offered me a discounted rate. Sipos would be around if I wanted to go surfing. He also informed me that Malfitani's surf camp was coincidentally slated to open the same week I'd be on the island; I emailed Malfitani to see if it was indeed true. He said yes, and, by the way, would I like to write a story about it?

Seated across the Guam airport room were five men who looked like surfers. They had Australian accents. Chuuk's barrier reef had a lot of surf potential, I thought—maybe they were headed there? Doubtful. They were photographer Simon "Swilly" Williams and professional surfers Tom Innes, Craig Warton, and Rique Smith, plus Global Surf Guides' David Scard (now the office manager of World Surfaris Kirra Surf). On behalf of *Tracks* magazine, Williams's group were the first official guests of the PSC, which Global Surf Guides advertised as "Caroline Islands." Some of the men appeared a bit miffed at the sight of another surfboard bag (mine) on the Pohnpei airport carousel, but Williams and Warton were friendly to me. Our paths crossed vaguely in the ensuing week, mostly because they and Malfitani went for dinners at the Village Hotel, and there was an awkward moment or two when we all ended up at the Nan Madol ruins one flat, blustery afternoon. Palikir Pass was nonexistent, and throughout the week Williams's crew surfed mediocre windswell at Mwahnd and Napali.

Things changed Sunday, November 14. A clean northwest swell rose, and the wind swung lightly from the southeast. The sky was blue and cloudless. Sipos, his 2-year-old son Andrew, FSM lawyer Shaun Simmons with his wife Felicia, and I headed out in Sipos's Mako 238. Palikir was sheet-glass, eight feet, and going off. Malfitani, his PSC crew, and Williams's group were all in the water, along with a few Seventh Day Adventist kids. It seemed crowded but I paddled out and caught a few. Later, sitting in the shade under the bimini of Sipos's boat, pondering the new surf camp, watching Williams document the pros in idyllic overhead blue barrels, I turned to Sipos and said: "You know what, Mike? This is it. We're witnessing the beginning of the end for Palikir."

It all added up to one photogenic cannonball for Williams that spawned the February 2005 cover shot of *Tracks*, followed by a 10-page feature called "Sweet Caroline" of which the magazine screamed: "World Exclusive!! The New Indo—Hundreds of islands, thousands of waves, not a surfer in sight...Welcome to the newest, sweetest surfing destination on Earth—the Caroline Islands." *Tracks* called the wave "P-Pass" and said it was in the Pacific; the article, like Shamlou's in *TSJ*, included two photos of Sokehs Rock and one of Nan Madol. In the back of the magazine was a Global Surf Guides ad that read, "Introducing the Caroline Islands—New Surf Camp."

News of the *Tracks* trip spread like wildfire. The surf media was hungry for a new elite tropical right-hander, and Palikir was it. In December a team from *Surfer* was greeted by Malfitani in the Pohnpei airport. *Waves, ASL, Surfing, Japan Surfing World, Fluir, Trip, Pacific*, ESPN, Fuel TV, Rip Curl, *Free Surf Hawaii, Hawaiian Skin Diver*, and *Surfing World* soon followed.

"We fought hard and tried our best to protect it and save it, but greed prevailed," Ben Schroer said. "With the greed came harsh, destructive feelings. The next time I surfed with Allois at Palikir, where earlier that year I'd taken him to four times for free, he deliberately dropped in on me in solid six-foot swell. My friends witnessed it. Then Allois said to me, 'Go learn how to surf, and stay the fuck away from my wave.'"

It didn't take a genius to pin Palikir's location. Malfitani named his camp "Pohnpei Surf Club," and a quick online search of "P-Pass" or "surfing Caroline Islands" revealed the island's name. Malfitani's fleet of pangas had "Pohnpei Surf Club" written on both sides. Even *Surfer* magazine, featuring Palikir (and another shot of iconic Sokehs Rock) in the July 2005 issue, called it "Ponapei" in the article's opening photo caption. Quickly, Palikir Pass became the surf media's worst-kept secret.

The wave became the subject of several commercial film shoots, most infamously the one in January 2006 that became part of "One

Track Mind," directed by Chris Malloy and released by Woodshed Films in October 2008. Controversy erupted in mid-2006 when, after Malfitani's and a local fisherman's urging, Malloy and his filming partners built an illegal scaffold on the reef at Palikir Pass to afford Malloy's filmers a frontal angle on the wave while it was surfed by Andy Irons, CJ Hobgood, Sunny Garcia, Tom Curren, and Mark Occhilupo. Still photos of the project were published in *Surfing* magazine's "Trip of the Decade" feature in its June 2006 issue. The November 2007 "Filmmakers" issue of *Surfing* contained a photo of Malloy atop the scaffold.

An employee of environmentally-conscious Patagonia, Inc., Malloy was branded a hypocrite, issued considerable heat from incensed Pohnpeians and dozens of others worldwide in a thread on *Surfer*'s website. The thread was later deleted. At the time of this writing, Malloy was not available for comment, though in an email to Sipos on July 11, 2006, Malloy wrote, "I will never argue that I should not have taken the camp's or the local fisherman's promise that it was alright (to build the scaffold). I never should have."

Malloy redeemed himself. "I think it's worthy to note," Ben Schroer said, "that Chris Malloy is the only surf pro who has ever done anything for Pohnpei to show some gratitude and put forth an effort to help the local culture in a sustainable way." Schroer and Malloy organized the September Swell Hits Gstaad charity event held September 6, 2006, in New York City. It was a successful fundraiser for Schroer's cousin's organization, MAHI International, which was thus able to give free health screening and solar energy technology to Pohnpei and Sapwuahfik Atoll. "For the record," Schroer said, "Chris told me that when he built his scaffold, all four of its legs were on sandy locations among the coral, not touching reef anywhere. I believed him, and although this didn't make it okay to do something illegal in Pohnpei, it was PSC who told him it was okay to do so, and when he did it, I think that he did it in a conservative and appropriate manner."

Between the hundreds of PSC guests, the magazine and surf company photo shoots, and the film crews, in February 2007 Palikir Pass hosted the Inaugural Hobgood Challenge (IHC), an ASP North

America-sanctioned specialty event at the so-called "craziest right-hander in the world." The IHC crew was hosted by Malfitani. The event became a major feature in *Surfing* and *Stab* magazines, the former including a full-length DVD with its June 2007 issue. Neither Pohnpei or Palikir were mentioned in the event's widespread coverage. "Our destination," *Surfing*'s Matt Walker wrote, "is one of the freshest finds in the sport— barely a few years old—yet already lauded as a world-class right by past visitors such as Pancho Sullivan and Kieren Perrow, whose guestbook entry brags he 'spent more time looking out of the tube than in.' Unfortunately, there's even more messages sadly scrawling, 'Sorry we didn't get to see what she can really do.'" The IHC itself had generally fair-to-poor waves, and to date is the only surf contest to be held on Pohnpei.

In the past few years, Palikir has entered the mainstream media, including Wikipedia, NBC, the BBC, and Apple, who, in its recent marketing campaign for the MacBook Pro, used a Grambeau photo of Shane Dorian (the same photo made the July 2007 cover of *Surfing*). "The Apple campaign started with my being sponsored by one of their photo software products called Aperture," Grambeau told me. "During one of the photo tradeshows, where I was invited to give a slide show, (Apple) expressed interest, and it just went from there." Surf photos of Palikir by Grambeau and Andrew Shield have also been featured on FSM postage stamps.

In its February 2009 issue, *National Geographic Adventure* listed Pohnpei as one of its "Best Island Vacations." In "Catch the Greatest Wave on Earth," Meg Noonan wrote that Palikir "is one hell of a wave," and quoted Aussie pro Dylan Longbottom as saying Palikir is "by far the best right in the world." It's safe to say Longbottom hasn't surfed every right in the world, but surfing, concluded Noonan, was the best reason to visit Pohnpei.

"The wave at Palikir Pass is worth hundreds of thousands of dollars annually," Mike Sipos said. "It's arguably Pohnpei's most valuable tourist attraction, and for some strange reason a foreigner finds himself the de facto overlord of the asset. What's the value added by the one foreigner selling access to Palikir Pass that could not just as easily be supplied by Pohnpeians? And how much of this money from the sale of Pohnpei's natural resource is going to Pohnpeians?"

"It's full packages," Malfitani said of his PSC business structure in *Guam Business* magazine. "The only money (guests) spend here is lunch, dinner, gifts, shopping."

The Entitlement

During his first FIP application hearing in June 2004, Malfitani pledged on the record that his camp would only bring small groups of 6-8 to keep the impact and crowds low. This did not happen.

Dennis Gearhart was from Pennsylvania. In 2001 he moved to Pohnpei to teach math at the College of Micronesia. "When Allois came here in 2004," Gearhart said, "I was just starting to surf. I knew nothing about the world of surfing, the rules, etiquette, etc., and when I heard Mike (Sipos) was filing a lawsuit against Allois, I thought that was totally fucked up, like Mike thought he owned the place. When I first met Allois, we talked about the lawsuit. He said he couldn't understand why Mike was so upset, that he intended to keep his operation 'low-key.' Since then, I've seen his advertised surfer 'limit' go from eight to 18; I've seen film crews, dozens of magazine covers and articles, an ASP contest, a scaffold built on the reef, and now the guy has his camp on the postage stamps here."

Not everyone is upset. *Surfing* photographer Rob Gilley put it this way: "It's a situation where you want to claim the death of secret spots and the decline of Western Civilization, but it's not applicable. My friend was just (at Palikir) and he said it was just them. Perfect barrels and no one around, just like in 2000. The only difference now is that you're staying at a surf camp instead of a seedy motel, and your rides out to the reef pass are more dependable. Plus, it's a boost to the local economy."

Sipos tends to disagree. "I can give you photos of the PSC boats pulling up to Palikir packed with people," he recently told me. "Even though that's a universally accepted breach of surfing etiquette, those guys think that because they are the first to exploit the wave commercially, it gives them the right to disregard the rules that apply everywhere else. And by doing so, they give the middle finger to anyone who doesn't stay at the surf camp, the average polite solo traveler or small groups who are often already there when PSC arrives each morning."

Dennis Gearhart: "PSC brings money and tourists into Pohnpei, no question about it. But I don't think you can judge the ethics of Chris's and Allois's actions based on that. Their motivation was not to help Pohnpei. It was to help themselves, and to do it, they had no qualms about walking over a handful of surfers who were already here."

Historically the Palikir Pass channel bottom had repeatedly been pierced by the anchors of surfers' and divers' boats. This was not a desired effect on a pristine ecosystem. So in early 2004 Sipos requested Tyler McAdams, a volunteer employee at the Conservation Society of Pohnpei (CSP), to install a mooring buoy in the passage to eliminate need for anchoring. The mooring was placed where the water rushed off the reef adjacent to a sandy break in the coral. According to Sipos, when PSC arrived in November 2004, it began "monopolizing" the mooring, "very much the same as they are now doing with the entire surfing area." Pre-PSC, the mooring saw light use by the local surfers. But with PSC came more boats, and there was no choice but to drop anchors onto the coral bottom. This concerned Sipos, who then boated CSP personnel out to the pass and arranged for the installation of two additional mooring buoys. "The other two were installed after Chris Groark yelled at me as I approached a PSC boat, skippered by Beru Mendiola, a friend of mine," Sipos said. Sipos had been surfing alone at Palikir, left briefly to troll for fish, then returned after Brendan Margieson arrived in one of two PSC boats. It was January 19, 2005.

"Beru's boat was tied to the mooring; Groark's boat was floating in the lineup with Andrew Shield, who was taking photos. After Beru waved me up to tie off on his boat, Groark started shouting to him not to let me tie off. I shouted back that I was going to tie off on that buoy one way or another since I arranged for its installation and that I wouldn't be intimidated or vibed off the spot." Sipos went to CSP the next day and arranged for the installation of two more moorings that very week. They were placed on both sides of the original mooring;

Sipos had personally picked the spots with divers in the water. "But on other occasions," he said, "Groark has been cordial to me. The only time things got ugly was when he tried to call me off that buoy."

Other non-PSC patrons, like Southern California's Mark Lovett, have had similar encounters with surf-camp territorialism. In October 2005, nearly a year after the camp's inception, Lovett set out to surf Palikir Pass alone. "Pohnpei was known elsewhere for its great women and for shipping marijuana out in taro plants," Lovett said, "so I knew it would be exciting." After arriving he shoved his surfboards and a mildewed duffel bag into a taxi and went looking for a hotel. Driving down the road in Kolonia, Lovett noticed a white guy in a truck with a boat in tow. He introduced himself to Sipos, who said Lovett was welcome to stay at his house for free until he got his bearings. Lovett surfed Palikir the entire 2005-2006 season. He witnessed "about 50 pros" sampling its barrels. "All-in-all," he said, "if the camps are giving a big portion of their profits to the local economy—like schools and hospitals and throwing big events for them—then it's great. But unfortunately I had the opportunity to surf with Allois and Chris, not as a paying member, but as a hard-core feral who would get dropped off by a fisherman every day. They were totally cold to me, pricks who acted like I was not welcome to surf 'their' wave that they'd been shown by Sipos just a few years before."

Despite all this, PSC has produced some happy guests, particularly those who lucked into good Palikir—never a sure thing. "Allois has all the qualities you would look for in a host and surf camp owner," said Henry Morales, director of Wavehunters Surf Travel. "He's a genuinely nice guy who puts his guests first, is by nature unselfish both in and out of the water, and well-intentioned in his management of the Pohnpei Surf Club. I have gotten to know Allois through regular correspondence as well as from my time on Pohnpei, and he could best be described as a low-key family man."

Several positive testimonials are published on the Wavehunters website. From Chris Ruotolo: "Thanks to all the boys—Allois, Chris, Sonden, Biro and Roro. The trip of my life. Best barrels and best time ever. Can't wait to see you all soon"; from Donny Valenzuela: "Just had the best surf trip of my life. Insanely sick barrels, great crew, and great people. Thanks for giving us a taste of paradise. Allois and Chris, Sonden, Biro and Roro—you guys rock"; from Gary Elkerton: "Been around the world a million times. Seen the best waves in the world, but this trip was one of the best. P-Pass is fucking sick at two feet or eight-to-10, the place (is) unbelievable. To all the boys at the camp: great work."

Two Can Play At This Game

After the 2004-2005 winter and resultant media frenzy, Steve Ware, like many surfers, learned about "P-Pass." Ware was a stonemason in Narrabeen, a suburb in northern Sydney, Australia, where surf magazines were commonplace. Inside one he saw a World Surfaris ad for a surf camp in the "Caroline Islands," and the connection was made. The following year Ware chose Pohnpei over the Mentawais, where he visited annually, because the Mentawais charter boat he booked had caught fire and sunk.

In October 2006 he visited Pohnpei for 16 days with PSC. "I didn't think the camp was very good value for the money," Ware said, "and the service wasn't very personal, but we did manage to have a good time."

He scored Palikir. It set the hook, and plans were made to return for an extended period of time each winter, sans PSC, which to Ware was "just another expensive surf camp." In the summer of 2007 he flew back to Pohnpei and spent three weeks determining how he could live on the island all winter. The idea was to return to the same house each season and invite his Australian friends to visit, stay, and contribute expense funds.

Damian Oswald was an old mate of Ware's. He too was a solid surfer and Narrabeen fixture, a deep-sea fisherman extraordinaire who sought waves of consequence. To Oswald, Ware described Palikir Pass being "Backdoor crossed with a big Burleigh Heads pit," which for Oswald was a dream come true. "It sounded like a spot to get to," he said.

For their first extended trip, Oswald and Ware filled and filled and shipped a container with 30 surfboards, fishing tackle, a small jeep, a ping-pong table, and a 60-horsepower outboard to affix to a boat once they arrived. All they needed was a house. They met Wilbur Walter, the genial owner of Nihco Marine Park, a pleasant waterfront nook catering to swimmers and weekend picnic groups. It was a fine, wind-sheltered place to while an afternoon away. Amongst the mangroves, the park had an enclosed lagoon where coral fill was once dredged; it had inner and outer beaches for swimming. And it was located on the closest point of land to Palikir Pass, its waves visible from the camp bungalows, a five-minute boat ride away.

A native Pohnpeian, Walter was married to a state senator and he owned an office supply business, retail shops, and a printing company. Financially he was quite well-off, particularly by FSM standards. He knew Palikir Pass was a natural resource being singularly exploited by foreigners to whom, by birthright, Palikir did not belong; Walter was displeased about this and asked Ware if he would like to become an employee of his, entering the realm of Pohnpei surf tourism. "I declined and told him that I was not there for that purpose," Ware said. "He asked me again and said he would buy whatever boat we suggested, within reason. I started warming to the idea of business and making an income surfing and looking after guests."

Inside the park Walter built a nice two-bedroom bungalow for Ware and Oswald. There were plans for five more. Wilbur freely offered the use of his boat. "He said I could handle everything," Ware said, "and all he wanted was the rental for his bungalows. Of course this has all changed now and he is after more than just rent. I think the general expectation from a local point of view is that a business of this kind should be very, very profitable. I think that is true, but maybe the fact that mortgages have to be serviced means that it could be five or 10 years before the business becomes profitable. Not everyone understands this point." Nonetheless, Walter was optimistic; he invested more than US$1 million in the property. "(Palikir) is among the Top Ten places to surf in the world," he told *Guam Business* magazine. "Every year there is a 10 percent increase of surfers coming to Pohnpei."

And, perhaps inevitably, Palikir Marine Adventures was born. "There's nothing wrong with a bit of competition, and Allois didn't discover Palikir," Oswald said.

"MICRONESIA IS ABOUT TO FIRE!"

ON SEPTEMBER 22, 2008, I received a promotional email from World Surfaris. The subject line was "Micronesia is about to fire!" and the text inside began with: "The swell is starting to brew in the Northern Pacific, the upcoming Pohnpei surf season is about to kick off next month. P-Pass has been unridden since last season and is ready to turn on. The crew of Pohnpei Surf Club eagerly anticipate the first surfers of the new season to arrive to share their tropical surfing paradise. Pohnpei offers a great balance and variety of waves for intermediate and advanced surfers, not just pit hungry pros. Pohnpei Surf Club have capped the surfer numbers to 20 for your enjoyment! That means NO CROWDS and MORE WAVES."

No crowds? *Palikir Pass + 20 surfers = no crowds* didn't compute, because although PSC was somewhat limiting its number of guests, there were also the island's resident surfers, plus the surfers from Nihco, plus the guys doing it on their own, using local fishermen to get out there.

"It's the slippery slope of exploitation," Sipos said. "Once things get pushed to a certain point, they tend to spiral out of control and it becomes a free-for-all. That's the reason places need to be respected for what they are before foreigners come in and turn them into something else."

And let's face it: Palikir Pass is the only reason any surfer will go to Pohnpei. If you book the PSC "Caroline Islands" trip through Wave-hunters, the basic package includes airport transfers, accommodation, daily breakfast, boat trips to "offshore reefs," use of snorkeling gear and fishing tackle, an island tour, and island transport ("conditions apply"). Not included is the guarantee of quality Palikir nor the expensive Continental Airlines ticket, from Los Angeles exceeding $2,000 for a cattle-class seat.

The seven spots listed on PSC's website are Palikir Pass, Sokehs Pass (which is actually Main Pass, a swell-magnet), Easy Pass (actually Lighthouse, best with summer typhoon swells), Freddos (the normally windblown left at Mwahnd Pass), Sondens (Mwahnd's equally windy right), Spaghettis (the ultra-rare left at Ohwa Pass), and Russell's Rights (the soft right at Nan Madol). Though Pohnpei's spots were already named and pioneered by others, PSC went public and claimed the names of Easy Pass, Freddos, Sondens, and Spaghettis. "Russell's Rights" was eponymous for Russell Hill, the Kiwi who wrote the erroneous Pohnpei *Surf Report* in 1998; the spot's real name was and is Napali.

Palikir Marine Adventures's website focuses on Palikir Pass, but its booking agent, The Surf Travel Company, a Sydney-based firm, also lists Lighthouse, Mwahnd, and Main Pass. The PMA surf package ranges from $185-$195 per night (no minimum number of nights); the price includes airport transfers, accommodation, daily breakfast, and daily surf transfers. The PSC package cost through Wavehunters is $185-$200 per night, minimum of six nights. World Surfaris' PSC prices are similar: $194-$204 per night, also a six-night minimum.

The Reality

"Surf camps are fine as long as they don't start thinking that they own the waves just because they provide a service," photographer Grambeau told me. "Saying you own the surf is like two fleas arguing over who owns the dog they live on."

For surfing's innate individualism and deliberate dodging of crowds, surf camps are a strange concept. But they serve a purpose.

"Surf camps are great for a guy who's an executive who's got two weeks per year to pack in as much surf as he can," said Randy Rarick, a famously hard-core traveler and director of the North Shore's annual Triple Crown series. He has never been to Pohnpei. "The camps allow people who don't have the time, the energy, or the wherewithal to maximize their surf experience. I think there should be a thousand surf camps where people could go and enjoy the surfing experience in different places."

Palikir Pass will never be what it was before November 2004. Even with its tiny crew of dedicated tube-addicts, the wave still existed firmly on the fringe and was a private haven for those in the know. But now everyone knows. Palikir is the latest addition to the elite world right-hand ranks of Jeffrey's Bay, Nias, and Lance's Right. It's the same thing that happened to Tavarua in 1984, though it took quite awhile longer for word to spread, because Palikir had the internet. It had surf forecasting sites, it had cell phones, it had a huge surf-travel world starving for something new to fixate on, something warm, hollow, and easy to reach. We'd all seen those green lefts of Indo, the blue bowls of the Fijis and the Tahitis and the Samoas—what else, besides Teahupo'o and Tavarua and Cloud Nine, was out there in the tropical Pacific? All those decades of surfers jetting across the Pacific to Indonesia or Australia or the Philippines, many flew right past Pohnpei and never gave it a thought. They didn't know it was there. Many had never even heard of Micronesia despite it consuming 4.5 million square miles of the Pacific, which possibly made it the world's most surf-rich fetch, with the largest number of reef passes, the most swell exposure, and the fewest surfers. Of course that's fantasy, because all of Micronesia—Pohnpei included—is as fickle as they come. But Palikir Pass has always been out there, barreling flawlessly, when it was able, in total solitude.

Last May, when I asked for his opinion about how things unraveled on Pohnpei in the past five years, Kosrae's Ken Miklos said: "I don't think Allois should be dished for starting something that someone else would have if he hadn't."

Which begs the question: *Would* there be two surf camps on Pohnpei right now if Malfitani had kept his promise of never to expose or exploit Palikir Pass? Further, *did* the first media coverage of the wave by Gilley, Shamlou, and Grambeau accelerate the process? Their articles mentioned nothing about Palikir, Pohnpei, or Micronesia, but there were those images of Sokehs Rock. Grambeau: "Places will evolve regardless of my impact, but from my perspective, the slower the better."

McIntosh, the guy who first surfed Pohnpei in 1971, reflects on the scenario with a hint of rue. "I've been back several times, but like any place, especially since they started the surf camp and they've got all the groups going there, it's not as fun as it was before. I have friends here on Guam who go down to Palikir every now and then, and they say the same thing." Hamilton: "When I heard about the surf camp, it broke my heart."

The good doctor Miklos, on a zen path of his own, shrugs and accepts what has happened to the premier wave of his neighboring isle. For all he knows, it could happen to his. "There are still a lot of perfect waves here and in Pohnpei (State) that go unridden," he said. "In fact, more that go *unridden*, by far. And it's true Micronesia is no longer very secret, but I guess that happens everywhere."

PART

IX

East Africa

33

SWAHILI COAST

2006

BROADLY, PUBLICLY, TANZANIA is many things. It is Serengeti cheetah, it is Maasai warrior, it is Zanzibari clove, it is pus-oozing Kilimanjaro foot blister. But surf? Nay, Tanzania is not surf.

Of course, convolution riddles dreams, and finding waves in Tanzania was testing. Hawai'ian Mikala Jones, Balinese duo Lee Wilson and Marlon Gerber, photographer Dustin Humphrey, and myself convened at gloomy Dar es Salaam International Airport one hot Tuesday last July, sans maps and surf guide, and after having flown directly over a serrated but lake-flat coast despite promise of swell, inklings of a Tanzanian J-Bay were quick to fade.

Next came the keys to the requisite Land Rover, and pointing south, our journey began, first with a hectic but short ferry across the harbor, then onward atop smooth asphalt which quickly deteriorated into a bumpy dirt track flanked by golden savanna, coconut palms, mud huts, birds, and barefoot locals—idle men, shrieking children, serene women burdened and carless but headed home from the city with a load of provisions on their heads and in sweat-stained rucksacks.

Suddenly our speeding posse had distanced from civilization, afar, deep into the southern bush. Immediately obvious was that coastal

Africa is the most authentic of African aura, remaining largely free of the balding missionaries, foreign aid workers, corrupt politicians, khakied tourists, slit-eyed thieves, frantic hawkers, pushy moneychangers, snarled traffic, factory clatter and exhaust pipes, gas stations and shimmering high-rises, dark hookers and shadowboxing shysters. African cities are pits—Dar es Salaam ("Haven of Peace") is nothing of its namesake—and, Durban exempted, few visit Africa to surf in suburbia. So after finding the rutted track and rattling out to our accommodation, the world fell away, and the atmosphere for which we had arrived presented itself amid acres of tall, swaying grass, damp and wheat-scented with the approach of black rain clouds, harbingers of good energy at sea. Then, briefly, the sun, a blinding cheddar half-orb, poked through the clouds above the horizon, and, lighting the scene, guided us in.

EVENTUALLY, WITH AN oceanfront vantage and fresh optimism, we went surfing. The sea was a greeny-brown murk but of pleasant temperature. Unfortunately the norm was smallish windswell, splintered briefly with spurts of good tide and offshore wind, never combined. From our house, a steep trail through dense pandanus and thornless flat-leaved cacti led to a private fetch of white-hot sand full of shattered seashells, pushed against the cliff by a series of jagged volcanic reefs. One featured a mushy left and a shorter but hollower right, both split by a channel. Another offered a slabby right, and another could have been a Tanzanian Trestles. To the north and south stretched point after refined point—potential for greatness was high; potential for swell was low. In the mornings, come high tide, our immediate reefs were flooded, the surf gutless but the wind offshore; at low tide each afternoon, the reefs lay bare, the surf rideable but torn by the monsoonal breeze.

Long ago, this same wind afforded one of history's richest trading histories—to be sure, today's Swahili Coast manifests the crossroads of ancient East Africa, and in its day, nowhere on the Dark Continent buzzed with such vibrancy. Between November and March, Omani and Indian merchant mariners arrived in lateen-rigged dhows loaded with incense, carpet, and dates from the desert; cloth, glassware, and pots from the markets of India; additional flotillas landed from Europe and the ever-distant Orient. Mainland Tanzanian harbors like Kilwa and Dar es Salaam hosted the sale and trade of these goods, which were compensated African-style with ivory, coconuts, cowrie and turtle shell, mangroves, slaves, and solid, shiny gold, which the Arabs and Indians took gleefully, reversing course homeward-bound utilizing summer's north wind.

Amid comings and goings, the foreigners lived with the Africans, the harmony and cultural bonding birthing the language of Swahili (*sawahil* is the Arabic word for "of the coast"), Tanzania's lingua franca, a blend of African, Arabic, Persian, and Asian. Today most bush Swahilis speak no English, but surprisingly they understood the sound and meaning of "money," evidenced one blown-out, low-tide afternoon as I attempted to snap a photo of two young men poking the reef for small octopus. "Surfing" was unknown to the men, but we shared the "of the coast" endemism, and late that day, while Marlon and Lee surfed Kiroko, the left-hander up the beach, the men watched with intrigue, ignoring the scuttling pink crabs they had targeted for supper, thinking nothing of the dhows sailing past, while contrarily the dhows seemed majestic and otherworldly to us in what truly was another world—another crossroads—completely.

BABOONS IN THE road were part of the landscape. Its unknown had us baffled. Questions were innumerable; directions were vague. And so the isolation was palpable, bushwhacking inevitable.

Darkness before dawn brought rain which greased the red-clay road, and, barreling past mud huts and naked children and brightly-dressed women, buckets and bundles of twigs on their heads, our Land Rover slid profusely en route to the maize-and-tomato-lined turnoff several miles from home. Amid the savanna were more crops—cotton, cassava, cashews, beans—and Africans walking slowly with sickles and shovels. One, a farmer near a red shack at the end of the road, pointed the way for us. His family was unacquainted with Caucasians; they were perplexed by our intent. Still we soldiered in, as close to the beach as possible—Lee had no shoes, there were snakes in the grass. For a final trail opening the farmer hacked at the weeds with a dull machete, and we walked out to the bluff's edge, which overlooked a sparkly, dhow-flecked ocean offering peaky waves over a boily, razorback reef. This was Smoka Point. Descending a thorny gulch to the white-sand beach, the boys were out there, because in the 21st century, this might be the best that Tanzania could do.

Eons from now, if Madagascar and the top two-thirds of Mozambique were to evaporate, Tanzania would become a marquee surf destination. The Indian Ocean is a reliable swell-maker, and Tanzania's refined reef-and-pointbreak-rich coast would be the perfect mitt—it's cleaner than Kenya, much safer than South Africa, far saner than anarchic Somalia. There are no land mines or tribal rivalries or political strife, the people are polite and reasonable, there is good infrastructure, it is scenic, the weather is perfect. Big animals (elephants, lions, giraffes) and Africa's tallest mountain (Kilimanjaro) are enough to lure thousands from abroad, but Tanzania's coastline is ignored, a visitor's experience limited primarily to arriving in and leaving from seaside Dar es Salaam, typically whisked off to Arusha, the country's main safari gateway, or offshore to the island of Zanzibar, widely touted in tourist rags as being "the ultimate Indian Ocean experience." For most, the mainland Tanzanian shore had nothing. Yet as Kiroko and Smoka Point pancaked terribly, we decided that we had to leave it, too.

MEDIEVAL SAILING SAVVY would have to suffice—after an expat kitesurfer told us that Tanzania's "best piece of reef" lay off Zanzibar, and that it was only reachable by boat, we had no choice but to go by dhow.

Lush Zanzibar had once dominated the western Indian Ocean, the island a powerful city-state that was the East African nexus of commerce, especially slaves, selling fifty thousand to Arabia each year, so impressing the Omani sultan that in 1832 he moved his capital from Oman to Zanzibar, ruling there for well over a century. This longtime connection created a rich cultural fusion, clear to us upon landfall at the harbor of fabled Stone Town, where Arabians, Africans, Indians coexist seamlessly.

In Stone Town's maze of narrow cobblestone alleys woven against tall whitewashed buildings, the foreigner without guidance would be easily lost. Led by Zanzibar native Mohammed, we culled spice shops and bustling bazaars, admired ruins and mosques and famously ornate doorways, breakfasted and sipped strong coffee with skullcapped, white-robed Muslim men. Then surfboards were stuffed into the rented van and we left for a long, potholed road through the island's interior out to a turquoise lagoon, where we would hire a dhow, traditional transport to hopeful surf glory. To the captain, this was new—centuries of major Indian Ocean seafaring have occurred aboard dhows; chartering one to find surf with was unheard of.

"Zenj"—our discovery—was what you made of it. It could have been purely mental, or it could be an actual place, an unmodern island, sunny and slow, sunken into the periphery of an equatorial ocean theater long revered for chance and mystique. But not for its waves, which, if you adhered to common belief, remain nonexistent. Because Tanzania is not surf. Tanzania is rich.

34

THE KENYA PROMISE
2007

"Always do sober what you said you'd do drunk. That will teach you to keep your mouth shut."
—Ernest Hemingway

BOOZING AND DEEP-SEA fishing have long been choice pastimes for visitors to seaside Kenya, the "Swahili Coast," East Africa's ancient crossroad that centuries ago was a kingdom of progress. In the 6th century a rumor of ivory lured Persians there, sailing south with the northeast monsoon, loading their wooden dhows with ivory and gold and animal skins, then reversing course and sailing north with the southwest monsoon, to growth and profit in the desert.

That was the beginning. Soon wealthy city-states like Lamu, Malindi, and Mombasa materialized, each teeming with trade goods like African slaves for Arabia, leading to intermarriages of Arabs and Indians and Kenyans, spawning the Swahili diaspora.

Border to border, Somalia to Tanzania, Kenya's sawahil is 360 miles of blue and white strewn with huge desolate beaches, dusty villages, weedy bays, cornfields, salt flats, coconut palms, mangroves, rivermouths, jagged cliffs, luxury resorts, mountainous dunes, mud huts, marshes, potholed roads, cargo ships, dhows, downtowns, and the dregs of an African-Arab-Muslim society today fueled by tourist cash, an ebb and flow which funds the entire coast, because today nothing is exported and because neither fishing nor alcohol can.

So came the tale when Hemingway blazed through in '33, when tourists were rare, the American author a sauced rogue from afar, a Great White Hunter, his goal to shoot big animals and get drunk and see the Kenya of legend, at the time a bizarre British colony. Between safaris he tried to hook billfish, eventually settling into smoky seafront pubs in Mombasa and Malindi, downing daiquiris with the tongue of Kiswahili surrounding him. Hemingway spoke none of the local language, yet absorption into the fray was never an issue, and he left an endearing if romanticized footprint 75 years before I decided to go there—but not for the fishing or safaris or iced fusions of rum.

IT WAS A promise done from a promise made a year prior in Zanzibar, the Indian Ocean island best known as the name of many pubs worldwide. ("Bullshit," you hear drinkers say. "There's actually an island called Zanzibar?") In July 2006 a surf magazine-sponsored crew to Tanzania eventually led me to that clove-scented isle. Our crew spent days searching in cars and dhows; we exhausted all resources and settled for less. We found surf but apparently were missing the point.

"If you want waves in East Africa, you've *got* to go to Kenya." This came from Troy, a white Kenyan who a few years prior had moved south to manage one of Zanzibar's most upscale resorts, just up the road from the small, dirty motel we were staying in.

We spent our last night on Zanzibar drinking inside his nice Zanzibari restaurant where'd he'd been "chefing"—cooking—all evening. Tall and blond, age 31, cocky, with a sharp British accent gained from an English education, Troy bought us rounds of Serengeti Lager noting our desperation wrested from the bad tides and bad winds, minds adrift in nearby places where photogenic surf existed—Madagascar, Maldives, Mozambique. Our Tanzanian surf timeframe had pinched shut, but word of another African wavescape spawned personal plans for the next season, a year distant.

"Where's the surf in Kenya?" I asked him.

"Don't worry about it. Just meet me there."

Immediately I vowed to contact Kenya Airways and see what they could do about getting me to Kenya at the prime nexus of wind, swell, and tide. From my home in southern California, Kenya's capital of Nairobi was easily accessible, but certainly the Swahili surf was fickle—an expensive and iffy trip.

Perhaps the beer had greased my decision to spend hard-earned cash to get there. But, a year later, it was still a promise, and as the plane from Nairobi sank toward the tarmac of Mombasa's airport, the shimmering blue Indian Ocean below with its brown barrier reefs laced in white, it became clear that Troy had spoken true.

"Kenya—just 39 years old and speaking at least 60 languages—has been many things for a very long time, but only one bewildered pretend nation for one generation."

THIS WAS BINYAVANGA Wainaina in the July 2007 issue of *Vanity Fair*. One of Kenya's new literary stars, Wainaina wrote with fire and aplomb, exposing and mulling the many problems and solutions of his great country. Kenya had been a sore victim of colonialistic centuries, freed at last from England in '63, but only recently it had morphed into somewhat of a positive place, economically and politically, something Kenyans gripped tightly, nurtured steadily—or so Wainaina said. "We have learned to ignore the shrill screams coming from the peddlers of hopelessness. We motor on faith and enterprise, with small steps. On hope, and without hysteria."

Hysteria was a bad thing to experience in Kenya, especially in the coastal towns where desperate thievery and violence seared through the local sector, targeting moneyed tourists who each summer flocked to the palmy beach resorts. Mombasa, Kenya's main seaport and the coast's largest city, was a smaller, saltier version of Nairobi, the energy and societal stink less visible, yet there was a certain charm to an African city built on an island in an idyllic natural harbor, for centuries a hub for Arabian and Indian merchants, now site of an interesting

Islamic heritage and a cultural complexity that was characteristic of all Swahili settlements.

"You buy spice?" an Indian merchant asked me in his dingy Mombasa shop, the kind of place that sold all sorts of useless souvenirs to tourists seeking a faux piece of Africa, something to show folks back home, boasting about where they went and what an adventure it was. "You were in Kenya?" their friends would gasp. "So dangerous there!"

But Kenya wasn't dangerous if you walked fast and had no valuables on you, if you didn't photograph Muslims, if you looked busy and far too important for the mundane pettiness of pickpocketing and ubiquitous beggars. You stayed indoors at night, and you certainly didn't coax or patronize the "beach boys," young fit black men who in daylight prowled the beaches in front of the resorts, seeking plucky Germans or Italians to beg from or to sell things to, or for keen white women—no matter how old or how fat—for whom sex with an African man might be something to also boast of.

"I don't need any spices," I told the Indian.

"Wood mask?"

"Nope."

"Maasai necklace?"

"Sorry."

"But you have money!" he cried. "Euros!"

"How do you know that?"

"Because you are German."

"American," I corrected him. "Besides, what's the difference? You must have plenty of money. Look at all these things you have in your shop."

"No customer," he said. "You first customer today."

"But I'm not buying anything from you."

He sighed and retreated to a chair in a corner of his store, which stunk of mold. I was more interested in the shop next door, which sold Tusker, Kenya's famous beer that, brewed with adjuncts like corn starch and sugar, wasn't very good. I bought a case anyway and took it to my hotel, where I found Troy and his Mombasan surfer friend George drinking alone at the downstairs bar.

"There he is!" George said. "We've just ordered you a Tusker. Looks like you brought your own."

"They're warm."

George was a school teacher, half Kenyan and half Omani. He was in his late 30s, short and thin, a dusky mix of Arab, African, and English, with green eyes and a long, gaunt face, his beaky nose supporting a pair of dirty eyeglasses. His black hair was wavy and medium-length, wiry gray hairs poking out.

"You look Indian," I said.

"Really?" he said. "Yes, I like Indians. We call them hindis. They own many businesses here."

"So, Omani and Kenyan—are you a Muslim?"

"Me? Ha! I've been drinking vodka-Cokes since eight!"

It was noon. I'd arrived at seven-thirty. Troy had deplaned from Zanzibar at ten. George was boozing because the wind was up and the tides were wrong, and for much of the previous night he had been in a long, costly telephone argument with his hippie English girlfriend vacationing up in Lamu, Kenya's north coast haven for freewheelers and aficionados of beaches and old Muslim culture, its women draped in blowsy colored fabrics, its men in the obligatory white robes and skullcaps.

Once an important trade stop in the string of ports from Mogadishu to Mozambique, mellow little Lamu has since had to settle for tourism to stay afloat. The town is too far from Kenya's population centers to be of any economical use, and when swamps of the useful mangrove tree were overcut by the 1970s, Lamu lost its main export. Recognizing the town's uniqueness, tourists became the big cash cow.

"During the 1970s, Lamu picked up a reputation as the Kathmandu of Africa," said my Lonely Planet guidebook, "a place of fantasy and other-worldliness, plucked straight from the pages of the Arabian Nights." The book went on to detail Lamu's tranquil beaches and that "for traditional surfing, there are real breakers at the mouth of the channel, although this is also the realm of some substantial sharks."

Kenya, it seemed, had never been short on sharks. Before I left Nairobi, people said that if I surfed Kenya I would likely be bitten by one, especially if I went to Lamu. I considered visiting that ancient town for its historical allure, but due to money and time constraints, I declined. Apparently Mombasa's waters held the world record for number of shark attacks (18) on humans in one year.

"When did those happen?" I asked George.

"It doesn't matter."

"I would think it would matter for you, being a surfer here."

"This place is shit, mind you," he said. "So is Lamu. So is Malindi. It is all shit. There might be some good waves along the coast that's inaccessible, like between Lamu and Somalia, or between Malindi and Lamu, but that's it."

"Troy told me it gets good here," I said.

"Ah, forget it."

I mentioned that I had studied numerous charts of the Kenya coast. "Have you noticed all of those curvy coral reef passes in the Lamu Archipelago? You can't tell me there isn't anywhere up in there that doesn't get swell and doesn't wrap around and blow offshore with the surf-season trades."

"Boat trip, mate," Troy said, chewing an ice cube. "That's the only way. Reckon it'd be windy as fuck."

"Those reefs look a lot more promising than what you have in Mombasa," I said to George.

"Mate, Mombasa is not a surf town," he said. "Malindi sucks, too. This isn't a surfing country. Look at this wind! Come here for a suntan or safari—that's it. I'm only here because my kids are. When they're old enough for university, I'm moving to Durban."

Apparently Kenya's surf was rideable for only a few months per year. East Africa typically shied from the crosshairs of a solid groundswell, jinxed by a long continental shelf and a shadowed bight, the majority of swells headed for the opposite direction, toward Indonesia. Madagascar blocked many swells, and the prevailing wind was stiffly onshore. Lack of roads made much of the coast unreachable, and the accessible parts were usually either too polluted, too windy, too sharky, or had no good reefs. Various rivermouths offered quality sandbars on occasion, but sea snakes and saltwater crocodiles were real threats. If you wanted to drive from

Lamu to Malindi, you would risk your life, and the coastal road north from Mombasa was so bad that Troy and George were reluctant to leave.

"Road is just terrible now," an elderly Kenyan told me at the bar. "Used to be quite good, but now I won't take my car on it. Better to hire a matatu—local bus—but those are dangerous."

"Why's that?"

"Crashes all the time, passengers dead, bandits, thieves, flat tires, breakdowns. Where you going?"

"North, I suppose. Malindi."

"Just hire a taxi."

"Don't waste your money," Troy said.

We walked outside and slouched around a cracked blue plastic table. George rolled a joint, which he and Troy smoked. My box of Tusker was opened, and soon I had finished three big bottles, making my head spin in the tropical midday heat. From the bar Troy continued ordering of double-vodka tonics; George stuck to vodka-Cokes.

"It's good to experience the world," George smirked at me, raising his glass, "under the influence."

Conversation drifted to road racing and about how many of George and Troy's friends have died because of Kenya's bad roads. Troy mentioned the problem of cars hitting animals. "I once hit five chickens in Zanzibar on the way from Nungwi to Stone Town," he said. The following week his brother-in-law, speeding through the Kenyan interior, hit an adult kudu, ripping the car's roof off. Not to be outdone story-wise, George's brother had hit five cows in one night. He explained the strategy: "You must continue straight on into the animal and just hit it. Otherwise you'll roll or crash if you try to do all this clever stuff and try to avoid the animal."

Troy finished the joint, snuffing it in the table's ashtray. "Speaking of driving," he said, "why don't we head up and do some fucking sandboarding on the dunes up north? Or kitesurfing?"

I said, "I thought you guys didn't want to drive anywhere."

"You're absolutely fucking right," George said, rolling another joint.

Troy looked around. "I knew a guy who once sat drinking at the bar of this hotel for 72 hours straight," he said. "It was quite impressive."

I scooted my plastic chair back, stood, and said, "I'm out of here."

"Where the fuck are you going?" Troy asked.

"Look, there's swell. I saw it from the plane. Didn't you see it when you flew in?"

"I couldn't see out the window. It's windy, mate—just hang here and get pissed."

"For 72 hours?"

"You won't find a wave today," George said.

"Maybe up north will have something."

"How will you get there?"

"I'm calling a *matatu*. Anyway, you guys will be asleep in an hour."

"Oh no no no," Troy scoffed. "Obviously you haven't met a true Kenyan. If we're here when you get back, you're in for a fucking big night out, eh."

I did not see them again.

35

THE FLANKS OF HOPE

2013

MONDAY AT THE MALIBU OF AFRICA. Walid, a white Ivorian, is a black dot on his shortboard thruster a thousand yards from land, floating in the brown Atlantic off the tip of a luxuriant point. Sent here to die, long-period groundswells afford overhead tubes and lengthy walls that croak as closeouts near the mouth of a lagoon. This is where the elephants play. Twenty-two of them, big and small, young and old, spraying themselves with their trunks of water, trumpeting, flaunting tusks, wallowing in mud laced white with seafoam. Sociable elephants on a desolate beach backed by a deep-green rainforest unaffected by poaching or illicit logging. Here at the Malibu of Africa, Walid shuns the chaos of Abidjan, his home city, the decaying Paris of Africa, a hive of crime and cocaine. The elephants don't notice the goofyfooted figure flirting with the wave, zipping along the glassy wall, smacking its lip, thrice burrowing into the barrel. He does this for them. The elephants. They squirt more lagoon water from their trunks as Walid is blasted with compressed tube spit, then bottom-turns and boosts a spectacular flyaway kickout over the closeout end section. Daily, the elephants see this wave. Right now, the Malibu of Africa is far better than California's Malibu, where it is near midnight yesterday. In Côte d'Ivoire—the Ivory Coast—today has just begun.

NEVER HAPPENED. No elephants on the beach. They are extinct.

Wartime dust seems unsettled as we leave a shaded alleyway home in the dense Abidjan commune of Marcory. Walid's English is bad, his French accent thick. He chainsmokes his hand-rolled marijuana cigarettes. He is 35 years old.

In his olive-green Renault station wagon, we weave through Abidjan, pass a big cocoa-processing factory—the air smells of chocolate—and blast out onto the A100, Voie Express de Bassam, under a hazy bluey-brown sky. The road is paved but crowded and lawless, noisy and dirty and stinky and loaded with litter. Walid says that, during the civil war two years back, nobody could drive their cars in or around Abidjan. "Here was many war, many sniper. People getting shot everywhere." He waves his left arm out the window. "Dead guys right here!"

We pass a gloomy French military camp, the 43rd BIMA (43rd Marine Infantry Battalion), ringed with razor wire. "They saved Ivory Coast," Walid says. "If no intervention from this army, Côte d'Ivoire was finished."

Flanking the A100 are several billboards in French and dozens of impromptu-looking stalls offering thousands of things for sale, almost everything imaginable for anyone with West African CFA francs. As in the rest of the Africa, the stuff is all the same—furniture, fruits and vegetables, lumber, clothes, tires, electronics, cell phones—things locals need, not tourists, because Côte d'Ivoire tourism is dead. During my trip, except for a few business travelers, I saw no foreigners.

At one of the road's many checkpoints, a soldier stops us. Says he's hot, implores Walid for cash for a bottle of cold soda. Walid informs the soldier that I'm an American tourist, and it would look bad if he palmed money to the unsmiling man in fatigues holding a loaded AK-47.

"If the military and police see me, a white Ivorian guy, not from France, they like this," Walid says as he resumes driving. "I born in Cocody *(an Abidjan suburb)* in 1977, my father Ivorian, my mother French. Côte d'Ivoire is many mixed. I have double nationality, Ivorian and French, but I don't want just Ivorian. Ivorian passport I want for go Ghana, go Liberia, for go Dakar. Is good. No visa. My big passport is France. Is better for travel. Is nice."

Two minutes later, we veer off into the dirt and stop in front of a yelping group of small, rag-clothed boys. Their arms and hands reach frantically into the car, pushing small cellophane-wrapped bundles of sugar cane at our faces, haggling with Walid. He buys two bundles and hands me one. "Good for chew, eh?" he says with a smile. "Delicious sweet."

"Yeah, sugar highs are great. I think those boys agree."

Aside from acres of coconut plantations, the road from Abidjan is essentially one long marketplace, stalls hawking all sorts of things. We stop aside one of the many roadside stalls to peruse a colorful spread of fresh, locally grown produce. In fertile Côte d'Ivoire, full of farms, such bounty prevails—nearly 70 percent of Ivorians work in some type of agriculture.

But no one really farms in Abidjan, and we're happy to leave. Exiting one of Earth's most dangerous cities is a retreat from pain, mental and physical. Muggings, robbery, burglary, and carjacking are common. The world's third-largest French-speaking metro (after Kinshasa and Paris), Abidjan's weary black heart throbs among the inlets and headlands that pierce Ébrié Lagoon. It is West Africa's largest, covering a surface of 120,000 hectares, one of three long, thin lagoons that parallel the Ivorian coast. Once the pristine "pearl" of the country's lagoons, the Ébrié is now a woeful cesspit of urban and industrial waste here in Côte d'Ivoire's economic hub.

For its first 33 years of independence, under its first president, Félix Houphouët-Boigny ("*Very* nice guy," Walid says), Côte d'Ivoire was famous for its cultural harmony and robust economy, the latter due to Côte d'Ivoire's status as the world's leading cocoa producer and Africa's main exporter of pineapples and palm oil. But when Houphouët-Boigny died from prostate cancer in 1993, a new president was needed, and the nation found itself struggling with its first democratic process and a new national identity, impeded by the divisive influence of the three Rs: region, religion, and resources.

Henri Konan Bédié, then-National Assembly President, succeeded Houphouët-Boigny, ruling until 1999, when he was overthrown by Ivorian military leader Robert Guéï in the nation's first successful coup d'état. At issue was Bédié's law, hastily drafted and approved before the 1995 election, that required both parents of a presidential candidate to have been born in Côte d'Ivoire.

Before the 2000 presidential election, Guéï sparked ethnic hate and xenophobia against his main political rival, Alassane Ouattara, who represented northern Côte d'Ivoire's immigrants, particularly Muslim plantation workers from Mali and Burkina Faso. Due to the parenthood clause, Ouattara was disqualified from the election by his mother's Burkina Faso heritage.

Guéï's rule lasted just 10 months, but it marked the beginning of conflict in once-peaceful Côte d'Ivoire. Defeated by Laurent Gbagbo in the 2000 election, Guéï refused to concede, and it took a citizen uprising to topple Guéï and lift Gbagbo to power. Still, the discontent over discrimination and voting rights exploded in September 2002, when Ivorian military troops, many from the north, mutinied and launched attacks in several cities, including Abidjan. Guéï was killed the first night, and thousands more died in the conflict. Ending in 2007, the war led to the death and displacement of thousands of Ivorians.

Still, Côte d'Ivoire stayed split. French and UN peacekeepers routinely patrolled the buffer zone that separated the rebel-controlled north and the government-controlled south. Finally, in October 2010, after repeated delays, elections aimed at ending the conflict were held. But the vote sparked chaos when incumbent Gbagbo refused to concede victory to Alassane Ouattara, who won with 54.1 percent of the vote. It escalated into a full-scale military conflict between those loyal to Gbagbo and Ouattara's people, and the ensuing stand-off stopped only when Ouattaran and French forces seized the Ivorian south, capturing and deposing Gbagbo. Since Ouattara's inauguration in 2011, Côte d'Ivoire has remained somewhat stable.

Political tensions persist, however, namely via Gbagbo supporters, who launched violent attacks near the Liberian border in 2012 and 2013. Then, four months before my visit, municipal and regional elections held were generally quiet aside from incidents of localized violence when results were announced.

TWO MONTHS BEFORE I dropped into Abidjan, the U.S. Department of State's Bureau of Consular Affairs website issued a warning:

> *The Department of State urges U.S. citizens to carefully consider the risks of traveling to Côte d'Ivoire. U.S. citizens who reside in or travel to Côte d'Ivoire should monitor conditions carefully, maintain situational awareness, and pay very close attention to their personal security. Although the security situation significantly improved in 2013, security conditions can change quickly and without warning.*

And, near the bottom of the page:

> *Swimming in coastal waters is dangerous and strongly discouraged, even for excellent swimmers. The ocean currents along the coast are powerful and treacherous, and several people drown each year.*

THOUGH GREAT FOR SURFERS, the latter is permanent on all travel warnings for Côte d'Ivoire. Fifty-five kilometers from Abidjan, near the Ghana border, are turbulent beachbreaks and leisure homes along a palmy sandspit between a canal and the muddy mouth of a lagoon, which Walid says it can be a fun place for longboarding. "Maybe we go there, but maybe not. Longboard, this I don't really want to."

"Same."

"Shark and crocodile there. Lagoon, you know?"

According to my guidebook, the area "tugs at the heartstrings of overlanders, washed-up surfers, and rich weekenders from Abidjan, who run their quad bikes up and down its peroxide-blonde beach." Today is Tuesday—"washed-up" or not, Walid promises we'll have the onshore, head-high closeouts to ourselves.

"If you come here in January, February, wind offshore all the spots," he says, lighting another spliff. "Now is onshore but bigger swells coming. Summer good for waves big, good no for wind normally. But is okay. We surf."

Soon the road deteriorates into a bumpy, palm-lined, red-dirt lane, its potholes filled with smashed coconut husks. Once in the village, we pass several colorfully painted, cement-walled bungalows, most with thatched roofs, but there are no people present aside from a woman walking and a small, dazed boy standing atop a large pile of husks. Walid pulls aside one of the bungalows and stops the car behind a small pickup with two shortboard thrusters in its bed.

"My friend staying here for today. Come, we surf."

The surf facing us is junky, the salt air soft and breezy. In an open veranda Walid's tattooed, non-English-speaking friend sits with a bikinied girl, both looking half-asleep, cross-legged on wicker chairs, drinking tea and smoking cigarettes. "*Salut,*" I say when they nod at me. "*Comment ça va?*"

The water is steps away; the soft white sand squeaks underfoot. The sunlight is wan and low, the air thick with the haze typical of coasts in the Gulf of Guinea. Needing to shed my travel grime, dumpy low-tide beachbreak or not. Mostly closeouts, strong currents, many duckdives. The biggest waves are slightly overhead, the water reddish-brown and murky, not as warm as I'd expected. Just past the surf line is a near-constant stream of local fishing canoes heading west, their outboard-motors humming through the windchop.

Toweling off post-session, Walid says the surf will be smaller but cleaner down the beach, where his parents' house is. To get there, he parks the Renault in a rocky, dusty lot on the north bank of the canal; we load our gear into an elderly smiling man's (Walid: "He my second father.") long blue wood canoe that will slide us a half-kilometer across to the canal's south bank, which initially appears to be a long wall of coconut palms, obscuring the pleasant oceanfront homes beyond. This is where upmarket Ivorians, including President Ouattara, often spend their days off. "On the weekends," Walid says, "*many* people here. Weekends is crazy—many jet skis, boats, wakes...." His eyes widen as he twists an imaginary jet ski throttle with his right hand. "*Vroom-vroom!*"

The water near this dock is vacant except for two other canoes, one with two squatting fishermen, the other with a small boy and his father slowly moving with a stick, pushing off the shallow sand bottom. The late-day sun coats the glassy water in liquid gold, silhouetting the land, and within minutes we step onto the rotting south-bank dock, walking with backpacks and surfboards along a mossy covered pathway directly to Walid's parents' tile-floored house, built in the 1970s, replete with beachfront swimming pool and exceptional peace and privacy. As Walid predicted, the surf here is smaller but much cleaner. We opt out of surfing and instead, while daylight fades, relax by the pool with sweating bottles of Flag beer.

Inside the main house, Walid's housekeeper is cooking dinner—barbecued chicken, *attiéké* (fermented and grated cassava, a Côte d'Ivoire staple), French fries, chilis, onion/tomato salad. Later, while heavy rain pelts the roof, we slouch on a too-soft sofa, our feet on the glass coffee table. On my laptop screen appear the six videos on Walid's YouTube channel, including a 39-second clip filmed from the inside of his Abidjan house—gunshots shatter the air outside; Walid gets his handgun; Walid shuts the sliding metal barrier fence around his front room; Walid is panicked. When the shooting stops, three men lay dead on Walid's driveway.

"Scared? *Oui.* Yes. Very." He drinks some beer. Long pause. "This thing happened all the time during the crisis."

"Did you ever grow numb to it? The public killings and chaos? Blood on the streets?"

"No. I never do this. Impossible. My country torn apart. Nobody want this."

"So how did you deal with the fact that your immediate domestic surroundings became a battlefield?"

In reflective resignation, perhaps, his right eyebrow lifts.

"I can do nothing."

Swallows another Flag swig. Shrugs. Blinks six times. Frowns. Coughs. Leans back and gestures at my computer screen.

"What we do? Not in military. Not politician. Can only wait. And hide in our homes. Not go outside any night for long time."

This night: windless, with near-constant rain. Can go outside, but we don't.

Next morning: dreariness, a gray haze. Muffled, like I'm wearing earplugs. Faint hum of fishing boats heading west. I peer through the fogged window. Surf: clean, a bit up from yesterday. Thirty minutes later, the end game of stove-boiled water is bad imported instant coffee, odd since Côte d'Ivoire is a big coffee exporter, once the world's third largest, behind Colombia and Brazil. While coffee remains its second biggest export (behind cocoa), the industry has been struggling for years, particularly after the turbulent 2010 election. Ex-president Gbagbo, who initially investigated corruption amongst so-called "coffee barons," tried to nationalize the coffee industry in 2011, suffocating production and export.

In Abidjan I'd bought a 500-gram bag of Café Malaga robusta beans (*"Coffees from the Ivory Coast are strongly aromatic with a light body and acidity,"* says the National Coffee Association of USA website. *"They are ideally suited for a darker roast and are therefore often used in espresso blends."*), planning to sample some here, but Walid's house holds no coffee grinder nor strainer nor anything of the sort. Could use a sock a la Pat Curren on O'ahu in 1955. But no socks, either.

Still, the hot cups of instant move us to surf. For an hour, the sun shines. In Atlantic murk, I admire the soft terrestrial backdrop of white sand and tall palms and nice homes. An exclusive, empty place when distanced from weekends.

We race closeouts till the wind comes. Walid and his helper take two hours to prepare an outdoor lunch (*taquitos de parra*, salad, mango for dessert) whence twice a butterfly landed next to me on the table. "Here, that is sign of good luck," Walid says. "*Oui*, maybe we get some good waves tomorrow, eh?"

Jet-lagged, I doze the afternoon away. Outside: cloudy and bleak, surf junky and smaller. Only sounds are occasional soft birdsong and the *whoosh* of waves, surreal and serene.

Floating through African dreams.

Sometime near dawn, Walid's neighbor leaves an expensive Italian coffee bean grinder on a small table near the swimming pool, near my room, in which a bag of Ivorian coffee beans scent the premises into an African Starbucks. Gone is the sound of the surf, shoved seaward by the offshore wind, a reversal of fortune for all, including the neighbor, a textiles magnate who lives in Bali now but keeps a home here for key getaways. When I wake at 9 a.m., I see him up the beach, wet-haired with surfboard underarm, giggling and skipping back toward Walid's house. Overnight, the waves had transformed from onshore closeouts to A-frame peaks, groomed to perfection, spitting kegs up and down the sandbars. Of course, there is no one out. Under the clear morning sun, this is heaven. "What a difference a night makes, eh?!" he shouts in excited French to Walid, who's doing yoga by the pool. "Let's drink some of Kew's coffee and get back out there!"

YEAH. THAT NEVER HAPPENED, EITHER.

Mid-day, mid-week, mid-August. Urban shantytowns—desperate poverty, squalor, impromptu disorder. Clothes being washed in brown rivers, then draped over to dry on roadside shrubbery. Broken glass and crushed beer cans. Scowls and rags. Twig fences and hollow eyes. Idle men and overworked women. Diesel-fumed, hazy air with a low gray sky that suffocates the earth. Endless roadside litter. A chaotic six-lane highway with older models of Mercedes and BMW swerving and speeding past ass-dragging taxis and crowded, top-heavy public buses.

West of Abidjan, civilization dissolves and the land opens. Verdant vistas and low hills, banana plantations, palm oil plantations, fields of maize and rice and passionfruit. Cassava, cocoa. Military checkpoints. People selling bottles of peanuts. Men pushing/pulling carts loaded with sticks. We're inland, inside Walid's Renault, blazing toward Liberia at 130 kph (80 mph) on Route de Dabou, the A3, a signed 70 kph-limit (40 mph) road that frequently slows us to a lurching crawl through its fields of wide, deep red-dirt potholes.

"Road is *shit*," Walid says as he leans forward over the steering wheel, gripping it with his right hand, his left thumb and index finger to his lips, steadying a hand-rolled marijuana spliff, one of several today. "It's not possible you dead from cannabis," he says. "Not like alcohol. You can smoke kilo-kilo-kilo. It's impossible you dead. Just smile." (laughs)

Sunglasses cover half his face and his right hand pilots us, the car shaking with the high speed, the horn getting a workout. Walid's seatbelt is fastened only before entering the numerous military/police checkpoints, uniformed Africans with rifles and a thirst for bribery, pointing and shouting at our car to stop.

"Because of the war," Walid says, exhaling pot smoke, "police just stop the big car, the big truck, for look, for control, but the white man is not stopped for bad. He stopped for just to take the money. But no control, you know? Just pay for take the road, give the money. Also give maybe food or water, a drink."

Liberia, a nation too resurfacing from civil war and economic death, is at road's end in the far west.

"Many-many-many Liberians come into Ivory Coast for the war, you know?" Walid says as we pass windswept fields of tall green grass and corn and *manioc* (cassava). "Mercenaries. They live here in the forest, in the jungle. On the frontier of Liberia and Ivory Coast, they have many army Ivorian, French army, USA army. The mercenaries go into Liberia and return to Ivory Coast village to kill many guys, to fuck many girls, take many riches. Mercenaries finish and return to Liberia.

"You have a big war for the frontier of Liberia and Ivory Coast. Liberian government and government Ivorian is working same for this problem. For three years, it not possible you come here on this road. It no possible. Oh, no. If you white guy come here? You finished." (laughs) "You finished."

"Police everywhere?" I ask.

"No police! Military, mercenary, Liberian, Angola, Sierra Leone—a mix. They don't like the white man. Long time I don't come here because of the war. *Many* problem. But it's nice now for return. Africa is the future, you know? The future of the world. It no have development, it no have many this, you know? Africa is very beginning."

At several areas along the road are machete-wielding men, hacking at tall green grass. Others are idle or walking aside the vast fields of manioc and maize and rubber trees and palm-oil groves, the scenery stained with incongruous billboards hawking luxury cars.

The rain that threatened all day now begins to fall, smudging the red dust on Renault's cracked windshield. The clouds mute the land and oppress the mud-hut villages we pass. The road is lined with fruit sellers, smoky fires, tall white rice bags of charcoal, naked kids, babies hanging off mothers' backs, women with bundles of sticks atop their heads, broken trucks, brown lakes. People strolling in zen daze, time irrelevant. No other roads, just dirt tracks that blend into the weeds and woods.

"This road no good to drive at night," Walid says, swerving to avoid potholes.

Soon he pulls over. We piss. The sun is sinking—orange hues on green. Back in the car, he rolls a joint while we listen to Alpha Blondy's spirited *Live Au Zénith*, recorded in Paris in 1992. A multilinguist singer known as the Bob Marley of Africa, Blondy (birth name: Seydou Koné) was born in 1953 about 160 kilometers due north from where we sit. For me, an Alpha Blondy fan since the '90s, it's fitting to hear his music in Côte d'Ivoire.

"This Alpha Blondy, he good, no?" Walid says after using his tongue tip to seal his new spliff. "You know Alpha Blondy in America?"

"Oh, yeah. I downloaded his new album (*Mystic Power*) before I flew here."

"He very nice man. When I was child, he was my neighbor in Cocody."

Among his vast discography, "Cocody Rock" is perhaps Blondy's nexus. I know it well. Millions do, because Blondy's reach is global, his message firm and up. In 2005 he was crowned Côte d'Ivoire's United Nations Ambassador of Peace; later, he launched his Jah Glory Foundation, a non-profit, non-partisan charity. Ironically, his 2010 "peace and unity" concert in Bouaké (Côte d'Ivoire's second-largest city and stronghold of rebels during the civil war) left two people dead and 20 injured.

"The workers let too many people into stadium at one time," Walid remembers. He lights his spliff. "I was there. Very sad." Inhales smoke. "So bad."

Exhale.

So good.

We are the rockers from Zion Ivory Coast
We're ready, ready, ready, ready to rock, we're sayin'
Coco, Coco, is Cocody Rock
Coco, Coco, is Cocody Rasta

CHILDREN SCREAM and wave as we rattle through another rural village, kicking up dust. "Michael, *this* is good," Walid says, smiling, tapping the ash from his spliff. "The young good, happy. They look the white man—*hello!*" He waves his left hand at me. "Happy. After years of war, it's very nice, you know? Future of Ivory Coast is good."

The swell has jumped. Sheltered right points entice. En route: plantation workers stroll along the track, holding machetes for coconuts. Many trails into the wilderness, in all directions, no signs—easy to get lost. Tall weeds and fields of maize. Walid has not ventured this way for a long time; he stops the car to chat with a hobbling old man and ask for directions to the beach. Walid hands him a cigarette; the man clasps his hands in thanks.

"Cigarette no easy for the villagers to buy," Walid says. "Everybody want the cigarette. I keep the ganja. Ha!"

He drives for a while. We listen to reggae. I eat peanuts and drink orange Fanta. Eventually we find the heavily rutted, overgrown track that winds to the edge of the forest, the glassy Atlantic offering large, severe shorepound.

"The jungle is quick to reclaim the road," I say. "This place was almost impossible to find."

"No problem, eh?" Walid replies with a wink. He parks in a small clearing between palms. "The spot is over there," he says, pointing left as he exits the Renault. It's a sharp bend in the coastline—a hidden right point—pounded with thundering whitewater, a place my guidebook describes thusly: "With its curling breakers, it's enough to inspire poetic musings."

We walk for a few minutes. The heavily eroded beach is littered with driftwood sticks and garbage, mostly plastic bottle caps. The sand is course and pink, the air thick with salt mist, the sky a low, ominous gray. Big, powerful groundswells explode along the uneven rock shelf. The lineup is a roiling mess of currents and closeouts, an odd corner off the edge of the channel. But the set-up looks nice for a smaller swell—the shelf piercing the straight backbeach, which falls away into a gradual beach curve before restraightening down to what appears to be another right point in the distance.

"Is shit, eh?" Walid says, relighting his spliff. "We keep going."

"Where?"

"Spots. Places need big swell like this."

Back at the car, I study the map where I'd marked 38 possible right points between Abidjan and Liberia. Most look inaccessible by land, but there is one southeast-facing nook in our general vicinity that looks like it would "need big swell." Finger on the map, I show Walid.

"Ah! This spot very good for fishing. Last time I there for surfing, one guy caught a snapper that was 45 kilos!"

"Does it need a big swell to be surfable?"

"The big swell, yes. Long time I went there."

The day itself is long, as are the drives to find anything remotely surfable. Checking this spot: misfire #1. Much time wasted.

Retrace north into the crickets and tall grass, to the main road, lined with maize, swaying in the wind. We are westbound again, this time in a national park. The route is marked by tall, deep-green trees, reminiscent of driving through Northern Californian redwoods. Twenty minutes of non-talking, just reggae on the radio.

Beach turn-off approaches. But first, a roadside stop: flyblown roasted corn, handled by filthy fingers.

Pass.

The seller, a man, in a black leather jacket, mildly offended: "You no eat this? You no belong in Africa!"

LUMPY PILLOW, BAD SLEEP in the empty three-story hotel on a hill overlooking a town and its harbor, once used to export timber from now-deforested Mali.

My gut shakes, result of last night's *langouste* feast with Solibra Bock beers in the hotel's restaurant, where Walid and I were the sole diners. This morning, the little town is abuzz—birds, honking cars, sawing, hammering, rap music, lumber being stacked, wind, people talking, kids yelling. The sky is sunny with some clouds; there is, of course, the smell of burning trash. Muezzin creeps into the airspace every so often. Shanty clusters are stacked up the hillside, little square boxes of white and brown smooshed unevenly aside one another, with sparse relief patches of green trees. Atop the main hill are the larger, richer homes. Many people walking—where are they all going?

The Atlantic shimmers in the heat, the low, hazy skyline a silhouette of immense jungle stretching eastward to infinity. Down on the steep beach, fishermen push their wooden canoes into the backwashed shorepound near a brown rivermouth that has a righthander mushing off of it. Last night, over the beers and lobster, Walid told me it can get good, "but many, many big fish."

Near noon today, he knocks on my door. "We go. Waves should be okay."

In town, we stop at a stall for an unrefrigerated bottle of Fanta, which soothes my stomach. The midday sun is searing, the track to the remote fishing village bumpy and overgrown, unsigned and obscure. Not obscure is the onshore wind, trashing the mushy, lumpy righthanders smashing off pinkish granite rocks that cradle a small cove, featuring a small fleet of fishing pirogues.

The wave here is a summertime favorite among Walid and his friends; they drive from Abidjan to surf and relax with bearded, cheerful Jules, a part-time bodyboarder who lives full-time with his family in a shack overlooking the cove, 200 yards west of the main village. The extent of Jules's English is "Yes I," something normally said by dreadlocked rastafarians.

We shake hands.

"*Je suis heureux de vous rencontrer*, Jules." (*I'm happy to meet you.*)

"Yes I!" And he laughs, in that crackly, deep-voiced, African-smoker way. He's happy. Walid brought cigarettes.

I survey the scene while Jules hacks a couple of coconuts open for us. Burning leaves scent the air, while on the small pocket beach fronting the wave, men hammer on a new *pirogue*. Aside from going to sea, the boat will never leave this village.

Drinking from the coconuts at Jules's shaded plastic outdoor table, while the wind eases, rustling palm fronds above us, Walid describes a great outside interest to develop the beach touristically. He suggests this would essentially corrupt and dull the shine of the place, so he's taking charge, donating money, helping Jules to establish a surf camp, which today is nothing but two flimsy rooms with sand floors but no beds, toilets, or running water.

"If we don't help Jules, in two or three years, here is finished. Hotel, you know? Place like this no change because of the war, but war is finished. Development now, you know?"

"So you think that, because the war is over, people are going to want to come here?"

"Yes! Many guy want this spot. Many opportunistic. Not now, but five years, 10 years, they come. So we preparing. It's not good to have *l'étranger* (strangers) to come here and take this place. Good for local person, long time life live here. I live here many war, many population, no problem."

An orange/white/green (Ivorian flag colors) pirogue with DIEU MERCI ("Thank God") painted on its bow sails around the headland, soon beached with its bounty of fish that look like big sardines. The whole village reacts—naked boys, giggling girls, women in colorful dresses and men in ripped soccer jerseys. (In rural Africa, attire fashion often contrasts between those preferring traditional [colorful sarongs, wraps, headdresses] versus western [straightened hair, counterfeited designer clothing]).

As if in a tug-of-war with the canoe, men chant and grunt as they drag it from the bluey-brown shorebreak and onto the sand, past the tideline. Commotion and haggling about who gets what and how much. A group of small boys clown for my camera. Three small girls cry and yell at each other; their moms yell at each other. Many goats and chickens, some dogs but no barking. One man divvies the fish, filling large stainless steel bowls and white plastic buckets (I LOVE AFRICA on one) into which the women pour seawater before carrying them to the village.

Back at Jules's, Walid rolls a joint while I wax my 5'4" Lovelace quad fish. The day is nearly over, but the tide has dropped and new swell has arrived. Long lulls. Appearing from the village is Édouard, the village's surfer, tall and shy, in prime physical shape but smoking a cigarette. Underarm is a thrashed, yellow, too-small (for him) 6'0" AXL thruster from Anglet, France. Walid gifted it 15 years ago, when Édouard was a boy. He speaks no English, so we communicate with hand gestures and facial expressions during the short walk to the slippery jumping-off spot on the nose of the point.

Backdrop: steep pink crescent beach, dense palm forest, colorful pirogues, sagging shacks in the square of village. A scene of purity, devoid of commerce or overcrowding, an innocence of subsistence owed to isolation, its absence of pavement, proximity to wilderness.

The ocean is cool, murky, like Southern California in summer. Despite whitecaps behind the point, the waves are smooth and playful, the good ones running for a while, past a large washrock, ending in shorepound at the edge of the village, where young boys clap and cheer.

The sets pulse; Édouard and I trade. No talking. His surfing is economic and smooth despite his anorexic board. At one interlude, he stands on the headland and hoots, pointing to sea at the approach of a rogue set. Nice one. Paddling back out, a turtle surfaces to my left. (Walid, later: "Shark like turtle. Turtle like surfer. Ha! But here, many food for the shark.")

During the session, fishermen in four pirogues row around the point and weave through the lineup before beaching in front of the awaiting folks, eager to assess the day's catch. Following this afternoon ritual, the women return to the village, buckets and bowls of fish atop their heads, followed by exhausted men, walking slowly with Yamaha outboards on their shoulders; the youths carry buoys, green nets, gas tanks. Each night, nothing but wet boats are left on the beach.

Gone since dawn, a blue pirogue slides into view. Four figures: two men frantically rowing; one man frantically bailing; a teenage boy lazily steering. The arrival causes a stir. Three men leap from the point to help the sinking pirogue, which surfs a wave sideways. Returning to the beach with their empty buckets and stainless steel bowls, women wait for fish; the men building the new pirogue don't bat an eye.

The sun drops and daylight fades. Villagers—Édouard included—return to their homes, most to stoke fires and embrace ambient darkness, the thunder of shorebreak filling the night. Tomorrow will be a repeat of today and yesterday, last week, last year. Because in the village, so somnolent and marginalized and self-sufficient, a world outside does not exist. Yet nothing but the outside can ever change it.

WE ARE HUNGOVER in a vile city, a lilliputian sketch of Abidjan, on the opposite side of the country, 350 kilometers from the Paris of Africa.

Its surf is not what I'd grokked via Stormrider Guide detail: *A black lava reef where waves break in crystalline waters surrounded by lush jungle. It also has a consistent low-tide shorebreak.* Reality: consistent, closed-out, onshore beachbreak. Polluted, murky water. Rusty, industrial setting. No jungle.

A late start today. Breakfast on the beach in front of our decaying hotel, which is empty. They all are.

Low overcast sky, looming rain, haze. As Walid navigates the city, honking the car horn and shouting at bad drivers, I shoot stills and video from the passenger-side window. "Wrap camera strap around your arm," he warns me. "People can take and run."

At the city border, a soldier (large bread crumb stuck to one side of his mouth) demands money for the surfboards stuffed in our car. Then, the stink of citified Africa: traffic, beggars, sellers, sewage, open drains, garbage, thick crowds of people. Lawless, impromptu, impermanent. At one intersection, where we are nearly broad-sided by a truck, a man is holding a chicken in one hand, using his other hand to publicly piss into the roadside weeds.

"The future of the road is very good," Walid says. "You look, you have many guys trucks, many guys work. The new government is very good. I see money, you know? I see money in the population working. Very nice for Ivory Coast."

Pens of live chickens for sale. Vegetables and roasted corn. Peanuts. Slabs of raw meat. Overcrowded blue taxis, oppressive low clouds, cocoa factories, diesel exhaust, vinegary scent to the air (chocolatey on the outskirts). More dusty red roads, more potholes, more skinny men on bikes hauling bundles of sticks behind them. "For barbecue," Walid says.

Hard rain. Liberia is near. Smell of burning leaves and Walid's spliff. Swamps, fields of maize and cocoa, splattered red mud on roadside foliage. Cassava rows growing up low hillsides. Dense jungle—palms, ferns. Earthen scent to the air, like what it must smell like inside the many homes in villages scattered throughout the bush. Women washing clothes in the rain, idle men and lurking kids beneath awnings and umbrellas.

Jagged with snags and dead trees, the road becomes singletrack and nearly impassable. The jungle suffocates, crowding our sight and scratching the car. Then the Atlantic appears, draped around a palmy headland doubling as a right point.

The water looks cool and dark, with fish traps several meters off the white beach, on which two men repair their green fishing nets. Behind them, two men with large machetes group freshly harvested coconuts into a pile. Behind them is a decrepit hotel, recently abandoned, now consumed by termites and the wild jungle it was built amongst. African idyll, returned.

The four men stop tasks and walk to us. Handshakes, smiles exchanged. Walid hands them cigarettes and there are words in French. He translates: *Where you come from? For why you come? Long time no guys come here. We want guys to come to our beach for surf and fishing, good for the people when we have money for barbecue.*

"I tell them in one year, maybe two maximum, you have many guy return in west Ivory Coast for tourist, because the road is finished."

I want to send message to white guy: you come. Ivory Coast problems finished.

Peace is precarious, perishable, like that ex-hotel over there. Like the reality of military truth. Like the majority of rural Ivorian homes. How long, really, do those mud huts last?

Walid has never surfed the African Malibu because, like the elephants and ivory tusks, it is fiction. Perhaps one will exist after a few thousand more years, when powerful South Atlantic swells have time to further fillet the rocks and bluffs of Côte d'Ivoire's many right points into something special. But only for Walid and his surfy ilk, not for Abidjan's devious government and its people trapped in desperate slums, lives of misery for whom there would be more time for civil war, more red stains of blood to drip and dry among their raped forests and dusty fields of fire.

But tomorrow is Independence Day in Côte d'Ivoire. National flags, flapping in the wind, are raised everywhere.

A hope Ivorians can embrace.

PART X

Northeast Pacific

36

COASTING

2005

"Me drunk practically all the time to put on a jovial cap to keep up with all of this but finally realizing I was surrounded and outnumbered and had to get away to solitude or die—"

Jack Kerouac, Big Sur, *1961*

KEROUAC AND I have much in common—by nature, writers are solitary souls. But the boozing, the women, the loose carousing with strangers in strange places—what was all of that? Here, for Jack nearly a half-century ago, it was but a rural respite.

Shrill of crickets, muted surf, crackle and hiss of a smoky campfire—*this* was an October night in south Monterey County, darkness dissolved by the waxing moon, filtered between boughs of pine and twisted cypress.

After dinner, with pen and paper and wine and fire, I was drunk but indeed working, wearing my jovial cap, much like Kerouac when he visited his friend in Bixby Canyon, thirty-five miles north of my grassy campground. Writing in a seaside forest on a cold mid-week night harkens back to an era of different auras, like Kerouac's in 1961, with cheap cab and damp air holding thoughts and focus to ground level.

For a coast that welcomes four million annual visitors, there is immense value to such peace.

I put another log in the fire and squinted at the flames, the heat warming my face, listening to the communications of owls and bats and crickets around me. One of life's finest scents is that of a healthy woodfire, snapping brightly into the night sky, lending comfort and warmth, stoking a writer's thirst for privacy and introspection.

There was sleep disturbance at 2 a.m. In the nearby cove, a regular thundercrack promised that there were waves to be ridden come daylight. Where remained the question, because Big Sur's jagged coast, from Carmel to Carpoforo, presents some of America's most complex geology, detailed in Paul Henson's *The Natural History Of Big Sur*:

> *Diverse rocks that formed under radically varied conditions are now mixed together in jumbled disorder. A complex network of faults fractures the range and blocks of rock have moved great distances along this network, further complicating the picture.*

BIG SUR COULD be networked also by woodsmoke, morning dew on green campground grass, loud surf, birdsong, and the sweet, earthy smells of the forest: fir, sap, moss, fungus, dusty poison oak, sagebrush, ripe berries, decayed, spongy bark, and the palpable stillness of wood.

Come dawn it was a sunny Thursday—crisp, windless, the sky vast. Songbirds and woodpeckers fussed in the trees. Soon, at the nearby school, small rural children would yak before the first class bell rang.

Imagine your life as a child in Big Sur—Monterey as New York City and Carmel as Manhattan. To the south lay the urban sprawl of San Luis Obispo and Morro Bay, and before you lay two hundred and fifty square miles of wilderness, the only land you could ever trust.

I FINISHED MY coffee, packed the car, and headed down the coast. Highway 1 was deserted. The first spot I checked was misty and equally empty, warbly with the high tide, bullwhip kelp clogging the lineup. Night had delivered the season's first real swell, the reef here at last redeemed from the flat months of summer.

A faded blue pickup truck pulled up beside me. Its driver was Billy, a ragged diesel mechanic, age forty-six, in overalls and a flannel shirt, short and stocky, with frizzy red hair and a round, bearded face punctured by two sensationally bloodshot eyes. He looked like an Irish sailor and reeked of sweat. He was smoking a joint. In his truck bed was a red 7'10" pintail.

"My winter special," he said.

For the last twenty years Billy had lived in a shack near the tiny retail strip at Gorda. I said I had been camping nearby for the past several days.

"People are always trying to get me to go camp out," he said, watching the waves, his faced shaded by his faded blue baseball cap. "But I live under the trees, off mountain water, off my generator and kerosene lamps. I camp out every day."

This day he left his shack at dawn to look for surf, first stopping at a beachbreak that was unsurfable because the swell was too big. At least twice weekly, he drove up to Santa Cruz, a two-hundred-mile round-trip and several hours spent in the car..

"That's a lot of driving just to surf," I said.

"Yeah, but the wind skirts the shit out of this place every day," he said, raising his voice, lifting his cap and rubbing his forehead. "It starts at about 10:30 in the morning, as soon as the sun heats up the land."

"You must surf early most of the time, then."

He scratched an eyebrow. Then he sucked on the joint, held the smoke in his lungs for a moment, and blew it at the gulls above us. "It's just such a waste of time checking all these spots, and then checking Carmel and the whole Monterey Peninsula. So I say screw it—just drive straight to Santa Cruz. Start at the east side and head north until I find a break. I'm telling you, ninety-eight percent of the time I go to Santa Cruz, I surf. Whereas here in Big Sur, okay, I go to the north end, which has, like, two fickle surf spots. And then down the coast, to this area, if there's any waves here. If not, then I go down to San Simeon, which is always windy. And it's like, what'd I just drive? Four hours to get shut out?"

"So being a surfer here is frustrating."

"It is for me."

"Why don't you move elsewhere?"

"That's too easy."

Despite the surfable waves in front of us, Billy left, probably bound for Santa Cruz, and I was again alone in the tiny parking lot. Gulls spiraled above, squawking at each other. As I considered the afternoon's combination of tide, wind, and swell, an abrupt onshore breeze pushed fog in from the west, the sea's greeny-blue vanishing within minutes. With that, I decided to bushwhack out to a little-known reefbreak in a tiny cliff-shrouded cove not far up the coast.

There the sea was sheet glass, and the inconsistent head-high peaks, tripped by shallow reef, pitched mere yards from black boulders lining the shore. Of course, ill-placed rocks are the bane of the Big Sur surfer's existence; a friend of mine once said that, wave-quality wise, the place is a million years from perfection.

The rides were brief but steep and challenging. Surfing backside, I had a good view of the rocks I would hit if I fell. The waves were laced with boils and kelp, but it was the kelp that kept the sea glassy, and sitting in the water between waves, I reflected about how special the whole experience was, surfing a hidden reef on a foggy weekday in remote Central California.

After the session, stuffing my board into the back of the small rented car, I was approached by a Spandexed pair of skinny male Asian cyclists. They were riding the length of Highway 1 from San Francisco to San Luis Obispo, a dangerous trip, especially through Big Sur.

"I didn't know there was a surf break here," one of them said. "Is it good?"

"Rarely."

His friend laughed. "Barely or rarely?"

"Same thing."

"Where is the spot?"

I said, "You must be kidding."

Cold and hungry and wanting to flee the fog, I drove north to a campground along the leafy banks of the Big Sur River. By nightfall I had made another fire with eucalyptus kindling and hunks of fir, crackling and spattering while I sat on a stump, swigging from another bottle of cheap cabernet. Only the racket of crickets for sound, with the occasional frog and the shooshing of wind through the redwoods. The fire boosted my spirits, chilly from the day, the torquing oranges and yellows thinning the darkness of my private campsite.

An hour later the sky opened, stars winking between shreds of cloud, framed by the trees and the silhouetted Santa Lucia Range. Eventually the fire reduced itself to a gentle murmur of ash, sparks rising in the smoke. The wine drowsed me, and as the clouds again claimed the sky, I thought of tomorrow.

Big Sur's natural world speaks loudest, I wrote in a notebook while cocooned in my down bag, minutes from sleep. *Its animals, its trees, its cliffs, its sea. There is nothing else. A soul's sanctity is born from not what is created, but what is innately inherited from eons of living time—a lifetime. A metaphor, Big Sur is life. And so existing here, ultimately, is a white canvas, a surfer's life the everlasting watercolor.*

37

HOURS OF DARKNESS

2007

"BETTER PUT YOUR jackets on," the stewardess warned. "It's a bit breezy out there."

Tyler Smith, Raph Bruhwiler, Josh Mulcoy, Chris Burkard, and I stepped through the Dash 8's door and were nearly blown off the airplane stairs. The wind was sharp, the air freezing. Black storm clouds loomed. Alaska lay within sight. Behind us were jagged, snow-covered mountains, and ahead lay shallow Hecate Strait, one of the world's most feared waterfetches, just wicked today, smeared white by the southeasterly gale.

"At least it's offshore somewhere!" someone yelled over the din.

This was expected. Daily, for months leading up to our departure, I'd monitored Haida Gwaii's weather online, and the forecasts were repetitive, like the one posted the day of our arrival:

STORM WARNING CONTINUED. Wind warning in effect.
Tonight..Rain. Amount 20 mm. Wind southeast 50 to 70 km/h increasing to 70 to 100 overnight. Low plus 5.
Thursday..Rain. Amount 20 mm. Wind southeast 70 to 100 km/h becoming south 40 to 60 in the afternoon. High 8.

Thursday night..Rain. Amount 10 to 15 mm. Wind southeast 50 to 80 km/h. Low 8.
Friday..Rain. Wind southeast 50 to 70 km/h increasing to 70 to 100 then becoming south 30 late this afternoon. High 10.

ON THE BUS into town, once he learned that Smith was a Maverick's junkie, a white fisherman with a redneck drawl promised us that there was a giant wave "just like Maverick's" that broke out in front of a fishing lodge his friend worked for, out on the west coast. "It breaks best when the winds are about 70 knots onshore," the man said. "Just comes up out of nowhere and boom, this huge roller, taller'n a cedar totem pole."

"Which way does it break?" Smith asked, eyebrows raised. "Left or right?"

"Oh, just straight in, right toward shore."

We were mocked by passersby outside our hotel; one woman thought we'd brought oversized snowboards. Three burly loggers in the café next door thought we were hippie tree-planters from Vancouver. Tree-planters are not particularly liked on Haida Gwaii, despite the island's forests being logged at twice the rate that is considered sustainable.

"In the past 50 years," says the Haida Nation homepage, "industrial logging has transformed the landscape of Haida Gwaii from diverse old forest to young, even-aged stands of one or two species. The major river systems that once provided Haida villages with salmon; large cedars for longhouses and monumental art; and, plants for food, medicines, fiber and animal habitat have been eradicated by logging without consideration for these values."

Still, we would not be digging holes for cedar saplings.

"You guys are here to go surfing?" the loggers asked, amused at our quest. "Good luck!"

Down at the quaint harbor, another local—a Haida—said we were out of our minds, that if we wanted to go surfing, we needed to go somewhere like California or Hawai'i. He suggested that we start drinking instead, joining him at a nearby cocktail lounge, where there would be "guaranteed fights."

Reputedly the Haida were fierce, physically large, historically feared by all other Indians in the northwest. Every Haida we met was extremely friendly, but, back in the day, the kin of these folks would routinely sail across the Hecate Strait in cedar canoes to terrorize mainland tribes, acquire slaves and provisions, and return to Haida Gwaii with the proud gaze of dominance.

"The Haida, and only the Haida, were immune from attack," Christie Harris wrote in Raven's Cry. "In consequence, the pride of the Haida shaded even that of their mighty neighbors [the Tsimshian and Tlingit]. They were lords of the coast, the aristocrats of their world."

While the offer of drinking and fighting proved nearly irresistible, we declined and repaired to a Chinese restaurant where we checked the online forecast and brainstormed between forkloads of MSG. West coast buoys reported a nine-meter swell. Otherwise, things looked grim.

"It might be stormy like this the whole time," Mulcoy said.

"Could get worse," Bruhwiler said.

"The west coast is going mental right now," Smith said.

"Only if it's blowing 70 knots onshore," I said.

Along Haida Gwaii's desolate and savage west side, the highest-energy coastline in North America, it's not a matter of getting swell—aside from finding a surfable spot, it's a matter of getting to that swell. There are no roads, no harbors, no hiking trails, nothing but deep, black fjords, vertical cliffs, impassable alpine ridges of rock and snow, and ancient forests averaging 20 feet of rain annually, pelted by furious winds and enormous seas. The island's refined, pointbreak-rich east coast is one big tease, receiving basically no swell, ever.

"I'll say that the east, or leeward, side…is the biggest waste of prime surf geography I have ever seen," Ben Marcus wrote when he visited the island in the late 1990s. And so, perhaps in desperation late one woolly afternoon, Smith braved 50-knot onshores and horizontal rain to surf rocky waist-high wind slop in 42-degree water at a spot that could be world-class. Considering the huge swell hitting the west coast at that very moment, if Smith could've flipped the island, turning east coast to west, he would have been surfing a gargantuan Malibu. Alas, in geographical terms, it is not meant to be.

The west coast's only car-accessible zone required a careful three-hour (each way) negotiation of a snowbound, signless logging road with many forks in it; eventually we reached the inlet, though sheltered it was. There we found a couple of pebbly beachbreaks, a flawless right point, and an enticing left rivermouth, but despite epic scenery and exposure to open ocean, these "spots" were flat while the truly exposed coast outside was bombing left and right. Smith's binoculars confirmed this. "We need jet skis!" came the consensus.

But there are few jet skis in Haida Gwaii. Renting one was impossible. Even if we had our own, trailering it out atop that road would likely bang the thing to bits; having nowhere to launch it was another problem. Bruhwiler had considered bringing his two skis on the ferry from Port Hardy, but that would've been bloody expensive.

For all the world's surfers, Haida Gwaii is a cruel and unusual place. We had a good crew for the task: Vancouver Island's Raphael Bruhwiler really needs no introduction, a gritty lifelong soldier of the Pacific Northwest; Santa Cruz's Tyler Smith, a Billabong XXL Global Big Wave Award finalist, top-placing Maverick's competitor and Ghost Tree charger, is fearless; fellow Westsider Josh Mulcoy is a core coldwater freak, actively seeking juice along some of the globe's harshest coasts—Norway, Alaska, Iceland, Oregon. "Still," Mulcoy said, "Haida Gwaii is definitely the coldest place I've ever been."

Cold was not an issue when it came to accessing the west coast. One day Raph and I lunched on Reubens and coffee in the Purple Onion Deli; soon Mulcoy arrived and the conversation returned to boats. A cute brunette named Lindsey overheard our plight; she handed me a scrap of paper containing the phone number of her friend, a local fishing-charter guy who just might be stoked to take us out yonder for a look-see.

"He's got a killer, brand-spankin'-new Boston Whaler," Lindsey said. "He just christened it the other day. Super fun guy, knows where to go out there—he works for the Coast Guard. Give him a call."

A lifetime of cigarettes bespoke Chumma's even, disc-jockey-modulated voice. It suggested that he knew his stuff, and I could tell he was keen for a real bluewater chance to test his new vessel before salmon season started.

"If it's big water you're after," Chumma said, "the west is the place. I've spent my whole life trying to avoid the damn breakers out there."

We arranged to meet Thursday at the dock at 5:30 a.m. Today was Monday—Thursday seemed an awfully long way off considering the severe but mesmerizing weather we were having. Locals said it would ease. The myth was, if you don't like the weather, wait 10 minutes. Unfortunately we had to wait much longer than that.

MYTHOLOGY SATURATES NORTHWEST Indian culture, and true to universal theme, supernatural entities are created to explain the unknowable, interpreted through generations via intricate art, dance, and detailed verbology. For the Haida, the most prominent figure of myth and legend is the jet-black raven, something we saw every day. Technically the raven is a hawk-sized songbird, a skilled predator and scavenger, never short on food or wit, and, mythologically, the raven is a transformer, able to become anything, anytime, anywhere. "As a transformer he is responsible for the present order of the universe," Martine Reid wrote in *The Children of the Raven*. "He discovers mankind, acquires and controls food, brings the light into the world."

Episodes of raven myth are illustrated on totem poles throughout Haida Gwaii, and the one we found of most interest, considering the violent weather we faced, was how the raven discovered a man who possessed a small box containing a ball of light, which was all the light in the universe. The raven, cunning as he was, managed to steal the ball and use it to illuminate the entire world, previously an "inky, pitchy, all-consuming dark, blacker than a thousand stormy winter midnights, blacker than anything anywhere has been since," Bill Reid and Robert Bringhurst wrote in *The Raven Steals the Light*. "The world was at once transformed. Mountains and valleys were starkly silhouetted, the river sparkled with broken reflections, and everywhere life began to stir. The Raven flew on, rejoicing in his wonderful new possession, admiring the effect it had on the world below, revelling in the experience of being able to see where he was going, instead of flying blind and hoping for the best."

Halfway into the trip, staring out at clouds and rain and distant snowcaps, listening to the wind shriek past the hotel windows, we could almost—almost—relate. We'd found fun albeit gutless waves at one rivermouth, but really, until then, searching for waves, we'd driven an average of 150 miles a day, very slowly, with no music, in a rented four-wheel-drive truck, progressively coating the cab's floor with food wrappers and empty water bottles. Five of us in the truck for hour upon hour, fidgeting and farting and letting the comedy flow freely. "Let's see what's down that road" became a common utterance, the driver (me) repeatedly and abruptly veering the truck off the main road and down sketchy singletracks in dense rain forest in the middle of nowhere, usually leading to an impassable hole or horizontal tree, or to another flat beachbreak, or to the cabin of a Haida family or hippie outcast who didn't want us there.

That night, crew morale threatened to plunge irreversibly. "We need something," Burkard said, glumly clicking through the Internet on his laptop. "It can't stay like this forever, can it?"

"We're definitely due for a change," I said.

"Check the forecast," Mulcoy said.

It had changed:

Wednesday..A mix of sun and cloud. Low 7. High 11.
Thursday..A mix of sun and cloud with 30 percent chance of showers.
Low plus 5. High 12.
Friday..A mix of sun and cloud. Low 6. High 13.

WE LOOKED AT each other. "High of 13? A mix of clouds *and* sun?"

Buoyweather.com confirmed a swing in swell angle, from southwest to west, optimum for both the entire west coast and a certain beachbreak up north. Our luck had bloomed.

Since hiring Chumma's boat for the next day was unlikely, we settled for the beachbreak, which turned out to be an impressive score.

Moss Landing or Hossegor—either, only minus crowds and traffic and topless girls, and the water was much colder, the driftwood much bigger. Aside from a brief shower, the sun shone warmly all day and the offshore wind puffed gently, grooming the consistent and overhead lines, which, based on their orderliness, had come from afar. Only problem were the extraordinary tides, which in Haida Gwaii range 25 feet. So one sandbar that was good for 45 minutes would send us down the beach to sample another bar for maybe 30 minutes, then another, and another, and so forth.

For lunch, in total solitude, we lounged in the dunes and roasted sausages over a driftwood fire, and the sweet scent of woodsmoke in the lineup that golden afternoon accented what had actually been a very good day, better than most in terms of any surf trip any of us had ever been on.

"Weather-wise," said Smith upon sunset, "we probably just got the nicest day of the year. We got sunburned in a place where that normally doesn't happen."

AND THEN IT was Thursday. Chumma and deckhand Gary finished prepping the Whaler as we pulled onto the wooden dock an hour before first light, the scene faintly aglow under the orange harbor lights. As luck would have it, our hours of darkness—figuratively and literally—were about to end for good. Surfing beneath sun for an entire day at an empty, hollow beachbreak proved prescient for the second half of our trip—from now until departure, we would bid farewell to the darkness, dissolved by the raven, perhaps, and quickly forgotten.

On the last day, waiting for our airport taxi, a woman in a coffee shop said, "From the looks of your tans, you're definitely not from around here." Actually, we weren't quite sure where we were, I told her, but we weren't ready to leave it behind.

"I know what you mean," the woman said, turning her face up toward the midday sun, smiling and squinting into the warmth.

In his book *Haida Gwaii*, Ian Gill wrote that there is "nowhere more beguiling, more hypnotic, more intoxicating and infuriating and enigmatic, more ineffable" than where we found waves, and, fittingly, nothing could better describe our path and our eventual taste—our feast—of it on Haida Gwaii, a.k.a. Xhaaidlagha Gwaayaii to native elders, these "islands of the people" where climatic traits are not mythical, the rain perpetual, the darkness vast. Yet Haida Gwaii is no site of true monotony. Nothing remains the same for long.

38

SPIRIT OF PLACE

2006

OWLS HOOTED IN darkness, frogs croaked in the marsh, wind swooshed loudly through the pines and gnarled cypress. At the campground it was a cold, heavy night—nights behind storms are always so, the sky impenetrable, moonless, starry, and with cold hands I held cold bottles of beer, drinking one after another, until finally the frogs and wind and roar of surf knocked me out.

At first light I smelled cow dung—the wind was offshore. Quickly I rose and walked out to the beach, where large swell broke in mass confusion. There was no one around, no runners or dog walkers, no coffee drinkers, no fishermen, no surfers. It was six-thirty on a freezing Tuesday morning in late January, night mist still clinging to the beach, gulls huddling together at the mouth of Salmon Creek, flowing fast and fat with rain and brown farm silt. My grandfather once fished here, and my mother, a Sonoma native, would frequent this beach as a child, the beach where the water was dark and the surf fierce, an environment with enough grit to shape one's life into a soul forever spliced with nature.

East was a psychedelic sunrise, orange and pink swirls painting the sky above the ridges of Mount Roscoe and Irish Hill, the grassy slopes specked with silhouettes of sheep and black beef cattle. To the north was rocky coast easing eastward into these soft hills, unspoiled by homes or wineries, and to the south lay a thousand acres of sand dunes, rimming Bodega Harbor, leading into the low sheared mound of Mussel Point, piercing the Pacific.

I was standing on the north spur of California's infamous "Red Triangle," an ocean fetch extending seaward from Bodega Bay to the Farallon Islands, twenty-seven miles west of San Francisco, before veering southeasterly to Año Nuevo Island, near Santa Cruz. Hence a problem for surfers: since scientists began monitoring shark encounters and the species responsible for them, the Red Triangle has been the world's leading site of great-white attacks on humans.

Sonoma County's Department of Fish and Game believes Salmon Creek Beach to be particularly "high-risk" for surfers. This morning, just beyond the breakers, rising and falling slow-motion in the swells, a small commercial fishing boat from Bodega Harbor motored north, circled by a squawking cloud of white gulls. Watching the boat, nets and lines cluttering its decks, out to kill fish, I thought that conversely the DFG should declare any ocean near humans as "high-risk" for the sharks.

> *"I find myself hoping that it may yet be my lot to pass a year or two in some region of almost perpetual storm; where sunshine will be a phenomenon, color will be reduced to the all-satisfying range of the grays, and sound limited to the solemn fugue of wind and sweeping rain."*
>
> *—Joseph Smeaton Chase, Sonoma coast, c. 1911*

SIMPLE CAMPERS AND well-heeled lovers often coexist when visiting the Sonoma coast, because there is no middle ground: either you camp or you book a costly inn or vacation home.

I slept outside. Of the Sonoma coast's campgrounds, five were private, four were county-owned, and six were run by California State Parks. These, the most popular, were also the costliest, up considerably from just a few years ago: one black-ice winter night in 2002 I paid ten dollars to camp at Salt Point State Park. Four years later, I paid thirty.

The reason was obvious. First elected in 1998 and re-elected in 2002, California governor Gray Davis was recalled in 2003, when citizens accused him of tax and utility corruption and shameless fibbing about the state's $35 billion deficit. This greatly affected outdoor recreation: during Davis's reign, State Parks lost nearly $20 million and about two hundred jobs, reducing its twenty-three park districts to eighteen. In Davis's shadow State Parks lay badly wounded, requiring a fee spike to ensure park maintenance. Now the camper must pay more if he or she wants to hike, bike, picnic, or jab a tent into a dirty, piss-scented square of dirt.

I mentioned this to a sweating maintenance worker at Fort Ross.

"For just camping, yes, it is expensive," he said, lobbing black trash bags into the bed of a white State Park truck. "But people pay—everyone pays. Nobody complains. I figure it's because the people are just happy to be here. They're usually vacationing families from the city or somewhere inland or they're abalone divers, and they're willing to spend money."

"Where are you originally from?" I asked.

"Sacramento."

"Would you pay thirty dollars a night to sleep here in a tent?"

"No way."

Many people do, though, because besides natural beauty, the Sonoma coast offers the world's best red abalone fishery. Each year, starting April 1 and lasting seven months, throngs of far-flung folks arrive wielding drysuits and lead weight belts and flat iron bars, eager to submerge themselves into the frigid ocean to pry tasty mollusks from rocks and reefs. Selling Sonoma abalone is forbidden, and of course poaching is a problem, with only a handful of rangers patrolling the coast.

Many of Sonoma's surf spots are in or around abalone beds that are in or around state parks, which is why I again camped for several nights at Salt Point, a six-thousand-acre paradise of rocky coast and second-growth forest in which it is legal to also gather five pounds of mushrooms every day (poaching is not a problem). The cliffside campground was serene and empty and not far from the frontier village of Gualala, with its supermarkets and gas stations and wireless Internet.

In recent years California's rich Bay Area has changed many of the North Coast's old logging towns. The closer to San Francisco a town is, the more it is developed and the more its costs intensify. Homes—the majority for summering—have become expensive, on par price-wise with those in Santa Cruz and Southern California, which enjoy the bonus of mild climate, unlike Sonoma.

In *Coastal Living* magazine I found a Gualala depiction that would have also worked well for Malibu or Carmel, if only Gualala too had good waves:

> *In the Surf Supermarket parking lot in the center of Gualala, a violet Mercedes convertible, waxed and shining like a jelly bean, sits next to a vintage Volkswagen van, its painted sides a nod to Picasso. The two autos appear perfectly comfortable as neighbors. Inside the grocery store, and elsewhere in town, surfers mingle with millionaires.*

BUT IN GUALALA I saw no surfers—there are no surf spots—and there was a palpable sense of newly imported wealth. A month after my trip, Santa Rosa's *Press Democrat* called Gualala "the new hot spot," and *Men's Journal* touted Gualala as an "outpost of adventure lifestyle," one of America's "50 Healthiest, Sexiest, Most Adventurous Towns", urging readers to pack up and relocate to "one of California's best below-the-radar places to a make a move on before the word gets out." I found this funny, also a bit sad. But due to its Bay Area proximity and the scope of rich Sea Ranch, homely little Gualala, recuperating on the soiled heels of the logging industry, has since proved invaluable as a commerce hub, today well-stocked with everything one could need, including surfboards at the new mid-town surf shop.

"Half the homes around here are vacant except on weekends and during the summer," said a woman who was walking her dog in grassy Gualala Point Park.

"It's mostly urban Johnny-come-latelies," another man said. "They bring money, but a lot of them are assholes, to tell you the truth."

His name was Steve. He was sixty-three. He was gaunt and ancient-looking, tall, bearded, and solidly built. He looked like a longtime resident because he was one. As a logger, Steve had spent his entire life in the woods on the north Somona coast, and at the twilight of his career, on his fifty-fifth birthday, he tried surfing for his first time.

"I wasn't getting any younger," Steve said. "I used to dive for abalone, so I was comfortable in the ocean. But an old urchin-diving friend of mine was a surfer and he always talked about how great surfing was, so I borrowed a board of his one day and started messing around."

On this rainy morning we were sitting in the lineup of an ice-cold Sea Ranch beachbreak, where the south wind blew offshore into powerful, overhead waves, backdropped by relatively new development. Once, between sets, in the rain, grimacing at the pale, boxy homes behind us, Steve spat and shrugged.

"Just a bunch of cloned cubes."

It wasn't supposed to turn out like this, he said. In the early 1960s a San Francisco landscape planner named Lawrence Halprin envisioned an attractive, unique, small-scale development, a handful of inconspicuous homes to blend with the coastal scenery. Initially all went according to Halprin's plan, which quickly tanked once greedy Bay Area realtors got wind of the project.

"That," Steve said, "was when it all went to shit."

The development (with golf links and private airstrip) consumed ten miles of Highway 1 coast and wrecked ocean views for passing motorists. Today public access is limited to five muddy pathways and a bit of rocky beach.

At home a few weeks later, I offhandedly mentioned Sea Ranch to my friend Mark Massara, an environmental lawyer who has surfed Sea Ranch many times.

"That place stands as an example of a failed development and land-use strategy," Massara said. "It's monotonous, unimaginative architectural blandness punctuated by luxury automobiles and occupied by out-of-town retirees, world-famous for decidedly unimpressive, inadequate public parking, access, and hiking trails. Public beaches and rural coastline as spectacular as Sea Ranch should never again be sacrificed to this sort of mind-numbing, mediocre suburban-style sprawl."

I found a much different perspective on the Web site of the Sea Ranch Association:

> *...the building design constitutes an architectural vernacular that is world-renowned. Its hallmark is the attempt to blend man-made structures with their natural setting, and to live lightly on the land.*

—and this in the *San Francisco Chronicle*:

> *If you rent one of the condos at Sea Ranch, you will experience being close to other people, but at the same time feeling like you're a million miles from the Bay Area. Wildlife cruises in and around the property, barely noticing the stressed-out people seeking peace.*

INDEED SEA RANCH was tranquil, and on its public beach paths I had only pleasant encounters with pleasant residents, mostly retired urban refugees, the sort of serene, plucky folk you meet on cruise ships and boardwalks, strolling with hands clasped behind their backs on cold and windy winter mornings, a morning similar to when I surfed with Steve at one of Sonoma's rarefied beachbreaks.

"You got lucky," he said. "It's only been in the past week that the waves here have had any shape. Shit will change after the next big swell."

Which wasn't far off, based on the Internet forecast hyping an impressively large, long-period westerly, due in the next few days.

Less than an hour after we'd paddled out, the wind stiffened and swayed to the west, trashing the waves, and it began raining so hard that it blurred our sight. So for heat and replenishment I followed Steve's red rattletrap truck to the parking lot of the Sea Ranch Lodge, and it was at a corner table in the lodge's nice restaurant, overlooking the stormy Pacific, where we talked and swigged strong black coffee, working through plates of bacon and eggs and big steak omelettes.

A retired logger, Steve was thoughtful and articulate, his countenance expressing a great deal of regret. This came from a life spent in the watershed ("checkerboard of clear-cuts") of the Gualala River, felling prehistoric redwood trees and trucking them to the mill. Steve had no family or children; years ago, his marriage ended bitterly.

"Logging will do that do you," he said, chewing bacon, lips shiny with grease. "It just beats on your body and brain. Sometimes when I surf I get so cold and stiff that I wonder if I'll be able to make it back to the car."

After breakfast we drove north, crossing the Gualala River bridge into Mendocino County. We parked in a dirt turnout above the swollen estuary. Whitewater sloshed into the rivermouth. A few people walked on the sandspit, bracing themselves in the wind, moving stiffly and slowly, small dark splotches in the gray, weighted with boots and big jackets, looking robotic and clubfooted.

I asked, "Does it ever get good out there?"

"No. Something perpetually wrong with the sand flow and the currents—they never line up right. Too much swell and too deep and not enough downtime to ever let a sandbar form."

Federal experts consider the Gualala to be an impaired river because of its excessive logging-triggered sediments and, because of shade loss, its relatively warm water temperatures, fatal for fish. (California's Forest Practice Rules now require preservation of trees in any riparian zone, but until those rules were written in the 1970s, loggers cut right to the water's edge, eliminating all shade.) Once recognized for its seemingly inexhaustible fishery, today the thirty-two-mile-long river sulks in the mud from a hundred-and-fifty years of logging, so damaged that its famed steelhead and coho salmon are virtually extinct. Run-off of mud and gravel from stripped hillsides suffocated the river's spawning beds, turning the teeming Gualala into a fallow, fishless murk.

"Years ago you could walk down to that sandspit with a pitchfork and just stab it in and yank out some real nice salmon," Steve said. "You wouldn't believe how full of fish that river was. Whole different deal now."

I said, "But as a logger you contributed to this problem."

"We all did. It was our attitude. Denial was easy—you cut the trees and you haul them to the mill, and since you don't see an immediate impact besides the stripped land, you tell yourself nothing bad is happening downhill, although you know that you and everyone else working with you is trashing that river, that entire ecosystem, something that had been there since the beginning of time. We ruined it. But the money was there—the work was there. I earned a steady paycheck. Around here, there weren't many options otherwise."

"How about selective-tree logging instead of clear-cutting?"

"Not economical. Everyone knew that logging a whole chunk of land made things more profitable for the company. It was a normal job—supply and demand. Redwoods can grow back, but the damage might be permanent. These forests are incredibly abused."

"What's next for them?" I asked.

"Depends on who you ask."

Late afternoon came quickly. From Gualala I drove south, exiting the community's rainy-day ghost-town facade, passing Sea Ranch. Near Stewarts Point I drove into a gale, gusting from the southwest. Here the sea was a dense gray-brown smeared with white, the swell blown to shreds. I parked in a small turnout and grabbed a beer from the cooler; I sat in the car drinking it, the wind so strong it shook the car.

The surrounding sheep pastures and coastal meadows were on the market for fifteen million dollars. Stewarts Point, once an important lumber settlement, had long been reduced to a few decayed barns and cabins, a mobile home, a tiny post office, and an interesting general store that was being renovated for the upcoming abalone season. For several generations the property had been owned by the Richardson family, who used the land for sheep ranching. The property couldn't have looked much different today than when England's Joseph Smeaton Chase rode through here on his horse in 1911, chronicling everything he experienced in California Coast Trails, a rare book first published in 1913. In Chapter 19 Chase described his Stewarts Point layover:

> *As it was Sunday, no work was going on, and the rain had sent the entire population to the saloon, where three poker games were in*

progress. Money passed freely, and by no means all I saw was as low as silver. They were a cosmopolitan lot. I could distinguish Mexicans, Indians, Irishmen, Germans, and Swedes, besides Americans. The thirst was general and unremitting, and the language frightful, even for "lumber-jacks." I suppose that most of these poor fellows saw no more harm in the hideous oaths they rapped out every moment than we see in reading the newspaper. Rheumatic twinges sent me early to bed, and I awoke to find a clear sun shining and an Indian squaw looking seriously in at my window.

LOOKING IN AT my car window was a punished-looking gray-bearded man gripping a twelve-pack of beer. Staring blankly he tapped slowly on the glass, motioning for me to roll the window down. He needed a ride to Ocean Cove; I was headed that way. Mike was fifty-one and had walked ten miles from Gualala, where he'd bought the beer. He was dressed in rags and reeked of sweat and cigarette smoke, but despite his reluctance to speak, he was pleasant enough.

"Looks like we're in for some sun," was one of his few utterances. "On the television I saw five suns in the forecast. Never have I seen so many damn suns."

That night I slept in my car near his house, a mildewed shack deep in private property among second-growth redwoods. Come morning I took a walk and saw a rarefied right-hander, his personal and secluded surf spot—only Mike wasn't a surfer. He was a marijuana farmer.

LATE IN THE week I returned to the Sea Ranch beachbreak, which was unsurfable, flooded with swell. So instead of surfing I strolled through the soaked subdivision, trespassing on streets with names like Whitesurf and Wildberry. Amid the wind and hail and mist, the big houses looked forlorn, and I couldn't imagine Sea Ranch realtors selling this fierce face of weather to moneyed clientele from Phoenix and Sacramento. For most, Sonoma's north is all but habitable nor remotely recreational come winter.

Misperception is widespread. For surfers, the coastline is too young and climatically beaten to allow for reliable and refined surf quality.

Which isn't to say Sonoma's waves are perpetually bad, because like any surfy place, every dog has its day.

On this day I was badly hungover. The previous night, a torrential black wash from dusk to dawn, had confined me to my cramped car, trembling in the wind on a patch of campground pavement. To blend the hours I drank bourbon, flooding my system with alcohol for no reason other than to quicken time, listening to the storm rush through the trees above.

Suddenly it was daybreak and the storm was gone, followed by fog and silence. I woke nauseous, yet at six-thirty I started the car and drove a mile to the parking lot of a nearby trailhead, where I returned to the passenger seat to sleep again. Soon the rain resumed, and I dozed thinly, waiting for the rain to stop and the fog to clear, but neither did.

Near noon, uncomfortable and insomniac, I ventured inland up lush and unpaved Kruse Ranch Road. There I found a dripping stand of rhododendrons in a reserve of sorts, three hundred-and-seventeen previously logged acres given to the public in 1933 by rancher Edward Kruse, one of Sonoma's first settlers in the 19th century German Rancho land grant. Today it is a subtle hollow, ferny, leafy, mossy, dimmed with the dirt-scented dampness of redwood forest, soundtracked with birdsong and babbling brook, weightened with the stark solemnity of a wet winter day.

Serenity flows loosely from an ecosystem that has been otherwise ruined by commerce—nearly every forested acre here has been cut at least once in the past one-hundred-and-fifty years. A few miles from where I walked lay Sonoma's last remaining stand of ancient, extremely valuable trees, nearly nine hundred acres of old-growth redwoods in the Gualala River watershed. Recently the owner of this was denied in his proposal to log half of those trees on the sixty-five-degree slopes which lead down into Haupt Creek, a key fish-bearing stream, tributary to the Wheatfield Fork of the Gualala River.

Now grapes are worth more than wood, visibly obvious in nearby Annapolis, a remote hamlet that was once a boomtown of apple orchards, since converted to vineyards. The redwoods around Annapolis are sought by vintners, not for the trees, but for the land they occupy, which, if the vintners succeed, will be cleared for rows of pinot noir, one of the world's oldest cultivated grapes, further bolstering Sonoma County's annual grape revenue, currently a whopping two hundred million dollars, sixty-one percent of the county's agricultural base.

Sonoma's only truly "coastal" label is that of family-run Annapolis Winery, quaint and organic, situated on a green hilltop a thousand feet above the Pacific. And in Sonoma the color of money is either red or white, because with wine comes money, and with money come tourists and development, which bring more money, shedding the old reliance on trees and fish so that anyone with cash can buy a house here, freed from the city and traffic, toasting their luck with twelve-dollar glasses of Sonoma's finest. Ex-loggers like Steve are invisible, living in mildewed trailer parks, surviving on welfare checks, surfing in the cold rain, parking rusted pickups aside luxury sedans in front of the Gualala supermarket.

Around the rhododendrons I strolled, pondering all of this, breathing deeply, head slowly depressurizing, brow cooled by mist, hands behind my back, eyes up, senses roused by the simple act of walking outdoors. The forest wasn't ancient or marked for profit, yet among its serene innocence was holistic therapy for an aching head. Still, I felt greasy and itchy. Seeking warmwater therapy and a hangover cure, I went for a shower at a vacant campground nearby. But the campground had no change machine; I drove to the nearest store in search of quarters.

"I can give you two," the cashier said.

"I need six."

She frowned and crossed her skinny arms. "Can't do it. It's noon. We've just closed for lunch."

"I haven't showered in eight days. Please, a shower costs a dollar-fifty at Stillwater Cove Park, just down the road."

Mercifully she exchanged my two dollar bills for four quarters and the rest in dimes, which, as I soon discovered, the showers would not accept.

So I went for a pint down at the bar of Timber Cove Inn, a rustic joint on the headland of its namesake cove. I had the room to myself, as it was a rainy winter weekday afternoon. With a glass of Red Seal Ale, I read the *Independent Coast Observer*, studying the latest victories of the Point Arena High School basketball team.

"I played varsity there my senior year," the bartender said. "We weren't nearly as good as the team is now."

He was in his mid-thirties and looked like a surfer; I asked if this was true. He said he had never tried surfing, that his sun-bleached complexion came from other outdoor pursuits. Last weekend he had hunted blacktail deer in Jackson State Forest; this weekend he planned to shoot wild boars in the wine country; next weekend he planned to fish for black bass in Napa County's Lake Berryessa.

"Damn good for fishing," he grinned, showing stained teeth. "Good waterskiing out there, too."

"Growing up here, you never tried surfing?"

"No interest." He was still smiling. "Too cold, too sharky. I've never even dived for abalone. I think surfers here are crazy. Maybe not in someplace like Hawai'i, but here?"—he gestured out the window—"Shit, that ocean is nuts."

I considered his statement while driving back to the campsite at dusk, on an empty road, through drizzle and dense fog, listening to "December" by pianist George Winston, his music matching the somber and soothing forest scenery. At the deserted campground my oak firewood was too wet to burn, so I laid supine on the passenger seat, resting my eyes, dozing, eventually realizing that the hair-of-the-dog beers had worked: my migraine was gone.

CAMPING IN WINTER eliminates creature comforts and outdoor cooking, instead replaced by hot smoky campfires, tipsy postprandial walks, rough slumber without good shelter. It is time best spent alone. And so driving along Highway 1 in winter too may harken of times preceding Sonoma's chambers of commerce and expensive Sea Ranch homes, before the vintners and abalone pickers and gargantuan RVs, before elegant art galleries and bed-and-breakfast romance, before retirees and southerners en masse fled their suburban sprawl, which people actually needed to escape so they could revisit nature. But when the south was rural, why go north? It was much colder, much darker, vastly remote—decades ago, to Southern California surfers, Santa Barbara was a fringe, Santa Cruz was arctic, and nobody seemed to know what lay north of San Francisco.

On my final night camping in Sonoma I ate cold pizza and drank beer in fogbound darkness on the south bank of the Gualala River. The campground was flooded with rain beneath dripping redwoods, bordered by the fat river's muffled rush. There was no noise from insects or animals—only water. I sat on a wet picnic table and watched the wide river when the fog broke, illuminated dimly despite the absence of moonlight.

Around three in the morning I woke thinking a jet airplane was landing nearby. It was heavy shorepound, the booming thundercrack funneled to my campsite along the river corridor. Since dusk the wind had died and the swell had hit—a big westerly with a twenty-five-second period, strong and orderly, undoubtedly the winter's best swell.

At dawn I parked in the dirt pullout above the river, separated from the ocean by the narrow spit. The surf was huge, the sight impressive—because of the high tide and the beach's severe drop-off, sets slammed full-force onto the sand, immense wave energy accumulated over thousands of ocean miles at last terminating in violent fashion.

And so occasionally surfers are unavoidable, for good reason: it was a Monday, and, later, the air temperature hovered in the low seventies. The ebbing tide and epic swell were ideal for the windless day. The sea was blue and the sky was clear, and those who cared less for work were treated with sublimity at one of the north coast's finest reefs. If you closed your eyes, it could have been Southern California.

Certainly Sonoma in winter is no surfer's paradise. Then again, with the right swell, the right weather, and the right attitude, it could be.

39

MEMORY OF TREES

2010

MY FEET BLED lightly inside damp, ill-fitting boots. Skin was rotting. With two weeks of hikes, the blisters couldn't heal.

The air was cold, the forest concealing. An owl hooted softly from within. My legs were chafed by denim jeans, rain-soaked and mud-caked, my wet fullsuit and surfboard heavy underarm, straining the socket of my right shoulder. Backpack was a load of lead. The large road-rash scab on my left arm had worn off, its naked wound stuck to the inside of my sweatshirt. The trail was vague and overgrown, and after surfing all day, its length back to the campground—five miles—was painfully long.

Dusk killed the wan April light that at dawn had revealed mossy, centuries-old trunks of Sitka spruce. They were 200 feet tall. Beyond, down the hill and through the trees, the ocean was a dull gray, airbrushed with white spindrift from the swells bending and breaking into the cape at Bearpaw Gulch, a remote, rocky cove that turned onshore wind to off. The wave itself was poor, a sectiony, boily left-hander that broke over a shallow reef of sharp stones and spiny purple urchins. Dangerous snags of driftwood floated through the lineup. Yet in the moaning southwesterlies, Bearpaw lay sheltered.

Far from roads, the wave's access came from the hidden path over the spine of a bluff that reached into the sea with an impassable headland, one of the coast's many. The trail was difficult to follow; ferny, leafy, mossy, dimmed with the earthen murk of old-growth forest, a route taken more by elk than by humans, scented with sap, soundtracked with the squawk of gulls and bark of sea lions, the roar of the surf pounding the black-sand beaches below.

In terms of eternity, there was nothing else, no world outside. Few places could rival the forest's serenity. With its dirt and salt, the coast streamed idyll despite its austerity, a corner of Earth where nature was the champion, humanity the cancer.

> *"The people were here when the Pacific Northwest emerged from its icy womb and donned its forest raiment. Raven, Changer and Coyote, the demiurges of the myth-time, tamed its monsters, made it habitable for humankind."*
>
> *—David Buerge*

LIKE EVERYWHERE, THE woods were once virgin. From southern Alaska to northern California there lay vast tracks of temperate rain forest, huge conifers untouched since sprouting at the end of the last Ice Age. Later, humans arrived via the Bering land bridge and became the indigenous people of the northwest, settling and evolving into several cultures and societies, treading lightly and harmoniously in their rainy eden, living off and with the land and sea, the natural resources rich and widespread. And although the people warred amongst themselves, their pre-Columbian tribes and their forests flourished for 15,000 years.

Then came the 19th century and white men with big saws. Flat, open land surpassed trees in value, and the trees were simply large brown weeds that needed to be cleared. It wasn't long before settlers realized the terrain was unsuitable for anything but trees, however, so instead of building homes and seeding farms on the clearcuts, they made more. Large-scale industrial logging eventually leveled nearly 100 percent of the forests that covered the evergreen coast.

The natives had no involvement. They just lived there.

"My ancestors could do nothing," Sam said. I found him one morning squatting near the rivermouth on his tribe's beach, a beautiful place, cleaning a salmon he had just hooked. He tossed the guts into the river's clear running water. Like many around him, Sam was a die-hard fisherman, his gaunt face acne-scarred, his brown eyes weary. He loved adventure books and television shows like "Deadliest Catch." His hair was black and long and worn in a ponytail.

"I catch a lot of fish right here," he said. He pointed at some sea stacks. "We've got some good ling holes out there, too."

Nearly 30, Sam was thin and unemployed and grew up on his tribe's small reservation, a blustery and bleak patch of ramshackle homes, rusted cars on blocks, junked boats, bullet-holed street signs, roadside clearcuts, and lazy stray dogs howling into the wind. Trash was rampant. Alcoholism and precipitation were common. Tourists were not. There was no casino, no rustic riverside campground, no five-star resort—how could there be when the place sulked in squalor? Poverty beat the people down.

"This is what we have, you know? The reservation. The rez. What is happening around us, the logging outside the rez, we cannot control, but they really cannot control what is happening inside here."

"They" was the government. Indian reservations were exempt from normal bureaucratic protocol, sovereign entities that, like military bases, had the unique right to close beaches to the public. The tribe managed its own land. Sam's beach, covered with the largest pieces of driftwood I'd ever seen, had a wide gravel rivermouth sandbar that looked like it could form a good right-hander when the swell was small and clean. Today, preceding a storm on the horizon, the surf was huge and evil-looking.

"Have you seen surfers here?"

He lit a cigarette and took two tokes before answering. He looked pensive. His hands were spotted with fish blood.

"Surfers? No. This is not a place where you can do surfing."

Most of the northwest coast was like that. It was never a good surfing zone and never would be. Typically, miles of banal beachbreak alternated with inaccessible bays and fatally flawed reefs, nothing worth traveling for. Cradling the weather kitchen called Gulf of Alaska, the coast was typically overloaded with swell, the winds strong and foul, and with few roads leading to few beaches, a surfer was forced to hike or to avoid the place altogether.

"Want to come eat some of this salmon?" Sam asked.

"Yeah, sure."

I followed his old black Ford pickup for a mile inland to a small house that he shared with his mother and his two salmon-fishing brothers. At sunrise they had taken the family skiff upriver.

"They won't be back for awhile."

From outside, the home looked abandoned, with broken windows, a crumbling garage door, rotting walls, a mildewed roof smothered by thorny bramble bushes growing from the hillside that the house backed up against. Three wrecked pickup trucks, all flat-tired, were parked in tall weeds near a frail shed where fishing gear was stored. Stained laundry hung from pins on a fishing line strung between two skinny fir trees. Birds sang. A toppled basketball hoop lay on itself, pressing rust into the soil.

Sam's mother had gone for groceries. I caught a glimpse of the house innards, far cleaner and more organized than the yard. An untended fire burned in the kitchen woodstove; its smoke rose lazily from the rooftop chimney cowl.

Aside the front porch, a propane barbecue was ignited and Sam lay two small salmon steaks onto tin foil he'd set on the grill. The meat cooked quickly. Sam's black cat, Shadow, smelled the fish and crouched by my feet.

"Some in my tribe want to build a casino here, but I don't think it would do much good because we don't get tourists. The rez has nothing for them, no hotel, not even a restaurant. Maybe some river fishing. The beach is cold and windy. Nobody is going to drive all the way out here just to gamble. Alcohol is banned. Other reservations already have casinos and hotels, and they're a lot closer to the highways and cities. Tourists go there."

"Do you want tourists here?"

He chuckled. "I think they would ruin it for us. It is peaceful now. My mother thinks tourism would bring crime and traffic. Only a few people want a casino. My brothers do. But the rest of us know better."

With a metal spatula he lifted the steaks from the foil and soon we were pulling the tender pink meat apart with white plastic forks. It was delicious.

"Probably born in the fish hatchery," Sam said.

"It's kind of sad," I said. "Having to breed fish in a hatchery and later putting them into a lake or a river?"

"Better than nothing. Without hatcheries, there would be no fish. All the landslides and soil run-off from the logging areas have really trashed our creeks and rivers. Fish can't live in mud water."

The sky darkened fast and within minutes rain appeared, the drops hissing as they hit the hot barbecue grill. Shadow ran into the house.

"You think it will rain all day?" I asked Sam.

"Probably."

He was right.

AS THE DAYS and nights passed, my intimacy with the forest deepened. Sensory engagement with wild scents and sounds felt dreamlike, prescient, a portal to a primitive atmosphere disconnected from the present day. Inland, a few miles from the ocean, the silence and cold of the ancient trees soothed me into a meditation that numbed my physical discomfort, something that could never come from a clearcut or the dead soul of a city. It helped to be alone.

Awash in fog and rain and caressed by the damp breath of the sea, the ecosystem of the Pacific temperate rain forests was so fecund that their biomass was four or five times richer than the biomass of tropical jungles. In sheer volume of life and decay, the northwest woods triumphed over all ecosystems on Earth—the ranking a precious gift from the near-permanent clouds.

Sparrowhawk Creek was hellish to reach, especially in the rain. The wave was worthwhile. In two weeks I walked to it eight times. Just three miles each way, its trail was short, but steep grades—some nearly 45°—and slick mud linked the crossings of four waist-deep creeks. Dense foliage smothered much of the path, so most of the walk was done in my 5-mil fullsuit and 7-mil booties while holding my surfboard and backpack over my head. On separate occasions aside the trail, grazing elk and a foraging black bear were startled by my clumsy figure, but they didn't flee. They were unafraid because they were never hunted. Hiking to Sparrowhawk I saw no signs of humans, not a shoeprint or a bit of plastic trash. It was unknown when the last surfer had passed this way.

One somber morn the route remained dim beneath a frayed ceiling of mist, heavily shaded by the wraithlike crowns of huge Douglas firs and the vine maples draped in emerald moss. The trail itself was lined with dripping ferns and decaying nurse logs that supported new life; the ground was a plush carpet of rotten bark, fir needles, wood sorrel, moss, and false lily. The creeks were clear and clean and without purification I drank from them, their snowmelt water much colder than the ocean.

Then came through-the-trees vistas that exemplified the northwest surf experience: a gray Pacific, jagged black rocks, and some variation of rideable surf that typically couldn't justify the effort required to reach it. Or perhaps it could. State of mind leant reason to believe. Just ask brothers Bruhwiler or the middle Malloy. Believers, all.

ENDING A ROUGH dirt lane from a dirt spur road from an unsigned paved one, the trailhead to the wave at Gale Hollow was obscure and unmapped. Its trees were tall and ancient. Loggers hadn't been there. But they were good people. I liked them. On the outside, particularly in the environmentalist sphere, they had a bad rap.

In a nearby town one evening, I'd gone to a bizarre suburban garage advertised as a pizza parlor. A stenciled piece of cardboard in the window read *We Support The Timber Industry—This Business Supported By Timber Dollars*. Its cook was a fat hot-blooded white man wearing a stained yellow T-shirt. He was dirty, bearded, and he smoked a cigarette. He stood behind the counter and spoke loudly to his burly friend who slouched with a can of Budweiser in a plastic lawn chair across the echoey room. It looked like a school cafeteria.

"I got into a fistfight last night," the cook said. "I didn't want to, though. Fuckin' guy pissed me off. Guy was talkin' all *kinds* of shit."

"Must've been some fuckin' cowboy fisherman," the drinker said.

"I gave him two black eyes. He didn't get up, either. He just laid there, starin' at the ceiling. His buddy split real quick."

The cook inhaled from the cigarette and squinted at me sideways while blowing the smoke from the right corner of his mouth.

"Can I help you?"

"I'd like to order a pizza."

He pointed at me. "Hold that thought, man. I'm having a conversation here."

I left and walked to the center of the town, population 1,800. The air smelled of dirt and diesel. Drizzle dampened my clothes. The clouds were low and cold. Besides a gas station, Al's Saloon was the only place open, so I went inside and ordered peanuts and a beer—Alaskan Stout. The room was dim and smoky; a nicotine haze clung to the lights. The bartender was an elderly chain-smoking woman who didn't look like a bartender, especially in such a dive. She looked like she should've been knitting a quilt.

The saloon's rustic décor was classic, lodge-like: a ceiling of log beams, beer signs and old saws hanging from the walls, vintage logging photos, taxidermied fish and heads of elk and bear, a wood-burning fireplace, country music on the juke box. There was no TV or wireless Internet. The pool table was covered with a blue plaid blanket. The chairs were worn, the wood on the bar glass-smooth from years of human oils. Around the bar six men sat smoking cigarettes and drinking; as I took a first swig of my cool black brew, two of them got up to throw darts. Their Carhartt work clothes were filthy, smeared with mud and axle grease.

"Nice choice," Jeff, the middle-aged man next to me, said. He too had a stout. He wore a red flannel shirt with suspenders; a camouflage Stihl cap covered his shaggy brown hair. He was goateed, his hands were gnarled, and he looked every bit the clichéd image of a logger. He was there on a hunting trip, staying in the town's motel, but when not vacationing he worked down south in a softwood lumber mill run by

Weyerhaeuser, one of the world's largest timber companies that owned millions of forested acres in 18 countries. Weyerhaeuser had clearcut much of the Pacific Northwest, replacing it with dense, spindly renewable stands of spruce and fir and cedar no more than a few decades old. They looked like toothpicks.

"Why do you work for Weyerhaeuser?" I asked Jeff.

"They have a lot of land, a lot of mills, usually lots of jobs to offer. They're a big company, a good company. I worked at MacBlo before Weyerhaeuser bought 'em out in '99. I worked in a log-sorting yard. Before that, I was cutting a lot of big trees down. Mostly cedars."

In recent years Weyerhaeuser won several awards for its sustainable forestry management, safety, ethics, engineering, and apparently eco-friendly policies worldwide.

"They take care of us," Jeff said. "It's not all bullshit public-relations propaganda. And they do take care of the forests as best they can. The forests grow back. It's a science. Tree farming, just like Christmas tree farms, but bigger. Some people want logging to just die and go away, to never have another tree in the world cut down ever again, but they're living in a fantasy."

"Do you think the timber will eventually run out?"

"No. Jobs will go quicker than trees—that's for sure. Already so many guys are out of work. Timber harvesting has really been reduced."

"By how much?"

"I don't know the exact percentage, but it has a lot to do with the bad housing market down in California. The demand for wood is weak right now. Nobody's building homes. Weyerhaeuser closed some mills, too. Last year was real tough."

For 2009 Weyerhaeuser reported a net loss of $545 million on sales from operations of $5.5 billion, a huge decline from 2008's net loss of $1.2 billion on sales from operations of $8.1 billion. But in early 2010, things seemed to improve: on April 29 Weyerhaeuser reported a net loss of $20 million for the first quarter of 2010, on sales of $1.4 billion. The same period in 2009 experienced a whopping net loss of $264 million on sales from operations of $1.3 billion.

"After many difficult quarters, we're encouraged by the improvement in our performance," Dan Fulton, Weyerhaeuser president and CEO, said in a press release I found online. "While the pace of the housing recovery remains uncertain, we're moving in the right direction."

Weyerhaeuser did not harvest old-growth trees in the United States, likely because there were so few left, almost all within park boundaries, forever shielded from chainsaws. But old-growth trees in Canada were fair game and extremely controversial, particularly the celebrated cedar groves of British Columbia.

"Should Weyerhaeuser cut those cedars?" I asked Jeff as he finished his beer.

"It's not my decision."

"Do you want them to?"

He lit a cigarette and stared down at the bar—made of old-growth cedar—for 10 seconds before answering.

"No. I really don't. That would be bad for many reasons."

"As lush as any hobbit's realm...."
—National Geographic

TWILIGHT. AT BEARPAW Gulch I was surrounded by spruce, not cedar. Part of a park, this forest was protected. The grind of Weyerhaeuser chainsaws could never break its silence.

Dying batteries lent an annoying flicker to the bulb inside my headlamp; I hadn't been on the trail this late. Beneath the light diffusion and atmospheric dust, vision was compromised and a sort of autopilot blindness pushed me forward. As fatigue increased I became disoriented and careless with my footing, tripping and stumbling across the understory of downed logs and twigs and exposed roots, the tangles of bramble and salmonberry, the gardens of fern and the deep, trackless muck.

Mid-trail, over a stream and a yard of mud, lay an uneven log. In the morning light I had stepped across it sans incident. But in blurry darkness it looked suspect, a narrow, rickety plank over gently flowing water, a snow-fed tributary of Bearpaw, one of the coast's few creeks where coho salmon thrived despite siltation from the deforestation upstream.

Shifting the surfboard and wetsuit to my left arm, I took a deep breath and walked onto the log. Instantly I lost balance. The log rolled to the right and caused me to fall leftward and backwards, flat on my pack, face up. As I fell the board struck the log, denting a rail. The stream's frigid water was inches from my head. Frogs croaked nearby. Exhausted, I let go of the board, laid on my pack in the mud and gazed at the night sky, its lightless cycle of the new moon affording a view to a million stars, a serene celestial amphitheater framed by windswept treetops. My feet ached but welcomed the weightless relief. Cold mud oozed through the back of my pants and sweatshirt and across my hands, therapy for a satisfied but overheated soul.

I closed my eyes and listened to the voices of nature. Primeval spirits, visceral drama. I didn't want to leave. Sublimity of place never felt so true.

40

THIS IS WHERE YOU KILL THINGS

2012

TWENTY-EIGHT: Feet, length of the black Lincoln Town Car limousine in which Daniel Jones, Nico Manos, Trevor Gordon, and I are driven for three hours, starting at 3 a.m., from the seedy Anchorage hotel to the port of a deglaciated valley town, population 3,000.

"Just driving through that place makes me feel hungover, man."

Astride his broken captain's chair, gazing through thick glass at the fjord waters, bushy-browed Mike smiles and sips strong coffee. He's happy. I'm happy. We're on his boat. The back of his navy blue T-shirt shows a goofyfooter pulling into a tropical, head-high left over the words RIDE THE FURY. Yes, we'd like to.

The port, groggy and foggy at 6:39 a.m., shrinks astern. Flanked by tall, white peaks, we're southbound at eight knots inside the cramped third-story wheelhouse of this 48-year-old, 58-foot-long steel purse seiner. Built in Seattle, she spent her commercial life salmoning off the southeast Alaskan coast and off Washington, dragging for bottom fish.

We're not going fishing.

"Don't you guys feel that way, man? Hungover?"

No. The town was dead. I saw nil but the dotty headache of orange streetlights and their hazy glow on orange sidewalks and orange storefronts and orange parked cars, roofed with orange snow. No humans except the gaunt convenience store clerk who sold me weak coffee and a peanut butter Clif bar. She was high on meth. Thankfully, our fat chauffeur was not. Thankfully, I was not hungover — just one Alaskan Amber Ale in the hotel pub last night because, for a hophead like me, amber's a dull beer.

Mike sips more coffee, swallows, exhales. Smiles again. Smug. The new floor heater is working. It's warm in here. He leans over and taps a few laptop keys. On-screen, there's a tempting nautical chart. The Kenai Fjords look like shredded witch fingers. Eagle talons. Bold headlands, wide bays, beachbreaks, coves. Pointbreaks. Rivermouths — lots of rivermouths. Scenic grandeur. Attributing J. London, it's to be an odyssey of the north.

FIFTY-NINE: Degrees of north latitude which we occupy inside beanies and down parkas, sitting on black steel gunwales, grilling lingcod. There's ice on the deck. Holding strong ales in gloved hands, we admire the hallucinatory reflect of snowy cliffs across this tranquil, funnel-shaped anchorage that latitudinally drifts with Siberia.

Trevor is fly-fishing for his first time. *Swish-swish-swish.* He whips the line to and fro off the transom but hooks nothing. The bottom here is hard mud. The water is hunter green. The time is 10:30 p.m. but still the sky glows blue.

Pausing, Trevor looks shoreward and swigs from a bottle of stout. Halfway hidden on the forested beach, he sees three old wooden cabins that wait for summer.

"Somebody's idea of a good time right there," Captain Mike says from the barbecue, his chin bisecting the gray fish smoke.

"Lonely," Trevor says.

"Yeah, unless you've got it packed full of Bush Company dancers." *(laughs)*

The Great Alaskan Bush Company, Mike means. Look it up.

A shaggy white male mountain goat grazes fairly low above the pit of the anchorage, above the cabins, on that really steep cliff.

"It's amazing where you see them," Mike says, flipping fish fillets. "They do fall sometimes."

"Why would they be there and not up where it's not so steep?" Trevor asks.

"There's snow up there," Mike says, pointing at the top of the slope, then lowering his arm. "The grass is down here. Good munchin' spot."

In a month or two, this goat will laze in high alpine meadows, eating shrubs and herbs and grass at leisure. For now, though, he risks life to live. Like us. Sort of.

SEVEN: Millimeters of neoprene required to sheathe extremities whilst surfing. Hoods and six-millimeter fullsuits seal the encumbrance.

THIRTY-SEVEN: Degrees, Fahrenheit, of ocean water temperature, the going rate of glacial-stream-fed sting. My hands burn. It's bone-seeping cold.

We're sitting rib-deep in dense, black water at a playful, shapely spot that Trevor likens to Hammond's Reef, one of his (and Tom Curren's) preferred waves in California. Unlike sunny Hammond's, however, no surfers will flock to this beach. Unlike Hammond's, no billionaires sleep within sight. Unlike Hammond's, this reef is tucked in a primordial fjord, fronted with crumbling rock spires and seal-flecked pinnacles, shadowed by dark mountains and licked by the longest glacial ice tongue in Kenai Fjords National Park.

Over there, behind the gray-boulder moraine beach and its gray till and low, serrated green line of spruce, white icebergs float in the lake. Two miles behind that lake is a massive white glacier, cracked and fissured, which means this wave experiences katabatic winds howling off the icefield, 5,000 feet up and 12 miles in. Brash ice chunks often float in the lineup, which occurs regularly, per page 91 of my kayaking guidebook: STAY IN DEEP WATER AND AWAY FROM THE BEACH. THE BOTTOM RAPIDLY SHALLOWS AND ACCENTUATES THE SWELL AND SURF.

The windless morning's drizzle has become rain and hail and the ambiance is a cold, drab gray, the black mountain trees melding with quiet browns of nude earth and smatterings of snow.

Downstairs in the boiler room, full of wetsuits, Daniel, a creature of temperature, labors out of his. He rubs his nose and cheekbones with the back of his numb hand. Two days ago, he surfed Rocky Point in boardshorts.

"Yeah, we Hawaiians usually only come to Alaska to go snowboarding," he says to bearded Nico, another creature of temperature but, as a year-round Nova Scotian, he thrives on the opposite scale. Nico's already got his wetsuit/hood/booties/mittens off. He's used to surfing with snow on the beach. He says the vibe here is reminiscent of home, if only home had spell-binding glaciers and 4,000-foot sea cliffs.

FORTY-NINTH: State of the U.S.A., its largest and most northern. Also an exclave. Spiritually, Alaska is another country.

TWO: Huge icefields, named Harding and Sargent. Somewhere behind each estuarine spot we surf, they coat the Kenai Mountains up to a mile thick.

ZERO: Feet, in height, of the swell. We glide along. The other gents are belowdecks, sleeping or reading or drinking coffee. It's good coffee, from Homer, where Mike lives. He runs a fish-processing plant there.

Above, the sky is huge and blue. The mountain snow is blinding. Aloud, I wonder if such weather is rare.

With a small rag, Mike wipes his sunglasses. "Maybe *rare* is not quite the word," he says, "but it's nice to take advantage of 'em when you see 'em. That's for sure. Doesn't really do much for swell, though." *(laughs)*

The fjord water is silty green and glassy-smooth — a little too glassy, too lake-like for a boatload of surfers. Last night, Trevor suggested we try wakeboarding.

"Are we going to get some big breakers today?" I ask Mike as he pulls the throttle back with his right hand. With yellow binoculars in his left, he's studying the gravel beach we've approached.

Neighbored by a wooded peninsula and steep talus cliffs, this beach is bereft of whitewater but strewn with driftwood logs. The adjacent lagoon is serene. There are ducks and river otters and harbor seals, bushes of lupine and salmonberry amongst the moss-bearded spruce and alder. I'd like to stay and sunbathe and beachcomb, perhaps pitch a tent and wait for swell.

"Not a lot of confidence that we'll find big breakers today," Mike says. "We'll take a look here mainly to put some new info into the memory bank. I know guys have camped out and surfed along this beach here, but I don't think we have the right swell conditions today, by any means."

Awesome.

SEVEN: Million dollars, for which Alaska was purchased from Russia in 1867. That's two cents an acre.

FIFTEEN THOUSAND: Acres, densely forested, comprising the biggest island here. It is jagged and lung-shaped, rife with eagles and seals. There's surf, too — peaky, punchy beachbreak, its black-sand shore poked with bear tracks among the driftwood logs and stray container-ship flotsam: orange basketballs, black fly swatters, blue aluminum water bottles. A ghost forest, immortalized after 1964's four-minute, 9.2-magnitude Great Alaskan Earthquake, tops the steep beach.

The surf is fun before the sky bleeds gray and the air is seized by an onshore gale. We're done. Tea and books in the anchorage. Cozy downtime again.

This afternoon, we buzz the skiff to the hidden entrance of a tiny cove. Along the shore are the skeletal remains of a bulldozer, a barn, and a termite-wrecked cabin. Through falling snowflakes, I see "Herring Pete" and Josephine Sather tending to their noisy fox farm here. But they abandoned this place in 1961, and the barn's decay, scented with river-otter dung, makes me sneeze. Pete too was a reputedly ripe and eccentric guy, his rarely washed clothes afoul of rotten fish. His wife was an obsessive clean-freak, forcing Pete to take cold showers after his fishing trips, even mid-winter.

Admiring his view out over the cove, I picture Pete shivering wet in the bathroom while Josephine stirred a hot pot of fox stew. But, foolishly standing in snow, I realize I'm the one shivering.

TWO THOUSAND: Years ago, when the first humans migrated from the Alaskan interior to the Kenai Fjords coast. These were the Unegkurmiut, a hardy Eskimo breed of maritime subsistence who so excelled in boat-making that they were exploited by Russian fur traders to hunt sea otters. The Russians, who'd arrived in July of 1790, also brought smallpox, which trashed the once-harmonious Unegkurmiut population. Ensuing panic, starvation, and Russian bullying contributed to complete Unegkurmiut demise by 1912, one century removed from us.

THREE: Days, consecutive, which are too flat to surf. Vexing in a such a storm-washed place.

"Maybe we should go fishing or hunting," Nico says over his oatmeal in the galley. "Get some deer or moose or something."

"Most people *do* come to Alaska to kill things," deckhand Scott says.

Fresh halibut sounds good. The white inflatable skiff is launched with fishing gear and Scott and Trevor aboard. Their bright orange and yellow rain jackets contrast well with the gray of the sea and the dark, conical headland, which flattens into a long gravel beach and berm that supports a large tree-lined lagoon and a foraging black bear. And topography for a perfect left pointbreak. Mike says he's surfed it — slabby up top, ropey through the middle as it wrapped around the crescent-shaped barrier beach.

Later, black lingcod and rockfish are hooked, cleaned, and served for dinner. Salmon season is two months off.

The next morning, Trevor confides to me that the west side of the fjord, three miles opposite the left point, has a long, tapered right cobblestone beach, also with a lagoon behind it. "If we had swell, that place might be just like El Cap," he says, referring to another perfect wave he surfs at home.

"El Capitan of Kenai Fjords" has a nice ring to it, I say. A dead ring.

FIVE HUNDRED NINETY-TWO THOUSAND: Square miles, surface area, comprising the Gulf of Alaska. Plenty of room to cause trouble. In winter, the Gulf is a weather kitchen, a sea of severity, a near-constant stream of cyclones and anticyclones. Sixty-foot waves with 100-knot winds are routine. Depressions twist east from Japan, stalling once they hit the Gulf and, trapped, they mutate and shove swell down to western North America and eastern Oceania. North swells deny the south-facing Kenai Fjords. We need south.

But this is a fjord and there is swell in this afternoon's marine forecast, the charts showing a pair of modest, local low-pressure systems with favorable fetch.

"It's a good reason to feel optimistic instead of just feeling hopeful," Mike says, watching a bald eagle soar in the updraft, its spearing blackness contrasted by the white snow bowl of a hanging valley. Below the raptor are steep slopes and shale landslides, chalky brown, laced with thin snowmelt waterfalls. It's late April — Alaska is beginning to thaw. Soon, bears will be everywhere. Post-Memorial Day until September, this fjord will be flush with cruise ships and fishing boats because Seward is a major fishing hub, the ninth most-lucrative fisheries port in the United States. (In 2011, $79.5 million worth of fish passed through it.)

A diehard surfer and ex-merchant marine, Mike isn't thrilled about other dingy fishing towns — Yakutat and Dutch Harbor, for example — he's had to work in and around since he moved from Hawaii to Alaska to work at a fish cannery in the summer of '76.

"What's Yakutat like?" I ask.

"Small. Some good waves over there."

"Dutch Harbor?"

"Drunk." *(laughs)*

He leans and starts steering the ship with its wooden wheel, the first time I've seen him do this.

"Don't you always steer with the compass?"

He nodded. "It just started acting funny. Maybe it blew a fuse, or a wire's loose, or there's a bunch of iron in that mountain and it threw the compass crazy. Happens sometimes."

We approach the fjord's entrance, or, in this case, the exit. Instantly the scene shifts. Out here, the wind howls from the east, deeply corrugating the open ocean. The boat dips and lurches in the raw sea.

"At least we're looking at waves now," Mike says. "It's a start!"

ONE HUNDRED TWENTY-SIX: Feet, in height, of the rock pinnacle that looms at the reefy fore of this exposed bay, a two-mile-long stretch of black sand of which my guidebook states: BEACH LANDINGS ARE DIFFICULT AND UNRELIABLE BECAUSE OF THE CONSTANT SURF.

We anchor 100 yards out. The beach fronts another deglaciated valley and an icy glacier lake below a glacier. Mike has surfed in front of this, at a shifty sandbar west of the faux left point we're paddling to. It looks good from behind, the whitewater tapering in the proper direction for an ideal length of time. Stroking shoreward, there's a nice backdrop of spruce and alder. In the rockbound lineup, we're looking at two big, horn-shaped spires which may or may not dilute the head-high sets as they hump in from the southeast. The waves are clean but soft, the sun warm, the sky blue, the air temperature mild — our exhaled breath is invisible. The scene implies Carmel, Monterey, even Big Sur.

EIGHTY: Times the crabber's fatality rate of the average worker. On average, one crabber dies weekly during Alaska's crab-fishing seasons.

TWELVE: Feet, in height, of the swell. A certain rivermouth cove could massage it, Mike says, the region's "crown jewel" of the spots he knows about. He's been talking about it all week. Studying his poster-sized nautical charts, I reckon that, on the right day or hour, there could be dozens of crown jewels along the 250 miles of Kenai Fjords seacoast. Goodness knows there is ample daylight this month.

"We can get there at 8:30 p.m. and still have a two-hour session," he says with a grin.

But first, it's a rough ride. Huddled in the wheelhouse, we pound west through the rain, rounding an exposed cape, a balding head of granite with hairs of spruce trees and smears of dirty snow. Its base has 13 tall, narrow black sea caves placed like sharp teeth. Joy for a spelunker. Thousands of murres and kittiwakes swoop about. Three sea lions bark. We slosh past porpoises and a pod of orcas.

Out the starboard exterior, a large gray trawler steams east, likely for shelter as fishing today would be tough. Daniel, lounging on the couch aside Mike in an unzipped black hoodie, takes a swig from his bottle of Alaskan Black IPA.

"You think that's a crab boat?"

"Nah, not around here," Mike says. "They're probably out for halibut. Salmon in summer. Crab season doesn't start till October."

"How many crab seasons are there?"

"The opilio and the king crab are the two big ones, but then there's a different king crab way up north, near St. Matthew Island, and there's the Adak brown crab. Some years, there's a crab I see that's a cross between the king crab and opilio."

"How do the dudes know which one they're fishing for?" Nico asks.

"Crabs live in different areas and at different depths."

"Do the same boats hit them all up?" Daniel asks.

"Pretty much. Some of them, there's only a couple of boats that fish."

"A lot of the boats aren't on that one TV show, right?" Trevor asks, referring to *Deadliest Catch.*

"Yeah. For the most part, the dudes on that show are a bunch of real frickin' idiots."

"Really?" Daniel asks.

"Yeah. I've bought crab from all those guys."

"Does the TV channel pay them?" Trevor asks.

"Nope."

"Why are they doing it if they're not getting paid?"

"Just trying to get famous."

"So why do they pick the dickheads?" Nico asked. "Just to make for a more interesting cast?"

"Yeah. A bunch of 'em are crackheads. One night after the show was done taping, one of the guys was found dead in a hotel room."

"Do a lot of those fishermen have to smoke crack to stay awake?" Daniel asks.

"In the old days, they were all cokeheads, when there was a lot of money, and nobody knew how dangerous it was. You had to pretty much go around the clock to catch your share, or more than your share."

In three hours: Lumpy rivermouth tubes. Shallow and hard-hitting. East-wind slag bump. Rain.

Daniel: "Coldest session *ever.*"

ONE: Little-known fact: Two beachbreaks cradled by the ragged, most swell-exposed barb of the Kenai Fjords can be almost flat, like they are the day our marine forecast had promised a 16-foot southeast swell. Guidebook: HERE, THE SURF IS CONSTANT. THE WATERS ARE RENOWNED FOR THEIR INTENSITY.

Previously unknown: The largest Alaskan seas Captain Mike has faced. "I don't know," he says, chewing a bite of banana muffin. "I try to avoid them." Later he reveals: "There were these white lines, standing waves, and all I could do was steer right into them. My pilothouse was 60 feet above the water, and for three waves in a row, I couldn't see a thing."

What you probably know: Sixty-foot waves are big waves.

Partially true fact: The Kenai Fjords possess many slabs and at least one world-class surf spot. This wave may or may not employ Jeffrey's Bay, Mangamaunu, Malibu, Scorpion Bay, or Rincon Point.

Unequivocally true: I left Alaska with a hangover.